I0797302

We the Women

We the Women

THE HIDDEN HEROES WHO SHAPED AMERICA

by

NORAH O'DONNELL

with

KATE ANDERSEN BROWER

Ballantine Books

NEW YORK

Ballantine Books
An imprint of Random House
A division of Penguin Random House LLC
1745 Broadway, New York, NY 10019
randomhousebooks.com
penguinrandomhouse.com

Photo credits are located on pages 333–335.

Hardcover ISBN 978-0-593-72702-7
Ebook ISBN 978-0-593-72703-4

Printed in the United States of America on acid-free paper

3rd Printing

First Edition

BOOK TEAM: Production editor: Cassie Gitkin • Managing editor: Pam Alders
Production manager: Sarah Feightner • Copy editor: Amy J. Schneider
Proofreaders: Cyrus Chin, Marissa Earl, Dan Goff, Pam Feinstein, Barbara Jatkola

Book design by Sara Bereta

The authorized representative in the EU for product safety and compliance is Penguin Random House Ireland, Morrison Chambers, 32 Nassau Street, Dublin D02 YH68, Ireland.
https://eu-contact.penguin.ie

For my mother and my daughters,
and for the women in history
who remind us that nothing is impossible.

Contents

We the Women

Introduction

On July 4, 1876, celebrations of America's centennial were planned all across the country, with the grandest event taking place in Philadelphia. Thousands stood in the blistering sun to hear the reading of the Declaration of Independence, but a small group of women gathered in America's birthplace had their own patriotic message to deliver.[1]

Elizabeth Cady Stanton, Susan B. Anthony, and other prominent suffragists from all over America had been denied the right to participate in the day's activities. Elizabeth had been told by the man in charge that the program was full, but the women insisted they must be heard and decided to storm the stage.[2]

Outside Independence Hall, Richard Henry Lee of Virginia, whose grandfather had proposed independence from England a century earlier, read from the original Declaration of Independence, which promised equal rights. When he finished, Susan and four other women rose from the audience and marched their way to the front of the platform, which was adorned in red, white, and blue for the holiday.

The crowd was caught off guard and, remarkably, Susan encountered no resistance, only the stunned, pale face of the presiding officer, Senator Thomas W. Ferry. She handed him their pamphlet, titled "Declaration of Rights of the Women of the United States," which he begrudgingly accepted, thus making it an official part of the day's proceedings.[3] It was a groundbreaking four-page list of grievances that equated women's oppression with the treatment of the colonies under King George III.

The group of women caused such a stir that men in the audience stood on their seats to see what was happening. As the women quickly exited the stage, they handed extra copies of their manifesto to men who eagerly reached for the documents.

We ask justice, we ask equality, we ask that all the civil and political rights that belong to citizens of the United States, be guaranteed to us and our daughters forever.

—Susan B. Anthony

The women had created their own fireworks—too much for General Joseph R. Hawley, who shouted, "Order! Order!"[4] As head of the U.S. Centennial Commission, Hawley was the man who had denied Elizabeth's request for the women to participate. "We are crowded for time," he had written in a letter. Those words had come back to haunt him.

Elizabeth Cady Stanton, president of the National Woman Suffrage Association (NWSA), and her colleagues had hoped to use the occasion to highlight the hypocrisy of celebrating independence while half the population were still denied their right to vote. "We thought it would be fitting for us to read our Declaration of Rights immediately after that of the Fathers was read, as an impeachment of them and their male descendants for their injustice and oppression," Elizabeth later recounted.

The six NWSA members who had stormed the stage then moved to the front of Independence Hall for the next dramatic moment of the day. In her memoir, Elizabeth described the scene:

> Here, under the shadow of Washington's statue, [behind] them the old bell that proclaimed, "liberty to all the land and all the inhabitants thereof," they took their places, and to a listening,

applauding crowd, Miss Anthony read the Women's Declaration.

Susan B. Anthony's remarks began, "While the nation is buoyant with patriotism, and all hearts are attuned to praise, it is with sorrow we come to strike the one discordant note, on this one-hundredth anniversary of our country's birth."

Standing in the sweltering noon heat, wearing a heavy Victorian petticoat, Susan reminded the crowd that women had no right to vote, no marriage rights, no real legal protections, and were subject to taxation without representation.[5]

"We ask justice, we ask equality, we ask that all the civil and political rights that belong to citizens of the United States, be guaranteed to us and our daughters forever."

Our daughters forever.

This courageous call for universal suffrage, delivered on the centennial celebration of the Fourth of July, helped inspire the struggle that would culminate in the passage of the Nineteenth Amendment more than four decades later. It was a profound American moment that helped ensure we *all* now have the right to vote.

I didn't learn about this extraordinary day in school or from the many history books I've read. It took following my curiosity about America's Independence Day through the years, and a lot of research, to uncover this story. That led me to wonder: Why is this moment a mere footnote to our country's story rather than a centerpiece of our lessons? Most of the history I learned in school was, well, pretty boring—or should I say more politely, difficult to relate to! But I can relate to these bold and brilliant women who had not been given a seat at the table or an equal opportunity and had to force their way to the stage. Many of their voices have been silenced and their contributions overshadowed by the privileged white men, who . . . well, wrote the history books.

As I learned more about these prominent suffragists, I began to wonder what else was missing from my understanding of our nation's founding document and the centuries-long struggle for civil rights and women's rights. I was curious about other women who helped change the course of history in America who we know little about; the hidden heroines who against all odds fought for the freedoms outlined in the Declaration of Independence and the Constitution. How did their actions lead to my freedoms today? Most important, I can vote. I can also own my own property and have my own bank account. I can work as a journalist and ask tough questions to people in positions of power.

Those rights were not afforded to women at our country's founding. They had to be hard-won over the past 250 years.

"We hold these truths to be self-evident, that all men are created equal." Those very words created this country and are the spark that lit every revolution in American history. Yet for the women at America's centennial, more than half of the population were still denied the inalienable rights of "Life, Liberty, and the Pursuit of Happiness." Susan, Elizabeth, and their fellow suffragists were not equal. In *their* declaration, they affirmed a belief in human rights *for all*, which they called the "corner stones of a republic."[6]

As you'll learn in this book, women have never given up the fight to realize a more perfect union. The heroes in this book powerfully illustrate the 250-year struggle they have fought to achieve that better version of America. Their persistent defense of this country's ideals at home and abroad has forced our nation to live up to its promises.

Women are the real architects of society.

—***Harriet Beecher Stowe***

Women have bled for their country during every war in our nation's history. Some women took a bullet for America when they didn't even have the right to vote. Women also built this country—from bridges to banks to hospitals—and they birthed movements, not just suffrage but also the Civil Rights Movement. As Harriet Beecher Stowe famously put it, "Women are the real architects of society." Many of these great early female reformers were abolitionist leaders. Again and again, women have demanded their place, their rights, *and* rights for others. Yet they were imperfect, and their mission to achieve greater equality came with its own fissures and flaws.

"We the People" is the phrase that begins the U.S. Constitution, and it is meant to remind us all that the authority of our government comes directly from all of its citizens; that our government is by and for the people. This book is titled *We the Women* as a reminder of the shared struggle, the collective fight, *by women and for women*, to make sure that our government recognizes all of its citizens.

It's a story often missing from our history books. The National Women's History Museum found that less than 15 percent of what is taught in America's schools highlights the achievements and history of women. We want to change that. This retelling of the American narrative puts women in their rightful place on the pages of history.

On a more personal note, I wonder how my own sense of self, power, and courage might have been shaped if I had learned more about these women as a young girl.

As America celebrates its 250th birthday, a more perfect union is still a work in progress. Even still, the United States of America's democratic ideals are the envy of the world. The promise of the American dream is what brought my grandmother to the United States in the 1930s.

Mary Teresa Monaghan O'Kane was the oldest girl of nine children, a Catholic living in Protestant-controlled Northern Ireland. My grandmother started working at age twelve in a linen factory in Belfast, traveling through barbed wire and barricades every day, not to school but to a job to support her family. She never made it past the eighth grade, but she was smart enough to know she had to leave Northern Ireland.

So she did what so many young Irish women did in the early twentieth century: She gathered her courage, boarded a boat, all alone, and set sail for America inspired by a dream for a new life. The week-long transatlantic voyage on a steamship was notorious. James Joyce, the renowned Irish author, once described the Atlantic Ocean as a "bowl of bitter tears," to capture the sorrow of immigrants leaving their homeland.[7]

My grandmother arrived at Ellis Island in 1930. When she entered New York Harbor, she was greeted by the Statue of Liberty. Think about that! A woman—Lady Liberty!—holding a torch, welcoming people like my grandmother to America's shore. What did this 150-year-old country offer a young woman? Certainly my grandmother believed there would be opportunities for women not provided for them in Ireland.

If I could travel back in time, I'd hold my scared grandmother's hand and say, "It's going to be okay. Look at this bronze plaque on the pedestal of Lady Liberty." It reads in part, "Give me your tired, your poor / Your huddled masses yearning to breathe free." I'd say, "Grandma, that was written by a young female poet. Her name is Emma Lazarus. America is the land of opportunity."[8]

You might think my Irish grandmother's story is only remembered as part of my family history, and yet she is recorded in America's narrative. I found her name in a book at the National Archives in Washington, D.C., where upon arrival in America she listed her profession as a hemstitcher. She had just $20 to her name.

The bold spirit and bravery that brought my grandmother across the Atlantic lives inside the women that we feature in this book. Each woman represents the historical significance of the period in which she lived. Some fought in wars; others fought in the courtroom or for equality in sports and business. All of them are changemakers.

For nearly three decades, I've spent my career as a journalist amplifying the stories of women. This book is an expansion of that work. It was not easy to unearth these stories of hidden heroes. Fortunately, I worked with bestselling author Kate Andersen Brower to bring them to life. Julie Morse, a senior producer at CBS News, was invaluable with research and as a thought partner. Together we spent nearly two years interviewing dozens of people and reading hundreds of books and scholarly articles. Through the process, we learned that these women are complicated. They are imperfect—but find me a person who is not. They pushed limits, they didn't take no for an answer, and they imagined a future where they had equal standing with men. Our research led us to uncover some pretty astounding women. It was a difficult process to narrow down whom to feature across 250 years of American history, where women's contributions have been not only extraordinary but often overlooked or diminished.

Mary Katherine Goddard is the only woman whose name is on the Declaration of Independence; Belva Lockwood was the first woman to argue before the U.S. Supreme Court and the first to mount a full national campaign for the U.S. presidency; Susette La Flesche spent her life advocating for Indigenous peoples' rights as a speaker and writer, and as an interpreter during a landmark Native American civil rights case; Mary McLeod Bethune was a visionary educator who led the Black Cabinet during FDR's presidency and opened the first Black hospital in Florida; and Frances Perkins was the architect of the New Deal and the nation's first female Cabinet member.

Many held the distinction of being the first in their field, breaking barriers like Phillis Wheatley, the first African American woman to publish a book of poems; Dr. Elizabeth Blackwell was the first woman admitted to a medical school; and Agnes Meyer Driscoll is the "First Lady of Naval Cryptology." One of them was not just the first, but to this day is the *only:* Dr. Mary Edwards Walker is the only woman to receive the Medal of Honor, the nation's highest military decoration, awarded by the president of the United States.

Through this journey, I developed a personal connection to each of these women, a sense of admiration for what they endured and for the courage it took for them to keep going in the face of adversity, discrimination, and hatred. I hope they inspire you the way they inspired me.

Our goal is not to deliver a full biography of the women we are showcasing but to paint a picture of their grit and determination to be treated equally—not just under the law but by society. We wanted to highlight women who pushed America to live up to its founding promises: liberty, equality, and the pursuit of happiness.

We relied on historians who have made it their life's work to rediscover these women. But *we* are not historians. So if *something* or *someone* is missing, I hope that you too will help share their stories. We didn't include every famous woman you've heard of; there's no chapter on Abigail Adams, though she is a widely influential founding mother. But there is a chapter on Abigail's friend Mercy Otis Warren, an Anti-Federalist who wrote the first history of the Revolution. Many women throughout history exemplify America's values, and we couldn't possibly write about all of them. We wanted, as much as possible, for each profile to feel like a gem we were uncovering—something new, and valuable, with a significant history worthy of discovery.

Each of us plays a role in the arc of history. I love that phrase. Dr. Martin Luther King, Jr., said, "The arc of the moral universe is long, but it bends towards justice." King often used the quote, which had its origins in the nineteenth-century abolitionist movement.[9] The push for civil rights was a continuation of those earlier social justice movements. By examining American history, we see how progress and transformation take place. It can be agonizingly slow. These women have been central to bending that arc toward justice. Throughout this process, when I felt discouraged by challenges in my own life, these women filled me with a sense of grit and resilience. My hope is that you, too, are inspired by their lives.

PART I

THE FIRST FIFTY YEARS: THE WOMEN BEHIND AMERICA'S FIGHT FOR INDEPENDENCE, 1776–1826

1.

Mary Katherine Goddard: *The Printer*

Two days before Christmas in 1789, Mary Katherine Goddard was seething with anger—and for good reason. She was not a member of the nascent country's elite, but she knew that she had done enough to justify taking her case straight to the top. In a letter to the newly elected president, George Washington, she decried an "extraordinary Act of oppression towards her."[1]

At age fifty-one, she had earned her position as the first female postmaster in the United States. Yet after fourteen years of service, she was suddenly dismissed due to political cronyism, cast aside so that a powerful man could return a political favor.

What stung even more was that she had risked everything for her country, including her life. A dedicated patriot, Mary Katherine Goddard was the woman Congress had trusted in the early days of the Republic to complete one of the country's most important jobs: printing and distributing its founding documents.

On January 18, 1777, the Second Continental Congress ordered the printing of an authentic copy of the Declaration of Independence, with the names of the signers, so that each of the states could put the founding document into its archives.[2] It was the first time that the country would learn the names of almost every signer of the Declaration. America was at war, and they needed to know the men leading the charge.

The lawmakers were meeting in Baltimore because British troops were in New Jersey, and getting close to Philadelphia, "the seat of war"[3] and the nation's then capital. Baltimore was the home of Mary Katherine Goddard, and the printing shop she had inherited from her family was just a few blocks away from the new Congress. Since the move south, Mary Katherine had printed a number of resolutions and notices for Congress, so when it was time to quickly print the country's most important document, they called on her.

In just two weeks, she gathered the names, printed copies, and sent them to the thirteen colonies. Earlier versions of the Declaration had circulated without all the signatories' names to avoid British detection.[4] Printing the version with nearly all the signers' names was an act of defiance and extraordinary bravery.

And that's not all. There under the large signature of John Hancock, clearly printed, is the name *Mary Katherine Goddard.* Mary Katherine stood alongside the nation's founders, taking a tremendous risk at a time when the outcome of the American Revolution was uncertain.

Today her work is known as the Goddard Broadside, and only a handful of copies still exist, including ones at the New York Public Library and at the Library of Congress.[5] It was the first printed version of the Declaration of Independence specifically intended for preservation.

How ironic that Mary Katherine's work was meant to be remembered forever, yet she herself has largely been forgotten.

The broadside was the first to use the title "The Unanimous Declaration of the Thirteen United States of America." It is also the first version to contain almost every signer's name, fifty-five of them—all men, including John Hancock, Benjamin Franklin, and Thomas Jefferson. And then at the bottom, in bold type, is the only woman's name on the nation's founding documents: Mary Katherine Goddard.[6]

It's significant that she used her full name. She could have left it blank or used her initials, as she had done earlier when signing her newspapers as "MK Goddard." Including her full name opened her up to the risk of being imprisoned by the British. That's not an overstatement, as Richard Stockton, one of the signers from New Jersey,

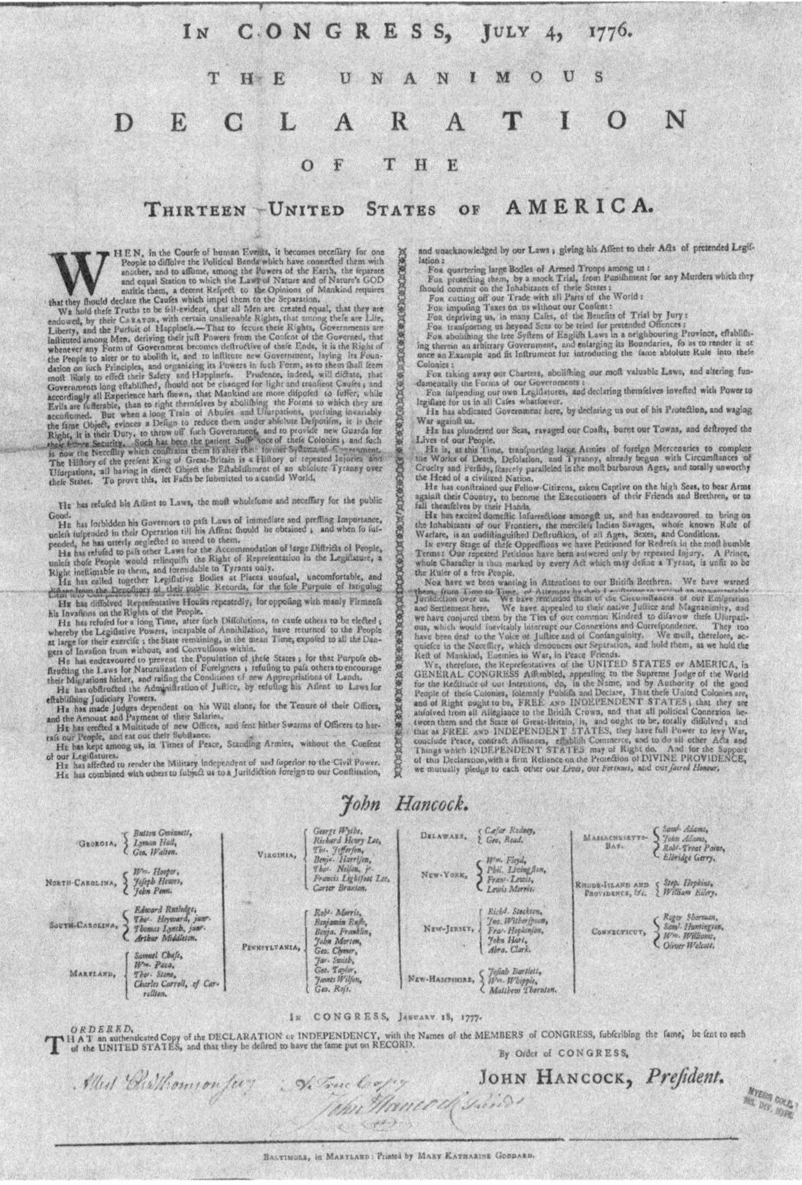

IN CONGRESS, JULY 4, 1776.

THE UNANIMOUS

DECLARATION

OF THE

THIRTEEN UNITED STATES OF AMERICA.

WHEN, in the Course of human Events, it becomes necessary for one People to dissolve the Political Bands which have connected them with another, and to assume, among the Powers of the Earth, the separate and equal Station to which the Laws of Nature and of Nature's GOD entitle them, a decent Respect to the Opinions of Mankind requires that they should declare the Causes which impel them to the Separation.

WE hold these Truths to be self-evident, that all Men are created equal, that they are endowed, by their CREATOR, with certain unalienable Rights, that among these are Life, Liberty, and the Pursuit of Happiness.—That to secure these Rights, Governments are instituted among Men, deriving their just Powers from the Consent of the Governed, that whenever any Form of Government becomes destructive of these Ends, it is the Right of the People to alter or to abolish it, and to institute new Government, laying its Foundation on such Principles, and organizing its Powers in such Form, as to them shall seem most likely to effect their Safety and Happiness. Prudence, indeed, will dictate, that Governments long established, should not be changed for light and transient Causes; and accordingly all Experience hath shewn, that Mankind are more disposed to suffer, while Evils are sufferable, than to right themselves by abolishing the Forms to which they are accustomed. But when a long Train of Abuses and Usurpations, pursuing invariably the same Object, evinces a Design to reduce them under absolute Despotism, it is their Right, it is their Duty, to throw off such Government, and to provide new Guards for their future Security. Such has been the patient Sufferance of these Colonies; and such is now the Necessity which constrains them to alter their former Systems of Government. The History of the present King of Great-Britain is a History of repeated Injuries and Usurpations, all having in direct Object the Establishment of an absolute Tyranny over these States. To prove this, let Facts be submitted to a candid World.

HE has refused his Assent to Laws, the most wholesome and necessary for the public Good.

HE has forbidden his Governors to pass Laws of immediate and pressing Importance, unless suspended in their Operation till his Assent should be obtained; and when so suspended, he has utterly neglected to attend to them.

HE has refused to pass other Laws for the Accommodation of large Districts of People, unless those People would relinquish the Right of Representation in the Legislature, a Right inestimable to them, and formidable to Tyrants only.

HE has called together Legislative Bodies at Places unusual, uncomfortable, and distant from the Depository of their public Records, for the sole Purpose of fatiguing them into Compliance with his Measures.

HE has dissolved Representative Houses repeatedly, for opposing with manly Firmness his Invasions on the Rights of the People.

HE has refused for a long Time, after such Dissolutions, to cause others to be elected; whereby the Legislative Powers, incapable of Annihilation, have returned to the People at large for their exercise; the State remaining, in the mean Time, exposed to all the Dangers of Invasion from without, and Convulsions within.

HE has endeavoured to prevent the Population of these States; for that Purpose obstructing the Laws for Naturalization of Foreigners; refusing to pass others to encourage their Migrations hither, and raising the Conditions of new Appropriations of Lands.

HE has obstructed the Administration of Justice, by refusing his Assent to Laws for establishing Judiciary Powers.

HE has made Judges dependent on his Will alone, for the Tenure of their Offices, and the Amount and Payment of their Salaries.

HE has erected a Multitude of new Offices, and sent hither Swarms of Officers to harrass our People, and eat out their Substance.

HE has kept among us, in Times of Peace, Standing Armies, without the Consent of our Legislatures.

HE has affected to render the Military independent of and superior to the Civil Power.

HE has combined with others to subject us to a Jurisdiction foreign to our Constitution, and unacknowledged by our Laws; giving his Assent to their Acts of pretended Legislation:

FOR quartering large Bodies of Armed Troops among us:

FOR protecting them, by a mock Trial, from Punishment for any Murders which they should commit on the Inhabitants of these States:

FOR cutting off our Trade with all Parts of the World:

FOR imposing Taxes on us without our Consent:

FOR depriving us, in many Cases, of the Benefits of Trial by Jury:

FOR transporting us beyond Seas to be tried for pretended Offences:

FOR abolishing the free System of English Laws in a neighbouring Province, establishing therein an arbitrary Government, and enlarging its Boundaries, so as to render it at once an Example and fit Instrument for introducing the same absolute Rule into these Colonies:

FOR taking away our Charters, abolishing our most valuable Laws, and altering fundamentally the Forms of our Governments:

FOR suspending our own Legislatures, and declaring themselves invested with Power to legislate for us in all Cases whatsoever.

HE has abdicated Government here, by declaring us out of his Protection, and waging War against us.

HE has plundered our Seas, ravaged our Coasts, burnt our Towns, and destroyed the Lives of our People.

HE is, at this Time, transporting large Armies of foreign Mercenaries to complete the Works of Death, Desolation, and Tyranny, already begun with Circumstances of Cruelty and Perfidy, scarcely paralleled in the most barbarous Ages, and totally unworthy the Head of a civilized Nation.

HE has constrained our Fellow-Citizens, taken Captive on the high Seas, to bear Arms against their Country, to become the Executioners of their Friends and Brethren, or to fall themselves by their Hands.

HE has excited domestic Insurrections amongst us, and has endeavoured to bring on the Inhabitants of our Frontiers, the merciless Indian Savages, whose known Rule of Warfare, is an undistinguished Destruction, of all Ages, Sexes, and Conditions.

IN every Stage of these Oppressions we have Petitioned for Redress in the most humble Terms: Our repeated Petitions have been answered only by repeated Injury. A Prince, whose Character is thus marked by every Act which may define a Tyrant, is unfit to be the Ruler of a free People.

NOR have we been wanting in Attentions to our British Brethren. We have warned them, from Time to Time, of Attempts by their Legislature to extend an unwarrantable Jurisdiction over us. We have reminded them of the Circumstances of our Emigration and Settlement here. We have appealed to their native Justice and Magnanimity, and we have conjured them by the Ties of our common Kindred to disavow these Usurpations, which would inevitably interrupt our Connexions and Correspondence. They too have been deaf to the Voice of Justice and of Consanguinity. We must, therefore, acquiesce in the Necessity, which denounces our Separation, and hold them, as we hold the Rest of Mankind, Enemies in War, in Peace Friends.

WE, therefore, the Representatives of the UNITED STATES OF AMERICA, in GENERAL CONGRESS Assembled, appealing to the Supreme Judge of the World for the Rectitude of our Intentions, do, in the Name, and by Authority of the good People of these Colonies, solemnly Publish and Declare, That these United Colonies are, and of Right ought to be, FREE AND INDEPENDENT STATES; that they are absolved from all Allegiance to the British Crown, and that all political Connexion between them and the State of Great-Britain, is, and ought to be, totally dissolved; and that as FREE AND INDEPENDENT STATES, they have full Power to levy War, conclude Peace, contract Alliances, establish Commerce, and to do all other Acts and Things which INDEPENDENT STATES may of Right do. And for the Support of this Declaration, with a firm Reliance on the Protection of DIVINE PROVIDENCE, we mutually pledge to each other our *Lives*, our *Fortunes*, and our *sacred Honour*.

John Hancock.

GEORGIA, *Button Gwinnett, Lyman Hall, Geo. Walton.*

NORTH-CAROLINA, *Wm. Hooper, Joseph Hewes, John Penn.*

SOUTH-CAROLINA, *Edward Rutledge, Thos. Heyward, junr. Thomas Lynch, junr. Arthur Middleton.*

MARYLAND, *Samuel Chase, Wm. Paca, Thos. Stone, Charles Carroll, of Carrollton.*

VIRGINIA, *George Wythe, Richard Henry Lee, Ths. Jefferson, Benja. Harrison, Thos. Nelson, jr. Francis Lightfoot Lee, Carter Braxton.*

PENNSYLVANIA, *Robt. Morris, Benjamin Rush, Benja. Franklin, John Morton, Geo. Clymer, Jas. Smith, Geo. Taylor, James Wilson, Geo. Ross.*

DELAWARE, *Cæsar Rodney, Geo. Read.*

NEW-YORK, *Wm. Floyd, Phil. Livingston, Frans. Lewis, Lewis Morris.*

NEW-JERSEY, *Richd. Stockton, Jno. Witherspoon, Fras. Hopkinson, John Hart, Abra. Clark.*

NEW-HAMPSHIRE, *Josiah Bartlett, Wm. Whipple, Matthew Thornton.*

MASSACHUSETTS-BAY, *Saml. Adams, John Adams, Robt. Treat Paine, Elbridge Gerry.*

RHODE-ISLAND AND PROVIDENCE, &c. *Step. Hopkins, William Ellery.*

CONNECTICUT, *Roger Sherman, Saml. Huntington, Wm. Williams, Oliver Wolcott.*

IN CONGRESS, JANUARY 18, 1777.

ORDERED,

THAT an authenticated Copy of the DECLARATION OF INDEPENDENCY, with the Names of the MEMBERS of CONGRESS, subscribing the same, be sent to each of the UNITED STATES, and that they be desired to have the same put on RECORD.

By Order of CONGRESS,

JOHN HANCOCK, *President.*

BALTIMORE, in MARYLAND: Printed by MARY KATHARINE GODDARD.

At the bottom of the Goddard Broadside, you can see Mary Katherine's name. You'll notice a different spelling; variations like this were very common in the eighteenth century.

was captured and imprisoned "under harsh conditions" for adding his name to the Declaration.[7]

In 1777, many women could not write; they often signed documents with an *X* because they were not literate. Even decades later, French political observer Alexis de Tocqueville noted that American society confined women to domestic roles, writing that "inexorable public opinion carefully keeps woman within the little sphere of domestic interests and duties."[8]

Mary Katherine defied those expectations, becoming one of the most prominent publishers during the nation's founding. Even before the statement of freedom from the king of England, Mary Katherine's newspaper, the *Maryland Journal and Baltimore Advertiser*, published editorials and documents that challenged unpopular taxation and control of the colonies by the British monarch. She devoted pages of her newspaper to Thomas Paine's "Common Sense"—the Revolutionary pamphlet that galvanized support for independence and rebuked the tyrannical rule of the king.

Furthermore, she wrote editorials *herself*. Following the battles of Lexington and Concord in 1775, considered the beginning of the Revolutionary War, she wrote, "What think ye of Congress now? That day . . . evidenced that Americans would rather die than live [as] slaves!"[9] As a wartime printer, she brought the front lines of the battlefield to the front pages, telling the colonies about the "savage barbarity" of the British soldiers.[10] Printing these words was clearly dangerous. Yet she persisted.

An established printer and publisher, she was appointed the postmaster of Baltimore in 1775 just as the Revolution started, serving under the leadership of Postmaster General Benjamin Franklin. That alone was a tremendous accomplishment for *anyone* at the time. Her duties were critical: ensuring the timely delivery of mail, often at her own expense, frequently using her own money to pay the people who were delivering letters and packages.[11] Writing letters was the only form of long-distance communication, and it allowed for the coordination of resistance during the war.[12]

Despite her service, in 1789, the new postmaster general replaced her with a man who, in her words, "never had a Day's previous knowledge of the duties he undertakes."[13] The reason given for her dismissal? Postmaster General Samuel Osgood claimed that in the role, "more travelling might be necessary than a Woman could undertake."[14] *A woman can't travel? It makes my blood boil.*

Baltimore citizens were outraged. Over 230 businessmen, including Maryland governor John Eager Howard, signed a petition demanding her reinstatement.

Mary Katherine's own letter to President Washington in 1789 was a plea for justice. She protested not only her removal but the humiliating way she had been treated as "an unfriendly delinquent, unworthy of common Civility, as well as common Justice."[15] When she called her dismissal an "extraordinary Act of oppression towards her," she was making it clear to Washington that she expected better from the republic she had helped to create.

It might very well have been the first time that a woman used the word *oppression* in a political context.[16] Her words still resonate today, echoing in the demands for equal pay, workplace equity, and recognition of women's contributions.

Sadly, President Washington's response on January 6, 1790, was dismissive: "I have uniformly avoided interfering with any appointments which do not require my official agency."[17] But Mary Katherine did not stop advocating for herself; she asked the U.S. Senate to reinstate her, but they never responded.[18]

She never got her job back. She never married or had children, but let us remember, *she helped birth a nation.* Her life was devoted to her work. Though no portraits of her survive today, her name is set in capital letters on the Goddard Broadside, an indelible mark on the history of the United States. For those who look hard enough, she is still there—forged in ink on parchment, a founding mother of America.

2.

Phillis Wheatley: *The Poet*

Mary Katherine Goddard printed the Declaration of Independence, but it was the poetry of Phillis Wheatley, an enslaved young woman, that helped inspire it.

In 1772, when Phillis was just nineteen years old, she penned a consequential poem that reflected her commitment to the cause of the colonies. In what is considered one of her most important political pieces, she expressed hope that there would be a new era where "*Freedom's* charms unfold."[1]

The poem was in the form of a letter, "To the Right Honourable William, Earl of Dartmouth," welcoming his appointment as the new secretary of state for the colonies. In it, she makes an impassioned plea for freedom and the end to British tyranny:

> Should you, my lord, while you peruse my song, Wonder from whence my love of Freedom sprung, Whence flow these wishes for the common good, By feeling hearts alone best understood, I, young in life, by seeming cruel fate Was snatch'd from Afric's fancy'd happy seat: . . . Such, such my case. And can I then but pray Others may never feel tyrannic sway?[2]

Phillis used rhyme and verse to draw a parallel between her personal experience as a Black girl born in West Africa and kidnapped as a child and the colonies' struggle against British rule. Through powerful prose, she highlighted the pain of slavery and urged Dartmouth to use his influence to abolish it. Her courage is extraordinary, given her age and the context of eighteenth-century America. That she would publish poems linking her experience as an enslaved woman to the need for America's independence from England was truly revolutionary, positioning her as a voice of her generation. In fact, no other poet at the time contributed to the cause of independence through verse like Phillis, and few other poets received such public praise or direct engagement from Revolutionary leaders like George Washington.[3]

Phillis's writings earned her the distinction of being called the "Poet Laureate of the American Revolution."[4] Her work spanned from the early protests against British oppression to the celebrations of American independence in 1784. Despite the adversity she faced, she managed to intertwine the themes of liberty, equality, and patriotism in her poetry. She not only supported the ideals of the Revolution but also highlighted its contradictions, particularly regarding slavery. And that makes her a hidden hero of America.

Phillis Wheatley arrived on America's shores on a slave ship from West Africa at age seven. She was born in Senegambia, which is part of modern-day Senegal and the Gambia. We don't know the name her parents gave to her because she was stolen from them and transported to Boston.

She spent two months aboard the *Phillis*—which would become her namesake—in the most horrific conditions, in a cramped hold with little to no ventilation or sanitation, leading to outbreaks of dysentery and smallpox. She emerged from the ship frail and nearly naked, except for a "quantity of dirty carpet" wrapped around her, and missing her front baby teeth.[5] Her survival in itself was remarkable, as nearly one out of four enslaved Africans died aboard that ship during the Middle Passage.[6]

Purchased in 1761 by John Wheatley, a prominent merchant, and his wife, Susanna, Phillis was initially brought into their household to be a domestic servant, according to Wheatley's biographer David Waldstreicher.

Ultimately, the Wheatleys encouraged her education, allowing their daughter Mary to tutor Phillis in reading and writing.[7] Within sixteen months, Phillis was fluent in English. By age eleven she was writing poems. "As soon as she could read well, she began to make Rhymes," said Susanna's grandnephew.[8] She quickly mastered the alphabet and went on to read English literature, Latin, and the Bible. Education was rare for any woman in the eighteenth century, let alone an enslaved girl. The Wheatleys recognized Phillis's extraordinary intellect and curiosity and considered her education to be their own spiritual obligation—although we'll never truly know their motivations.

In 1768, when Phillis was in her early teens, she wrote two notable poems that reflected the themes of freedom. The first was "To the King's Most Excellent Majesty," which praised King George III for the British Parliament's repeal of the hated Stamp Act, a direct tax on the colonies.[9] The second was "On Being Brought from Africa to America," a poem that directly addressed slavery through the framework of Christianity. The poem's final words were a rebuke to enslavers:

> Some view our sable race with scornful eye,
> "The color is a diabolic die."
> Remember Christians, Negros, black as Cain,
> May be refin'd, and join th' angelic train.[10]

By the time Phillis was fourteen years old, her fame had spread across the Atlantic, as her poetry was circulated among American and British elites. In 1770, when she was seventeen, a poem she wrote on the death of prominent English preacher George Whitefield was widely published and received acclaim.[11]

She closed out the elegy by addressing the English Countess of Huntingdon, a close friend of the preacher Whitefield, directly. This move proved pivotal for Phillis's future. A few years later, the countess sponsored Phillis's travel to London so she could publish her first collection of poems, called *Poems on Various Subjects, Religious and Moral.* The book was published in 1773 and was dedicated to the countess.[12]

Portrait of Phillis Wheatley sitting at a desk with pen and paper

The book included a note "to the public" by several notable Bostonians, attesting to the authenticity of Phillis's authorship. Reflecting the racist beliefs at the time that a Black woman couldn't possibly be the writer of incredible poetry, it reads: "AS it has been repeatedly suggested to the Publisher, by Persons, who have seen the Manuscript, that Numbers would be ready to suspect they were not really the Writings of PHILLIS . . . WE whose Names are under-written, do assure the World, that the POEMS . . . were written by Phillis, a young Negro Girl, who was but a few Years since, brought an uncultivated Barbarian from Africa, and has ever since been, and now is, under the Disadvantage of serving as a Slave in a Family in this Town."[13]

One of these supporters was none other than John Hancock, who would later sign the Declaration of Independence.

With this book, Phillis Wheatley became the first published African American poet and the third colonial American woman to have her work published.[14] Ironically, Phillis had to go to England, a country that her fellow patriots felt was too repressive, to get published.

During her visit to London, Phillis met Benjamin Franklin, who was living there at the time. This meeting was more than just a professional visit; some historians suggest there were discussions of emancipation or the idea of Phillis staying in England so that she could be free.[15]

According to the Constitution Center, Phillis returned to America with the understanding that the Wheatley family would grant her freedom. A month after her return, she was indeed freed—although her freedom was still constrained by the racial and gendered limitations of the time.

With her newfound independence, she continued to write. In 1775, she sent a patriotic poem to General George Washington, congratulating him as the commander in chief of the Continental Army:

> Proceed, great chief, with virtue on thy side,
> Thy ev'ry action let the goddess guide.
> A crown, a mansion, and a throne that shine,
> With gold unfading, WASHINGTON! be thine.[16]

Washington clearly liked it and replied praising her "great poetical Talents." He called her "genius" and invited Phillis to his headquarters, an unprecedented gesture at the time for a Black person.[17]

"If you should ever come to Cambridge, or near Head Quarters," he wrote, "I shall be happy to see a person so favourd by the Muses, and to whom nature has been so liberal and beneficent in her dispensations."[18]

Washington sent Phillis's letter and poem to his aide, Lieutenant Colonel Joseph Reed, who had it published in the pro-American newspaper the *Virginia Gazette*.[19] It was a carefully considered decision because at the time the British were offering freedom to enslaved people who would fight with the redcoats. The goal was to stop Black Americans from joining the English after hundreds had already signed up. "In ways she never anticipated, [Phillis] became a political actor in one of America's worst crises," according to scholar James G. Basker. The poem showed once again that Phillis was committed to the American cause, praising soldiers for joining the Continental Army.

Phillis's patriotic words would also have been considered treasonous by the British monarchy, punishable by death. Phillis was a Black woman and "she might be summarily transported to the Caribbean and sold into slavery," Basker observed. "By writing this poem and others like it over the next eight years, Wheatley as much as Patrick Henry or any other American patriot was risking her liberty and her life."[20]

By writing this poem and others like it over the next eight years, Wheatley as much as Patrick Henry or any other American patriot was risking her liberty and her life.

—James G. Basker

As the Revolution raged on and the slave trade flourished, she wrote a poem in 1778 that was never published during her lifetime.[21] It's an elegy called "On the Death of General Wooster"—an American war hero who died in battle and was supportive of ending slavery. Through her words, General Wooster speaks from the grave, criticizing the enslavement of Black people while the country fights for freedom:

> But how, presumptuous shall we hope to find
> Divine acceptance with th' Almighty mind—
> While yet (O deed ungenerous!) they disgrace
> And hold in bondage Afric's blameless race?
> Let virtue reign—And thou accord our prayers
> Be victory our's, and generous freedom theirs.

Phillis hoped that freedom for the colonies would mean freedom for everyone. She believed that freedom was an intrinsic human right, clearly enshrined in the Declaration of Independence, but not in practice in the new nation.[22]

Not all the signers of the founding document were fans of Phillis. Thomas Jefferson—the notorious slaveowner and future president—dismissed her. "Religion indeed has produced a Phyllis Whately [*sic*]; but it could not produce a poet," he wrote in his 1787 book, *Notes on the State of Virginia*. "The compositions published under her name are below the dignity of criticism."[23]

Over two hundred years later, that criticism of Phillis would be the inspiration for America's first National Youth Poet Laureate and activist Amanda Gorman. She wrote in 2021, "Whenever I feel unable to write, I remember that Thomas Jefferson singled out young black poetess Phillis Wheatley with shallow disdain. . . . Then I crack my knuckles and get to work."[24]

> ***Whenever I feel unable to write, I remember that Thomas Jefferson singled out young black poetess Phillis Wheatley with shallow disdain. . . . Then I crack my knuckles and get to work.***
>
> ***—Amanda Gorman***

Despite Phillis's literary success, life remained difficult. Her works continued to push for freedom and equality for all, though she faced many challenges, including financial struggles and the limitations placed on her as a Black woman in early America.[25]

In 1784, she died shortly after the birth of her third child at just thirty-one years old. Her obituary, published in the *Worcester Gazette*, was brief and dismissive: "At Boston, Phillis Peters (formerly Phillis Wheatley), an African, aged 31, known to the literary world by her celebrated miscellaneous poems."[26]

Phillis deserved more recognition then and now. She was a genius by any measure. Her bold messages of freedom—and her hope that this new nation would be free for more people—were alchemized and translated into the writings of the founding fathers, including in the Declaration of Independence, where the singular spirit of American liberty was crystallized. She helped create the idea of America and she inspired the men who take up the most space in the history books, including George Washington and Benjamin Franklin. Even so, they denied her the freedom she wrote about so eloquently.

Today, her voice lives on through the work of modern poets and activists, as Phillis Wheatley is now rightly known as the "founding mother of African American literature."[27]

3.

Mercy Otis Warren:
The Intellectual

"History is not the Province of the Ladies," John Adams declared dismissively.[1]

These bitter words were aimed at a particular woman, Mercy Otis Warren, who is considered the leading female intellectual of the Revolution and the early Republic. Her pen had wounded Adams's pride and shattered their decades-long friendship just a few years after he finished his term as the second president of the United States (and lost re-election to political rival Thomas Jefferson).

The irony of his rebuke was striking. The same John Adams had been one of Mercy's greatest early champions, praising her political acumen, and once calling Mercy "the most accomplished Lady in America."[2]

Now he sought to undermine Mercy's greatest achievement: *History of the Rise, Progress and Termination of the American Revolution,* published in 1805. Over three decades she had meticulously crafted a comprehensive three-volume history of the Revolution, and Adams was furious over Mercy's candid assessment of him in the work.[3]

The pair had known each other for most of their lives, and the origin of their conflict was seeded almost twenty years earlier, during the constitutional debates of 1787–1788. Mercy, a staunch Anti-Federalist, believed that the proposed Constitution betrayed the republican ideals of the Revolution by centralizing too much power in the federal government. Adams, whose political philosophy influenced the Constitution, took her criticisms personally. Mercy's pamphlet "Observations on the New Constitution" was published anonymously in 1788 and circulated widely.[4] It not only articulated a powerful case against ratification without a Bill of Rights but also implicitly criticized men like Adams who supported it.

In 1805, she described him in her seminal history as having a "partiality for monarchy" and offered this scathing critique: "A statesman of penetration and ability; but his prejudices and passions were sometimes too strong for his sagacity and judgment."[5] The criticism stung Adams deeply, and he felt he had been stabbed in the back.[6]

What's more, Mercy refused to back down. If Adams wanted to correct the record, she suggested in their exchange of heated letters following the publication, he should write his own memoir.[7] The book's publication was the final blow to a friendship already strained by political disagreements that were at the heart of America's founding ideals.

The depth of their intellectual relationship makes his dismissive "not the Province of the Ladies" comment all the more revealing: *He was threatened by her independent thinking.* Though they would eventually reconcile, their relationship never fully recovered. For Mercy, principles always came before personalities, even when it cost her dearly. That is why the poet, playwright, and pamphleteer is today known as the "First Lady of the American Revolution."[8]

Mercy Otis Warren was a revolutionary intellectual, and admittedly I was surprised to learn just how influential she was. Not only did she have direct sway over the founding fathers, but she has been called the "secret muse of the Bill of Rights."[9]

Mercy was born in Barnstable, Massachusetts, in 1728, the third of thirteen children and the first daughter of Colonel James Otis and Mary Allyne Otis. Her father was a merchant, farmer, and wealthy district judge who took an unusual interest in his daughter's education. When she was approximately nine years old, she forcefully made her case to sit in on her brother's school lessons, and her father granted permission—a highly unorthodox decision for the time.[10]

While some privileged girls of her era learned only to read, Mercy received a comprehensive education in history, classical literature, and mythology alongside her brother. She was especially close to her brother James Otis, Jr., who became Boston's leading advocate for colonial rights.[11]

In 1754, at age twenty-six, she married James Warren, a Massachusetts politician she had met eleven years earlier through her brother's Harvard connections. They would have five sons together between 1757 and 1766.[12] You could say the Warrens were one of the original political power couples at the center of the radical anti-British movement in Massachusetts. They hosted frequent salons where they discussed British tyranny and America's path to independence with influential men, including George Washington. Their Plymouth, Massachusetts, home became a strategic meeting place where Boston radicals planned newspaper coverage to incite rebellion against British rule.

What made their marriage remarkable was James's encouragement of his wife's "unfeminine" interests in politics and writing. Her husband said she had a "Masculine Genius"[13] along with the "Weakness which is the Consequence of the Exquisite delicacy and softness of her Sex."[14]

As biographer Rosemarie Zagarri noted, "Mercy Otis Warren came to be who she was because the men in her life allowed her to violate the established boundaries of womanhood."[15] Remember, women during this time period were politically invisible; they had no vote and no voice in politics.

Mercy initially published her writings anonymously under pen names like "A Columbian Patriot." But in 1790, she became one of the first American women to publish political works under her own name, something she did until her death.

Her first play, *The Adulateur,* appeared in Boston's *Massachusetts Spy* newspaper in 1772, signaling her fierce belief in America's need for autonomy.[16] Her patriotic writings were partially fueled by a long-standing grudge against the colonial governor Thomas Hutchinson, her family's nemesis. She resented him for defeating her father for the position of chief justice in 1760 and believed Hutchinson would do anything to win King George III's favor. In *The Adulateur,* she warned that a time would come when "murders, blood and carnage / Shall crimson all these streets."

> ***The origin of all power is in the people, and that they have an incontestable right to check the creatures of their own creation.***
>
> ***—Mercy Otis Warren***

After the Boston Tea Party, John Adams specifically requested that she write a poem using mythical "sea-nymphs and goddesses."[17] Her resulting work, "The Squabble of the Sea Nymphs," supported the tea protests, portraying Neptune's wives discussing which teas are best when protesters pour them into the water, and thereby "bids defiance to the servile train, / The pimps and sycophants of George's reign."[18] *Today, we might call this a "diss track" of King George III.*

Mercy was a Jeffersonian Republican—opposing a powerful centralized government.[19] She wanted power centered in the states, believing that strong local governance was the best defense against tyranny. For example, she wrote in "Observations on the New Constitution," "The origin of all power is in the people, and that they have an incontestable right to check the creatures of their own creation."

When Massachusetts ratified the Constitution on February 6, 1788, Governor John Hancock sent a number of amendments, many of which were suggestions Mercy had made. Her insistence on explicit protections for individual liberties created a model for the Bill of Rights.[20] Her 1788 pamphlet, written anonymously, "Observations on the New Constitution," was instrumental in pressing Congress to

Painting of Mercy Otis Warren at age thirty-six or thirty-seven

adopt the seminal document. Mercy's critique was comprehensive and prescient. Her essay warned that the Constitution lacked a bill of rights—no guarantees of a "free press, freedom of conscience, or trial by jury." Mercy complained that the Constitution didn't protect citizens from arbitrary warrants giving officials power to "enter our houses, search, insult, and seize at pleasure."[21, 22]

Her writing provided the intellectual and emotional foundation for demanding explicit protections of individual rights. Her pamphlet became a rallying cry for the Anti-Federalist cause, with 1,700 copies distributed in New York alone in response to the 500 copies of The Federalist Papers.[23]

In today's vernacular, Mercy would be called an intellectual influencer. She played a public political role that was extraordinarily rare for women of her time, writing scathing satires, poems, and plays that took on the British monarchy. She treated Americans loyal to the British crown—known as loyalists—with equal venom. Mercy was taken very seriously by the men who were decision-makers, at a time when women were not meant to participate in political discussions.

Thomas Jefferson praised her "high station in the ranks of genius."[24] Alexander Hamilton, upon receiving her book of poetry, wrote that her work makes it clear that "female genius in the United States has outstripped the Male."[25]

While she wasn't always *in the room where it happened,* she and her good friend Abigail Adams stood in the doorway offering their own opinions and critiques that shaped the nation's founding.

Mercy had a long and prolific career, culminating in the publication of her signature work when she was almost eighty years old: the three-volume history of the American Revolution.

With all her accomplishments, what remains surprising is that even as the "muse of the Bill of Rights," someone who went toe-to-toe with John Adams, Mercy was not an advocate for greater legal rights for women. The leading intellectual of her time would instead be remembered for promoting what's known as "Republican Motherhood"—the idea that women's key role was educating their sons (not their daughters) to become active citizens and future leaders.

Today, Mercy is often considered a hero by those who value the principles of limited government, individual liberty, and republicanism. Her writings championed Enlightenment principles and republican virtues, emphasizing sacrifice for the common good over personal greed. Her role as a defender of the Revolution and her critiques of centralized power continue to resonate with those who admire America's founding values.

As she aged, Mercy worried that her mind would deteriorate before her body. She prayed this wouldn't happen—and it didn't.[26] Until her death at age eighty-six in 1814, she remained engaged with the new country she had helped create.

Perhaps the most enduring aspect of Mercy's legacy is her unwavering commitment to principle. When her portrayal of John Adams cost her a valued friendship, she never backed down. She stood by her convictions, even when they came at a personal cost. Mercy demonstrated that the highest form of patriotism sometimes requires speaking uncomfortable truths to those in power—even when they're your friends. And in doing so, she proved definitively that history was, indeed, the province of this lady.

4.

Elizabeth Ellet: *The Historian*

Like Mercy, Elizabeth Ellet was a well-known author, historian, and cultural influencer. By the time she passed away in 1877, she had certainly accomplished enough to be considered worthy of a comprehensive obituary in the venerated *New York Times.* Yet what was written about her on June 4, 1877, was disappointingly brief. In fact, the obituary devoted a good bit of space to her father, who was praised as "a gentleman of refined tastes and studious habits," an irrelevant detail that overshadowed Elizabeth's achievements. According to the *Times,* she was "in every way a true woman" whose "professional pursuits, much as she was attached to them, did not rob her of interest in domestic affairs."[1] One could only imagine Elizabeth's horror if she knew how her prolific body of work would be remembered.

Elizabeth Ellet's true legacy lies in being the first writer to record the lives of women who contributed to the Revolutionary War in her 1848 book, *The Women of the American Revolution.* With a single-minded determination, she researched and chronicled the experiences of the women from an era several decades before her own. It is because of her meticulous work that we know the hopes, fears, and challenges faced by Revolutionary-era women.

These "patriotic mothers," Elizabeth eloquently wrote, "nursed the infancy of freedom." What makes her achievement even more remarkable is that she was researching and writing women's history more than a hundred years before America's universities began formally teaching the subject.[2]

The challenges Elizabeth faced in telling the stories of these influential women were vast—something I've learned while working on *this* book and is likely familiar to anyone who has attempted similar historical recovery work. We remain indebted to women like Elizabeth who created the blueprint for future historians. In the early nineteenth century, women's lives were considered largely unimportant to the historical record, making it extraordinary that a woman would undertake such a daunting research project. The idea itself was bold; achieving it was a remarkable feat.

Elizabeth herself acknowledged this difficulty in her preface, writing, "The apparent dearth of information was at first almost disheartening." She continued, "The actions of men stand out in prominent relief, and are a safe guide in forming a judgment of them; a woman's sphere, on the other hand, is secluded, and in very few instances does her personal history, even though she may fill a conspicuous position, afford sufficient incident to; throw a strong light upon her character."[3] Through her work, Elizabeth attempted to correct this historical imbalance.

Elizabeth's ambition to tell these unheralded women's stories would become a three-volume history containing more than 160 biographical sketches. Through her work, she offered contemporary nineteenth-century readers a window into a time when women, who were expected to stay at home and take care of the house and children, stepped outside their traditional roles to help secure America's freedom.

The Women of the American Revolution was truly the first of its kind of women's history. Elizabeth approached her work not only as a historian but also as a journalist.

She traveled extensively around the country, seeking out and interviewing surviving women who had lived through the Revolution. For those who had died, she diligently tracked down their descendants. She undertook this monumental task to ensure that their stories would not be lost.

"Many incidents and scenes of Revolutionary times are remembered, of the actors in which little is known beyond what is contained in the anecdotes themselves," she wrote. "A few of these are subjoined as aiding our general object of illustrating the spirit and character of the women of those days. Fragmentary as they are—they have some interest in this light, and it seems a duty to preserve them as historical facts."[4]

Elizabeth Ellet

The Revolution, as told through Elizabeth's research, revealed how circumstances expanded female opportunities out of sheer necessity. Determined to reimagine American history through the eyes of women, Elizabeth spent many mornings at the New York Historical Society gathering facts and anecdotes. She traveled to libraries and historical societies throughout parts of the South and the Northeast, often facing significant challenges in transportation and accommodations as a woman traveling alone for scholarly purposes.

With tremendous effort and a sense of urgency, Elizabeth solicited aid from other scholars, writers, and descendants of the Revolution's participants. She corresponded with prominent figures such as Lydia Sigourney, Henry Wadsworth Longfellow, and Jared Sparks, appealing to their patriotic sentiments to assist her work. Almost everyone she approached responded with anecdotes, advice, or encouragement.[5]

Elizabeth understood what was at stake: If she did not seek out relatives or the few remaining survivors of the Revolution, these women's stories would vanish forever.

Elizabeth Fries Lummis Ellet was born in western New York in 1818 to Dr. William A. Lummis and his wife, Sarah Maxwell.[6] Elizabeth was raised in an upper-middle-class home and educated at a female seminary in Aurora, New York.[7]

As with most women of her race and class, her education was mainly intended to prepare her for marriage and motherhood, not a professional career. The value of her schooling was seen primarily in what she could impart to her future children. Yet Elizabeth clearly wanted more, despite living in a society that considered a "woman with brains" who thought or wrote to be somehow diseased and abnormal.[8] She showed early literary talent; in her teens, she started publishing her poetry and translating European literature for the *American Ladies' Magazine.*[9]

In 1835, at age seventeen, she married Dr. William H. Ellet, a professor of chemistry at Columbia College in New York City. That same year, she published *Poems: Translated and Original.* Soon after their marriage, the Ellets moved to Columbia, South Carolina, where her husband took a position as a chemistry teacher at South Carolina College.[10]

Elizabeth believed that literary success required a presence in New York City, which was already the center of the publishing industry. By 1820, New York was America's fastest-growing city with a population of over two hundred thousand, which would quadruple by 1860.[11] Elizabeth was entering the literary world at a time when publishers were eager to promote American authors with their own unique style.

By 1843, Elizabeth was making regular trips between South Carolina and New York. She strategically invited the most prestigious authors and editors for dinners at her apartment, which was located within the eight-block radius that was home to New York's publishing community.[12] She became a frequent and welcome guest at literary salons.[13]

Elizabeth was remarkably prolific; between 1835 and 1870 she published at least seventeen books spanning poetry, biography, history, and domestic guides.[14] Despite her success, she confided to friends that she felt constrained by her marriage and wished she hadn't married so young.[15] She never had children, but her legacy lived on through the breadth of her work.

One of the remarkable stories Elizabeth preserved was that of Emily Geiger. In the summer of 1781, Emily volunteered as a messenger for General Nathanael Greene when no one else would risk the dangerous journey through territory controlled by British forces. Greene needed to deliver a message to General Thomas Sumter requesting that they combine forces to attack British lieutenant colonel Francis Rawdon's army. Greene gave the young woman a letter for Sumter and read it aloud to her so she could memorize it in case she needed to destroy the physical evidence.

Riding sidesaddle through the countryside, Emily was intercepted by Lord Rawdon's scouts on the second day of her journey. While waiting for a woman to search her, Emily ate the letter, destroying the evidence. *What quick thinking!* Finding nothing incriminating, the British eventually released her. Taking an indirect route to avoid further capture, she successfully reached Sumter's camp and delivered General Greene's message verbally, exactly as she had memorized it.

Elizabeth concluded Emily's story with hope that "her name will descend to posterity among those of the patriotic females of the Revolution."[16] Thanks to Elizabeth's work, it has. The South Carolina State House has a memorial plaque dedicated to Emily Geiger.[17]

The Women of the American Revolution was a tremendous commercial success, going into multiple printings after the first volume was published in 1848.[18] The book received nearly universal praise from critics and readers alike. The *North American Review* called it "delicious . . . bits of private history fished up from the vast sea of things forgotten."[19] By 1850, after her book had gone through five printings, Elizabeth added a second and third volume with additional biographies.

By profiling so many previously unknown women, Elizabeth made the profound point that women who participated in the founding of the country deserved historical recognition. The women of Elizabeth's era could look to these revolutionary women of the past and find inspiration to challenge their own contemporary limitations. Through her writing, Elizabeth helped shape the evolving narrative of the young American nation.

Her historical work, while groundbreaking, had significant limitations. Though she told the stories of women from every colony and from various ranks of society, she chose to ignore the role of Black women in the Revolution, reflecting the racial prejudices of her time. It's unfortunate that she did not include Black women like Phillis Wheatley and Elizabeth Freeman in her volumes.

While Elizabeth is best remembered for her revolutionary histories, her work extended to many domains. In 1857, she published *The Practical Housekeeper: A Cyclopaedia of Domestic Economy*, a comprehensive cookbook and encyclopedic treatise on all aspects of homemaking.[20] This impressive volume would no doubt impress Martha Stewart, as it contained five thousand recipes, capturing American culinary arts just before the Civil War.

> ***Patriotic mothers nursed the infancy of freedom.***
>
> ***—Elizabeth Ellet***

The book included everything from home furnishings, table setting, and napkin folding to childcare and food storage. It also featured sections on carving, culinary utensils, foreign cooking terms, and seasonal foods for each month. It shows Elizabeth's versatility. Some of the recipes had entertaining names like "Salmon-To Pickle Undressed," "A Fresh Neat's Tongue and Udder," and "Mutton China Chilo." *Not rushing to try those.*

Despite her significant contributions to American historical writing, one of the first things modern readers might discover if they Google "Elizabeth Ellet" is her alleged romantic entanglement with Edgar Allan Poe. She became involved in a public scandal involving the famous writer when, reportedly jealous of Poe's relationship with Frances Sargent Osgood, she exposed the affair to Poe's wife. Poe, for his part, publicly denounced her, and this imbroglio has unfortunately become a distracting footnote in her biography, overshadowing her substantial intellectual contributions.

At a time when women were publishing anonymously and using pseudonyms, Elizabeth always used her real name. This choice, combined with her unprecedented historical research, reveals how strongly she believed in her own intellect and the value of her contributions.

Elizabeth Ellet died in 1877, having published works across multiple genres and established herself as a pioneering voice in women's history. While her contemporaries may not have fully appreciated the significance of her achievements, her contributions laid essential groundwork for future generations of women's historians.

Over the next decades we see women taking increasing pride in and ownership over their intellectual contributions, eventually gaining the seats at historical and academic tables that Elizabeth herself had rightfully claimed. More than simply a historian, Elizabeth Ellet was a visionary who understood that a nation's story is incomplete without the voices of its women.

5.

Elizabeth Freeman: *The Freedom Seeker*

An unusual resting place exists for an influential family in Stockbridge, Massachusetts, in the bucolic western part of the state. Known locally as the Sedgwick Pie, several graves are arranged in a circle around prominent judge Theodore Sedgwick and his wife, Pamela.

The story goes that the eccentric arrangement is because Judge Sedgwick wanted his family's feet facing the center so that, on Judgment Day, they would stand and see only Sedgwicks gathered around them. Elizabeth Freeman is the only person buried among them who is not related to the family by blood. Her tombstone stands in the innermost circle of the pie. She earned her place of prominence among the Sedgwicks, but she's also earned her place of distinction in American history. Elizabeth Freeman was the reason slavery ended in the Commonwealth of Massachusetts—which was effectively the first state to abolish slavery.[1]

Elizabeth was born enslaved around 1742–1744 and given the name Bett. Enslaved people in the Northeast often did domestic work, cleaned, cooked, and gardened, and they participated in spinning and weaving. She grew up with her younger sister on a plantation in a small town in the New York colony. Her enslaver was Pieter Hogeboom, who was related to the first Dutch settlers in the region.[2] When Hogeboom's daughter, Hannah, married Colonel John Ashley, Elizabeth and her sister were given to the couple. The sisters were forced to move and start a new life of servitude in Sheffield, Massachusetts, thirty-four miles away from everything and everyone they had ever known.[3]

Elizabeth was only a teenager when she arrived in Sheffield. Before the American Revolution, Sheffield was the largest town in Berkshire County, with a population of nearly two thousand people—nineteen of them enslaved.[4]

One day, Hannah Ashley was enraged after apparently finding Elizabeth's sister (although some historians say it was Elizabeth's daughter) using leftover dough to make bread. Mrs. Ashley picked up "a large iron shovel red hot from cleaning the oven" and tried to hit her.[5] Elizabeth raised her arm to protect her family member and received a deep wound that left a long scar on her forearm for the rest of her life. She never covered it, and when visitors to the house asked her what happened, she said simply, "Ask Madam."[6] Elizabeth intended to make sure *no one* forgot how she was treated.

While Elizabeth lived in the Ashley household, a revolutionary moment happened there. Colonel Ashley hosted the committee that drafted the Sheffield Resolves, a declaration of individual rights and a protest of British rule over the colonies drawn up in 1773.

The Sheffield Resolves began with the powerful words "RESOLVED, That Mankind in a State of Nature are equal, free, and independent of each other, and have a right to the undisturbed Enjoyment of their Lives, their Liberty and Property."[7] These ideals were later echoed in the Declaration of Independence.

Elizabeth was serving the white revolutionaries who gathered at the house. Here she was surrounded by discussions about individual liberty and freedom, and yet she herself was being enslaved by one of the men promoting equality.

Though she could neither read nor write, she heard these documents read aloud, and their principles resonated deeply with her. "By keepin' still and mindin' things," she's recorded as saying, she realized she should seek her own freedom.[8]

When she heard a public reading of the newly ratified Massachusetts Constitution of 1780, written by John Adams, proclaiming in Article I, "All men are born free and equal and have certain natural, essential, and unalienable rights," Elizabeth knew she deserved the same freedom the patriots were fighting for.[9]

"Any time while I was a slave," she reportedly later said, "if one minute's freedom had been offered to me, and I had been told I must die at the end of that minute, I would have taken it—just to stand one minute on God's earth a free woman."[10] Her yearning for freedom was so powerful that the day after hearing the Declaration of Independence read aloud, Elizabeth walked about five miles to the home of attorney Theodore Sedgwick, who had helped write the Sheffield Resolves.[11]

There she approached Sedgwick. "Sir," she said, "I heard that paper read yesterday that says 'all men are born equal—&, that every man has a right to freedom'—I am not a dumb Critter, wont the law give me my freedom?"[12] She understood perfectly the contradiction between the ideals being espoused and her own condition of enslavement. She used their own language against them, asking why she should be excluded from the ideals that were shaping this new country.

Sedgwick agreed to represent her, though he had his own abhorrent relationship with slavery. A bill of sale recorded in 1777 shows that Theodore Sedgwick purchased a "negro woman" named Ton, about thirty years old, from a neighbor.[13] Even after representing Elizabeth, Sedgwick helped co-author the Fugitive Slave Law of 1793, which made it a crime for northerners to aid or abet escaped enslaved people. That law set the precedent for the Fugitive Slave Law of 1850, which contributed to the Civil War.[14]

One of the first choices made by Sedgwick in the case was to include a man named Brom, who was enslaved by the Colonel Ashley of the suit. Women had limited legal rights in Massachusetts courts at the time, and the thought was that an enslaved woman might not have the same credibility as a man.[15] The case became known as *Brom and Bett v. Ashley*.

Ashley was ordered to turn over Brom and Bett to the local sheriff, but he refused, and the case went to a jury trial. The trial opened at the

County Court of Common Pleas in Great Barrington on August 21, 1781; it lasted only two days and neither plaintiff took the stand.[16] The jury ruled in Brom and Bett's favor, making them the first enslaved people to be emancipated in Massachusetts as a result of the 1780 state constitution.[17] Colonel Ashley was also instructed to pay thirty shillings in damages plus trial costs.[18]

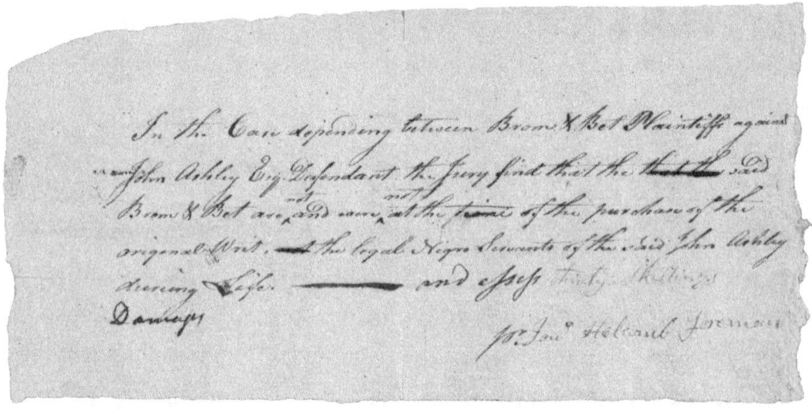

In the Case depending between Brom & Bet Plaintiffs against John Ashley Esq Defendant the Jury find that the ~~that the~~ said Brom & Bet are not and were not at the time of the purchase of the original Writ, the legal Negro Servants of the said John Ashley during Life. —— and assess thirty shillings Damages

pr. Saml Holcomb Foreman

The jury verdict form that found Brom and Bett were not Ashley's property and set them free

At first, Ashley appealed the decision to the Supreme Judicial Court of Massachusetts, the highest court in the commonwealth, but he dropped it before his appeal reached the court. This was likely due to the intervening decisions in the Quock Walker trials, which made it clear that slavery was not legal under the Massachusetts Constitution.[19]

Elizabeth's landmark case paved the way for the state to effectively outlaw slavery in 1783, and when the state Supreme Court upheld Walker's freedom, the ruling was considered to have informally ended slavery in the state.[20] Massachusetts was, in effect, the first state to abolish slavery and stood as a moral compass for the rest of the country during the Civil War.[21]

After winning her freedom, Elizabeth made a powerful statement of self-determination by changing her name from Bett to Elizabeth

Freeman, rejecting her enslaved name and claiming her identity as a free woman.[22] She then became the paid domestic servant of Theodore and Pamela Sedgwick and their seven children. The family adored her—but we can never know how Elizabeth felt about them. She did not read or write, so her story has always been told through the eyes of her white employers.

The Sedgwick children did not call her by her chosen name and instead called her Mumbet, or "Mother Beth."[23] Pamela was often sick in bed with debilitating depression, and Elizabeth essentially raised the children and also worked as a midwife and nurse. She proved her courage during Shays' Rebellion in 1787, when she defended the Sedgwick house from a small mob of rebels.[24]

The Sedgwicks' youngest daughter, Catharine Maria, described Elizabeth as "the main pillar of our household."[25]

Catharine became a well-known novelist; among other Sedgwick family celebrities are one of Andy Warhol's stars, Edie Sedgwick, and Hollywood actress Kyra Sedgwick.

Catharine's 1853 essay "Slavery in New England" is the most often cited source about Elizabeth's life. However, it delivers a romanticized vision of the relationship between the Sedgwicks and Freeman. In her essay, Catharine explained that she and her siblings referred to Freeman as "Mumbet," a name "contracted by lisping lips from Mammy Bet, to Mum-Bett, by which name she was best known." Her nickname, by which she is widely referred to in history texts, was given to her by white children whom she effectively worked for; it is not the name she gave herself.[26] There was an undeniable power structure in place.

Catharine wrote about Elizabeth as a maternal figure for her and her siblings and only mentions Elizabeth's own family in harsh terms, describing her as "weakly indulgent to her riotous and ruinous descendants."[27] One can't imagine Elizabeth referring to her children that way.

In 1808, when Elizabeth was in her sixties, she bought her own property, where she practiced as a midwife, farmed, and devoted herself to caring for her grown child, grandchildren, and great-grandchildren. She became economically independent and successful. When she died, she was the second-wealthiest Black landowner in her town.

Portrait of Elizabeth Freeman painted in 1811

We know from her will, which she dictated to Catharine's brother Charles and signed with an *X* two months before she passed away, that she had managed to buy nineteen acres of land as well as furniture, jewelry, and expensive clothing. Unsurprisingly, she left it all to her family and nothing to the Sedgwicks.[28]

Her influence on the country cannot be overstated. According to historian Ousmane Power-Greene, "One can challenge authority, and end up shifting the way people think about the world."[29]

Elizabeth was buried not with her family but with the Sedgwicks, and the epitaph on her gravestone was written by Catharine:

> ELIZABETH FREEMAN, also known by the name of MUMBET died Dec. 28 1829. Her supposed age was 85 Years. She was born a slave and remained a slave for nearly thirty years; she could neither read nor write, yet in her own sphere she had no superior or equal. She neither wasted time nor property. She never violated a trust, nor failed to perform a duty. In every situation of domestic trial, she was the most efficient helper and the tenderest friend. Good mother, farewell.[30]

The one existing portrait of Freeman was painted in 1811 by Catharine's sister-in-law Susan Ann Livingston Ridley Sedgwick. I think the most striking thing about it is that her scar is covered up by the long sleeves of her dress, an artistic choice I can't imagine she made herself. According to Catharine's "Slavery in New England," Elizabeth made a point of never covering up her scar, which she may have considered symbolic of her own strength and ability to protect others.[31]

I wish that we could hear Elizabeth Freeman's story in her own words. I wish we could know how she found the courage to demand her freedom. I wish we knew how she felt about the Sedgwicks. Even though her story is incomplete, she left behind a legacy of great courage, wisdom, and tremendous love. She showed that one individual, without formal education or social standing, could understand profound principles of justice and freedom and, through her actions, change the course of history.

6.

Deborah Sampson: *The War Fighter*

Deborah Sampson was one of the first women to take a bullet for America, after she secretly joined George Washington's army when she was twenty-one years old.[1] Until her death in 1827, she had a musket ball lodged in her body—one of the many injuries she endured as a trailblazing woman warrior.[2]

But for Deborah, the pain of her injuries was nothing compared to the "sickening terror" she felt at the possibility of being discovered. She would rather die on the battlefield than have it be known that she was a woman disguised as a man.[3] Deborah was a patriot who was forced to fend for herself at a young age.

Born around 1760 in Plympton, Massachusetts, Deborah was raised in poverty. She was told her father died in a shipwreck, although it is believed he deserted his family. Her mother could not afford to support her children, so she sent them away to live with families that could give the kids proper care. Deborah went to the home of a "respectable farmer."[4] This practice of placing children with foster families was not uncommon in eighteenth-century New England.[5]

From age five, Deborah worked as an indentured servant. While she didn't attend school, she borrowed books from the children she took care of and taught herself how to read.[6]

Alfred F. Young, her biographer, describes Deborah as a "masterless woman," emphasizing her independence and resilience. Her refusal to be controlled by any man was striking, and this attitude would define her life.[7]

In 1779, as a young woman, she left to strike out on her own. She worked as a teacher and a weaver, paid by the piece. It was one of the rare occupations that paid men and women equally. She stood out physically—at five feet, seven inches, she was taller than most men of the time.[8] One man in her town described her as "tall, muscular and very erect and considered one of the very best specimens of womanhood among the hardy and vigorous population of Middleboro of that day." People thought she had masculine qualities, which likely aided in her ability to disguise herself as a man.[9]

It is impossible to know why she joined the Continental Army, but it is logical to think that her place in the world led her to take risks that other women wouldn't. She had no close family, no reliable source of income, and very little to lose. As the war dragged on it became harder and harder to find young men willing to sign up to fight. Massachusetts had to enact a draft to meet its quota of Continental troops. This made it easier for Deborah to enlist under the name Timothy Thayer in 1782.[10] There was no physical examination; all she had to do was show up.

According to Elizabeth Ellet's book chronicling the women of the American Revolution, Deborah stitched her men's clothing for herself and hid it in a stack of hay until she was ready to leave. "Alone in the world, there were few to inquire what had become of her, and still fewer to care for her fate. She felt herself accountable to no human being."[11] It must have felt liberating and terrifying at the same time.

But she was quickly discovered after she was recognized by a local resident and had to pay back her bonus for signing up.[12] Soon, everyone in town was talking. It was illegal for a woman to dress as a man in Massachusetts. She was excommunicated by the local Baptist church after she was accused of "dressing in men's clothes, and enlisting as a Soldier in the Army," and for behaving in a "very loose and unchristian like" manner.[13]

But Deborah was not about to give up. "She was a person with enough of a sense of herself to become someone else," her biographer wrote.[14] She ran away, forty miles to Bellingham, Massachusetts, to re-enlist.

There were rumors back home that she had eloped with a British soldier or that she had died. But, in fact, on May 20, 1782, she snuck into George Washington's Continental Army as "Robert Shurtleff" and served in the 4th Massachusetts Regiment for seventeen months.[15] She lived as an ordinary soldier, sleeping in barns, always on the lookout for the enemy.

She was a person with enough of a sense of herself to become someone else.

—Alfred F. Young

In her first battle, at Tarrytown on July 3, 1782, she was injured—shot twice in the leg and wounded on the forehead. She feared her true identity would be exposed if she sought medical treatment, so she begged her fellow soldiers to leave her there to die. Instead, they brought her to the hospital; she let a doctor treat her head wound but left before they could examine her thigh injury.[16]

After she recovered, she continued to serve in the army, even working as a waiter, or officer's servant, for a general at New Windsor and West Point. As a waiter, Deborah would have helped dress the general and wash his clothes, but there's no indication that her commanding officer suspected anything was amiss.[17]

In the summer of 1783, Deborah traveled with the troops to Philadelphia, where she fell ill just before the Treaty of Paris ended the Revolutionary War. Had she remained at the general's home, her secret might never have been uncovered.

Engraving of Deborah Sampson from 1797

The story of how she was discovered was told by newspaper publisher Herman Mann, who wrote and released *The Female Review* in 1797, with Deborah's consent. In his exaggerated and overly dramatic retelling, he recounted a scene where undertakers were getting ready to remove an unconscious Deborah for burial when she "came to some degree of consciousness" and a nurse declared that she was still alive.[18] It was all too theatrical to be true.

"Doctor Bana at that instant entered; and putting his hand in her bosom to feel her pulse, was surprised to find an inner waist-coat tightly compressing her breasts. Ripping it in haste, he was still more shocked, not only on finding life, but the breasts and other tokens of a *female.*" It was then that she was sent to the women's unit.[19]

Deborah was discharged in October 1783. She was not the only woman to disguise herself as a soldier to fight in the war, but she may have been the most successful. Excitement and danger surrounded her every day. I can imagine that Deborah may have felt that for the first time in her life she *mattered.* After she had been abandoned by her own family at such a young age, the army gave her a sense of community and—ironically enough—a sense of belonging.

She did not shy away from the attention she received after she left military service. On January 10, 1784, four months after the Treaty of Paris, the *New York Gazette* published the first report of a woman who dressed as a man in the army. The story refers to Deborah as "a lively comely young nymph, 19 years old," who dressed as a man because her parents had tried "to induce her marriage with a young man she had conceived a great antipathy for."[20] Some of the reported details are known to be wrong—she didn't have contact with her parents when she enlisted—and they were possibly even supplied by Deborah to create a stronger story for the press.

What we know for certain is that when she returned to Massachusetts in November, Deborah went to live with an uncle. She married Benjamin Gannett, a farmer, on April 7, 1785, and had three children with him, and they adopted a fourth.[21] But even then, she did not live a conventional life. She used her experience to become the first woman in America to go on a national lecture circuit. In 1802, she started traveling around the Northeast—including Massachusetts, Rhode Island, and New York—connecting her personal odyssey to the country's journey to independence. Her presentation was quite a spectacle. She dressed in uniform and drew applause when she showed how comfortable she was handling a musket.

Part of the tour was to make the point that she deserved a pension. Unlike male soldiers, Deborah had to fight to be compensated for the role she played during the war. She had powerful allies to help her make her case, including Paul Revere. In 1804, the famous patriot tried to make Deborah more palatable to a member of Congress by describing her as "a small, effeminate, and conversable Woman, whose education entitled her to a better situation in life."[22] It's a strange way to describe Deborah, who was known to be tall and have masculine features. Either way, it worked. In 1805, she received her pension from the Commonwealth of Massachusetts, making her one of the first women to receive a pension for her service.[23]

Deborah Sampson lived her final years in Massachusetts, where she died in 1827 at age sixty-six. Congress would later recognize her heroism, declaring that the Revolutionary War "furnished no other similar example of female heroism, fidelity and courage."[24] She is one of the earliest examples of a woman serving in the U.S. military. Her headstone in Sharon, Massachusetts, honors this, referring to her as "the Female Soldier."[25]

7.

Patience Lovell Wright: *The Sculptor*

When John Dickinson, a Pennsylvania delegate to the First Continental Congress, sent a letter to an American spy living in London, it wasn't addressed to a hardened young member of the militia or a diplomat. Instead, it was sent to a middle-aged mother of four—a brash, ostentatious artist who made her living creating wax busts of the most recognizable faces of the time, including George Washington and Benjamin Franklin.[1] Her dramatic performances while sculpting served as the perfect cover for her side work as a spy with a die-hard commitment to the patriots' cause.

Patience Lovell Wright was one of the earliest professional female sculptors in America, creating disarmingly realistic life-size wax figures three decades before anyone had heard of Madame Tussaud.[2] She earned fame, but her work was not without controversy. Such lifelike imagery was rare in the eighteenth century and had an air of danger and witchcraft about it. Some called it a mockery of God, even blasphemous. Yet this gutsy woman managed to place herself in the highest circles of British society, even considering herself to be on a first-name basis with royalty. She would address King George III as "George" rather than using his formal titles, like "Your Majesty" or "Your Royal Highness," that were strictly required. One can only imagine the look on the royal couple's faces when she addressed them with such familiar impertinence in their palace.

What few knew was that Patience lived a double life; she was a self-appointed spy. As she crafted her renowned wax busts, she secretly embedded messages with intelligence inside them. Her portrait head of Lord Chatham may have been the first to travel stuffed with dispatches from her London studio to the Continental Congress in Philadelphia in 1774.[3] Benjamin Franklin was one of the people receiving her secret information.

"I heartily thank you for the Intelligence you have been pleased to give me," Dickinson, who would later serve as president (the equivalent of a governor) of Pennsylvania and Delaware, wrote to Patience.[4]

Like many of the influential women of early America, Patience followed an unexpected path to become a key player in the American Revolution.

A drawing of Patience Lovell Wright holding one of her lifelike wax figures, apparently representing George Washington

Born in 1725 in Bordentown, New Jersey, she was raised in a Quaker family and received little formal education. At age sixteen, she moved to Philadelphia, where she married Joseph Wright, an older Quaker farmer, in 1748. When he died in 1769, Patience was forty-four years old and pregnant with their fourth child.[5] Never one to adhere strictly to convention, she shaved a decade off her age by telling people that she was thirty-five when her husband died.

Faced with the sudden need to support her family—women did not inherit their husbands' wealth and property at this time—Patience turned to an unusual solution. Rather than taking in boarders, as many widowed women did, she and her sister Rachel Wells, who was also recently widowed, transformed their childhood hobby of making small figures out of tinted clay into a lucrative profession.

It was a remarkably bold move for the time. With encouragement from her neighbor Francis Hopkinson, who would later sign the Declaration of Independence and is credited for designing the American flag, Patience began molding portrait busts in tinted wax.[6] The sisters soon opened waxworks establishments in Philadelphia and New York, with Patience proving herself the more audacious of the two.

Disaster struck in June 1771 when a fire ravaged Patience's Manhattan studio, destroying most of her work. Once again facing financial ruin, she made the daring decision to relocate to London in 1772. There Benjamin Franklin's sister Jane Mecom proved instrumental in helping Patience enter London high society and secure commissions.[7]

Patience established a studio in the epicenter of luxury between St. James's Palace and Pall Mall. Despite her provincial American background—she wrote phonetically in what one can imagine was a thick New England accent, spelling *dear* as "dea" and *Philadelphia* as "Philadelphy"—she managed to make herself indispensable to the most powerful and influential people on both sides of the Atlantic.

Her reputation grew so great that four years before he became president, George Washington himself wrote to her: "If your inclination to return to this Country should overcome other considerations, you will, no doubt, meet a welcome reception from your numerous friends: among whom, I should be proud to see a person so universally celebrated; & on whom, nature has bestowed such rare & uncommon gifts. I am—Madam Yr Most Obedt & very Hble Servant."[8]

Patience was famous, publicly, at the time for her art. A 1775 issue of *London Magazine* described Patience as a "Promethean composer," noting, "While the head lies upon her knee, it hath so strongly a human appearance, that, at the first sight, it looks like a fresh head severed from the body."

Patience was not merely a visual artist but a performer who turned the act of creation into theater. When working in her studio, she wore a simple dark dress with a white cap and apron, but her methods were anything but modest. To the shock and fascination of onlookers, she occasionally lifted her apron and used her body heat to warm the wax between her thighs—scandalous then and provocative even now.[9]

Far from deterring visitors, this audacious behavior kept crowds flocking to her performances. During these sessions, she would dramatically call to her assistant for ingredients: tobacco to darken the skin and red pigment for the cheeks.[10] Over her career, she created at least fifty-five life-size sculptures and many smaller wax pieces. Remarkably, only one sculpture survives today: a life-size effigy of the first Earl of Chatham, now housed in Westminster Abbey—a testament to her artistic skill and her strategic political connections.[11]

As tension between the thirteen colonies and Great Britain escalated, Patience's position in London society gave her unprecedented access to valuable intelligence. The Boston Tea Party in 1773 had provoked harsh British reprisals, including the closure of Boston's port and the imposition of military rule. Following Parliament's passage of the Intolerable Acts, which further restricted colonial rights, Americans were forced to choose complete submission or war.

But not Patience. Her straight-talking American style and undeniable talent had impressed royalty. In the summer of 1773, she was summoned to Buckingham Palace to make wax portraits of the king and queen.[12] According to correspondence at the time, she would spend hours with the king, talking about "politics & the distresses of the People."[13] *Can you imagine that this American artist was bending the monarch's ear about the plight of the American colonies?*

As the colonies began to revolt during the spring of 1775, Patience offered to send intelligence back home, noting in a letter: "I will give you a Compleat List of the names of all your friends and Enemies."[14]

In that same letter she provided specific military intelligence: "The fleat is any moment to sail and new Constructed Cannon, lite, Portable on horse Back, 32 Inches Long, wide muzzle to fire at the Inhabitants and kill many at a shot."[15]

Her method of gathering information was ingenious in its simplicity. She offered private studio sessions, where she collected gossip from wealthy and well-connected subjects, as well as public shows that established her as a fixture in London society. According to Benjamin Franklin's grandson William Temple Franklin, her espionage work was invaluable: "As soon as a general was appointed, or a squadron begun to be fitted out, the old lady found means of access to some family where she could gain information, and thus without being at all suspected, she continued to transmit an account of the number of troops and the place of their destination to her political friends abroad."[16] Patience was no doubt one of America's earliest patriots.

> ***Women are always useful in grand Events.***
>
> ***—Patience Lovell Wright***

Patience's sister Rachel later confirmed the extent of her espionage, noting that "she [made] her Country her whole attention" and sent "Letters in buttons & pictures heads to me, ye first in Congress attended Constantly to me for them in that perilous hour."[17] Patience herself embraced her clandestine role, observing that "Women are always useful in grand Events," for people don't expect them to be spies.[18] Beyond gathering intelligence, she also fundraised for American prisoners of war and hosted pro-Revolutionary meetings.[19] Eventually, her open support for the American colonial cause led her to fall out of favor with the royals.

Like many women of her era, Patience found that once the Revolution ended, her services were no longer in demand. Her waxwork reportedly diminished, and by 1785, she yearned to return to America, the land of "peace and liberty."[20]

Her sister Rachel wrote an anonymous plea to Benjamin Franklin, dated December 16, 1785, requesting that Patience be given land in

America: "She Can't be Content to have her bones Laid in London."[21] Rachel argued that her sister had fought for her country in its most "perilous hour" and deserved recognition.

The request was denied. Undeterred, Patience sought out John Adams in person while he was serving as minister to the Court of St. James. Tragically, on her way home from court, she suffered a bad fall. She died during the winter of 1786 at age sixty-one, never having returned to the nation she had served so cleverly. She was buried in London and her story has largely faded from American history.

In a poignant letter to Thomas Jefferson in 1785, shortly before her death, Patience wrote: "I most sincerely wish not only to make the likeness of Washington, but of those *five* gentlemen, who assisted at the signing the treaty of peace, that put an end to so bloody and dreadful a war. The more public the honours bestowed on such men by their country, the better."[22] Jefferson never responded to her request to help honor America's founding fathers—like Benjamin Franklin, John Jay, and John Adams—through her art.

Years after her death the American poet and diplomat Joel Barlow paid tribute to her:

> Grief, rage and fear beneath her fingers start,
> Roll the wild eye and pour the bursting heart[23]

Through her artistry, innovation, and daring espionage, Patience Lovell Wright helped the patriots win their war for independence and build a new country in perhaps the most unusual way possible. She was not merely one of America's first professional sculptors but a woman who molded history itself, a revolutionary artist whose greatest masterpiece may have been her own extraordinary life.

PART II

RISK TAKERS AND RULEBREAKERS: SENECA FALLS AND THE CIVIL WAR, 1826–1876

1826–1876

On July 4, 1826, Presidents John Adams and Thomas Jefferson died just hours apart. This date marked the fiftieth anniversary of the Declaration of Independence, the founding document they both played pivotal roles in creating. The remarkable coincidence of their deaths symbolized the end of the founding era, a time that has long been defined by the stories of white men.

The truth is that women also stood on the dangerous precipice between liberty and death during the Revolution. Their words and actions inspired the men taught in our history books. These women, as we have learned, were integral to the founding of America, and each, in her own way, stretched the limits of her power to play a critical role in the fight for independence.

The next five decades would become among the most tumultuous in our nation's history, with the struggles for civil rights and women's equality at the forefront. Women were bringing their unique cultural experiences to the fight for representation.

Perhaps the most inspiring aspect of this period was the cumulative effect of women joining forces—as sisters, mothers, aunts, and friends—to demand that America live up to its founding ideals.

Power came in numbers, and as you'll read in this section, these women created strong networks and sisterhoods, sometimes because of family ties or because they were united by a common experience as outsiders in the democratic system. Charlotte Forten drew strength from her grandmother and her aunts, who devoted their lives to lifting up fellow Black women in Philadelphia. Sisters Elizabeth and Emily Blackwell saw the need for women in medicine, believing they would better understand their female friends and neighbors. Well-to-do women attended a tea party in Waterloo, New York, that resulted in the first convention to discuss women's rights. These women did not always agree on the best path to achieve equality, but their shared commitment to change transformed American society.

Most women living in the early nineteenth century could not imagine a world in which their opinions mattered. "Woman's duties are within the quiet seclusion of home," author Mrs. A. J. Graves wrote in her influential book, *Women in America,* in 1841. "Whenever she neglects these duties, or goes out of this sphere of action to mingle in any of the great public movements of the day, she is deserting the station which God and nature have assigned to her." The book was part of the broader "cult of domesticity" movement championed by Catharine Beecher.

This sentiment sounds limiting today, but it expressed the common beliefs of the time. When you read about the remarkable women of this era in this section, you must remember how much they risked and how truly revolutionary their actions were. They were fighting against a culture that didn't allow women to vote or pursue higher education, that limited women's professions to teaching and nursing, that didn't allow women to own property, and, of course, that didn't allow women to share their own opinions.

The Declaration of Independence had enshrined the idea that America was a place where "all men are created equal" with "unalienable Rights" including "Life, Liberty and the pursuit of Happiness." The pressing question from women and people of color became: Why don't those unalienable rights apply to us?

The abolitionist movement provided the first major platform for women to enter public discourse. The aforementioned Fortens, the most prominent Black family in Philadelphia, exemplified how women could organize for change. The Forten women formed the Philadelphia Female Anti-Slavery Society, one of the first abolitionist societies led by women and a model of interracial cooperation.

The Grimké sisters, Sarah and Angelina, were unique as perhaps the only Southern white women in the early abolitionist movement. Their advocacy was considered scandalous, as they spoke out publicly against slavery in 1837, a quarter century before Lincoln's Emancipation Proclamation. Their writings and speeches helped open the way for women to participate in public affairs, inspiring future generations of activists and even Supreme Court Justice Ruth Bader Ginsburg.

Maria Stewart, a freeborn Black woman living in Boston, rose to prominence in 1832 when she became the first American-born woman of any race to give a series of public lectures. In Maria's final speech, she delivered a line that would become famous when she asked, "What if I am a woman?" affirming her right to speak publicly about politics. This phrase was later echoed and transformed by Sojourner Truth, who declared, "Ain't I a woman?" in her famous 1851 address—now considered one of the most important abolitionist and women's rights speeches in American history.

These women asked over and over again: Why don't the principles of this new nation apply to us?

When women of this time were doing something "radical"—like speaking their mind—they were sometimes forced to undertake their activism in the most conservative ways possible to simply move the needle. The American movement for women's rights—demanding equality and the right to vote—officially began at Jane Hunt's tea party. In July 1848, just weeks after giving birth, Jane gathered the country's most prominent female suffragists in her mansion in Waterloo, New York: Elizabeth Cady Stanton, Lucretia Mott, Martha Coffin Wright, and Mary Ann M'Clintock.

This was no ordinary social gathering. These women had let their frustrations steep for too long. They were fed up with women's lack of rights: They couldn't vote, own property, or even speak publicly in many places. Elizabeth later recalled that at that tea party, she poured out her long-standing anger with such indignation that "I stirred myself, as well as the rest of the party, to do and dare anything."[1]

To do and dare anything is exactly what they did.

That same day, they wrote an unsigned notice for the local *Seneca County Courier* newspaper, advertising what was then considered revolutionary: the first women's rights convention in the Western world. Advocating for suffrage in 1848 was highly controversial, and these women risked ridicule, social rebuke, and worse.

The Seneca Falls Convention would be followed by many more public meetings and help build a sustained movement for women's rights. However, women would wait another seventy-two years for the right to vote, and women of color would wait even longer. Seneca Falls was a step in the right direction but part of incremental change that was sidelined by seismic events like the Civil War.

The Civil War lasted more than four years and claimed an estimated 750,000 American lives, making it the deadliest conflict in U.S. history.[2] During this period, the women's rights movement was often set aside as the nation focused on the all-consuming battle.

Historian Christine Stansell notes that women who had thrown themselves into the abolitionist movement "were assigned to the sidelines along with the rest of their sex, knitting and rolling bandages."[3] However, Susan B. Anthony and Elizabeth Cady Stanton formed the Women's National Loyal League, showing that women could support the Republican Party and the war effort while still advancing their cause. The Republican Party supported social reforms, including suffrage and the abolition of slavery.

The war also created new opportunities for women to prove their capabilities. Women managed farms and industries in men's absence, served as nurses on battlefields, and, in some cases, even fought in disguise. Dr. Mary Edwards Walker, who worked as a surgeon and spy during the conflict, was captured by the Confederacy and spent

THE COURIER.

Semi-Weekly—Circulation One Thousand.

FRIDAY, AUGUST 4, 1848.

Women's Rights Convention.

A Convention to discuss the social, civil and religious condition and rights of Woman, will be held in the Wesleyan Chapel, at Seneca Falls, N. Y., on Wednesday and Thursday the 19th and 20th of July current, commencing at 10 o'clock A. M.

During the first day, the meeting will be exclusively for Women, which all are earnestly invited to attend. The public generally are invited to be present on the second day, when LUCRETIA MOTT, of Philadelphia, and others both ladies and gentlemen, will address the Convention.

The following is the Declaration of Sentiments made at the Woman's Rights Convention, held in this place on the 19th and 20th inst.

DECLARATION OF SENTIMENTS.

When in the course of human events it becomes necessary for one portion of the family of man to assume among the people of earth, a position different from that which they have hitherto occupied but one to which the laws of nature and nature's God entitle them, a decent respect to the opinions of mankind requires that the should declare the causes that impel them to such a course.

We hold these truths to be self evident—that all men and women are created equal, that they are endowed by their Creator with certain inalienable rights—that among these are life, liberty and the pursuit of happiness—that to secure these rights governments are instituted, deriving their just powers from the consent of the governed. Whenever any form of government becomes destructive of these ends, it is the right of those who suffer from it, to refuse allegiance to it and to insist upon the institution of a new government laying its foundation on such principles and organizing its powers in such form as to them shall seem most likely to effect their safety and happiness. Prudence indeed will dictate that governments long established should not be changed for light and transient causes, and accordingly all experience hath shown that mankind are more disposed to suffer while evils are sufferable, than to right themselves by abolishing the forms to which they are accustomed:—but when a long train of abuses and usurpations, pursuing invariably the same object, evinces a design to reduce them under absolute despotism, it is their right—it is their duty, to throw off such government, and to provide new guards for their future security. Such has been the patient sufferance of the women under this government and such is now the necessity which constrains them to demand the equal station to which they are entitled.

The history of mankind is a history of repeated injuries and usurpations on the part of man toward woman, having in direct object the establishment of an absolute tyranny over her. To prove this let facts be submitted to a candid world.

He has never permitted her to exercise her alienable right to the elective franchise.

He has compelled her to submit to laws in the formation of which she has had no voice.

He has withheld from her rights which are given to the most ignorant and degraded men—both natives and foreigners.

Having deprived her of this first right of a citizen, the elective franchise, thereby leaving her without representation in the halls of legislation, he has oppressed her on all sides.

He has made her, if married, in the eye of the law, civilly dead.

He has taken from her all right in property, even to the wages she earns.

He has made her, morally, an irresponsible being, as she can commit many crimes with impunity, provided they be done in the presence of her husband. In the covenant of marriage she is compelled to promise obedience to her husband, he becoming to all intents and purposes her master—the law giving him power to deprive her of her liberty and to administer chastisement.

He has so framed the laws of divorce as to what shall be proper causes of divorce, in case of separation to whom the guardianship of the children shall be given, as to be wholly unjust and regardless of the happiness of woman—the law in all cases going upon the false supposition of the supremacy of man and giving all power into his hands.

After depriving her of all rights as a married woman, if single and the owner of property, he has taxed her to support a gov-

The Declaration of Sentiments was published in the *Seneca County Courier,* along with the original advertisement for the convention.

time as a prisoner of war. For her remarkable service, she received the Medal of Honor—the highest honor for military service. To this day, among the more than 3,500 recipients of this distinction, Dr. Walker remains the only woman.

In 1864, Anna Dickinson, called "America's Joan of Arc," became the first woman to give a political address before Congress. Two thousand people—including senators, representatives, Cabinet members, First Lady Mary Todd Lincoln, and President Lincoln himself—crowded into the hall for her speech. For over an hour, Anna, who campaigned for pro-Union Republicans, held her audience spellbound, assailing the institution of slavery and rarely looking at her notes. Her performance earned a standing ovation and was dubbed the "sensation of the season."[4]

After the Civil War, new constitutional amendments aimed to secure rights for formerly enslaved people. This prompted female activists to develop innovative legal strategies for obtaining the right to vote for their gender, as a next step in America's journey to become a more perfect union.

In the 1870s, the National Woman Suffrage Association (NWSA) championed a novel approach called the New Departure. Virginia Minor, along with her lawyer husband, Francis, developed the legal theory behind it, arguing that the newly passed Fourteenth Amendment granted women citizenship and equal rights—including the right to vote. This sparked protests across the country as women attempted to cast ballots at polling places.

The New Departure movement led to two landmark Supreme Court cases. In 1872, Myra Bradwell sued Illinois after the state rejected her application for admission to the bar because she was a married woman. Her appeal resulted in the infamous Supreme Court decision *Bradwell v. Illinois* (1873). Along with *Minor v. Happersett* (1875), these were the Court's first considerations of women's constitutional rights. The Court rejected both cases, crushing the New Departure strategy and upholding gender discrimination, delaying progress for women's suffrage and professional equality by decades. A century later,

Ruth Bader Ginsburg would often quote from then Justice Bradley's concurrence in *Bradwell*, in which he claimed, "The paramount destiny and mission of woman are to fulfill the noble and benign offices of wife and mother. This is the law of the Creator." Ginsburg would respond with her sharp wit: "Neither Justice Bradley, nor lawmen who recapitulate his exposition, provide enlightenment on the method of communication between jurist and Creator."[5]

This fifty-year period also saw remarkable advances in women's education and professional opportunities. Ohio's Oberlin College opened in 1833 as the first coeducational institution of higher learning anywhere in the world. Mount Holyoke College was established in 1837. Following the Civil War, land-grant colleges, which formed the basis for state universities, also began admitting women.

Rising literacy rates strengthened women's ability to participate in public life. Elizabeth Blackwell became the first woman to earn a medical degree in America; her younger sister Emily followed in her footsteps, and together they established hospitals to care for women and children living in poverty.

Belva Ann Lockwood became the first woman admitted to practice law before the Supreme Court. She ran for president in 1884 and 1888 on the National Equal Rights Party ticket and was the first woman ever to appear on official ballots (Victoria Woodhull was the first woman to run for president, but at age thirty-three, she wasn't old enough).[6] At fifty-four, Belva ran for president nearly four decades before women could vote, pointing out the irony that she could not cast a ballot but was eligible to receive votes. Her platform focused on women's rights: "We shall never have equal rights until we take them, nor respect until we command it."

> ***We shall never have equal rights until we take them, nor respect until we command it.***
>
> ***—Belva Lockwood***

Some pioneering women have been nearly forgotten. In the 1850s, amateur scientist Eunice Foote conducted experiments with glass cylinders containing moist air and carbon dioxide, discovering what we now know as the greenhouse gas effect. But a male colleague read her 1856 paper at a scientific meeting, and three years later, another male scientist in England received credit for the same findings, relegating her work to obscurity.[7] There are no known photographs of Eunice Foote.[8] It's no surprise that Eunice was also a feminist who helped organize the Seneca Falls Convention and was the fifth signature on the Declaration of Sentiments in 1848.[9]

By being deprived of basic rights, women learned a critical lesson: Change came when they banded together to challenge conventional wisdom. During the Civil War era, they created strong networks of family ties and sisterhood—through blood or shared beliefs—to amplify their voices. They were united by their common experience as outsiders in the democratic system, with varying degrees of exclusion from the political process, whether white or Black, rich or poor. There was strength in numbers, a lesson that courage is strengthened by community.

Through their collective efforts, we see America's evolution clearly, with all its faults and contradictions. When Kate Gannett Wells wrote in an 1880 *Atlantic Monthly* article called "The Transitional American Woman" that "women do not care for their home as they did," for "the simple fact is that women have found that they can have occupation, respectability, and even dignity disconnected from the home," she was acknowledging a fundamental shift in American society that these pioneers had helped bring about.

These women's stories remind us that democracy is always unfinished work, that progress requires both individual courage and collective action, and that the struggle for equality continues with each generation. By understanding their achievements, we can better honor their efforts to shape America into a nation that truly lives up to its founding promise—that all people are created equal.

8.

The Grimké Sisters: *The Truth Tellers*

Sarah Grimké was just a teenager when she was riding in a carriage between the cotton fields of her family's sprawling South Carolina plantation and came across a sight that would forever be seared in her mind: an enslaved man's head on a stake. His crime? He tried to run away from her family.[1]

The head was there, in plain sight, to deter other enslaved people from trying to escape. Sarah was horrified by that murder and by other acts of extreme violence that she saw on her family's plantation.

When Sarah and her sister, Angelina, reached their twenties, they individually made the extraordinary decision to reject their privileged upbringing, betray their Southern heritage, and move north. They made it their mission to tell people just how brutal slavery truly was. By doing so, the sisters became pariahs in their home state but heroes to the abolitionist movement.

Sarah and Angelina Grimké stand as revolutionary figures in American history—the only white Southern women to become prominent abolitionists. Through their fearless public speaking and powerful writings, they helped forge a path for women's participation in public affairs while challenging both slavery and gender inequality with unwavering determination. They fought to transcend the system they were born into and made huge strides in fighting against it.

Born into one of the wealthiest slaveholding families of their state, as two of fourteen children, they witnessed slavery's brutality firsthand

Sarah Grimké

during their childhood. Their father, Judge John Grimké, the chief justice of the South Carolina Supreme Court, demanded he be addressed as "Colonel" for his Revolutionary War service. He wielded tremendous power, enslaved hundreds of Black men, women, and children, and often made his own children work in the fields among enslaved people. Sarah later reflected, "Perhaps I am indebted partially to this for my life-long detestation of slavery, as it brought me in close contact with these unpaid toilers."[2]

They were raised in the most compromised moral system imaginable, and their family tree shows how complicated and imperfect their story is. For instance, they did not cut ties with their brother Henry, who had children with one of his slaves and kept his sons enslaved for some time. It is important to recognize how the Grimké sisters' lives were affected by the sins of their family. They left their family's plantation, but they could not erase their heritage. It is an undeniable part of their legacy.

Angelina Grimké

The people enslaved by the Grimkés experienced abhorrent brutality: Their mother, Polly, once tied an iron collar around an enslaved woman and pulled out her front teeth so that she would be easy to identify if she ran away again.[3]

In 1805, when Sarah was thirteen years old, Angelina was born. Sarah threw herself into taking care of her little sister, alongside the enslaved women who raised the Grimké children. Sarah insisted on being Angelina's godmother, and Angelina even called her "Mother" throughout her life.[4] It is clear that Sarah was Angelina's moral compass and opened her eyes from a young age to the evils of slavery. Angelina lamented in her diary about her family's wickedness and their support of a system that was "altogether contrary to the spirit of the Gospel."[5]

Sarah had always wanted to be a lawyer, but her father would not permit her to go to college like her brother Thomas, who went to Yale. Her father appreciated Sarah's intelligence and reportedly told her that if she had been a man, she would have been the greatest lawyer in South Carolina, or according to some sources, "the greatest jurist in the country."[6] This thwarted ambition would later fuel her passionate arguments for women's equality.

In 1830, slavery was rampant, with more than two million enslaved people in the United States.[7] Sarah, at age twenty-eight, left Charleston for Philadelphia. Her sister would join a few years later. In 1830, slavery was rampant, with more than two million enslaved people in the United States. Angelina realized "it was impossible to act effectively against slave society while living within it. Self-imposed exile was her final gesture of protest in the South."[8]

The sisters became Quakers and were part of a community that was naturally aligned with the abolitionist movement. The Quaker tradition largely considered women equal to men under their general belief that every human being deserves respect. Quaker women supported abolitionist activists in the Black urban middle class. Angelina and Sarah were active members of the Philadelphia Female Anti-Slavery Society (PFASS), working alongside Black women activists, including the daughters of James Forten, a prominent Black businessman and abolitionist.

This collaboration represented one of the earliest examples of interracial cooperation in reform movements. The sisters participated in PFASS-sponsored petition campaigns, fundraising events, and educational initiatives for free Black children. The experience of working as equals with Black women abolitionists deepened the Grimkés' understanding of how racial and gender oppression were interconnected. The philosophy expressed by James Forten that freedom was "the birthright of the human race" became central to the sisters' own developing views on both abolition and women's rights.

> ***Slavery is contrary to the declaration of our independence.***
>
> —*ANGELINA GRIMKÉ*

In 1835, Angelina wrote a letter to William Lloyd Garrison, editor of the abolitionist newspaper *The Liberator*, about violence against abolitionists. In it, she declared, "It is my deep, solemn, deliberate conviction, *that this is a cause worth dying for*."[9] Garrison published her note in his popular paper immediately. The letter caused a huge controversy. Even Angelina's Quaker friends advised her to retract it or tone down her words. A woman was not meant to speak so passionately on any issue—let alone abolitionism. But Angelina refused to change a single word.

A year later, Angelina was more outspoken than ever. She used the foundations of American democracy to make her case against enslavement, just as women's rights activists later used the founders' arguments to advocate for suffrage.

In her 1836 pamphlet "Appeal to the Christian Women of the South," Angelina spoke directly to the slaveholding society that she and her sister had fled, and her family had profited from. She implored Southern women "to arise and gird yourselves for this great moral conflict" to "overthrow this horrible system of oppression and cruelty." She continued, "Slavery is contrary to the declaration of our independence."[10]

It's worth taking note of her deliberate phrasing: "*our* independence." She reminded people in power that the country belonged to everyone. The deeply religious sisters argued that slavery was fundamentally unchristian. It went against the "example and precepts of our holy and merciful Redeemer, and of his apostles," because it made human beings into "chattel personal" and took away "all his rights as a human being."[11]

The pamphlet was burned in Charleston and Angelina was threatened with prison in South Carolina.[12] This reaction was hardly surprising. At this point, the Grimké sisters had become an embarrassment to their powerful family, still slaveholders in the South.

They invited further criticism by embarking on a public speaking tour to advocate for liberty and freedom.

The reaction to their public speaking was swift and severe in both the North and the South. Their critics objected not only to their abolitionist message but to the very idea of women speaking publicly on political matters. You have to remember the time; they were advocating against slavery a quarter century before the Emancipation Proclamation, when such views were considered not merely controversial but dangerous, especially coming from Southern women of their social standing. A group of northeastern ministers published a letter stating that women who speak in the public sphere were "unnatural" and brought "shame and dishonor" to their communities.[13]

> ***I ask no favors for my sex. I surrender not our claim to equality. All I ask of our brethren, is that they will take their feet from off our necks.***
>
> ***—Sarah Grimké***

Sarah responded by broadening her argument and publishing *Letters on the Equality of the Sexes.* "Men and women were CREATED EQUAL," she wrote; "they are both moral and accountable beings, and whatever is *right* for man to do, is *right* for woman."[14]

In what would become a famous phrase a century later, Sarah declared: "I ask no favors for my sex. I surrender not our claim to equality. All I ask of our brethren, is that they will take their feet from off our necks."[15]

In fact, Ruth Bader Ginsburg quoted this passage from Sarah in her oral argument before the Supreme Court in the 1973 case of *Frontiero v. Richardson,* a landmark case against sex discrimination.[16] Ginsburg, who would become only the second female justice on the nation's highest court, found inspiration in Sarah's words—a fitting tribute to a woman who had been denied the legal career she desired.

As Angelina built her new life in the North, she found like-minded allies in the abolitionist movement.

Among them was Theodore Dwight Weld, a prominent abolitionist who fell in love with Angelina. However, even Weld encouraged Angelina to moderate her advocacy for women's suffrage, suggesting she "give it time" and that men would "begin to be converted" gradually.

Angelina's response was characteristically direct: "What is the matter with thee?" She believed there was no time for waiting. The moment for action was now.[17] She needed him to stand by her side in solidarity, not only for Black people's freedom but also for women's rights. The tension in their correspondence reveals the larger debate within the progressive movements of the time. Angelina wondered, "How can we expect to be able to hold meetings much longer when people are so diligently taught to despise us for thus stepping out of the sphere of woman?"[18]

At age thirty-three in 1838, Angelina married Weld in Philadelphia before a mixed-race group of guests in a building not far from where the Declaration of Independence was conceived. One Black and one white minister oversaw the ceremony. Their vows were more progressive than traditional at the time, and Weld explicitly spoke against the stifling expectations of coverture, the legal doctrine that merged a woman's rights and identity with her husband's upon marriage. Angelina refused to include the word "obey" in her vows.[19] They were what in modern terms would be described as a power couple, though the world around them was not changing as quickly as they'd hoped.

Days after their wedding, Angelina was onstage speaking at the annual anti-slavery convention at the newly constructed Pennsylvania Hall, a meeting house for abolitionists. The Anti-Slavery Convention of American Women had refused the mayor's request that only white women attend the meeting. While she spoke, an angry mob threw rocks that crashed through windows and hurled insults from outside. But Angelina held court for more than an hour, and when people got up to leave, she urged them to stay. She would not be intimidated. At the end of her speech, white and Black women walked arm-in-arm out of the building.[20] Tragically, the anti-abolitionist mob returned the next day and burned Pennsylvania Hall, a monument to free speech, to the ground.[21]

Just days after it was opened, Pennsylvania Hall was set on fire by an anti-abolitionist mob.

In February 1838, Angelina became the first woman in the country to speak before a legislative body when she presented a petition calling for an immediate end to slavery, signed by thousands, before the Massachusetts state legislature. She insisted that lawmakers include women in political debates. "Are we aliens, because we are women? Are we bereft of citizenship, because we are the mothers, wives, and daughters of a mighty people? Have women no country . . . no partnership in a nation's guilt and shame? Let the history of the world answer."[22]

Such a bold public speech by a woman was unprecedented. No woman had ever stated the case so aggressively and so simply. The reaction was harsh, not just from pro-slavery activists but from much of society. Again, the sisters were criticized not only for what they were saying but for speaking up at all. Women were expected to be ladylike and to refrain from wading into controversial matters, particularly in public forums.

Throughout their lives, the Grimké sisters maintained contact with one of their brothers, Henry, who was a cruel enslaver. From a modern perspective, their continued relationship with him is troubling and has led critics to argue their complicity. Henry had three children with an enslaved woman named Nancy Weston. Henry left his Black sons to his white son in his will, which made Henry the architect of their fate. Archie, Frank, and John were enslaved by their white half brother after their father's death.

Are we aliens, because we are women? Are we bereft of citizenship, because we are the mothers, wives, and daughters of a mighty people?

—Angelina Grimké

Archie and Frank left the South as the Civil War was ending. In 1868, they came North and to the attention of Sarah and Angelina. The Grimké sisters sponsored Archie's and Frank's education, and both men went on to successful careers. Archie became a lawyer and diplomat, later serving as the national vice president of the National Association for the Advancement of Colored People (NAACP). Frank became an influential Presbyterian minister at a Black church in Washington, D.C., and married the noted activist Charlotte Forten.

Sarah and Angelina insisted that the young men focus on their future, not the trauma of their past. Yet, as historian Kerri K. Greenidge contends, "the tragedy of the Grimké sisters' lives was the fact that they never acknowledged their complicity in the slave system they so eloquently spoke against."[23] As with many white abolitionists, their advocacy had blind spots and contradictions.

The Grimké sisters never stopped pushing for social change. On the bitterly cold day of March 7, 1870, fifty years before the passage of the Nineteenth Amendment, seventy-seven-year-old Sarah and sixty-four-year-old Angelina joined a group of women who tried to vote in a local Massachusetts election. Their votes were stored in a separate box and left uncounted. The *Norfolk County Gazette* recorded the historic day: "The delay of the women in making their appearance led to the rumor that their courage had failed them and the anti-female suffrage masculines were in high glee." When the men learned that the women were indeed coming, "their joy . . . soon turned to sorrow." Their votes weren't counted, but "their ticket was elected."[24]

Nothing could stop the Grimké sisters, who had seen so much—and told the world the truth of what they saw—in their long and audacious lives. Their legacy lives on in the ongoing struggles for racial justice and gender equality, reminding us that moral courage often means standing apart from one's time, one's community, and even one's family to advocate for what is right.

9.

Charlotte Forten: *The Abolitionist*

For Charlotte Forten, July 4, 1855, was no time for celebration. As fireworks exploded in the night sky and exuberant crowds lined the streets outside her family's brick home in Philadelphia, she sat in quiet frustration. In her diary, she wrote bitterly about the hypocrisy of their jubilation: "The patriots, poor fools, were celebrating the anniversary of their vaunted independence. Strange that they cannot feel their own degradation—the weight of the chains which they have imposed upon themselves."

As a young Black woman whose grandfather had fought in the American Revolution, Charlotte understood far too well that the promise of freedom did not extend to all Americans. One can imagine her looking out the window, her anger swirling with a dream that one day her country could live up to its ideals.

Charlotte Forten's extraordinary life and insights are known to us today because she was a prolific writer who kept a diary. Her personal journals provide a rare glimpse into the life of a free Black woman in the antebellum North. What's also remarkable is that her diary was preserved. Many writings by women from that era were lost. People doubted their historical significance. One historian we spoke with said many letters and diaries from women were frequently destroyed, because people at the time believed that women's thoughts were unworthy of reading or saving.

It was Charlotte's husband, Reverend Francis J. Grimké (the nephew of Sarah and Angelina Grimké), who ensured that her writings were saved. However, they remained unpublished until the 1950s, when historian Dr. Ray Allen Billington transcribed and edited them, releasing them as *The Journal of Charlotte Forten: A Free Negro in the Slave Era.* Today, her words are considered invaluable by historians and journalists alike.[1]

The patriots, poor fools, were celebrating the anniversary of their vaunted independence. Strange that they cannot feel their own degradation—the weight of the chains which they have imposed upon themselves.

—Charlotte Forten

Born in 1837 in Philadelphia, a city deeply entwined with the ideals of liberty and democracy, Charlotte was raised in a family of free Black elites. Her grandfather James Forten was the patriarch.

James Forten was born just before the American Revolution to free parents. He was nine years old when he heard the Declaration of Independence read aloud at the Pennsylvania State House (now Independence Hall) on July 8, 1776. James Forten was likely one of the first Americans to hear the words "all men are created equal," which had been written by the founders and published just days earlier. Later, James Forten would write passionately to legislators that the Declaration's core sentiment that every American had inalienable rights should be applied to Black people as well.[2]

He would help fight for America's independence at age fourteen as a privateer in the Revolution. On his second voyage he was captured by the British and held for several months on the infamous HMS *Jersey* in New York Harbor. The prison ship was notorious for inhumane conditions and thousands of men are estimated to have died aboard.

He was freed as part of a prisoner exchange. James Forten returned to Philadelphia and embarked on a career as a sailmaker, becoming an apprentice in 1785. Thirteen years later, the white owner left James Forten his business, which ultimately made him one of the wealthiest Black people in the city during the early 1800s. Philadelphia was a port city, and sail-making, which involved designing and repairing sails for shipbuilders, was a key part of the economy.

When he wasn't managing a racially integrated staff of around thirty men, he and his wife, Charlotte Vandine Forten, who was also an abolitionist, were taking care of their nine children. They invited the most important progressive thinkers of the time to their elegant home on Lombard Street, including Lucretia Mott, Angelina Grimké, and William Lloyd Garrison, who was the influential founder of the anti-slavery newspaper *The Liberator,* which James Forten helped fund.

At the time, Philadelphia had a significant free Black population of some twenty thousand people. This was because of Pennsylvania's Gradual Abolition Act of 1780, and the city's status made it a haven for those escaping slavery in the South.

Charlotte Forten Grimké

Charlotte Forten grew up in her grandparents' large home, a hub for abolitionist activity and influential thinkers. Charlotte's mother, Mary Virginia, died of tuberculosis when Charlotte was just three years old. Charlotte was raised by her grandmother and her aunts, a powerful matriarchy who were founding members of the Philadelphia Female Anti-Slavery Society.

Despite the privileges her family's wealth afforded, Charlotte was not insulated from racism or sexism. She was acutely aware of the racial violence that shaped their lives. In 1834, before she was born, her family watched as white mobs terrorized Philadelphia's Black community in a brutal, days-long riot. Marked by these scarring experiences, her family instilled in Charlotte a lifelong commitment to activism and education. When she was denied admission to Philadelphia's white schools at age sixteen, Charlotte was sent to Salem, Massachusetts, where she studied Latin, French, poetry, and art at an integrated school (although she was the only Black student).[3]

In 1855, Charlotte followed in her aunts' footsteps and joined the Salem Female Anti-Slavery Society, deepening her activism. During visits home, she faced overt racism, experiences that fueled her "suspicion and distrust" of white society. In her diary on July 17, 1857, she wrote about getting turned away from an ice cream shop with her friend, Mrs. Putnam: "Oh, how terribly I felt! Could say, but few words, Mrs. P told one of the people, some wholesome truth, which cannot be soon forgotten. It is dreadful! Dreadful! I cannot stay in such a place long for New England."[4]

Her writings from this period reveal her internal struggle—a sophisticated, well-read young woman torn between love for her country and disillusionment with its racial injustice. On September 12, 1855, when she was eighteen years old, she wrote: "Oh! It is hard to go through life meeting contempt with contempt, hatred with hatred, fearing, with too good reason, to love and trust hardly anyone whose skin is white."[5]

She didn't just keep her thoughts to her private diaries, she published them in poetry and essays.

In response to the infamous *Dred Scott* decision of 1857, which denied citizenship to Black Americans, Charlotte published the poem "Parody on 'Red, White and Blue,'" condemning the country's failure to uphold its founding principles and its promise that all men are created equal.[6]

She wrote the poem when she was just twenty years old, and it was published as a broadside in 1858 for an event commemorating the Boston Massacre, specifically remembering the death of Crispus Attucks, the African Indigenous man who was the first victim.

> Oh, when shall each child of our Father,
> Whatever his nation or hue,

Be protected throughout thy dominions,
'Neath the folds of the red, white and blue.[7]

A few years later, the Civil War broke out, and as with many Americans, Charlotte's life was shaped by the deadly fight, which lasted from 1861 until 1865.

The war opened new opportunities for women, and Charlotte seized the moment. In 1861, the Union had captured South Carolina's Sea Islands and freed approximately ten thousand enslaved people. Abandoned plantations were converted to schools, and an early effort began to integrate formerly enslaved people into American society as free citizens.[8] Northern missionaries worked together with the newly freed people to create schools and an economy for paid labor. Thousands were part of this effort, which was an early foray into what would become Reconstruction.[9] In 1862, Charlotte became the first Northern Black teacher to travel south to educate freed slaves as part of the Port Royal Experiment in South Carolina.

Teaching formerly enslaved people was both a professional and personal awakening for Charlotte. Just twenty-five years old, she admired their resilience and deep spirituality. "I wish some of those persons at the North who say the race is hopelessly and naturally inferior," she wrote in an article describing her time as a teacher, "could see the readiness with which these children, so long oppressed and deprived of every privilege, learn and understand."[10]

Charlotte hoped to inspire her students with stories of Black heroes like Toussaint Louverture, a general who led the Haitian Revolution: "It is well that they should know what one of their own color could do for his race. I long to inspire them with courage and ambition (of a noble sort) and high purpose."[11] By harnessing their curiosity and by getting an education, she believed, her students could one day overcome the brutality of their lives as enslaved people.

She documented her experiences and published her writings in *The Atlantic Monthly* in 1864, becoming the first Black woman to publish in the prestigious magazine.[12] That was where the country read her essays

"Life on the Sea Islands," Parts I and II. By writing about the physical beauty of the Sea Islands and the culture that the Black community had created there, historian Kerri K. Greenidge says, "Charlotte Forten staked a claim for Black women in the intellectual discourse of the time by assuming the role of cultural commentator and journalist rather than Romantic author focused on Black suffering."[13]

Charlotte was still in South Carolina when President Abraham Lincoln signed the Emancipation Proclamation in 1863, which freed enslaved people in the Confederate states—though the war would not end until 1865. She wrote in "New Year's Day on the Island of South Carolina, 1863," which was published in *The Liberator,* it was "the most glorious day this nation has yet seen, I think. . . . As I sat on the [viewing] stand and looked around on the various groups, I thought you had never seen a sight so beautiful. There were the black soldiers, in their coats and scarlet pants, the officers of this and other regiments in their handsome uniforms, and crowds of lookers-on, men, women and children of every complexion."

The Black soldiers did "a dress parade," she wrote. "It was a brilliant sight—the lone line of men in their brilliant uniforms, with bayonets gleaming in the sunlight. . . . The dawn of freedom which it heralds may not break upon us at once; but it will surely come."[14]

After the war, Charlotte's life took her to Boston, Charleston, and finally Washington, D.C., where she married Reverend Francis James Grimké, the twenty-eight-year-old nephew of the abolitionist Grimké sisters. Francis was formerly enslaved. He graduated from Princeton and became a Presbyterian minister.[15] Famous abolitionist Frederick Douglass was one of the wedding guests, after helping to make the match that brought together two of America's most influential abolitionist families.[16] They had one child, a daughter named Theodora Cornelia, who died in infancy.

Charlotte's writings from later in her life denounced Jim Crow laws and racial violence, emphasizing that prejudice was "essentially unchristian."[17] In an 1885 letter to the *Boston Commonwealth,* she warned against moral compromise, declaring that "this nation has well-nigh been wrecked upon that rock of expediency" and encouraged them to consider "simply what is right."[18] Her words remained just as powerful during the civil rights era as they were in her own time.

Charlotte helped establish the National Association of Colored Women in 1896, and her husband was a co-founder of the NAACP in 1909.

Charlotte Forten passed away at age seventy-six on July 23, 1914. Though her life ended before the full realization of the Civil Rights Movement, her work as a teacher, writer, and activist left an indelible mark. Today, she is remembered as a trailblazer who fought tirelessly for justice and education. Her work provided future generations with a firsthand account of both the struggles and triumphs of the era.

10.

The Women of Seneca Falls: *The Signers*

We hold these truths to be self-evident;
that all men ***and women*** *are created equal;*
that they are endowed by their Creator
with certain inalienable rights."
—DECLARATION OF SENTIMENTS, 1848

When Lucretia Mott and Elizabeth Cady Stanton went to the World Anti-Slavery Convention in London in 1840, they were told to keep their mouths shut. They were even made to sit behind a curtain. Can you imagine how that must have felt to two educated abolitionists who just happened to be women? They were understandably furious.

But something history-changing came out of that day. Elizabeth's and Lucretia's shared outrage over their exclusion from that one event sparked a friendship that led to the first organized women's rights convention and ignited a national movement in support of women's rights. It was the beginning of an eight-decade-long fight that achieved the passage of the Nineteenth Amendment—which finally granted women the right to vote 144 years after America's founding. If they hadn't met under those humiliating circumstances, who knows how much longer women would have been denied their rights.

It took several years for the two to reconnect once they got back to America, but when they did, there was no stopping them. On July 13, 1848, Elizabeth, a women's rights activist, and Lucretia, a Quaker and social reformer, gathered at Jane Hunt's house in Waterloo, New York, with a small group of Quaker women. This was where they hatched their plan.

Elizabeth recalled that she sat at the table and "poured out . . . the torrent of my long-accumulating discontent with such vehemence and indignation that I stirred myself, as well as the rest of the party, to do or dare anything."[1] They agreed that women needed to be given the vote in a country founded on freedom and equality. Elizabeth picked up the Declaration of Independence from a stack of papers sitting on the table. *This was it,* she told her friends. The Declaration was the foundation of their argument. The first thing they needed to do was fix the first line to make it reflect the point: "We hold these truths to be self-evident, that all men *and women* are created equal, that they are endowed by their Creator with certain unalienable Rights, that among these are Life, Liberty and the pursuit of Happiness."

I stirred myself, as well as the rest of the party, to do or dare anything.

—Elizabeth Cady Stanton

The women were fired up, and they only gave themselves a few days to plan the convention. They wanted to take advantage of the momentum they were building. Within a couple of days, they placed the first of several ads in local newspapers.[2] They published an announcement for the convention in the *Seneca County Courier:*

> A Convention to discuss the social, civil and religious condition and rights of Woman, will be held in the Wesleyan Chapel, at Seneca Falls, N.Y., on Wednesday and Thursday the 19th and 20th of July current commencing at 10 o'clock A.M. During the first day, the meeting will be exclusively for Women, which all are earnestly invited to attend. The public generally are invited to be present on the second day, when LUCRETIA MOTT, of Philadelphia, and others both ladies and gentlemen, will address the Convention.[3]

The convention was held on July 19 and 20, 1848. They did not expect many people to show up at the height of summer and with so little notice. But they were pleasantly surprised when more than three hundred people attended over the course of two days.

Just as at the small table with her friends, Elizabeth's determination was palpable when she spoke at the convention. "We are assembled to protest against a form of government, existing without the consent of the governed—to declare our right to be free as man is free, to be represented in the government which we are taxed to support, to have such disgraceful laws as give man the power to chastise and imprison his wife, to take the wages which she earns, the property which she inherits, and, in case of separation, the children of her love," she said on the first day.[4]

The history of mankind is a history of repeated injuries and usurpations on the part of man toward woman.

—Elizabeth Cady Stanton

Elizabeth Cady Stanton wisely decided to tie the fight for women's rights to the most distinguished political statement the nation had made: the Declaration of Independence, ratified on July 4, 1776. And thus, the Declaration of Sentiments was born.

We celebrate America's birthday every year because of that document and the words written largely by Thomas Jefferson that declared "all men are created equal." Elizabeth mimicked that same line but added "all men *and women* are created equal."

That wasn't the only cribbing of the text by Elizabeth. She deliberately altered the language to make the case that women's demands were no more or less radical than those made during the American Revolution, and as historian Linda K. Kerber has asserted, they were in fact an implicit fulfillment of the commitments already made.

Whereas America's thirteen colonies fought for independence from

British rule, women wanted independence from a patriarchal U.S. government.

Look how closely Elizabeth mirrored the text. The original Declaration of 1776 stated: "Such has been the patient sufferance of these Colonies; and such is now the necessity which constrains them to alter their former Systems of Government." Elizabeth changed that to: "Such has been the patient sufferance of *the women under this government,* and such is now the necessity which constrains them *to demand the equal station to which they are entitled.*"

Could it be said that these women, in the same spirit of the 1776 document, were making it clear that their grievances were not against a tyrannical king but against tyrannical men who were denying their rights and liberties? The document then states that "the history of mankind is a history of repeated injuries and usurpations on the part of man toward woman."

Don't take my word for it, you should read it yourself. It goes on to list sixteen bullet points of proof of the "absolute tyranny" of man over woman.

The first is: "He has never permitted her to exercise her inalienable right to the elective franchise."

Another one: "He has made her, if married, in the eye of the law, civilly dead." *Wow.*

The final bullet point is the one that *really gets me.* I admit I had never read it until writing the introduction to this book. And as I sit here retyping it, *I am in tears.*

"He has endeavored, in every way that he could to destroy her confidence in her own powers, to lessen her self-respect, and to make her willing to lead a dependent and abject life."

He has endeavored, in every way that he could to destroy her confidence in her own powers, to lessen her self-respect, and to make her willing to lead a dependent and abject life.

—Elizabeth Cady Stanton

Destroy her confidence in her own powers.

Remember when I said this was revolutionary? The women fully anticipated "misconception, misrepresentation, and ridicule," but also made clear they would use "every instrumentality within our power to effect our object."

The Declaration of Sentiments says, "We insist that they have immediate admission to all the rights and privileges which belong to them as citizens of these United States." They wanted, no, they *demanded*, the right to vote.

It was Elizabeth who insisted that women's suffrage be part of the Declaration of Sentiments. Some attendees thought it was too controversial. It was eventually included thanks in part to abolitionist Frederick Douglass, whose support of the resolution was critical to its inclusion. At a later commemoration of women's rights, Douglass reflected, "When I ran away from slavery, it was for myself; when I advocated emancipation, it was for my people; but when I stood up for the rights of woman, self was out of the question, and I found a little nobility in the act."[5]

The convention was considered a huge success. And the powerful Declaration of Sentiments was bravely signed by one hundred convention attendees, including men like Douglass. He published the first known copy in his newspaper *The North Star*.[6] The public response was another story; reaction was so harsh that some people who signed it later removed their names. The *Worcester Telegraph* called the women who signed the Declaration of Sentiments "Amazons." Some newspapers mocked them with crude political cartoons and called the convention "a most insane and ludicrous farce."[7]

But they were undeterred. Elizabeth and Lucretia knew from experience that there would be blowback to the movement they were creating. Because of Seneca Falls, women's rights conventions became annual events throughout the Northeast and Midwest until the Civil War began in 1861. They were gathering places where like-minded women connected and strategized. These intellectual incubators created a new generation of reformers.

This wasn't by accident. In fact, the signers of the Declaration of Sentiments hoped for "a series of Conventions, embracing every part of the country."[8] A month later, the same group of women hosted a larger women's rights convention in Rochester, New York, where more than a hundred additional signatures were added to the Declaration of Sentiments. Elizabeth and Lucretia had started a trend.

Lucretia argued that women were not asking for any favors, they merely wanted their God-given rights. "The question is often asked, 'What does woman want, more than she enjoys? What is she seeking to obtain? Of what rights is she deprived? What privileges are withheld from her?' I answer, she asks nothing as favor, but as right; she wants to be acknowledged a moral, responsible being."[9]

> ***She asks nothing as favor, but as right; she wants to be acknowledged a moral, responsible being.***
>
> —LUCRETIA MOTT

Fighting for God-given rights and asking for acknowledgment as a human being was at the heart of Seneca Falls, yet Black women were denied the same respect. In fact, no Black women were even invited to Seneca Falls. One of the most important activists of the day, Sojourner Truth, did not attend the convention but regardless became a powerful voice in both the abolitionist and women's rights movements.

Sojourner was born in 1797 in upstate New York, where her parents were enslaved. She was given the name Isabella Baumfree. She was first sold at auction at nine years old, and she had a series of enslavers before she escaped in 1826 with her baby daughter. When she learned that her son had been sold to an Alabama slaveholder, she dedicated her life to bringing him home. She said she summoned the strength of her faith in God and it made her "so tall within, as if the power of a nation was within [her]." She won her groundbreaking case to bring her son home, and in 1829, she moved to New York City, where she became an important figure in the women's rights and abolitionist movements. Her preaching was tied deeply to her Christian beliefs.

She never learned to read or write, but she dictated her memoir, *The Narrative of Sojourner Truth,* and traveled the country speaking about slavery. She was bold and outspoken. Sojourner said, "There is a great stir about colored men getting their rights, but not a word about the colored women."[10]

You need not be afraid to give us our rights for fear we will take too much.
—Sojourner Truth

Sojourner was eventually included in women's rights meetings, and when she spoke, people listened. On May 29, 1851, in Akron, Ohio, at the Woman's Rights Convention, Sojourner made her most famous speech. Her words "Ain't I a woman?" have lived on long since her death in 1883 at age eighty-six.

While the exact wording has been debated by historians (with some suggesting the Southern dialect in which it was recorded may not accurately represent Sojourner's New York–accented speech), the power of her message remains clear.[11] She boldly challenged arbitrary gender stereotypes when she said, "I have heard much about the sexes being equal; I can carry as much as any man, and can eat as much too, if I can get it. I am as strong as any man that is now. . . . You need not be afraid to give us our rights for fear we will take too much."[12]

The early women's rights movement would have benefited greatly from more actively including Black women like Sojourner Truth, whose perspectives and experiences could have strengthened and broadened the movement from its inception.

It is extraordinary to realize that women would have to wait *seventy-two* years after Seneca Falls for the Nineteenth Amendment. Only one of the sixty-eight women who originally signed the Declaration of Sentiments in 1848 was still alive when women finally got the right to vote. Her name was Charlotte Woodward Pierce, but she was in her nineties on Election Day 1920 and too ill to make it to the polls.[13]

Our Roll of Honor

Containing all the

Signatures to the "Declaration of Sentiments"

Set Forth by the First

Woman's Rights Convention,

held at

Seneca Falls, New York

July 19-20, 1848

LADIES:

Lucretia Mott
Harriet Cady Eaton
Margaret Pryor
Elizabeth Cady Stanton
Eunice Newton Foote
Mary Ann M'Clintock
Margaret Schooley
Martha C. Wright
Jane C. Hunt
Amy Post
Catherine F. Stebbins
Mary Ann Frink
Lydia Mount
Delia Mathews
Catherine C. Paine
Elizabeth W. M'Clintock
Malvina Seymour
Phebe Mosher
Catherine Shaw
Deborah Scott
Sarah Hallowell
Mary M'Clintock
Mary Gilbert
Sophronia Taylor
Cynthia Davis
Hannah Plant
Lucy Jones
Sarah Whitney
Mary H. Hallowell
Elizabeth Conklin
Sally Pitcher
Mary Conklin
Susan Quinn
Mary S. Mirror
Phebe King
Julia Ann Drake
Charlotte Woodward
Martha Underhill
Dorothy Mathews
Eunice Barker
Sarah R. Woods
Lydia Gild
Sarah Hoffman
Elizabeth Leslie
Martha Ridley
Rachel D. Bonnel
Betsey Tewksbury
Rhoda Palmer
Margaret Jenkins
Cynthia Fuller
Mary Martin
P. A. Culvert
Susan R. Doty
Rebecca Race
Sarah A. Mosher
Mary E. Vail
Lucy Spalding
Lovina Latham
Sarah Smith
Eliza Martin
Maria E. Wilbur
Elizabeth D. Smith
Caroline Barker
Ann Porter
Experience Gibbs
Antoinette E. Segur
Hannah J. Latham
Sarah Sisson

GENTLEMEN:

Richard P. Hunt
Samuel D. Tillman
Justin Williams
Elisha Foote
Frederick Douglass
Henry W. Seymour
Henry Seymour
David Spalding
William G. Barker
Elias J. Doty
John Jones
William S. Dell
James Mott
William Burroughs
Robert Smallbridge
Jacob Mathews
Charles L. Hoskins
Thomas M'Clintock
Saron Phillips
Jacob P. Chamberlain
Jonathan Metcalf
Nathan J. Milliken
S. E. Woodworth
Edward F. Underhill
George W. Pryor
Joel Bunker
Isaac VanTassel
Thomas Dell
E. W. Capron
Stephen Shear
Henry Hatley
Azaliah Schooley

A souvenir list of the sixty-eight women and thirty-two men who signed the Declaration of Sentiments at the first Woman's Rights Convention, in July 1848

Even if most people don't know the details of the Seneca Falls Convention, it is one of the landmark events in women's history that historians have thankfully recognized. In fact, the table on which the first draft of the Declaration of Sentiments was written is now part of the Smithsonian's collection. This is one of those rare occasions where, I believe, history has given Seneca Falls the place it deserves, but it has not always done justice to the women who made it happen.

DECLARATION OF SENTIMENTS

When, in the course of human events, it becomes necessary for one portion of the family of man to assume among the people of the earth a position different from that which they have hitherto occupied, but one to which the laws of nature and of nature's God entitle them, a decent respect to the opinions of mankind requires that they should declare the causes that impel them to such a course.

We hold these truths to be self-evident; that all men and women are created equal; that they are endowed by their Creator with certain inalienable rights; that among these are life, liberty, and the pursuit of happiness; that to secure these rights governments are instituted, deriving their just powers from the consent of the governed. Whenever any form of Government becomes destructive of these ends, it is the right of those who suffer from it to refuse allegiance to it, and to insist upon the institution of a new government, laying its foundation on such principles, and organizing its powers in such form as to them shall seem most likely to effect their safety and happiness. Prudence, indeed, will dictate that governments long established should not be changed for light and transient causes; and accordingly, all experience hath shown that mankind are more disposed to suffer, while evils are sufferable, than to right themselves, by abolishing the forms to which they are accustomed.

But when a long train of abuses and usurpations, pursuing invariably the same object, evinces a design to reduce them under absolute despotism, it is their duty to throw off such government, and to provide new guards for their future security. Such has been the patient sufferance of the women under this government, and such is now the necessity which constrains them to demand the equal station to which they are entitled.

The history of mankind is a history of repeated injuries and usurpations on the part of man toward woman, having in direct object the establishment of an absolute tyranny over her. To prove this, let facts be submitted to a candid world.

- He has never permitted her to exercise her inalienable right to the elective franchise.
- He has compelled her to submit to laws, in the formation of which she had no voice.
- He has withheld from her rights which are given to the most ignorant and degraded men—both natives and foreigners.
- Having deprived her of this first right of a citizen, the elective franchise, thereby leaving her without representation in the halls of legislation, he has oppressed her on all sides.
- He has made her, if married, in the eye of the law, civilly dead.
- He has taken from her all right in property, even to the wages she earns.
- He has made her, morally, an irresponsible being, as she can commit many crimes, with impunity, provided they be done in the presence of her husband. In the covenant of marriage, she is compelled to promise obedience to her husband, he becoming, to all intents and purposes, her master—the law giving him power to deprive her of her liberty, and to administer chastisement.
- He has so framed the laws of divorce, as to what shall be the proper causes of divorce; in case of separation, to whom the

guardianship of the children shall be given, as to be wholly regardless of the happiness of women—the law, in all cases, going upon the false supposition of the supremacy of man, and giving all power into his hands.

- After depriving her of all rights as a married woman, if single and the owner of property, he has taxed her to support a government which recognizes her only when her property can be made profitable to it.
- He has monopolized nearly all the profitable employments, and from those she is permitted to follow, she receives but a scanty remuneration.
- He closes against her all the avenues to wealth and distinction, which he considers most honorable to himself. As a teacher of theology, medicine, or law, she is not known.
- He has denied her the facilities for obtaining a thorough education—all colleges being closed against her.
- He allows her in Church as well as State, but a subordinate position, claiming Apostolic authority for her exclusion from the ministry, and with some exceptions, from any public participation in the affairs of the Church.
- He has created a false public sentiment, by giving to the world a different code of morals for men and women, by which moral delinquencies which exclude women from society, are not only tolerated but deemed of little account in man.
- He has usurped the prerogative of Jehovah himself, claiming it as his right to assign for her a sphere of action, when that belongs to her conscience and her God.
- He has endeavored, in every way that he could to destroy her confidence in her own powers, to lessen her self-respect, and to make her willing to lead a dependent and abject life.

Now, in view of this entire disfranchisement of one-half the people of this country, their social and religious degradation,—in view of the unjust laws above mentioned, and because women do feel themselves aggrieved, oppressed, and fraudulently deprived of their most sacred rights, we insist that they have immediate admission to all the rights and privileges which belong to them as citizens of these United States.

In entering upon the great work before us, we anticipate no small amount of misconception, misrepresentation, and ridicule; but we shall use every instrumentality within our power to effect our object. We shall employ agents, circulate tracts, petition the State and national Legislatures, and endeavor to enlist the pulpit and the press in our behalf. We hope this Convention will be followed by a series of Conventions, embracing every part of the country.

Firmly relying upon the final triumph of the Right and the True, we do this day affix our signatures to this declaration.

11.

The Blackwell Sisters: *The Doctors*

In 1847, when she was twenty-six years old, Elizabeth Blackwell applied to nearly thirty medical schools. She was rejected by all but two of them. When she got an acceptance letter from Geneva Medical College in western New York, it was a happy surprise. She had just about given up hope, writing in her journal about her "immense sigh of relief and aspiration of profound gratitude."[1] She couldn't wait to pack up her bags and do something that no other woman had ever done in America: attend medical school. Elizabeth became the first woman to earn a medical degree when she graduated at the top of her class in 1849.[2]

Yet the awful truth is that, unbeknownst to Elizabeth, her acceptance was supposed to be a joke.

The story behind Elizabeth's admittance reveals the deeply entrenched gender bias of the time. The notion of admitting a female medical student to Geneva was considered so absurd that the faculty left the decision up to the all-male student body, assuming they would reject the idea. The strategy backfired spectacularly. The male students, considering the application a university prank, voted unanimously to let her in.[3] They never expected she would actually attend. Their miscalculation opened the door to medical history. *And is a reminder to us all, never underestimate a woman.*

On November 4, Elizabeth departed Philadelphia for New York, blazing a path that countless women, including her own sister, would eventually follow.

Elizabeth was born near Bristol, England, on February 3, 1821, the third of nine children in a family of Quaker abolitionists. Her family valued education highly and gave equal lessons to the boys and girls, a progressive idea at the time. Her father, Samuel Blackwell, was a sugar refiner and an anti-slavery activist. Her parents were friends with the editor of *The Liberator*, William Lloyd Garrison, a name that comes up again and again in this period. Her brother Henry became a famous abolitionist and women's suffrage supporter who married women's rights activist Lucy Stone.

In 1832, the Blackwells moved to Cincinnati, Ohio. When Elizabeth's father died in 1838, the family was destitute, and her mother and her two older sisters had to work. Like many women of the time, they became teachers, one of the few acceptable professions for women. Elizabeth also taught to help her family and to raise money for medical school.

In her autobiography, Elizabeth wrote that growing up, she "hated everything connected with the body, and could not bear the sight of a medical book." But something made her change her mind. Elizabeth says she was inspired by a friend dealing with chronic illness who once told her, "If I could have been treated by a lady doctor, my worst sufferings would have been spared me."[4] It marked a turning point in her life.

Going to school with members of the opposite sex was extremely rare at the time. Ohio's Oberlin College, the first coeducational school in the country, didn't open until 1833. So Elizabeth's first day at Geneva Medical College was uncomfortable at best. She was entering an environment that was considered completely off-limits to women. It was outlandish for a proper lady to have her hands on a corpse or to talk about the human body alongside men.

A Geneva medical student named Stephen Smith remembered the reaction of the male students on Elizabeth's first day. "The Dean came into the classroom, evidently in a state of unusual agitation. The class took alarm, fearing that some great calamity was about to befall the College. . . . He stated, with a trembling voice, that . . . the female student . . . had arrived. . . . With this introduction he opened the door to the reception room and a lady . . . entered, whom the Dean formally introduced as Miss Blackwell. She was plainly but neatly dressed in Quaker style, and carried the usual notebook of the medical student. A hush fell on the class as if each member had been stricken with paralysis. A death-like stillness prevailed during the lecture, and only the newly arrived student took notes."[5]

Dr. Elizabeth Blackwell

Elizabeth often sat separately from the rest of the class during lectures and endured the jeers of people in her college town.

"I had not the slightest idea of the commotion created by my appearance as a medical student in the little town. Very slowly I perceived that a doctor's wife at the table avoided any communication with me, and that as I walked backwards and forwards to college the ladies stopped to stare at me, as at a curious animal," she wrote. "I afterwards found that I had so shocked Geneva propriety that the theory was fully established either that I was a bad woman, whose designs would gradually become evident, or that, being insane, an outbreak of insanity would soon be apparent."[6]

Elizabeth had to argue with her professor to be included in surgical observations and to take part in dissections. In an entry dated November 15, 1847, she wrote in her journal, "Today, a second operation at which I was not allowed to be present. This annoys me. I was quite saddened and discouraged by Dr. Webster requesting me to be absent from some of his demonstrations. I don't believe it is his wish. I wrote to him hoping to change things."[7] Sticking up for herself worked, and she wrote, "No further difficulty ever afterwards occurred" in the class.[8]

Elizabeth's persistence in gaining full access to medical education wasn't just about personal achievement—it was essential for addressing the glaring gaps in women's healthcare. Her presence in those previously forbidden surgical demonstrations was critical because there was basically no understanding of women's reproductive system at the time. It's horrifying to consider that male doctors would sometimes use a device called a metrotome to cut the cervix to help treat fertility issues.[9] When one of Elizabeth's relatives told her that she was contemplating trying the procedure, Elizabeth told her that the scarring it caused would make it even more difficult to get pregnant.[10] This highlighted why more women needed to be in the medical profession—and it was why Elizabeth decided to push through and break the glass ceiling to become a doctor.

In general, it was still a primitive time in medicine. The American Medical Association had just been established and antiseptics and antibiotics were not widely in use. There were midwives and nurses who basically served as doctors, but they did not receive the same training, level of respect, or income.

Elizabeth's research was groundbreaking. Her thesis about an outbreak of typhoid among immigrants called "ship fever" was published in the *Buffalo Medical Journal and Monthly Review*.[11] Her work was grounded in her belief that better sanitation and education, especially among poor communities, would save lives.

"When the laws of health are generally understood and practiced," she declared, "when a social providence is extended over all ranks of the community, and the different nations of the earth interlinked in a true brotherhood—then we may hope to see these physical evils disappear with all the moral evils which correspond to and are closely associated with them."[12]

Elizabeth's sister Emily, who was five years younger, wanted to follow her path. But, as it turned out, Geneva Medical College had decided that it had had enough female medical students. Women's medical colleges were beginning to be established, and because men and women training as doctors together was still considered so controversial, women like Emily were told to go to an all-women's school instead.

Dr. Emily Blackwell

The problem was that neither Blackwell sister thought those schools offered the same level of education. Many focused only on midwifery.[13] Emily suffered rejection after rejection; eleven medical schools refused to admit her because she was a woman. Although she was accepted by Rush Medical College in Chicago, pressure from the Medical Society of Illinois led the school to discontinue her studies at the end of the first year.[14]

She eventually graduated from the institution that would become Case Western Reserve University in Cleveland.[15] Emily was only the third woman in the United States to earn a medical degree, after her sister and Dr. Mary Edwards Walker (more on her later).[16]

After graduation, Elizabeth worked in clinics in London and Paris for two years and studied midwifery. She contracted purulent ophthalmia, an infection that caused her to lose sight in one eye. In 1851, she moved to New York City. Her left eye was surgically removed and replaced with a glass prosthesis; in a cruel twist of fate, she could no longer work as a surgeon.[17]

One challenge the sisters didn't anticipate was that after overcoming so many obstacles to obtain their degrees, they'd face just as many practicing medicine. The public wasn't ready to trust its health to fe-

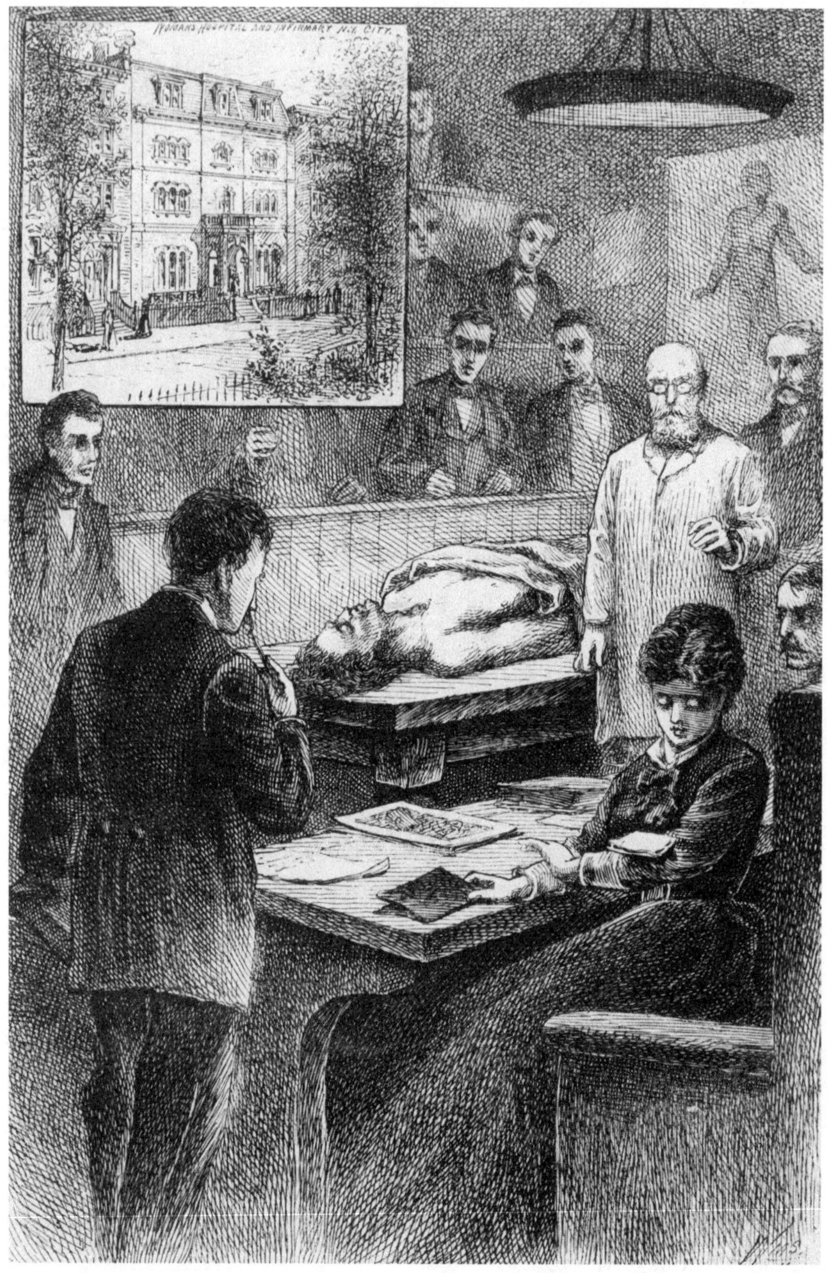

An illustration from 1847 shows Elizabeth Blackwell during a lecture in Geneva Medical College's operating room.

male physicians. But one sector of the population was desperate; poor people were grateful to receive medical care, even from a woman.

In 1857, Elizabeth and Emily founded the first American hospital staffed by women, the New York Infirmary for Indigent Women and Children. The institution was groundbreaking, with each sister playing a vital but different role. Although Elizabeth was largely responsible for founding the hospital, the credit for its growth belongs primarily to Emily. After just two years of operation, Elizabeth and their colleague Dr. Marie Zakrzewska left to work elsewhere, leaving Emily in charge.[18]

For the next forty years, Dr. Emily Blackwell took over management of the infirmary, overseeing surgery, nursing, and bookkeeping. Her advocacy took her to Albany, the capital of New York, to convince the legislature to provide the hospital with funds that would ensure its long-term financial stability. Her remarkable skills helped transform an institution housed in a rented sixteen-room house into a large hospital.[19] By 1874, the infirmary served over seven thousand patients annually.[20]

The hospital charged a few dollars a week, or nothing at all, to patients who could not afford to pay. And the hospital allowed female physicians, who were rejected from residencies at other places, the opportunity to practice their skills as physicians. Over time, the infirmary evolved into NewYork-Presbyterian Lower Manhattan Hospital. During the first hundred years of the infirmary's existence, it cared for more than one million men, women, and children.[21]

As the infirmary established itself, the sisters recognized that their vision couldn't be fulfilled through clinical care alone, so they took their next ambitious step. In 1868, they opened the Women's Medical College of the New York Infirmary, with Elizabeth serving as professor of hygiene and Emily as professor of obstetrics and diseases of women.[22] It was among the first four-year medical colleges in the United States, and operated until 1899, when its students transitioned to Weill Cornell Medicine, which had begun admitting women.[23]

Through a modern lens, some of the Blackwells' views are not at all progressive. Elizabeth was not particularly supportive of the women's suffrage movement because she thought that women needed to be better educated before they had the power to sway elections. She was also against contraception. And she was horrified by the idea of abortion, deeming it a "gross perversion and destruction of motherhood."[24]

The Blackwells' biographer Janice Nimura noted that the sisters were "complicated, prickly, sometimes self-contradictory people." It seems to me that our society expects female leaders to be nice and ladylike, but history shows that women in male-dominated arenas are often judged by a double standard. Disruption is rarely comfortable—but it is how revolutions begin.

In 1869, Elizabeth returned to England, where she founded the National Health Society with the motto, "Prevention is better than cure." She died in 1910 at age eighty-nine, just months before her sister Emily.

The Blackwell sisters would be heartened to know that, though it took time, women have made remarkable strides in medicine—today they make up the majority of U.S. medical school graduates.[25] Every February 3, National Women Physicians Day honors their contributions, timed to Elizabeth Blackwell's birthday.[26]

In their day, the idea of a woman doctor was met with open mockery. In 1859, the *British Medical Journal* scoffed at "the idea of a female practitioner" and asked, "imagine, good reader, if you can, a British lady" performing a doctor's duties.[27] Thanks to the Blackwells, no one had to imagine for long. They proved it could be done—and opened the door for generations who would do it even better.

12.

Dr. Mary Edwards Walker: *The Medal of Honor Recipient*

On April 10, 1864, Dr. Mary Edwards Walker was captured by Confederate soldiers. She was riding alone behind enemy lines on horseback, searching for wounded Union Army soldiers who needed her help. As the first female U.S. Army surgeon, she was used to being on battlefields by herself. But this time, she was detained and taken to the infamous Castle Thunder prison in Richmond, Virginia—a place where female prisoners were chloroformed and raped.[1] Four years into the war, Dr. Walker was well-known not only as a surgeon but also as a spy for the Union Army. Her treatment at Castle Thunder would be especially harrowing.

Her appearance was the talk of the prison guards. One Confederate captain described Dr. Walker as a sight that "both amused and disgusted" the crowd, noting that she was dressed in the full uniform of a federal surgeon and was "not good-looking."[2] The captain's remarks reflected their disdain, but the focus on her appearance and assertiveness was typical sexism.

The food was filled with maggots, and mice were everywhere. After four months, Dr. Walker was released in exchange for a Confederate surgeon. While in prison, she was malnourished and ill and left with partial muscular atrophy. She never fully recovered from the experience, which ended her surgical career but not her pioneering legacy.

Dr. Walker was a larger-than-life character. She was intensely patriotic. When she was imprisoned, her stated crime was her work as an undercover intelligence officer aiding the North during the Civil

War. She declared, "Let the generations know that women in uniform also guaranteed their freedom."[3] Her story is a reminder of how long women have been in military service and how little we know about their sacrifices. It's also a warning not to forget them.

More than 3,500 people have received the Medal of Honor, the highest military decoration for bravery in combat awarded in America by the president. Dr. Walker is the only woman among them. Despite that unique distinction, and the incredible actions that earned her the medal, it was taken away from her. However, her resilience and courage ignited her fight to win it back.

Mary was born in 1832 in Oswego, New York, on the banks of Lake Ontario. She was the fifth of six surviving children and the youngest of five daughters. Her parents were abolitionists who emphasized the importance of education. As a young girl, Mary dreamed of becoming a doctor, and with so few women in medicine, she embraced the challenge. She was briefly a teacher before being accepted to Syracuse Medical College in 1853. Mary graduated with honors in 1855, becoming one of the first women in the United States to graduate from medical school, a few years after Elizabeth Blackwell.[4]

Let the generations know that women in uniform also guaranteed their freedom.

—Dr. Mary Edwards Walker

During the Civil War, Mary moved to Washington, D.C., and requested a commission as a medical officer in the Union Army. Even though the government was desperate for trained physicians, she was denied the posting because of her sex. But she would not take no for an answer. She served as an unpaid surgeon at a makeshift hospital in the unfinished U.S. Patent Building, which is now the National Portrait Gallery and the Smithsonian American Art Museum in downtown Washington, D.C.[5]

What she did to earn her Medal of Honor shows her true grit and patriotism. In the fall of 1862, she moved to Virginia, where the fighting was intense. She served on the battlefields of Bull Run—the first major battle of the war—and Fredericksburg—one of its bloodiest—placing herself near the front lines where few civilians, let alone women, dared to go. Her presence there was significant: It meant she was treating the wounded amid the chaos and danger of major Civil War engagements, at a time when battlefield medicine was primitive and perilous. Determined that soldiers would recognize her as a surgeon, not a nurse, she designed her own blue uniform with a green sash, modeled after those worn by official army doctors. She continued working without pay for two years, never ceasing to push for an official, paid position. Each rejection only deepened her resolve.

She could have been given the title of nurse, but that was not an accurate description of her work. The *New York Tribune* was intrigued by her and wrote this of her in December 1862: "Dressed in male habiliments . . . she carries herself amid the camp with a jaunty air of dignity well calculated to receive the sincere respect of the soldiers. . . . She can amputate a limb with the skill of an old surgeon, and administer medicine equally as well. Strange to say that, although she has frequently applied for a permanent position in the medical corps, she has never been formally assigned to any particular duty."[6]

Dr. Mary Edwards Walker pictured with her Medal of Honor

In 1863, she finally received the recognition she had been seeking and was formally named as the only female acting assistant surgeon in the U.S. Army during the Civil War. She was assigned to the 52nd Ohio volunteers and was paid $80 a month, the equivalent of almost $2,000 today. Surgery was not the only thing she was known for. In fact, she crossed enemy lines to provide medical care to civilians. It was a risky job, so initially she was accompanied by two officers, two orderlies, and the added security of "two revolvers in her saddlebags."[7]

Mary was a risk taker who was willing to give her life for her country. Her trips into Confederate territory had a dual purpose: They also allowed her to gather intelligence and spy for the Union Army.[8] In 1864, when Union general William Sherman was getting ready to march on Atlanta, it was Mary's information that provided strategic benefit to the general. Sherman's famous capture of Atlanta damaged the Confederacy and helped President Abraham Lincoln's re-election campaign. Sherman reportedly changed his strategy because of information Mary collected.[9]

After her capture and subsequent release, President Lincoln invited Mary to Washington to learn about her time as a prisoner of war. She was still a civilian in the U.S. Army, but she hoped that meeting with the commander in chief would help her earn a commission to become an official member. Unfortunately, that didn't work because women were still not allowed to join the U.S. military.[10]

Her biographer Sara Latta wrote, "Mary hoped that her commission would pave the way for other women who wanted to serve in the military. Military officials were well aware of her goal, and they didn't want to set such a precedent." However, President Andrew Johnson—who had taken office after Lincoln's assassination—wanted to honor Mary's valiant service. President Johnson, along with the secretary of war, "settled" on the Medal of Honor.[11]

Her Medal of Honor citation is remarkable, especially when you consider that it was issued in 1866, nearly fifty-five years before women were given the right to vote and eighty-three years before women could officially join the U.S. military.[12] It commended her for committing herself "with much patriotic zeal to the sick and wounded soldiers, both in the field and hospitals, to the detriment of her own health."

The commendation noted the suffering she endured as a prisoner of war for four months in a Southern prison while she served as a contract surgeon. It continued: "Whereas by reason of her not being a commissioned officer in the military service, a brevet or honorary rank cannot, under existing laws, be conferred upon her; and Whereas in the opinion of the President an honorable recognition of her services and sufferings should be made; It is ordered, That a testimonial thereof shall be hereby made and given to the said Dr. Mary E. Walker, and that the usual medal of honor for meritorious services be given her."[13]

What truly astounds me is that she was the *first* and the *last* woman to ever receive the nation's highest military honor for actions in war.

In 1917, the government changed the criteria for who was allowed to receive the prestigious Medal of Honor—removing it from civilians, including Mary. Hers was rescinded along with more than nine hundred others. In keeping with her spirit, Mary refused to return the medal, which she reportedly wore every day until her death.

Walker, Dr. Mary E.
Date of award: January 24, 1866. Medal of Honor.
Date of action: 1861 to 1865.

Stricken from list Feb. 15, 1917.
Adverse action Medal of Honor
Board - A. G. 2411162.

Restored by ABCMR
in 1977

Dr. Mary Edwards Walker's U.S. Army "award card" shows the dates of when she received the Medal of Honor, when it was taken away, and when it was restored.

Like so many unsung heroes, she had to fight for recognition. It would take another sixty years for her to officially have it (long after her death). On June 10, 1977, President Jimmy Carter legally restored the medal to Dr. Mary Edwards Walker.

Even people who have never heard of Dr. Mary Edwards Walker have benefited from the life she lived. And that's not only because of her work during the Civil War to keep the Union together. It may seem trivial, but the way she dressed is also part of her legacy. She rejected the Victorian style of the times that dictated that middle- and upper-class white women wear tight-fitting corsets, creating tiny waists, and heavy floor-length layered skirts. These cumbersome skirts sometimes weighed up to fifteen pounds![14] Corsets, meant to give women hourglass figures, were painful, causing deformed ribs and lowering lung capacity.

Dr. Walker became one of the first women to wear trousers in public in a shocking act of defiance of gender norms. It was much more than a fashion statement, or a desire to be comfortable; to Mary, wearing pants was about outwardly declaring her freedom to do as she pleased. When she married, instead of an elegant white dress, she wore her usual trousers and short skirt. She would not use the word *obey* in her vows and she kept her maiden name professionally. After four years, she and her husband separated, and for good reason: He had impregnated at least two patients. And yet it took a decade until the divorce was granted.[15] Dr. Walker was infuriated by the delay. "Without proper divorce laws, virtue is robbed of her rights, vice encouraged, noble aspirations rushed, love turned to hate, and marriage made wretched beyond the power of human expression," she said.[16] "If it is right to be legally married, it is right to be legally divorced."[17]

> ***If it is right to be legally married, it is right to be legally divorced.***
>
> ***—Dr. Mary Edwards Walker***

In 1870, during a speaking tour, she stopped in New Orleans, where she was arrested for impersonating a man. But she never backed down or apologized. "I don't wear men's clothes," she said, "*I wear my own clothes.*"[18] She dedicated her 1871 book, *Hit: Essays on Women's Rights,* to the "practical dress reformers." In her dedication, she thanked the women "who have *lived* the precepts and principles that others have only *talked*—who have been so consistent in your ideas of the equality of the sexes, by dressing in a manner to fit you for the duties of a noble and useful life."[19]

Her dress was her rebellion, and she was courageous. But the criticism still stung. "Every jeer has cut me to the quick," she wrote. "Many times have I gone to my room and wept after being publicly derided. No one knows, or will ever know, what it has cost me to live up to my principles, to be consistent with my convictions and declarations; but I have done it, and am not sorry for it."[20]

Later in life, Dr. Walker became a well-known women's rights activist, but her views placed her at odds with many suffragists.

Mary was a proponent of the New Departure strategy in the women's suffrage movement, which argued that women already had the constitutional right to vote, and that no additional amendment was needed. In 1907, she published her "Crowning Constitutional Argument," which was based on the idea that the U.S. Constitution's reference to "We the People" specifically avoided gendered nouns and did not prohibit women from voting.

Her vehement opposition to the Susan B. Anthony Voting Rights Amendment led her to testify before Congress. I wish we had video of the hearings because what we know is that Dr. Walker was seventy-nine years old. She wore a tall black top hat, a medium-length black coat, crisp white gloves, and a tight wingtip collar around her neck.

No one could miss the star emblem adorning her chest that was the Medal of Honor decoration.

"We do not want any amendment to the Constitution," she argued. "We do not want any such sort of trash as that."[21]

Five years later, in 1917, Mary slipped on the steps of the Capitol in Washington and never fully recovered.

She died at age eighty-six in her hometown of Oswego, New York;

true to herself, she was buried in a black suit. An American flag was draped over her casket. She passed the very same year of the passage of the Nineteenth Amendment that guaranteed women the right to vote.

Today Dr. Mary Edwards Walker is still the only woman to have received the Medal of Honor. Her medal is displayed at the Richardson-Bates House Museum in her hometown of Oswego, New York.

13.

Susan and Susette La Flesche: *The Advocates*

The Declaration of Independence proclaimed that "all men are created equal," yet for Indigenous peoples in the late nineteenth century, this promise remained hollow. Native Americans were actually referred to as "merciless Indian Savages" in our nation's founding document.[1] Equality was reserved for a privileged few. Two sisters from the Omaha Tribe would challenge this contradiction through radically different paths—one through the examination room and hospital ward, the other through the courtroom and lecture circuit. Susan and Susette La Flesche became changemakers who fought for their people's rights and survival in an era of profound injustice.

When Susan La Flesche was a young girl, she witnessed an event that would shape her entire life. A desperately ill Native American woman was refused treatment by a white doctor and later died because of the lack of care. This moment of callous discrimination planted the seeds of Susan's revolutionary ambition: She would ensure that her people had access to quality healthcare, even if it meant becoming a doctor herself.[2]

Susan's path to medicine required extraordinary dedication and resilience. At Virginia's Hampton Institute, and later at the Women's Medical College of Pennsylvania, she excelled academically while maintaining her cultural identity, graduating in 1889 as valedictorian.[3]

What she was doing was not new for Indigenous women. Many tribal cultures encouraged women to be involved in medicine, and in

Dr. Susan La Flesche Picotte

line with the matrilineal nature of many tribes, women held significant political and economic power. They were midwives and healers. They were often held in high regard as having important knowledge about plant-based medicines and childbirth. In fact, many tribal nations believed that women had greater healing power than men.

At a time when women were still considered "too delicate" to be doctors, Susan used her experience and grounding in Native cultures to propel herself into the medical field. Susan's education was financed by the Connecticut Indian Association, which supported "Christianization" of Native Americans.[4] She wore her hair in an updo and dressed like her white classmates.

Before the first surgery, male medical students teased the female students that they would faint at the first sight of blood. But Susan wasn't fazed. Instead, she leaned in farther to see every bit of the surgery. Ironically, the male student who had teased her the most collapsed shortly after surgery began.[5] Susan later wrote to her sister Rosalie, "I wasn't even thinking of fainting."[6]

Today Susan La Flesche is known as the first Indigenous woman to earn a medical degree.[7]

Returning to the Omaha Reservation at age twenty-four, Susan became the sole physician for over a thousand people scattered across four hundred miles.[8] Her practice was demanding—she walked miles in harsh weather to reach patients, eventually saving enough money to buy a horse and buggy for her rounds. Some days stretched from

8 a.m. to 10 p.m. as she battled cholera, malaria, and other diseases ravaging her community.[9]

But Susan's influence extended far beyond individual patient care. As the only medical professional serving her tribe, she possessed unique authority to speak about the health conditions on the reservation and their causes. Her daily work revealed the devastating impact of government policies on Native American health and well-being.

Initially, Susan believed that adopting certain aspects of mainstream American life might benefit her people. In her salutatorian speech at the Hampton Institute she had said, "We have to prepare our people to live in the white man's way, to use the white man's books, and to use his laws if you will only give them to us." She worked with the Office of Indian Affairs, hoping to improve living conditions through cooperation with federal authorities.

However, her medical expertise gave her a unique perspective on how government politics were affecting Native American communities. She began to see connections between the disruption of traditional ways of life and poor health outcomes. Government-mandated frame houses created overcrowding that accelerated disease transmission. The stress of cultural displacement contributed to alcoholism and mental health issues.[10] By 1907, Susan observed with growing alarm: "The physical degeneration in 20 years among my people is terrible."[11]

Susan's reputation gave her unprecedented influence. In 1894, she married Henry Picotte, a Yankton Sioux, and they had two sons, whom she occasionally brought on house calls. She had become what historians call a New Woman—financially independent, professionally accomplished, and unwilling to confine herself to traditional domestic roles.

Her disillusionment with the federal policies deepened as she witnessed the hardships caused by land allotment policies.[12] She traveled to Washington, D.C., on behalf of the Omaha people to meet with the Secretary of the Interior and the Attorney General. When Senator Elmer Burkett of Nebraska dismissed her concerns, Susan delivered a response that captured decades of neglect: "Mr. Burkett, we have lived on broken promises."[13]

Susan joined the temperance movement, recognizing that alcohol abuse was both a symptom of cultural destruction and a tool of continued oppression. Her approach to healing expanded beyond individual patients to encompass systemic advocacy for her community's rights and well-being.

The pinnacle of Susan's influence came with the establishment of the first privately funded hospital on any Native American reservation. When the federal government refused to support general hospitals for Indigenous peoples, Susan raised the funds herself, creating an institution that would serve her community long after her death. The hospital, declared a National Historic Landmark in 1993, stands as a testament to her vision of Indigenous peoples' self-determination. There is no doubt that Susan was a force for change.

Susette La Flesche

Before Susan started building her medical practice, her older sister, Susette, had already begun her own form of advocacy on a different path.

That journey began on the morning of April 30, 1879, in a packed courtroom in Omaha, Nebraska, in a case called *Standing Bear v. Crook*. Susette was present to help translate the testimony of tribal leader Chief Standing Bear, whose emotional speech left the crowd in tears and resulted in a landmark victory.

The case arose from the forcible removal of the Ponca Tribe from their ancestral lands in Nebraska to a distant reservation, followed by the government's refusal to allow Chief Standing Bear to return home to bury his son. At that time, Native Americans could not leave their reservations—designated lands for Indigenous tribes—without the government's permission. When Standing Bear defied this order and was arrested, the government argued he had no legal standing to challenge his detention because, as a Native American, he was not a "person" under American law.

In the courtroom's most electrifying moment, Chief Standing Bear held out his hand and spoke words that Susette would translate with profound impact: "That hand is not the color of yours, but if I pierce it, I shall feel pain. If you pierce your hand, you also feel pain. The blood that will flow from mine will be of the same color as yours. I am a man. The same God made us both." The courtroom erupted in emotion, with spectators weeping and clamoring to shake the chief's hand.

Susette's translation proved decisive.

The judge ruled in Standing Bear's favor, declaring that "an Indian is a PERSON within the meaning of the laws of the United States." The judge also quoted the Declaration of Independence: "Indians possess the inherent right of expatriation as well as the more fortunate white race, and have the inalienable right to 'life, liberty, and the pursuit of happiness.'" It was a significant ruling.

Yet even this victory revealed the depths of prejudice Indigenous peoples faced—the same judge who granted them personhood also called them a "weak, insignificant, unlettered and generally despised race."

The moment crystallized a strategy that would define both sisters' approaches to advocacy: They would excel in the institutions of the dominant culture (created by their oppressors) to fight for their people's survival and rights.

With this case, Susette helped Standing Bear become the first Indigenous person to win a civil rights victory in a U.S. federal court. Chief Standing Bear's story, in part, became known because of Susette. And today, he has a statue in the U.S. Capitol.

The courtroom triumph transformed Susette into "Inshata-Theumba"—"Bright Eyes"—a name her tribe bestowed for her clarity of vision to exposing injustice.[14] Recognizing that legal victories meant little without broader public support, she embarked on a speaking campaign across the eastern United States.

> ***I shall always fight good and hard, even if I have to fight alone.***
>
> **—*Susan La Flesche***

Wearing a traditional Omaha deerskin dress, Susette toured the country calling for a new direction in federal Indian policy. The tour was organized by her husband, Thomas H. Tibbles, and included Standing Bear and her half brother Francis. Her choice of attire was deliberate—she presented her authentic Omaha identity in a way that would engage white audiences while delivering speeches that challenged their fundamental assumptions about Indigenous peoples.

Her message was clear and revolutionary: Native Americans wanted citizenship and the freedoms that were promised to all Americans in 1776. They did not want to be told who they could trade with or where they could live.

In Boston in 1880, she exposed American hypocrisy with surgical precision: "When the first settlers in this country fought for their property, liberty, and lives, they were called heroes. When the Indian in fighting this great nation wins a battle, it is called a massacre; when this great nation in fighting the Indian wins a battle, it is called a victory."[15]

Susette's advocacy contributed to the passage of the 1887 Dawes Act, legislation initially intended to protect Native American property rights. However, the law's actual consequences—the breakup of tribal lands and the erosion of tribal sovereignty—would later reveal the complex challenges facing Native Americans in this era and would be used to disenfranchise them.[16]

Both sisters drew inspiration from their father, Joseph La Flesche, known as "Iron Eye," who was the last recognized chief of the Omaha Tribe. He often said, "It is either civilization or extermination," reflecting the impossible choices facing Indigenous leaders of his generation.[17] His daughters would prove that survival could take many forms. The statue of Susan La Flesche in Lincoln, Nebraska, bears her own words: "I shall always fight good and hard, even if I have to fight alone."[18] Yet the La Flesche sisters never fought alone—they fought together, each using different forms of advocacy that would pave the way for future generations of Native American leaders.

The stories of the La Flesche sisters were introduced to us by Shelly Lowe, the first Native American chair of the National Endowment for the Humanities. Their legacy reminds us that assimilation was never a simple choice but rather a complex decision.

14.

Anna Dickinson: *The Orator*

The year was 1864. The U.S. House of Representatives' chamber was packed with two thousand people—including President Abraham Lincoln and First Lady Mary Todd Lincoln. They weren't there for a State of the Union address or a speech from a foreign politician visiting America. They were gathered to hear from a twenty-one-year-old firebrand named Anna Dickinson, an eloquent abolitionist who left the country's politicians hanging on her every word as she spoke for more than an hour denouncing slavery.

Anna had become a major celebrity, and her youth and self-confidence only added to her allure. She was nicknamed "America's Joan of Arc" because of her passionate speeches.

Speaking out against slavery ran in Anna's family. She was raised by Quaker parents who were fierce abolitionists and she grew up in the wake of the 1848 Seneca Falls Convention. Her family hosted Frederick Douglass and sheltered enslaved people who had run away. As a teenager, Anna had read an article about a teacher from Kentucky who was beaten and covered in tar and feathers for his stance against slavery. She was outraged and sent a letter in 1856 to the editor of the abolitionist newspaper *The Liberator* railing against the "barbarous atrocity."[1]

She discovered her gift for public speaking at a Quaker meeting in 1860 when she spoke in support of women's equality with men. Anna jumped to her feet to deliver a rebuttal to a man who suggested that a woman's only sphere of influence was in the home. Throughout her career as an orator, she rarely glanced down at her notes.

Public speaking was risky for a woman. In fact, Anna was fired as a teenager from a job at the Philadelphia Mint for criticizing a Union general. No one wants to be fired from their job, but it led Anna to embark on a career as a paid public speaker that would cement her legacy as one of the Civil War's most important orators.

Anna had impressed William Lloyd Garrison, the *Liberator* editor who published her scathing letter in his newspaper. Garrison helped organize a speaking tour for Anna. At the time, it was considered unseemly for a woman to have such strong opinions. Anna was sarcastic, determined, and passionate onstage.

One of the most noteworthy things to me as a journalist who covers politics is that this young woman was then recruited by the Republican Party to campaign during a pivotal time, when Lincoln's party was concerned about waning support for the Civil War. It's amazing that, at a time when women didn't have the right to vote, *any* political party believed that a woman would be influential enough to sway elections and public opinion.

Anna barnstormed the country, giving twenty speeches for the Republican cause, mostly in small towns. Republican leaders credited her with helping the party win statewide races.[2] That landed her an invitation from Senator William D. Kelley to speak in the nation's capital. The letter was signed by the vice president of the United States, twenty-three senators, and seventy-eight members of the House of Representatives.[3]

She accepted and became the first woman to give a political address to the U.S. Congress on January 16, 1864. The twenty-one-year-old was in the middle of denouncing President Lincoln's Reconstruction plans when the president and his wife walked into the chamber. In Anna's mind, Lincoln's plans and his protections for Black people weren't strong enough. She felt there was no room for compromise with the South because it had tried to destroy the country when it seceded. Lincoln sat with his head hung low as she spoke, "Let no man prate of compromise! Defeated by ballots, the South had appealed to bullets. Let it stand by the appeal! There was not an arm of compromise in all the North long enough to stretch over the sea of blood and the mound of fallen Northern soldiers to shake hands with their murderers."[4]

The audience erupted in applause and someone in the balcony waved an American flag. But even after her criticism of Lincoln, and any plans of compromise with the South, in that same speech, she offered him her full endorsement for his re-election: "This was pre-eminently a people's war. It was guided by the man of the people, who had never been behind the great heart of the people. We had done much, and all was hopeful before us. Granted that we had much yet to do, we had the man to complete the grand and glorious work, *and that work was left for his second term of office*."

The surprised crowd erupted again, and Lincoln must have been pleased because what Anna said carried great weight. No one knows if this was planned or if she had a change of heart when she saw the president.[5]

Shortly afterward, she privately met with President Lincoln. She spoke about the meeting in public lectures in which she made fun of him—"his figure—his dress—his old coat, out at the elbows which look[ed] as if he had worn it three years and used it as a pen wiper—his stocking limp and soiled."

She said that she told Lincoln his Reconstruction plans were " 'all wrong; as radically bad as can be.' " He ended the conversation, according to Anna, by telling her, " 'All I can say is, if the radicals want me to lead, let them get out of the way and let me lead.' " With that, she told one Boston audience, "I came out and remarked to a friend—'I have spoken my last word to President Lincoln.' " She was disappointed that he wouldn't consider her ideas more seriously, though it's remarkable that he met with her at all.[6]

Even after all she accomplished, her words weren't always the focus of articles about her. In fact, reporters debated whether she was beautiful. She was thin and her face was round. She wore her short brown hair in waves and she had expressive gray eyes. Not everyone approved of a woman taking the stage. A London correspondent was amazed that Congress would allow a "crazy Jane in a red jacket" in its halls. A journalist from the *Philadelphia Evening Bulletin* who saw her speak wrote, "We were sorry to hear the lady damaging her cause by claiming intellectual equality with men."[7]

Anna Dickinson

She was a shrewd businesswoman. In 1872, she earned $23,000 from the lecture circuit, which is notable because the president's yearly salary at the time was $25,000! She made $300 or $400 a night, which means she earned more money than Mark Twain in the year when he published his book *Roughing It*.[8]

Her most popular speech was "Jeanne d'Arc" or "Joan of Arc," a nod to her nickname, which she delivered many times after the Civil War. In it, she made the case for women's suffrage. She likened Joan's military ability to Napoleon's, making the point that Napoleon was considered a brilliant strategist whereas many thought Joan was just lucky: "Of the man, the world says, 'What august power! What commanding genius!' Of the woman, under precisely similar conditions, it cries, 'Why what a lucky accident it was, she should happen to hit upon that plan.' "[9] Given her rhetorical skill, if she had been born a century later, she would have made a good candidate herself.

Black and white women abolitionists like Sojourner Truth and Lucretia Mott made it possible for someone like Anna Dickinson to get the kind of attention she garnered. Like them, she faced questions about whether she should be an influential speaker. She was earnest and persuasive. She was spellbinding when she spoke about Reconstruction and the need to give Black people more rights. She thought members of the Confederacy needed to be held to account for their attempt to tear apart the nation. She wanted the formerly enslaved to be given rebel land seized by the government, and she wanted them to have the right to vote.

Dickinson's story highlights both the extraordinary possibilities and the harsh challenges for pioneering women in the mid-nineteenth century. She struggled with poor health and depression, and her life took a dramatic turn in 1891 when her sister had her committed, against her will, to a state-run mental institution.[10] Anna spent years fighting to restore her reputation, filing numerous lawsuits and eventually winning several of them.[11]

But Anna Dickinson's legacy extends far beyond her personal struggles. At just twenty-one, she had commanded the attention of lawmakers with her eloquence. She proved that a woman could earn a fortune through her intellect and oratory—making nearly as much as the president himself. She demonstrated that female voices could sway elections and shape national discourse on the most pressing issues of her time. Anna was helpful to the Republican Party and to Abraham Lincoln's re-election bid.

Most important, Anna blazed a trail for generations of women who would follow. Every woman who has taken a political stage, delivered a keynote address, or commanded a lecture hall owes something to the fearless young Quaker who refused to be silenced. Her passionate advocacy for abolition and Reconstruction helped shape a more just America, while her defense of women's intellectual equality challenged a nation to expand its vision of what women could achieve. "See to it . . . that no man take your crown," she said during an 1869 lecture series.[12]

See to it . . . that no man take your crown.

—Anna Dickinson

When Anna Dickinson died in 1932, women had finally won the right to vote—a victory she had championed decades earlier. The shy thirteen-year-old who once wrote an outraged letter to an abolitionist newspaper had grown into America's Joan of Arc, proving that one voice, raised with courage and conviction, could indeed change the world. In that transformation, she left us a powerful reminder that barriers exist to be broken, and that sometimes the most unlikely revolutionaries leave the most lasting mark on history.

15.

Belva Lockwood: *The Lawyer*

Article II of the U.S. Constitution lays out *who* can be president of the United States. You must be a natural-born citizen, be at least thirty-five years old, and have lived in America for fourteen years. Nowhere does it say you can't be a woman—and Belva Lockwood was the first to try to crack that glass ceiling.

Long before Shirley Chisholm and Hillary Clinton, Belva Lockwood ran for president twice—first in 1884 and again in 1888—as the candidate of the National Equal Rights Party.

It was a full-fledged campaign for president with her name on the official presidential ballot. If that wasn't impressive enough, she was also the first woman ever admitted to practice law before the U.S. Supreme Court. Her gutsiness in all things led one newspaper to call Belva "the nerviest woman in the United States,"[1] while Justice Ruth Bader Ginsburg referred to her as "principal among way pavers."[2]

Belva Ann Bennett Lockwood was born in 1830 and raised on a farm in a remote county in upstate New York. She was the second of five children, worked as a teacher, and married young. Her first husband died a few years after their wedding, leaving her widowed at twenty-two with a three-year-old to support on $3 a week.

The moment that crystallized her awareness of systemic gender inequality came with brutal clarity when she discovered that the male teachers in her hometown of Royalton, New York, earned twice her salary—despite doing identical work. This wasn't merely an oversight or individual unfairness; it was a deliberate system that valued men's work at double that of a woman, regardless of competence or need.

Belva Ann Lockwood

Determined to fight the injustice, she protested to the school trustees. But the response she received revealed how deeply those inequalities were embedded in society's consciousness. When Belva asked for equal pay, the wife of the local Methodist minister delivered a response that encapsulated the era's resigned acceptance of gender discrimination: "I cannot help you; you cannot help yourself, for it is the way of the world." This dismissal marked a turning point in Belva's understanding. She never got the raise, but as the *Farmington Times* later noted, "This experience determined her future career."[3] The barriers were not just economic; they were ideological, wrapped in the assumption that women's lesser status was simply "the way of the world."

Her move to Washington, D.C., and remarriage in 1868 at age thirty-eight provided temporary stability, but when her second husband, a Civil War veteran and retired dentist, passed away less than a decade later, she was once again the sole provider for her family.[4] Recognizing the importance of education for women, she later encouraged audiences to support girls' schools so the students could support themselves like she had to.

The cultural barriers became even more apparent when she entered National University Law School (now George Washington University) in her forties. Of the fifteen women who enrolled, only two, including Belva, graduated. But the real revelation came when she and the other female students were barred from attending lectures because of complaints from male students who simply didn't want to go to school with women. This wasn't about academic capability or preparation—it was about the fundamental belief that certain spaces belonged exclusively to men.

When she feared she might not receive her diploma despite completing all the requirements, she appealed directly to President Ulysses S. Grant in 1873, writing with characteristic directness:[5] "SIR, You are, or you are not, President of the National University Law School. If you are its President, I desire to say to you that I have passed through the curriculum of study in this school, and am entitled to, and demand, my diploma. If you are not its President, then I ask that you take your name from its papers, and not hold out to the world to be what you are not. Very respectfully, Belva A. Lockwood."[6]

The fact that she had to lobby the president of the United States to receive a diploma she had rightfully earned illustrates how the barriers extended far beyond individual prejudice into the very institutions meant to uphold fairness and merit.

She never received a reply from President Grant, but days later, her diploma arrived in the mail. That same year, she was admitted to the D.C. bar, becoming only the second woman, after Howard University graduate Charlotte Ray, to achieve this distinction.

Belva opened her own law practice, specializing in pension claims against the government and divorce cases. Over her forty-three-year legal career, she helped resolve thousands of pension cases and even represented people charged with burglary and murder.

In 1876, she applied for admission to argue before the U.S. Supreme Court but was denied. Undeterred, she personally drafted a bill allowing women to practice before the Court—and single-handedly petitioned Congress to pass it. It was an effort that a reporter described as requiring "an unconscionable deal of lobbying."[7]

I never stopped fighting. My cause was the cause of thousands of women.

—Belva Lockwood

This represented a crucial evolution in her thinking: from seeking individual accommodation within an unjust system to challenging the system's very foundations. As she later wrote, "I never stopped fighting. My cause was the cause of thousands of women." At the time, most courts in the country still barred female lawyers.[8]

We shall never have equal rights until we take them, nor respect until we command it.

—Belva Lockwood

Her persistence paid off. On March 3, 1879, at age forty-nine, she became the first woman admitted to the U.S. Supreme Court Bar, sworn in amid "a bating of breath and craning of necks."[9] The following year, she argued *Kaiser v. Stickney*, making history as the first woman to present a case before the nation's highest court.[10] Belva's appearance made front-page news in the *Evening Star*, which detailed her speaking for about twenty minutes.[11]

By the early 1900s, an employee of the Supreme Court's Office of the Clerk started to keep a running record of women admitted to practice there. The first name on the list was Belva Lockwood. It was kept inside an envelope with "In Re Lady Lawyers" written on it. The list grew to include ninety-seven names before being discontinued in 1920.[12] Today there is an exhibit at the U.S. Supreme Court that pays tribute to the rise of female attorneys, and the envelope is a key part of the display.

Practicing law was of course more lucrative than her earlier career as a teacher, which was one of the few professions deemed acceptable for women. She earned between $3,000 and $5,000 a year as a lawyer, equivalent to more than $100,000 today.[13]

Despite Belva's breakthrough, there are still a relatively small number of women who make arguments before the highest court in the land. In the term that ended in June 2022, less than a quarter of arguments were presented by women.[14]

What's fascinating is that Belva was not content with her groundbreaking legal career. She had greater ambitions. At fifty-four, Belva ran for president—nearly four decades before women could vote. She pointed out the irony: She could not cast a ballot, but people could vote for her! But this wasn't just about personal political ambition—it was a fundamental challenge to society's assumptions about women's capabilities and proper roles.

Her platform focused on the rights of working women, who were paid significantly less than men and had limited professional opportunities. "There is no use in attempting to avoid the inevitable," Belva declared. "It is quite time that we had our own party; our own platform, and our own nominees. We shall never have equal rights until we take them, nor respect until we command it."[15]

Running on the National Equal Rights Party ticket, Belva made history alongside her running mate, Marietta L. B. Stow, who was a women's rights activist and newspaper editor. Belva had to write letters to newspapers correcting misinformation about her campaign. The *Buffalo Evening News* noted that jokes and puns about her—including her choice to smoke a pipe—received more coverage "than her ideas for women and the country."[16] In the 1884 election, the ticket won fewer than five thousand votes.

National Equal Rights Party electoral ticket for the presidential election of 1884

Still, she paved the way for future politicians.[17] When she ran for president again in 1888, she told reporters, "Men always say, 'Let's see what you can do.' If we always talk and never work we will not accomplish anything."[18]

Her influence extended to the next generation, as her daughter, Lura, and her niece, Clara Bennett, worked as her legal assistants.

Even her daily choices became acts of quiet rebellion against gender limitations. What raised more eyebrows in Washington than employing her female family members was her decision to ride a tricycle for several miles each day as she traveled to the Capitol and the courts. In that era, riding a bicycle was considered unsuitable for women, but Belva purchased hers after observing that male attorneys who used them were finishing their work more quickly.[19]

Her final Supreme Court case came in 1906, at age seventy-five, when she represented the Cherokee Nation and secured a $5 million settlement—one of the largest payments from the federal government to a Native American tribe at the time. At age eighty-one, she was still practicing law, earning the distinction of the "oldest practicing lawyer in the world."[20]

Belva remained active on the lecture circuit into her eighties. In 1912, she told an audience in Columbus, Ohio, that if women were given the same responsibilities and pay as men, then society would be more productive. Toward the end of her life, a reporter asked her if she thought a woman could ever become president of the United States. She still firmly believed a woman would someday occupy the Oval Office. "It will be entirely on her own merits," she replied. "No movement can place her there simply because she is a woman. It will come if she proves herself mentally fit for the position."[21]

Even before her death, and despite her prodigious and historic career, her legacy was fading. A couple of days after the *New York World* erroneously published her obituary, they printed a letter Belva wrote to the editor in which she stated that she was very much alive and living in Washington, D.C.![22] She corrected them on her age too; they said that she was eighty-five, but she was actually eighty-six years old, *thank you very much.*

She passed away shortly after that in 1917, three years before women could vote. Her legacy is the path she opened for many women in the legal profession and beyond. As Justice Ruth Bader Ginsburg noted, Belva Lockwood's life reminds us that "ideas once taken as fixed can be changed." Her story shows how one person's refusal to accept "the way of the world" can transform what the world believes is possible.

"Resilience, wit, and good humor, Lockwood's work and days reveal, can turn put-downs and slights into opportunities," wrote Justice Ginsburg. "With optimism and tenacity, may we continue to strive as she did to advance in our Nation and World the ideals of liberty, equality, and justice for all."[23]

PART III

BLOOD, SWEAT, AND TEARS: THE GILDED AGE AND THE GREAT DEMAND, 1876–1926

1876–1926

The Gilded Age is known for its robber barons and materialism, but it was also marked by tremendous achievements in engineering and an awakening of social consciousness. It was an opulent time for the fortunate few, and it was a chance for women to prove themselves. At the turn of the twentieth century women made themselves so indispensable that it became acceptable for women to take on new roles as inventors, athletes, and leaders of a movement that eventually won them the right to vote. Our country is still staggering toward full equality; without these women I can only imagine how little progress we would have made.

During this era, the baton was passed from the women who were behind the Seneca Falls Convention to the activist generation who took voting rights over the finish line, seeing the Nineteenth Amendment ratified on August 18, 1920. This period marks the end of the hard-fought journey for the right to vote, which took several generations of women, and men like Frederick Douglass who supported their activism, an astonishing seventy-two years to complete. Women found their voice, and once they had the vote, men no longer had the luxury of not listening to them.

The women in this section were impossible to ignore: They were entrepreneurs, they withstood attacks on the front lines during World War I, and they risked their lives to access the freedom that has always been the great promise of our country. But while we still feel the effects of their work, whether it be the bridges they built or the businesses they started, society's memory of them sadly has been fleeting. Most of us don't know the name of the woman who made train travel more comfortable or that Wilbur and Orville Wright had a sister who made their work possible. My goal here is to bring them back into the light.

One of these changemakers was a woman named Emily Warren Roebling. On May 24, 1883, Emily rode in the first carriage across the Brooklyn Bridge with her teenage son beside her and a rooster on her lap. The squawking animal symbolized victory and good luck. She didn't need luck, though; she had guts.

Building the world's first and longest steel suspension bridge had been an incredible achievement, and it seemed the whole country was celebrating. It would not have happened without Emily. The bridge took fourteen years to complete, an arduous feat that had incapacitated her husband and subsequently made her the bridge's de facto chief engineer. Few knew the personal price that Emily had paid and the rules she had broken to complete work on the bridge. But someone knew enough to ensure that she was one of the first people—male or female—to cross the modern marvel.

Women making it possible for men to do their best work, either by running the household or by actively participating in their careers, is a theme that comes up repeatedly during this era. But managing a home or workplace doesn't fit into our historical perspective of who deserves credit. Leaders, bold thinkers, pioneers, generals, presidents, they are the people we lionize. But what about the people who stand behind them and make great things happen? That is the story of Katharine Wright, the sister of the famous Wright brothers, who have gone down in history for the first successful airplane flight on December 17, 1903. If Katharine, who fundraised for the flights and ran the business that supported them, had been the third Wright brother, we certainly would all be familiar with her today.

There is not enough space here to adequately describe the women of the Gilded Age, a term coined by Mark Twain to describe the decadent years between the Civil War and the turn of the century. The 1870s through the early 1900s was a time when the great divide between the haves and the have-nots in America was put in sharp relief. The rich were getting richer and the poor—the women, children, and new immigrants to the country—were being exploited for very little pay in the manufacturing industry. It was not uncommon for them to work ten-hour shifts, seven days a week.

What followed was the Progressive Era, which continued into the early twentieth century and was marked by widespread social, political, and economic reforms aimed at addressing the excesses and inequalities that developed during the Gilded Age.

> ***The way to right wrongs is to turn the light of truth upon them.***
>
> ***—Ida B. Wells***

Women played a central role in these reforms, advocating for women's suffrage, better schools, labor regulations, improved working conditions, and prohibition. Women of diverse backgrounds joined national organizations and clubs, which became powerful forces for change. The rise of the National American Woman Suffrage Association and the National Association of Colored Women occured as part of this new organizing movement. The Women's Christian Temperance Movement was among the most popular, with 150,000 dues-paying members.[1] Their strength led to the nationwide prohibition of alcohol in 1919.

Women's activism during this period allowed them to break from traditional domestic roles and exert significant influence on public life and policy, in what Jane Addams called "civic housekeeping." For example, Jane established Chicago's Hull House, a settlement house that educated and provided services for immigrants. And Ida B. Wells-Barnett led a campaign against the lynching of Black Americans. "The way to right wrongs is to turn the light of truth upon them," Ida said.[2]

Women were proving that they could be innovators too. They wanted to make the country better by bringing their own ideas to life, and although you've probably never heard of some of them, their work has undoubtedly helped you.

Maria Beasley patented a life raft in 1882 that saved an inestimable number of lives. Her original design featured collapsible metal floats and airtight containers so that it could be stored and taken out in an emergency.[3] Maria had already established herself as an inventor, having filed more than a dozen patents for a different invention—a barrel construction machine—when an 1888 article in the *Newton Enterprise* made note of her success.[4] "Mrs. Marie E. Beasley, of Philadelphia, has made a fortune from the most remarkable invention which the mind of a woman has ever conceived."[5]

Olive Dennis is not a household name, but chances are you've benefited from her innovations. Olive was only the second woman to graduate from Cornell, the first coeducational Ivy League school. (Most Ivy League schools went coed in the 1960s, but Columbia University was shockingly late to open its doors to women, waiting until 1983 to do so.) In 1920, Olive became the first woman ever hired in the engineering department for a major rail line.

She went on to transform what was then the leading form of cross-country travel. "She took the pain out of the train," as a 1997 *Baltimore Sun* article put it.[6]

Her job was to make trains more comfortable; she rode more than forty thousand miles in one year to determine what needed changing.[7] Olive lowered the seats because many people's feet couldn't even touch the floor. She also made it so that seats could partially recline, and she designed them using plush, stain-resistant material.[8] She recommended that lights with dimmers be installed so that people could take naps, and she added free paper towels and drinking cups for women in the dressing rooms. Olive also invented window vents that let in fresh air: the Olive W. Dennis Ventilator.[9] We found her patent from December 13, 1927. In it she wrote, "Another object of my invention is to provide a ventilator for cars which is entirely under the control of the passenger."

"Being a woman practicing a profession in which there are few women is both an advantage and a disadvantage," Olive said in an interview for the February 24, 1921, edition of Baltimore's *Evening Sun.* "It is an advantage in that if your work is good, it will be recognized quickly because of your conspicuousness; it is, however, a distinct disadvantage in obtaining employment. I think one counterbalances the other."[10]

Our daily lives have also been vastly improved by Josephine Garis Cochran, another unsung woman who invented the first practical dishwasher.[11] Josephine wanted to find a solution after plateware was getting chipped from hand-washing. The machine was showcased at the Chicago World's Fair in 1893—catching the attention of hotels and large restaurants. The dishwasher was, and is, a huge time-saver that freed up women, who were usually the ones doing the dishes, to spend their time doing other things.

Another pathfinder is Maggie Lena Walker, who was the first Black woman to be the president of a bank in the United States. She organized and led the St. Luke Penny Savings Bank until her death in 1934. The bank was part of her vision for the Independent Order of St. Luke (IOSL), a society founded in the 1860s by a formerly enslaved woman.[12] The IOSL and St. Luke Bank formed the foundation of a financial powerhouse that, at its height in the 1920s, provided financial services to one hundred thousand members in more than twenty states.

Maggie's message of sisterhood struck me. At the 1906 Negro Young People's Christian and Educational Congress she said, "Faith in God and faith in ourselves can work miracles. Sisters, let us join hands. Let us trust each other, let us believe in each other and half of the battle is won."[13]

We found that there were so many remarkable women during this period that we had trouble deciding which to write about.

Often, when discussing the turn of the century, history books focus on women seeking the right to vote, but the progress of this era was also about women advocating for equality more broadly. The 1890s came to be known as the nadir of African American history. That's in part because of the Supreme Court decision *Plessy v. Ferguson* (1896), which gave constitutional legitimacy to segregation. The great writer and civil rights activist James Baldwin wrote in 1963, "American history is longer, larger, more various, more beautiful, and more terrible than anything anyone has ever said about it."[14] I've learned in working on this book just how much Baldwin's words ring true.

> ***The Negro woman is really the new woman of the times, and in possibilities the most interesting woman in America.***
>
> ***—Fannie Barrier Williams***

The abominable decision that codified "separate but equal" ushered in a new generation of Black suffragists that came to national prominence. Activist Fannie Barrier Williams was among those who refused to let their voices be drowned out. "The old notion that woman was intended by the Almighty to do not those things that men thought the youth to do, is fast passing away," Williams declared in 1904. "The Negro woman is really the new woman of the times, and in possibilities the most interesting woman in America."[15] Black suffragists wanted white women to work on behalf of *all* women.

This was also an age of immigration—and it was a woman who enshrined its meaning to the country. In 1903, Jewish American poet Emma Lazarus's famous sonnet, "The New Colossus," was displayed on a plaque inside the base of the Statue of Liberty. She spoke to the American dream and her poem still inspires Americans, many of whom can trace their family history to arrival at Ellis Island at the turn of the twentieth century.

Emma wrote the poem in 1883 when large numbers of Italian, Russian Jewish, and Greek refugees were coming to the United States. It was a time of hope and opportunity, but it was also marked by discrimination and hardship for these new Americans. Emma was from a wealthy family and worked to ease the difficult transition to life in a new country for exiles from Czarist Russia. The Statue of Liberty was intended to be a symbol of freedom; what Emma accomplished with her poem was to also make it a symbol of salvation.[16]

Not like the brazen giant of Greek fame,
With conquering limbs astride from land to land;
Here at our sea-washed, sunset gates shall stand
A mighty woman with a torch, whose flame
Is the imprisoned lightning, and her name
Mother of Exiles. From her beacon-hand
Glows world-wide welcome; her mild eyes command
The air-bridged harbor that twin cities frame.
"Keep, ancient lands, your storied pomp!" cries she
With silent lips. "Give me your tired, your poor,
Your huddled masses yearning to breathe free,
The wretched refuse of your teeming shore.
Send these, the homeless, tempest-tost to me,
I lift my lamp beside the golden door!"

Emma Lazarus
November 2, 1883[17]

The poem is famous today largely because of the efforts of another woman who made certain it wouldn't be lost to history. Emma died in 1887 and, like so many of the women we've written about, she was largely unknown during her lifetime. Emma's friend Georgina Schuyler, a composer and writer, lobbied for a plaque with the poem to be placed on the pedestal of the Statue of Liberty. Georgina was a descendant of Alexander Hamilton, and she understood the importance of symbolism in the ever-evolving country.[18] Like Abigail Adams and Mercy Otis Warren during the Revolution, Emma and Georgina were not in the "room where it happened," but today we know it was two women who helped make the Statue of Liberty a symbol of America as a land of immigrants.

The defining achievement of women's Progressive Era activism culminated in the passage of the Nineteenth Amendment—the largest enfranchisement in American history, giving twenty-six million women the right to vote, although women of color were often excluded.[19] Before that, many women in the West at the turn of the century could vote—in Wyoming in 1890, Colorado in 1893, Utah and Idaho in 1896.[20] But this wasn't because men realized the error of their ways. Instead, men wanted to entice women to move West and understood how coveted the right to vote was to most women. Men were willing to give women the vote when it was useful to them.

Women were bringing their unique cultural experiences to the fight for representation. Latina women were powerful political activists in the suffrage movement. Before the U.S. occupied and annexed territories on the border with Mexico, including Texas, New Mexico, and California, women living in those territories had more rights under Spanish and Mexican laws than they did under English common law. They could inherit land and own property, and they could even keep their maiden names after they got married. Latinas wanted to get back the freedom they once had when they were considered "persons" under the law. They joined protests, including one held on October 21, 1915, in Santa Fe, New Mexico. Spanish-speaking women made up at least half the female population in New Mexico. (New Mexico voted to ratify the Nineteenth Amendment on February 21, 1920.) Latinas joined women's clubs and organizations and insisted that their voices be heard.

It wasn't until women put their lives on the line, when democracy was at stake and a war raged across the Atlantic Ocean, that society started to acknowledge their worth. Women took on the most important job any full participant in a country can have: They went to war. It's incredible to track how women participated, first in the Revolutionary War, then in the Civil War, and in this era in World War I.

They fought to protect the freedoms promised in America's Declaration of Independence knowing that those promises did not apply to them. The freedom to vote, the freedom to divorce or to own property, these were all slow to evolve, and yet women confronted global conflicts again and again to stand up for America. All the while they were waiting for America to stand up for them.

During World War I, Grace Banker led more than two hundred women working as telephone operators on the front lines, known as "Hello Girls." They helped army officers communicate troop movements in the trenches. They left everything they knew behind in America and risked their lives in war, but when they returned home the government did not recognize them as veterans. Merle Egan Anderson led the charge to finally get the army to recognize their sacrifice. She had a simple motive that struck me. In her eighties, she wrote to another former telephone operator who served alongside her, "I love my country, consequently, I want that country to be worth loving."[21]

Finally, the country they wanted to be worthy of their service passed the Nineteenth Amendment in 1920. The bumpy road to get there was paved by activists, both peaceful and radical—sisters, wives, and mothers.

Sometimes it was paved by women who were not rowdy activists but who used their influence on their sons, brothers, and husbands to have a lasting impact.

> ***I love my country, consequently I want that country to be worth loving.***
>
> ***—Merle Egan Anderson***

Harry Burn was a twenty-four-year-old representative from eastern Tennessee serving in the all-male state legislature. On August 18, 1920, he was called to vote for ratification of the Nineteenth Amendment, which promised that "the right of citizens of the United States to vote shall not be denied or abridged by the United States or by any State on account of sex." Thirty-five states had already ratified it, and Tennessee would get it over the finish line, codifying the amendment as part of the U.S. Constitution. On the day of the vote, according to his great-great-grandson, Burn "had pinned to his jacket lapel a red rose representing his intent to vote against suffrage."[22]

It was a letter from his mother, Phoebe Ensminger Burn, that changed his mind. Known as Miss Febb, she implored her son to vote for suffrage. It worked; the young man listened to his mother. Harry Burn voted for ratification and the Nineteenth Amendment became the law of the land.

Today, one might ask: Where is Miss Febb's statue in the U.S. Capitol for finishing the decades-long fight for a woman's right to vote?

16.

Emily Warren Roebling: *The Builder*

The first person to cross the Brooklyn Bridge—a structure so awe-inspiring it was dubbed the "Eighth Wonder of the World"—was a woman named Emily Warren Roebling. She rode in a carriage with her teenage son beside her and a rooster on her lap, a symbol of good fortune. But what few knew then, and even fewer know now, is that the true symbol of the bridge's success was Emily herself. She was the good luck, the determination, and the brilliance behind its completion. She was the bridge's "silent builder."

In an era defined by engineering marvels, the Brooklyn Bridge stood as the crowning achievement. When it opened in 1883, it was the longest suspension bridge in the world. With the main span at nearly 1,600 feet, it surpassed any previous bridge by 50 percent. And it was the first bridge to use steel for its cable wires, a major innovation at the time.

The bridge took fourteen years to complete and claimed the lives of more than twenty workers, including Emily's father-in-law. Her husband, Washington Augustus Roebling, the project's chief engineer, was left severely incapacitated by illness brought on by the work. In his place, Emily stepped in as the bridge's de facto chief engineer for the last eleven years of the project, guiding it through to completion. Few understood the personal cost she bore, or the societal rules she had to defy, to see the project through.

I remember climbing to the very top of the Brooklyn Bridge in 2018, nearly 280 feet above the water. We were doing a story on the New York Police Department's only female countersniper. Even with my research then, I didn't know that a woman had been instrumental in the building of the iconic New York landmark.

The bridge's history has been written about exhaustively, including by the acclaimed author and historian David McCullough. His bestselling 1972 book, *The Great Bridge,* is more than five hundred pages long, but of its twenty-four chapters, only one of them focuses on Emily. Even in that chapter, there is scant mention of her work. Washington Augustus Roebling has gone down in history as the builder of the famous bridge, and Emily has been a footnote in the story. But it was Emily who rose to the challenge when her husband couldn't.

If ever there was a face that represented the saying "Behind every great man is a great woman," it should be Emily Warren Roebling's.

The saga of the building of the Brooklyn Bridge began when Washington Augustus Roebling's father, John Augustus Roebling, a German American cable manufacturer, was given the job of building the bridge. John had developed a method for weaving wire cables, and he had successfully built other suspension bridges, which were a novelty of nineteenth-century construction.

At the very beginning of the bridge's construction, the unthinkable happened. On June 28, 1869, while John Augustus Roebling was out surveying the construction site, his foot slipped and was crushed between a docking barge and the pilings of a pier. He developed tetanus and passed away less than a month later, on July 22, 1869. Emily was devastated. Her father-in-law had always respected her keen intellect and now her husband, who had been his father's assistant on the enormous project, would have to finish the job his father had started. The pressure to complete what his father had called "the greatest bridge in existence" was immense and difficult for the thirty-two-year-old son.[1]

The work was extremely dangerous. Washington Roebling felt it was necessary to have a doctor onsite. He was right: Over the course of four months, more than 110 men were diagnosed with caisson disease.[2]

Caissons are large airtight wooden chambers that were sunk into the riverbed, making it possible to excavate beneath the East River.

Functioning like underwater elevator shafts, they allowed workers to dig below so the bridge towers could be constructed above. Much like deep-sea divers, workers who ascended too quickly from the caissons risked severe illness, paralysis, or death. This condition, now known as decompression sickness, or "the bends," occurs when dissolved gases in the blood form bubbles in blood vessels during rapid ascent.[3]

Washington Roebling insisted on spending time in the caissons to personally oversee the work and show solidarity with his men—a decision that came with devastating consequences. In 1872, he suffered a severe case of decompression sickness. Bedridden and losing his eyesight, Roebling remained mostly incapacitated for the last eleven years of the bridge's construction. Reports from the time indicate he was partially paralyzed by the illness.

Someone needed to take over.

Enter Emily.

"I don't think that the Brooklyn Bridge would be standing were it not for her," Erica Wagner, a biographer of Washington Roebling, told *The New York Times.* "She was absolutely integral to its construction."[4]

Emily Roebling proved to be not only a skilled project manager but also a master negotiator. She worked closely with politicians, suppliers, and engineers, often devising creative solutions to unexpected challenges.[5]

Although bids for steel and iron had been placed several years earlier, new engineering requirements arose by the time Emily assumed her role as stand-in chief engineer. The existing plans were outdated and incompatible with the bridge's revised specifications.

It fell to Emily to inform mill owners that new patterns and components would be required. When representatives from the mills traveled to New York expecting to meet with Washington Roebling, they were surprised to find Emily in charge. Calmly and confidently, she met with each team, collaborated on the necessary redesigns, and selected the most suitable options for the bridge. What had previously been a source of weeks of frustration was resolved under Emily's leadership—efficiently and decisively.[6]

Painting of Emily Warren Roebling in 1896

In retrospect, Emily's life seemed destined for this moment. Born on September 23, 1843, in Cold Spring, New York, Emily was the second to youngest of twelve children born to Sylvanus Warren, a New York State assemblyman, and his wife, Phebe Lickley. Of the twelve children, only six survived. Her parents were not wealthy, but they were well educated. In 1858, she was sent to the prestigious Georgetown Academy of the Visitation in Washington, D.C., where she studied algebra, French, and astronomy, along with needlework. She was a natural at math, and although she did not have formal training, she later picked up the language of engineering, including physics, along with the complex details of cable construction and stress analysis. She met her husband through her older brother, G. K. Warren, who was a general in the Union Army. Washington was an engineer on her brother's staff. The two met at a military ball when Emily, then twenty, went to visit her brother at his encampment in Virginia during the Civil War in 1864.

Washington Roebling was so smitten that he bought Emily a diamond ring six weeks after their first meeting. They were married in Cold Spring in 1865. They moved to Cincinnati, Ohio, where Washington was helping his father design what was at the time the world's longest steel suspension bridge over the Ohio River. In 1867, the young couple left for Europe, where Washington Roebling studied caissons so that he could help his father in the construction of the Brooklyn Bridge. It was a challenge the father and son could not wait to take on. A pregnant Emily absorbed everything that was happening around her. Roebling called his wife "a woman of infinite tact and wisest counsel."[7] Emily gave birth to their son, John A. Roebling II, in Germany in 1867. He was their only child.

Formal engineering degrees were not common for anyone in the nineteenth century, which opened the door for talented women with family connections to learn the trade through osmosis. In the nineteenth century, but probably also well into the twentieth century, a few hundred women continued to manage their husbands' engineering work after their husbands' deaths, having received enough informal technical training to call themselves engineers.[8] Today only 14 percent of engineers are female.

Emily Roebling was uniquely equipped for any challenge. The daughter of a politician, she not only had a sharp engineering mind but also knew how to influence others and get things done. As she was working to complete the long-delayed Brooklyn Bridge, she was also fending off critics who sought to remove her husband as the project's chief engineer. She was determined not to let the Roebling name be forgotten.

In 1882, when construction was nearly complete, Brooklyn mayor Seth Low and a few engineers on the project attempted to replace Washington, arguing that he had been too absent because of illness. "We want in the position of chief engineer a live, energetic man, and not one who is too sick to give personal supervision to the work," Low said.[9]

Emily stepped in. It is widely believed that she lobbied the controllers of the Trustees of the New York and Brooklyn Bridge to save her husband's job. Mayor Low's resolution to replace Washington failed by a vote of 10 to 7.[10]

Some reporters caught on to her tremendous influence. In fact, on May 23, 1883, the day before the bridge opened and over a decade after the start of her husband's incapacitating illness, *The New York Times* ran a story that called Emily "chief of the engineering staff."[11]

I have more brains, common sense, and know-how generally than any two engineers civil or uncivil that I have ever met, and but for me the Brooklyn Bridge would never have had the name of Roebling in any way connected with it!

—Emily Warren Roebling

Imagine a woman in traditional Victorian dress wearing heavy petticoats and making routine visits to a dangerous all-male construction site. Some people might have worried about driving carriages across the bridge if they knew a woman had played a key role in its construction. The Brooklyn Bridge was the highest structure in New York—only the Trinity Church steeple on Wall Street was taller—and there was already concern about how safe it was.[12] For the most part the press presented Emily as a nurse to her husband who was mostly confined to his sickbed.[13] Some of society at the time was aware of her contributions, including Queen Victoria of the United Kingdom, who invited her to London in 1896 because of her work on the bridge.[14]

Although Emily was content with not being the star of the story, there was a part of her, I think, that wanted history to know. Fifteen years after the bridge was finished, when she was in her fifties, she wrote this to her son: "I have more brains, common sense, and know-how generally than any two engineers civil or uncivil that I have ever met, and but for me the Brooklyn Bridge would never have had the name of Roebling in any way connected with it!"[15] She made sure that her married name, Roebling, would always be etched in history books, even if her first name wasn't.

The accomplishment emboldened her to pursue a career of her own. She had shepherded the completion of the Eighth Wonder of the World, after all. In 1899, when she was fifty-six, she obtained a Women's Law Course certificate from New York University. Women were not required to take the exams to get the degree, but Emily insisted on taking them.[16]

She started using her voice more in public as she got older. In 1899, she won a $50 prize for her essay "A Wife's Disabilities," which was published in the *Albany Law Journal.* In it she made the case for equal property rights. "If man and wife are one being only in the eye of the law," she wrote. "Only one-half [of] that being should die when the breath passes from his body, and the other half should continue in full possession of all the rights and privileges of that original body until life is wholly extinct."[17]

Emily would spend the rest of her life advocating for women's rights until she died of stomach cancer at age fifty-nine on February 28, 1903. Her husband never recovered completely from caisson's disease, but he remarried and lived to be eighty-nine. In 1964, the bridge was designated a National Historic Landmark by the National Park Service.

In 1951, the Brooklyn Engineers' Club erected a plaque on the bridge honoring all three Roeblings. Emily's name is first—exactly where it should be:

THE BUILDERS OF THE BRIDGE
DEDICATED TO THE MEMORY OF
EMILY WARREN ROEBLING
1843–1903
WHOSE FAITH AND COURAGE HELPED HER
STRICKEN HUSBAND

COL. WASHINGTON A. ROEBLING, C.E.
1837–1926
COMPLETE THE CONSTRUCTION OF THIS
BRIDGE
FROM THE PLANS OF HIS FATHER
JOHN A. ROEBLING, C.E.
1806–1869
WHO GAVE HIS LIFE TO THE BRIDGE
"BACK OF EVERY GREAT WORK WE CAN FIND
THE SELF-SACRIFICING DEVOTION OF A
WOMAN"[18]

In 2021, Emily Warren Roebling Plaza was unveiled in Brooklyn Bridge Park.[19]

17.

Katharine Wright: *The Aviator*

We all know the story of the Wright brothers—Wilbur and Orville—pioneers of aviation. But what if I told you they had a sister, Katharine? And what if I told you she was part of the brain trust behind the pioneering American aviators?

Her two older brothers, Wilbur and Orville, are rightly enshrined in history. But without Katharine, they might never have achieved their dream flight. On December 17, 1903, they made the world's first powered, controlled flight of a heavier-than-air machine near Kitty Hawk, North Carolina. While Katharine's exact role in developing the airplane remains unclear because it wasn't recorded at the time (surprise!), contemporary newspapers recognized her importance. As one noted, there might have been "no Kitty Hawk without Kitty Wright."[1] I'm certain that had she been a man, she'd be remembered as the third Wright brother.

Born on August 19, 1874, in Dayton, Ohio, to middle-class parents, Milton and Susan Wright, Katharine was the youngest of five surviving children. Katharine was three years younger than Orville and seven years younger than Wilbur.

When her mother died in 1889, fifteen-year-old Katharine stepped into a caretaker role that would shape the rest of her life. As the only daughter, she held the family together—emotionally and logistically. She managed the household, cared for their father, Milton (a bishop in the United Brethren Church), and supported her brothers' work in countless invisible ways.[2]

She graduated from Oberlin College in 1898, the only Wright sibling to earn a college degree and one of the few women at the time to do so. She taught high school Latin and English in Dayton, becoming the family's only consistent income earner. While teaching, she also helped run the family's bicycle shop—the Wright Cycle Company—which funded the brothers' aviation experiments.[3] Katharine's practical support kept their dream alive.

Katharine also managed her brothers' growing business correspondence and media relations, especially after their first successful flights. In modern terms, she served as their COO, CFO, and head of public relations—all while holding down a full-time teaching job.

Everything changed for her family on September 17, 1908. Orville was severely injured in a plane crash during a demonstration for the U.S. Army at Fort Myer, Virginia. His passenger, Lieutenant Thomas Selfridge, became the first fatality in powered flight. Orville suffered a broken leg, a fractured pelvis, and back injuries that caused him tremendous pain until he died.[4] Katharine quit her job and went to the hospital to help nurse him back to health. An army surgeon said "it is dubious" that Orville would have survived without Katharine's care.[5]

At the same time, Katharine was needed to repair the brothers' relationship with the U.S. Army, which was deeply worried about the crash after just awarding the Wrights $25,000 for the first military contract for an airplane in U.S. history. Katharine helped negotiate a one-year extension, personally reassuring army officers of her brothers' capabilities despite the horrific accident. One lieutenant later referred to her as the "third member of the team."[6]

Today the Air Combat Command says the modern-day U.S. Air Force is a direct result of this contract and other efforts at the time.[7]

A few months later, Wilbur offered Katharine a chance to join the brothers in Europe. He and Orville would match her teaching salary if she helped market the Wright Flyer overseas. She leapt at the opportunity. "After spending a decade drumming Latin grammar and Roman history into the thick heads of Dayton teenagers," her step-grandson Harry Haskell said in his podcast, "she was eager to see the Old World with her own eyes."

Katharine never returned to teaching. In Europe, she became the Wrights' public face—meeting royalty, negotiating contracts, and managing their public image. Her charm and poise captivated European elites. "She was a smash hit," said Haskell. "Crowned heads of Europe and captains of science and industry soon succumbed to her unaffected Midwestern ways."

Her gregariousness was a perfect counterbalance to her famously shy brothers. "They're not the kind of guys you would want to invite to dinner," joked her biographer Richard Maurer. "You could picture them coming over and not saying a word."[8] Katharine was their translator, their advocate, and their star ambassador.

Katharine Wright flies for the first time while seated next to her brother Wilbur, and her brother Orville is standing nearby. Katharine's skirt is tied with a string.

In Europe, she became a celebrity in her own right. On February 15, 1909, near Pau, France, she made her first flight as a passenger with Wilbur. Photos show her in an open cockpit, coat and skirt tied with a string around her legs.[9] She would go on to take two more flights—becoming one of the first women in the world to fly.

While the French press speculated that Katharine might have helped with engineering or calculations, she always denied involvement in the technical side. She insisted there was no truth to that, but her influence was unmistakable.[10]

In recognition of her role, France awarded Katharine the title Officier de l'Instruction Publique—one of the nation's highest honors for contributions to education and culture.[11] Her brothers received the Légion d'Honneur. The Wrights were now global figures.

Katharine Wright stands alongside her brothers.

Katharine caught the eye of U.S. Air Force historian Lois E. Walker, who first noticed her in photographs from Europe. "There she was standing with the crowned heads of Europe, the elite of European society, the only woman at the banquet given by the Royal Aeronautical Society in London, going up in the airplane herself . . . going up in a hot-air balloon, going up in the dirigible, things that few women would have imagined doing," Walker observed. "She was smart. She was very observant. . . . I asked myself, who is this diminutive woman in these big hats and with so much on her shoulders?"[12]

> ***I get all "het up" over living forever in a "man's world," with so much discussion about what kind of women men like and so little concern over what kind of men women like.***
>
> —***Katharine Wright***

Thanks in part to Katharine's diplomacy, the Wright brothers received the Congressional Gold Medal on March 4, 1909.[13] Though she wasn't named in the citation, President William Howard Taft later publicly praised her as "the most important member of the family."[14]

After Wilbur's death from typhoid in 1912, Katharine became an officer of the Wright Company until it was sold in 1915.[15] She also served on the board of trustees at Oberlin (only the second woman elected), championed equal pay for teachers, and became a vocal suffragist.[16] In 1914, she marched in a parade alongside Orville and her father to push for a constitutional amendment for women's suffrage in Ohio.

In a letter, she once wrote: "I get all 'het up' over living forever in a 'man's world,' with so much discussion about what kind of women men like and so little concern over what kind of men women like. . . . [Orville] always used to say that woman suffrage was like Rome, in one respect. All roads led to it, with me."[17]

In 1919, Ohio was among the first states to ratify the Nineteenth Amendment. Katharine had played her part.

Later in life, she rekindled a relationship with Henry Haskell, a fellow Oberlin alum and editor at *The Kansas City Star.* Her letters to him reveal a fiercely independent spirit and an early feminist voice: "I am sick of hearing forever that women must do thus or mustn't do that or the men won't like them. . . . It's a game that I DESPISE."[18]

Katharine's engagement to Henry created a painful rift. Orville, who never married and depended deeply on her, saw it as a betrayal. "In his eyes, Katharine had violated an unspoken pact that she and her brothers would never marry," her step-grandson said. Orville refused to attend the wedding and told her that if she left, his door would be closed to her forever.[19] Katharine left with a single suitcase.[20]

I am sick of hearing forever that women must do thus or mustn't do that or the men won't like them. . . . It's a game that I DESPISE.

—Katharine Wright

The two did not speak again until she lay dying of pneumonia in 1929, just before a long-awaited honeymoon. Orville finally visited her bedside—but it was too late.[21] She died at age fifty-four.

Katharine's final resting place is between her brothers in Dayton, Ohio—but her contribution to history is quite literally buried. The signs directing visitors to their grave makes no mention of her. They simply read *Wright Brothers, 200 feet,* but there would have been no Wright brothers without a Wright sister.

18.

Inez Milholland: *The Suffragist*

On March 3, 1913, Inez Milholland sat astride a large white horse and led the first large-scale protest of suffragists in the United States. Dressed in a billowing white cape with her long dark hair cascading down her back and a golden tiara on her head, she looked like Joan of Arc. She led an estimated five thousand women down Washington, D.C.'s Pennsylvania Avenue. They were marching to demand a constitutional amendment enfranchising women, then known as the Susan B. Anthony Voting Rights Amendment.[1]

A photograph of her at the time helped inspire the celebrated comic book character Wonder Woman, which debuted at the end of 1941.[2] Never mind that Inez, a human rights lawyer, was dressed modestly, while Wonder Woman wore a cleavage-baring strapless bustier. Both wore a golden tiara with a "star of hope," a symbol of female strength and beauty. For Inez, the tiara symbolized her role as "the herald of the future" and embodied the ideals of the New Woman of the twentieth century. Sitting atop a handsome white horse named Grey Dawn, Inez literally portrayed "the suffrage movement's white knight."[3]

Famous suffragist Alice Paul organized the parade with Lucy Burns. Both women chaired the Congressional Committee of the National American Woman Suffrage Association (NAWSA). Alice hand-selected Inez to be the face of the march. She knew that Inez's beauty would attract press headlines. Inez, just twenty-six years old with a

Inez Milholland leads the 1913 Woman Suffrage Procession in Washington, D.C., atop a white horse named Grey Dawn.

dazzling smile, was called the most "beautifulest" suffragist by the *New York Tribune.*

Alice and Lucy also strategically chose the date—just one day before Woodrow Wilson's presidential inauguration—to draw maximum attention to the cause.

The energy and enthusiasm that day were contagious. Of the twenty floats displaying flags and banners, the first one was simply called "The Great Demand." It read: WE DEMAND AN AMENDMENT TO THE CONSTITUTION OF THE UNITED STATES ENFRANCHISING THE WOMEN OF THIS COUNTRY.

The marchers separated into different contingents—some carried banners of countries that had already granted women the right to vote, while others walked in groups representing professions such as librarians, nurses, and teachers.[4] Many joined their alma mater's group.[5] It was a triumphant moment for the suffragist movement. Photos show women smiling, chatting, and proud. It was a historic moment: the first major suffrage parade in Washington. It's also noteworthy that women staged what was the first large-scale organized political demonstration in the nation's capital.[6] Their message was clear: Every woman deserved the right to vote.

But the day took a very dark and unexpected turn. The cheerful banter soon turned into cries for help as a mob of angry men attacked the marchers. The inauguration of the first Democratic president in twenty years had attracted a massive crowd—estimated at over five hundred thousand—and many were hostile to the suffragists. Drunk men jeered, insulted, and assaulted the women.[7] Police did little to protect them. Some women locked arms or defended themselves with hatpins.[8] "We came to see chicks and not hens!" some men shouted.[9]

The crowd streams onto Pennsylvania Avenue, blocking the parade route.

According to *The Washington Post,* one police officer said, "There would have been nothing like this happen if you women would stay at home."[10]

Inez, undeterred, used Grey Dawn to carve a path through the crowd. "You men ought to be ashamed of yourselves," she yelled. "If you have a particle of backbone, you will come out here and help us to continue our parade."[11]

The next day, headlines covered both Wilson's inauguration and the women's march. Public outrage over the violence spurred a Senate investigation. More than 150 witnesses gave testimony over eleven days in hearings that brought national attention to the demand for women's rights and suffrage.[12] Inez declined to testify, but the coverage boosted the suffrage movement dramatically. One marcher testified, "They would have taken better care of a drove of pigs being driven through the streets by some farmer than they did of us."[13] The hearings also led to the resignation of the police chief.

The *Washington Post* headline the next day read: "Woman's Beauty, Grace, and Art Bewilder the Capital—Miles of Fluttering Femininity Present Entrancing Suffrage Appeal." Tangible results followed: On March 17, President Wilson met with Alice Paul. The Senate committee later produced a 745-page report concluding: "It is unfortunate that a quiet, dignified parade, composed mostly of women, could not be held upon the best known avenue in the Nation's capital without interference or insult."[14]

The march is considered a turning point in the fight for women's suffrage and the eventual passage of the Nineteenth Amendment.

Despite its significance, the march inflicted a deep wound for many Black suffragists. They weren't just attacked by the mob, they were ostracized by organizers. The NAACP's newspaper, *The Crisis,* described the experience: "The women's suffrage party had a hard time settling the status of Negroes in the Washington parade. At first Negro callers were received coolly at headquarters. . . . Finally an order went out to segregate them . . . but telegrams and protests poured in and eventually the colored women marched according to their State and occupation without let or hindrance."[15]

The Crisis reported that more than forty Black women marched—some at the very front of their delegations. Mary Church Terrell was there and more than two dozen students from Howard University's Delta Sigma Theta walked in cap and gown. Carrie Williams Clifford, a civil rights activist and poet, marched in the Homemakers section, where women wore white shawls and caps to honor domestic labor.[16]

Ida B. Wells, a prominent civil rights activist and journalist, was invited to march in the parade, as she was a founder of the Alpha Suffrage Club of Chicago. But organizers, afraid of offending Southern white suffragists, asked the Black women to march in the back of the parade. Ida defiantly refused. "I shall not march at all unless it is under the Illinois banner," she told fellow suffragists. "Either I go with you or not at all. I am not taking this stand because I personally wish for recognition, I am doing it for the future benefit of my whole race."[17]

Either I go with you or not at all. I am not taking this stand because I personally wish for recognition, I am doing it for the future benefit of my whole race.

—Ida B. Wells

On the day of the procession, Ida waited for her Illinois delegation and joined the front of the section. The next day, the *Chicago Tribune* published a picture of her leading her state's suffragists. It was a powerful statement against the exclusion of Black women and highlighted the hypocrisy of the movement's claim to inclusivity.[18]

"In spite of the apparent reluctance of the local suffrage committee to encourage the colored women to participate," *The Crisis* concluded, "they are to be congratulated that so many of them had the courage of their convictions and that they made such an admirable showing in the first great national parade."

Unfortunately, the 1913 parade did not lead to a widespread or lasting reconciliation between the main white suffrage organization and Black suffragists. In a recurring dynamic, the mainstream suffrage movement, including the NAWSA, often prioritized gaining support from Southern white politicians and voters, even if it meant excluding Black women.

Inez was already a revolutionary before that day in March.

Born in 1886 in Brooklyn to wealthy, progressive parents, Inez met Emmeline Pankhurst and participated in militant suffragette demonstrations one summer in England. She returned to Vassar College (then Vassar Female College) and held a series of protests, defying college bans to organize suffrage meetings. She first garnered attention by interrupting a New York campaign parade for soon-to-be President William Howard Taft with a megaphone demanding women's voting rights.

Inez was brilliant and wanted to attend an Ivy League graduate school but was rejected from Yale, Harvard, and Columbia because of her gender. Ultimately, she earned her law degree from New York University School of Law in 1912.[19] By that time, she was already prominent in the suffrage movement, a charismatic public figure who drew large crowds advocating for women's rights, labor reform, and prison reform. "I am so prepared to sacrifice every so-called privilege I possess in order to have a few rights."[20]

Her biographer Linda Lumsden describes a woman filled with impostor syndrome: "She was full of doubts about her abilities, but she would plunge ahead anyway. It's something that women still experience today."[21]

I am so prepared to sacrifice every so-called privilege I possess in order to have a few rights.

—Inez Milholland

In 1916, the National Woman's Party sent Inez, their most well-known suffragist, out west to campaign against President Wilson's re-election. At the time, women could vote in twelve Midwestern and Western states, from Illinois to California. Inez urged those women to support Republican nominee Charles Evans Hughes, who favored a suffrage amendment.

As always, Inez was tireless in her battle for equal rights. In twenty-eight days, she made fifty appearances in eight states while battling illness. She wrote to her husband about self-medicating with iron, arsenic, and strychnine.[22]

On October 23, 1916, Inez collapsed during a speech in Los Angeles, just after saying, "Mr. President, how long must women wait for liberty?" She died soon after, just thirty years old. Her death transformed her into a martyr. Women carried banners with her last words as they picketed the White House.[23]

Inez's official cause of death was pernicious anemia, though her biographer believes it may have been leukemia.[24] At the time, women's health was poorly understood, and exhaustion or hysteria was often cited in such deaths.

Mr. President, how long must women wait for liberty?

—Inez Milholland

Suffragists, including Alice Paul, continued her work. Two years after her death, President Wilson finally endorsed women's suffrage in a Senate speech. In 1920, the Nineteenth Amendment was ratified.

Inez Milholland was a singular force in American history—her life, brief but blazing, lit a path that others would follow.

"Her significance nearly a century ago has vanished like a ripple in a pond," Lumsden wrote. But ripples never truly disappear. And if we listen closely, one can still hear the meaning of her words echoing through history: *How long must women wait for liberty?*

19.

Maggie Lena Walker: *The Titan of Finance*

On November 2, 1903, in the heart of the former capital of the Confederacy, a Black woman did the unthinkable: She opened a bank—and not just any bank but one that sparked a movement of Black economic empowerment.

Nearly three hundred people gathered for the occasion, waiting patiently to open accounts in the St. Luke Penny Savings Bank.[1] The atmosphere was electric—music, speeches, and a steady stream of community members, from those with just thirty-one cents to others with over $100. By the end of the day, the bank had collected $8,000 in deposits.[2]

It was a crowning achievement for Maggie Lena Walker, whose vision would cement her legacy as the first Black woman to charter and successfully run a bank in the United States.

Maggie was born in Richmond, Virginia, on July 15, 1864—the daughter of Elizabeth "Lizzie" Draper, a formerly enslaved woman, and Eccles Cuthbert, a white Irish journalist. They never married. She was raised by her mother and stepfather, a butler named William Mitchell, who was robbed and killed when Maggie was just eight years old. She began working as a laundress at a young age to help support the family.

"My childhood became a struggle for something to eat, something to wear and a place to sleep," Maggie wrote in her diary. "I worked all day and way into the night. Work or starve, that was my mandate."[3]

Even so, she excelled in school and graduated from Richmond Colored Normal School in 1883. She became a teacher and soon after married Armstead Walker, a successful brickmason. They lived in Jackson Ward, a growing center of Black life in post–Civil War Richmond.

To fully grasp the significance of Maggie's achievement, we have to envision the South after the Civil War. White leaders erected monuments to Confederate generals and enforced Jim Crow and other means of discrimination against the Black community—which was almost 40 percent of Richmond's population. White-owned banks largely refused to provide financing and fair banking services to Black families. Many banks either did not accept deposits from Black customers or outright denied them loans, often citing racial stereotypes that Black borrowers would not pay them back. Even when Black customers were served, they were frequently charged higher interest rates or were paid less interest on their deposits.

Let us have a bank that will take nickels and turn them into dollars.

—Maggie Lena Walker

In 1902, Virginia revised its state constitution to disenfranchise most of the Black voters through poll taxes and literacy tests, effectively legalizing segregation, oppression, and second-class citizenship.

This hostile climate inspired Maggie to speak out forcefully against Jim Crow—and to act decisively to create institutions that empowered Black communities from within. Everything Maggie built in her life was about creating opportunities: the bank, a department store, a newspaper, and a scholarship fund to send young people to college.

At age fourteen, she joined the Independent Order of St. Luke, a mutual aid society, where she rose through the ranks and ultimately became its Right Worthy Grand Secretary. She would transform the organization from a struggling fraternal society into a thriving financial and civic institution for Black Americans. Black fraternal orders like the Independent Order of St. Luke were important job creators for the Black community. Because of segregation, Black Americans were forced to rely on one another. They founded banks, retail stores, insurance companies, and other Black-owned and operated businesses. They built a community and they created leadership training programs for their members.

Maggie helped the Order open the St. Luke Penny Savings Bank and she was its first president. This was more than a bank; it was a movement whose mission was to uplift the Black community through economic empowerment and self-reliance. In speeches, Walker explained her vision: "Let us put our money together; let us use our money; let us put our money out at usury among ourselves, and reap the benefit ourselves."[4]

Maggie Lena Walker

Maggie encouraged savings among people with modest means—literally starting with pennies. She even gave children penny banks to encourage saving—once they had a hundred pennies, they could open their own accounts. "Let us have a bank that will take nickels and turn them into dollars," she said famously.[5]

She believed that Black communities could thrive by circulating their dollars within their own institutions. That's why the bank's slogan was "Bring it all back home." Moreover, she ensured that much of the bank staff were Black women—and they were paid for every new member they recruited, giving them both economic power and agency.[6, 7]

Maggie Lena Walker set high standards. She was a demanding and disciplined leader. One former secretary recalled, "You had better be at your desk at ten minutes to nine."[8] She ran a tight ship, expecting accuracy and accountability. In one instance, when an audit came up one nickel short, Maggie instructed two employees to stay late—and they didn't leave until they found the missing coin at midnight.[9] She also enforced a formal dress code: White blouses and long dark skirts were required. Yet despite her strictness, Maggie was known for caring deeply about her employees' well-being, encouraging them to save 5 percent of their wages.[10]

Under her leadership, St. Luke Penny Savings Bank flourished. From 1904 to 1910, deposits grew from $21,362 to $85,183.[11] The bank financed hundreds of Black-owned homes and helped Black entrepreneurs start businesses. This wasn't inherited wealth or influence—Maggie was a self-made woman, and her clients were likewise creating wealth on their own initiative. She was likely the first woman in U.S. history to serve as a bank president without family ties to the institution.

She didn't stop there. Maggie also founded the *St. Luke Herald*, a weekly paper that published the organization's goals and took a strong stand against Jim Crow and injustice.

"What we need," she explained when starting the paper, "is an organ, a newspaper to herald and proclaim the work of the Order. No business, no enterprise, which has to deal with the public, can be pushed successfully without a newspaper."[12]

She also opened the St. Luke Emporium, a department store with Black mannequins and Black saleswomen—a bold and radical act in the early 1900s, when most Black women worked as housekeepers or in factories. She helped transform the idea of what was possible for Black women.

In civic life, Maggie served as vice president of the National Association for the Advancement of Colored People and founded Richmond's Council of Colored Women. In 1923, she joined the national board of directors of the NAACP. This belief in equality extended into her personal philosophy as well; she told the young women she mentored that marriage should be an equal partnership.[13]

Despite personal hardship—including the tragic accidental death of her husband and later her own declining health—she never stopped working. After a fall in 1908 and worsening diabetes, she eventually used a wheelchair.[14] She installed an elevator in her home and bought a car that could accommodate her wheelchair. Still, she traveled the country to expand St. Luke's membership and share her message of economic self-determination.

By the early 1920s, the Independent Order of St. Luke had grown to over one hundred thousand members and had become one of the most financially powerful Black institutions in America.[15] Even after the Great Depression, the bank she founded would remain open. It eventually merged with three other Black-owned banks to form the Consolidated Bank and Trust Company, where she served as board chair until her death.

Her efforts at the time were widely recognized. In 1925, Virginia Union University awarded her an honorary degree. In 1934, the City of Richmond named October "Maggie Walker Month."[16] First Lady Eleanor Roosevelt even wrote to her: "I cannot imagine anything more satisfying than a life of the kind of accomplishment that you have had. I congratulate you."[17]

Maggie's faith, community, and early exposure to activism through her church shaped her lifelong mission to uplift others. She entertained great thinkers like W.E.B. Du Bois, Langston Hughes, and Booker T. Washington in her home—but she always stayed focused on helping the people of Richmond, especially Black women, rise.

In 1931, she wrote: "I have indeed been happy in all these years of service; nothing encountered has lastingly impressed me as a hardship, weighed against the achievements of our splendid organization. My heart has sung out, 'Inspiration,' when physical strength has all but failed, but with eyes ever set to the golden horizon and the wonderful 'rainbow of promise' always just ahead, I've kept happy and traveled through the years to the music of the St. Luke drum tap."[18]

After she passed away on December 15, 1934, thousands gathered to mourn her—despite cold weather. Schools closed early. Flags flew at half-mast. The mayor attended. People lined the streets in the rain.[19]

It's incredible to comprehend all that she achieved. Maggie Lena Walker—born into poverty, shaped by struggle—proved to the world the importance of Black economic power. And she left behind institutions that would continue to uplift and empower generations to come. St. Luke Penny Savings Bank would become the oldest continuously operated Black-owned bank in the country by the twenty-first century.

20.

Mary Tape: *The Determined Mother*

Seventy years before the landmark case *Brown v. Board of Education,* there was *Tape v. Hurley,* a case that few Americans know but one that set legal precedent for educational equality. As the Library of Congress puts it, the 1885 case of *Tape v. Hurley* is one of "the most important civil rights decisions that you've likely never heard of."[1] *I know I hadn't!*

The case centers on Mamie Tape, an eight-year-old Chinese American girl born in San Francisco to recent immigrants Mary and Joseph Tape. Mary Tape's birth name has been lost to history, but what is well documented is how she changed our country. When she fought for her daughter's right to attend a better school, she wasn't just fighting for access to a better education—she was challenging the very meaning of equality first outlined in the Declaration of Independence.

Mary was born near Shanghai in 1857 and came to the United States by herself at age eleven. In Mary's homeland of China, girls were not valued as much as boys, and middlemen would sometimes arrange for girls to be sold to American couples in the United States for several hundred dollars. Mary is believed to have been a *mui tsai*—a Cantonese term that translates to *little sister* but in reality indicates a far darker truth.[2] These girls were often sold into servitude and subjected to abuse. What some considered "adoption" at the time is now viewed as human trafficking.[3]

During the Gold Rush, the demand for women in the American West led to the trafficking of thousands of Chinese girls. Between 1852 and 1873, six thousand women were trafficked in San Francisco. According to the 1870 census, prostitutes made up 61 percent of the city's Chinese female population.[4]

Mary ultimately escaped that fate. After her time as a servant in a brothel, she found her way to the Ladies' Relief Society outside Chinatown, either because she was rescued by a Presbyterian minister or because she ran away.[5] She may have felt safe in her new home, but she was the only non-white person there. She learned English and a woman named Mary McGladery took her under her wing and gave her the name we know her by today.

She met another Chinese immigrant named Jeu Dip when he was delivering milk to the relief society. They fell in love and got married in 1875.[6] Dip took the name Joseph Tape, built a successful delivery and import business, and later worked as an interpreter for the Chinese government.[7] They had four children: Mamie, Frank, Emily, and Gertrude.

Despite their assimilation—speaking English, dressing in Western fashion, and taking American names—the Tapes were still seen as outsiders. Discrimination against Chinese people had worsened with the Chinese Exclusion Act of 1882, banning new immigrants and making it nearly impossible for those already in the United States to find legitimate work or integrate into society. Still, the Tapes persisted.

Then came a turning point. In 1884, Mamie was eight years old when she was denied entry to Spring Valley Primary School—the school closest to her home—solely because she was Chinese. School officials claimed that no "provision" existed for Chinese students. Mary Tape was outraged.

She wrote that her family was the "same as other Caucasians, except in features."[8] Having fought her way out of servitude, learned English, and embraced American culture, she wasn't about to let the state tell her daughter she wasn't American enough. She and Joseph took the school principal Jennie Hurley, the superintendent, and the San Francisco Board of Education to court.

On January 9, 1885, the Superior Court of California ruled in

Portrait of the Tape family around 1884 or 1885. From left to right: Joseph, Emily, Mamie, Frank, and Mary

Tape v. Hurley that excluding "children of Chinese parents" from public schools went against state law and the Fourteenth Amendment.[9] "To deny a child, born of Chinese parents in this State, entrance to the public schools," the judge wrote, "would be a violation of the law of the State and the Constitution of the United States."[10]

On paper, it was a victory for Mary and her family, but officials found ways around the ruling. State lawmakers hurriedly introduced an "urgent" provision that created separate schools for children of "Mongolian or Chinese descent."

When Mamie again tried to attend Spring Valley Primary School, she was turned away for so-called technicalities—not having the proper vaccination records, the school was full, and so on. All excuses.[11]

Mary's fury erupted in a letter to the school board that was published in the local paper: "Will you please to tell me! Is it a disgrace to be Born a Chinese? Didn't God make us all!!! . . . It seems no matter how a Chinese may live and dress so long as you know they Chinese. Then they are hated as one. There is not any right or justice for them."[12]

Even though the Tapes did not want their children to attend a segregated school, they had no choice. Mamie and her brother, Frank, became the first students at the new Chinese Primary School in Chinatown. Around this time, some smaller school districts across California integrated, and eventually the Tapes moved to Berkeley, seeking integrated schools and better housing.

The press never gave Mary her due. In one condescending article from 1892, a reporter marveled that the Tapes' home "had nothing to make anyone believe it the home of a Chinese family." He asked why their children spoke English so well, and Mary replied that their kids were born in America and were citizens.[13]

When asked if she and her husband would ever return to China, she said, "We may some day . . . but it will only be as tourists visiting a foreign country. California is our home."

Mary Tape wasn't just fighting for her children—she was fighting for the promise of America. She showed that the battle for civil rights didn't begin in the 1950s; it started in homes like hers, with parents who believed that education, justice, and dignity weren't privileges—they were rights.

Will you please to tell me! Is it a disgrace to be Born a Chinese? Didn't God make us all!!!

—Mary Tape

The *Tape v. Hurley* case marked an early legal challenge to racial exclusion in public education, with the California Supreme Court affirming that children of Chinese descent were entitled to attend public schools under the law. However, instead of integrating schools, authorities responded by creating separate institutions for Chinese American children—foreshadowing the logic that would later define legally sanctioned segregation. Just over a decade later, in the unrelated case of *Plessy v. Ferguson* (1896), the U.S. Supreme Court upheld the constitutionality of racial segregation under the doctrine of "separate but equal." That ruling asserted that segregation did not violate the Fourteenth Amendment's guarantee of equal protection, so long as the separate facilities were considered equal—though in practice, they weren't. The decision provided a sweeping legal justification for systemic segregation across public life in the United States.

Mary Tape died in 1934, nearly fifteen years before California formally outlawed segregation in public schools. The governor who signed that bill may be familiar to you: Earl Warren.

Warren later became Chief Justice of the United States Supreme Court, and despite a mixed record on minority rights in his career, he would go on to lead the Court in one of its most transformative decisions. In *Brown v. Board of Education* (1954), Justice Warren delivered the unanimous opinion that finally struck down legalized segregation in public schools.

He wrote in his opinion, "We conclude that, in the field of public education, the doctrine of 'separate but equal' has no place. Separate educational facilities are inherently unequal."

Though Mary Tape did not live to see this landmark ruling, her fight for her daughter's education laid the crucial groundwork in the struggle for civil rights in America. She stood up against injustice at a time when few dared, and her legacy echoes in every step forward that followed.

21.

Zitkala-Ša: *The Writer*

During the winter of her freshman year at Earlham College, Zitkala-Ša delivered a speech titled "Side by Side," focused on women's rights, during a public speaking contest. Born on an Indian reservation and raised in a matriarchal tribe that valued women's contributions, she always believed her voice mattered. She spoke without hesitation, even though she was the only Indigenous student among her nearly five hundred peers in Richmond, Indiana.[1]

She won the schoolwide competition and advanced to the 1896 Annual Indiana State Oratorical Contest at the English Opera House in Indianapolis. Aware that she would be speaking before a large audience, she spent the night before rewriting her speech to focus on the violence inflicted on her people.[2] As she took the stage, she heard racial slurs being shouted at her, but she still spoke passionately. "The White Man's bullet decimates his tribes and drives him from his home. What if he fought?" she asked.[3]

Young Zitkala-Ša argued that Indigenous peoples have always been American and deserved equal rights. She declared that they come seeking "a new birthright to unite with yours our claim to a common country." Drawing on the ideals laid forth in the Declaration of Independence, she advocated for the inclusion of Indigenous peoples in the promise of equality: "America entered upon her career of freedom and prosperity with the declaration that 'all men are born free and equal.'" She asked, "Can you as consistent Americans deny equal opportunities with yourselves to an American people in their struggle to rise from ignorance and degradation?"[4]

While her speech received applause, it was also met with painful insult. As she finished, students from another school unfurled a banner with a crude drawing of an Indigenous girl and in big black letters the word *Squaw*, a slur against Native American women.

Despite this, Zitkala-Ša won one of the two prizes that night.[5] But the racism she faced stayed with her, fueling her determination as she became one of the most preeminent Native American activists of her generation. Systemic discrimination faced by Indigenous peoples was especially brutal at this time. They were not considered U.S. citizens, and many were subject to policies aimed at assimilation and land dispossession. Zitkala-Ša would spend her life working tirelessly on behalf of her people, and all Native Americans.

Born on the Yankton Indian Reservation in South Dakota on February 22, 1876, Zitkala-Ša was known by several names, including the English translation of her Sioux name, Red Bird, and her given name, Gertrude Simmons.

Zitkala-Ša's generation witnessed the aftermath of post–Civil War conquests of Native nations in the American West, a period marked by the widespread racist belief that the "only good Indian is a dead Indian."[6]

Native American governments were outlawed, and many of her people were placed under legal federal wardship. Their religious traditions and cultural celebrations were criminalized. After the forced selling of Native land to white speculators, most Indigenous Americans were living in extreme poverty.[7] The Lakota and Yankton tribes both belonged to the Sioux Nation in South Dakota, and Zitkala-Ša knew the horrors of the 1890 massacre at Wounded Knee, where hundreds of Lakota Native Americans were killed by U.S. troops.

The cruelty she experienced after delivering her college speech was certainly not her first experience with discrimination. In fact,

Zitkala-Ša once wrote that she had lost her spirit at the hands of white Americans.[8] At just eight years old, against her mother's wishes, she was taken from the Yankton Sioux Reservation in South Dakota and sent to White's Manual Labor Institute in Indiana, a boarding school over nine hundred miles away. Sadly, this was not uncommon in her community. It was part of a misguided effort to "civilize" Indigenous children by forcibly removing them from their families and placing them in government-run, missionary-operated boarding schools. The policy aimed to erase Native American culture and replace it with white European language and traditions.

By 1902, the federal government ran twenty-five off-reservation boarding schools, in addition to hundreds of day schools and reservation-based schools. The belief was that Indigenous boys should be trained as farmers while Indigenous girls were taught how to care for their homes and families so that they could raise a new generation of "Americans." However, as Zitkala-Ša pointed out in her writings, this assumption was ironic considering Indigenous peoples were, in fact, the *first* Americans.

One of the most traumatic experiences Zitkala-Ša faced at boarding school was the forced cutting of her hair, a practice imposed on Indigenous children to strip them of their cultural identity. In an essay published in *The Atlantic Monthly* more than a decade later, Zitkala-Ša recalled her anguish: "I cried aloud, shaking my head all the while until I felt the cold blades of the scissors against my neck, and heard them gnaw off one of my thick braids. Then I lost my spirit. Since the day I was taken from my mother I had suffered extreme indignities. People had stared at me. I had been tossed about in the air like a wooden puppet. And now my long hair was shingled like a coward's! In my anguish I moaned for my mother, but no one came to comfort me. Not a soul reasoned quietly with me, as my own mother used to do; for now, I was only one of many little animals driven by a herder."[9]

That event marked a pivotal moment in Zitkala-Ša's life. She would become an outspoken advocate for her people, fighting for both citizenship and voting rights for Native Americans, as well as women's suffrage.

Despite the adversity she faced, Zitkala-Ša excelled academically. After graduating from boarding school, she attended Earlham College, a Quaker school in Richmond, Indiana. According to her biographer Cathleen Cahill, the college experience was crucial in shaping Zitkala-Ša's political views. The college's "emphasis on spiritual equality meant that women and their ideas were also welcomed. . . . [it would] solidify her ideas about women's capabilities and strengthen her desire for equality, forging a foundation that informed her politics for the rest of her life."[10] It was during her college years that Zitkala-Ša began collecting the Native American stories that would become the hallmark of her literary career.

Zitkala-Ša was a woman of many talents, using her skills to challenge harmful stereotypes and express her cultural pride. She studied violin at the New England Conservatory of Music and in 1900, she performed at the White House for President William McKinley. In 1913, she co-composed *The Sun Dance Opera,* the first American Indian opera. Its namesake was the Sioux ceremony that the federal government had prohibited. Her collaborator only included *his* name on the title page of the opera and left her off the official copyright.[11]

Her most enduring legacy, however, comes from her writings—some of which were published in national magazines such as *The Atlantic Monthly* and *Harper's Monthly.* Zitkala-Ša's essays and speeches reflect her desire to instill the pride of her culture and challenge the racist stereotypes of the time. A columnist for the *Evening Star* wrote in 1906, "Her thought of [her people] was never

> ***We are here like other human beings and there is no reason why we should be afraid to hold up our heads. Let us stand up straight.***
>
> —Zitkala-Ša

Zitkala-Ša pictured in 1898

as of an inferior race, but as of a conquered people to whom the rights accorded by nature . . . were as sacred and should have been as inalienable as those of any race of men."[12]

Her 1921 book, *American Indian Stories,* was an important step in reshaping how white Americans viewed Native peoples. In a testimonial for the book, Helen Keller said the stories ignite "eternal wonder" in the minds of young readers.[13] That became apparent when at a book reading in Savannah, children waited two hours to hear Zitkala-Ša address cultural misunderstandings and read from the book.[14]

One of her most famous quotes, delivered at the Annual Convention of the Society of American Indians, encapsulates her message: "There is so much good in our people—everyone knows that when we give our word, we keep it. . . . We are here like other human beings and there is no reason why we should be afraid to hold up our heads. Let us stand up straight."[15]

In 1902, she married Captain Raymond Talefase Bonnin, a fellow Yankton Sioux.[16] During World War I, she used her husband's military service to highlight the contradiction in denying equal rights to Native Americans. "If the Indian is good enough to fight for America," she said, "he is good enough to be considered an American."[17] She understood how to use patriotism to make her point that the white men in power were betraying the tenets of the Declaration of Independence by denying freedom to Native Americans.

If the Indian is good enough to fight for America, he is good enough to be considered an American.

—Zitkala-Ša

Although much of her work focused on the issues facing her people, she continued her fight for equal rights for women. In 1918, she spoke at the National Woman's Party conference, urging attendees to support an Indian citizenship bill. They didn't, because they said they needed to focus on gender equality first, like the Equal Rights Amendment.

In 1920, when the Nineteenth Amendment was ratified, granting women the right to vote, many Native women were excluded from this right because of their lack of citizenship. Zitkala-Ša remained determined to secure voting rights for Native Americans.[18] For three years, she traveled around America asking white women to use their new voting power to support Native American citizenship.

She gave presentations in Washington, including to the Congressional Club, whose membership consisted of the wives of congressmen, wearing a traditional buckskin dress. She did not hold back. In her speeches she pointed out the irony that the first Americans were being deprived of the rights most other Americans had after the passage of the Nineteenth Amendment.

Her work culminated in the passage of the federal Indian Citizenship Act of 1924, which granted U.S. citizenship to all Native Americans. She also played a role in the Indian Reorganization Act of 1934, which sought to restore control over land and governance to Native tribes.

While the Indian Citizenship Act was passed in 1924, many states tried for decades to deny Indigenous peoples the right to vote. It wasn't until the Voting Rights Act of 1965 that most Native Americans were fully enfranchised. That moment came almost thirty years after Zitkala-Ša died at age sixty-one. But make no mistake, she was a full participant in helping her people realize that what the founding fathers promised in the Declaration of Independence should include them too.

Zitkala-Ša and her husband chose Arlington National Cemetery as their burial site.[19] She was the first Native American woman to be buried in the nation's most hallowed ground, because of her husband's military service. Her tombstone bears the inscription *Gertrude Simmons Bonnin, "Zitkala-Ša" of the Sioux Indians, 1876–1938,* along with a carving of a plains-style tepee.

This burial site embodies the very essence of Zitkala-Ša's life's work: the insistence that one could be both a proud American citizen and a devoted member of the Yankton Sioux Tribe. In death, as in life, she refused to choose between these identities, proving instead that they could not only coexist but strengthen each other.

For decades, her story remained largely untold. But as America approached the centennial of the Nineteenth Amendment in 2020, scholars and institutions finally began excavating her buried legacy. In 2024, the U.S. Mint released a quarter bearing her image alongside three words that barely contain her vast legacy: *Author, Activist, Composer.* But perhaps the most fitting tribute lies not only with her image on that coin, but in the countless Native voices that continue to rise because of her belief in the unalienable rights of all Americans.

22.

The Hello Girls of World War I
The Operators

The fire spread at lightning speed, quickly wiping out the flimsy wooden barracks where the few women stationed near the front lines were staying while working in twenty-four-hour rotating shifts.

Grace Banker knew they were in danger as the flames were getting perilously close to the main telephone switchboards. But the women she led continued to connect calls, ignoring repeated orders to evacuate. They would not abandon the soldiers on the battlefield who relied on them for communications. At the last moment, angry officers threatened the women with court-martial, compelling them to leave their posts.

"At last they came to us & told us to pull out our connections and escape by the back door," Berthe Hunt, an operator, wrote in her diary.[1]

The fire happened on October 30, 1918, in the midst of the American Meuse-Argonne offensive. The battle lasted for the final forty-seven days of the war and remains the largest and bloodiest engagement fought by the American Expeditionary Forces. There on the front lines were these pioneering female telephone operators, specifically assigned because they were considered the best in all of France. Their work was indispensable as they decoded and transmitted messages during the "Hundred Days Offensive," the final Allied effort that pushed German forces out of France and helped bring about the end of World War I.

The firefighters worked for an hour and were able to contain the blaze. Colonel Parker Hitt had ordered that the switchboards be dragged out to a nearby field for safekeeping, and Berthe and the operators rushed back into the wreckage of their headquarters to staff the remaining phone lines.

For her courageous heroism and leadership that day, Grace Banker received the Army Distinguished Service Medal, according to an order that noted her "untiring devotion to her exacting duties under trying conditions."[2] But according to Grace's diary, she believed the distinction should be shared with the other women: "Whatever glory May go with that Medal I have always felt belongs in large measure to the very small, but very loyal and devoted group of First Army Girls—Suzanne Prevot, Berthe Hunt, Adele Hoppock, Esther Fresnel, Helen Hill and Marie Lange."[3]

The switchboard operators, called the Hello Girls, were key to the Allied victory. A lifeline for American soldiers, these brave women helped army officers communicate with the troops in the trenches. They would ultimately become America's first official female soldiers.

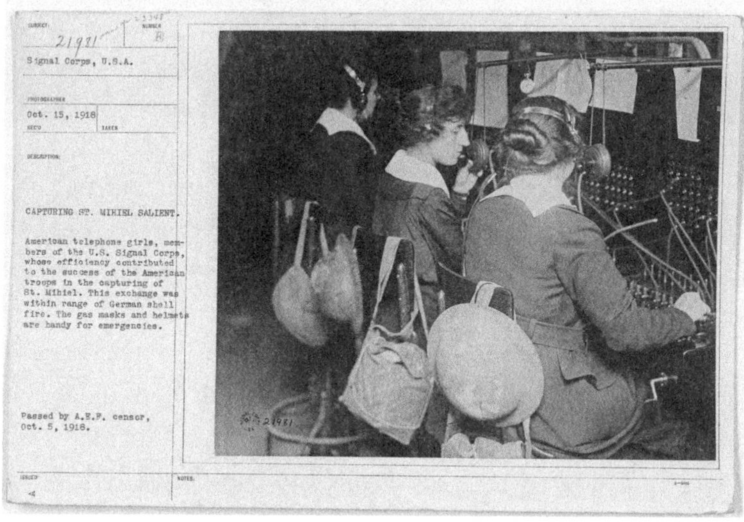
SUBJECT:
21981
NUMBER
Signal Corps, U.S.A.
PHOTOGRAPHER
Oct. 15, 1918
REC'D
TAKEN
DESCRIPTION:
CAPTURING ST. MIHIEL SALIENT.
American telephone girls, members of the U.S. Signal Corps, whose efficiency contributed to the success of the American troops in the capturing of St. Mihiel. This exchange was within range of German shell fire. The gas masks and helmets are handy for emergencies.
Passed by A.E.F. censor, Oct. 5, 1918.
ISSUED
NOTES:

Three members of the U.S. Army Signal Corps work near the front lines with gas masks and helmets on hand for emergencies, October 5, 1918.

Their story begins when General John J. Pershing, commander of the U.S. forces during World War I, arrived in France in 1917 and quickly grew frustrated with the inefficiency of communications. It often took sixty seconds after a call was placed to get someone to pick up the other end of the line. He made the urgent case for female operators, which the army lacked. Women had already proven their skill as switchboard operators back at home. It was one of the few professions dominated by women, who also worked as teachers and nurses.

He succeeded in getting female operators assigned to the front. After the women arrived at the front lines it took only ten seconds to connect. "In wartime," author Elizabeth Cobbs said, "50 seconds is the difference of getting killed or not."[4] The army later acknowledged that the women had better nerves than the men.

For Grace Banker it was a dream job. She had graduated from the all-women Barnard College with a double major in history and French. She was working at AT&T when she saw an advertisement in the paper for military switchboard operators. The next day, she applied.

Over 7,000 American women volunteered to be part of the Signal Corps, but only about 223 were sent overseas. In January 1918, Grace got the good news that she was one of the few hundred who met the strict qualifications, including fluency in both French and English. At age twenty-five, she was surprised to learn that she would become the chief operator, leading the first group of thirty-three women sent to France.[5]

After months of training, Grace and her unit set sail from New York Harbor. "Watched the Statue of Liberty fade from sight. For the first time, I suddenly realized what a responsibility I have on my young shoulders," Grace wrote in her diary. "I've crossed the Rubicon now. There can be no turning back." It was not only a dangerous mission but one that required discretion as the women would know the locations of Allied forces throughout France. Operators were told to destroy their diaries for security reasons. Thankfully for us, Grace ignored this order—or we might not know about her bravery!

When they first arrived in France, Grace and her unit stayed in Chaumont, which was the General Headquarters for the U.S. Army. Initially, they lived in a charming three-story home, but that comfort did not last long. Soon they were moved closer to the front lines, where they had to sleep on cots in a wooden shanty. France was a terrifying place to be in 1918. Air-raid signals rang out in the middle of the night, and after dark every light had to be turned off so that the enemy couldn't find them. The women ate the same rations as men—prunes, bread, and coffee. The operators trained with pistols and carried gas masks and steel trench helmets. "A lot depends on us," Grace wrote, "but I am sure of my girls."

A lot depends on us, but I am sure of my girls.

—Grace Banker

The name "Hello Girls" may sound demeaning today, but it was used to describe the highly skilled, cheerful, and efficient women who answered calls with "Hello" and swiftly connected them. The women, ages nineteen to thirty-five, proved better at the crucial job than their male counterparts. During the war they connected 150,000 calls a day at their busiest.[6]

"It would be impossible to brigade a troop without these girls," said Captain E. J. Wesson, who was a key figure in recruiting and organizing the Hello Girls. "They are going to astound the people over there by the efficiency of their work."

Their work was so vital that the army placed sandbags around the telephone exchange to reinforce its walls in case explosives struck. Like soldiers, they could not tell friends and family where they were stationed. If a line was blown up, they had to think on their feet. They were instructed to tell the caller that the line was "no longer in service" in case enemies were listening in. In all, operators worked at telephone exchanges in seventy-five cities and towns in France, as well as several in England.

The stakes were as high as they could be. The operators were the only link between generals and the front line. There was nothing that made "you feel like you were a real part of the army like knowing that Pershing can't talk to Colonel House, Wilson's adviser, or Lloyd George, unless you make the connection," one operator wrote to her mother in a letter from France.

By the end of World War I, the U.S. Army Signal Corps and the Hello Girls had connected over twenty-six million calls. Because they were so critically important to the war effort, the women were among the last American service personnel to leave Europe at the end of the war. The last telephone operators did not return home until January 1920.

When they were in Chaumont in 1918, General Pershing, the Allied commander, visited them and inspected their headquarters. When they saluted him, he called them "real soldiers." Every man, Pershing later said, wanted to feel looked after by a woman.[7]

Grace and her team helped secure the victory at the Meuse-Argonne offensive, the final major battle before the armistice was signed on November 11, 1918. It was the deadliest campaign in American history, with 26,000 soldiers killed in action.[8]

Two days after the armistice, Colonel Hitt told his superiors that the women outperformed almost every man in the job. "They had a most uncanny way of finding routes to strange places and it seemed impossible for them to give up a call after it had once been filed. . . . [The American Expeditionary Forces] were indebted to these women who gave their labor so cheerfully for its success."[9]

The Hello Girls were celebrated at the front, but when they finally returned home, they were told they were not soldiers. Despite praise from the top military officers, there was no fanfare for them in America.

Much worse, because they were classified as civilians, not soldiers, they were denied military benefits. That meant no government-provided healthcare or the right to be buried in a military cemetery.[10] It would take one Hello Girl from Montana, Merle Egan Anderson, who had served in France, to lead the fight for recognition at home.

Each woman had sworn a loyalty oath to America and wore a uniform, which included a blue hat, a skirt, and black shoes. This was long before pants were common attire for women. Imagine having to wear a skirt while trudging through a battlefield. The skirts had to be cut nine inches above the ground to avoid skimming the mud. The army also required that they wear black sateen bloomers in case a breeze lifted the hems of their skirts!

A woman in uniform was still a rare sight in America. Merle recalled, "As we sailed out of the New York Harbor, a young aviator asked me, 'Why are you in that uniform?' I looked him straight in the eye. 'Same as you. I'm on my way to France to help win the war.' "[11]

Unlike Grace Banker and the other operators, Merle didn't speak French, but she was an experienced phone operator and was needed on the front lines to teach the soldiers how to use a Magneto switchboard. She trained sixty men in three days.

" 'Where's my skirt?' was their standard greeting," Merle recalled. "[After] I reminded them that any soldier could carry a gun, but the safety of a whole division might depend on the switchboard one of them was operating, I had no more trouble."[12]

Merle used that same grit and spent the rest of her life fighting for recognition and veterans' benefits, not just for herself but for the women she served with. It's heartening to read letters from powerful men who supported them. Brigadier General George Squier, chief signal officer of the U.S. Army Signal Corps, wrote a letter to Secretary of War John Weeks making the case that the Hello Girls deserved military benefits: Female operators "rendered conspicuous service during the war under trying conditions and [they were] exposed to the hazards of submarine and aerial warfare and are deserving of recognition of their splendid and unselfish service." But their requests were repeatedly denied. The War Department was already paying benefits for millions of eligible men, and they didn't want to add any more. Between 1927 and 1977, members of Congress introduced several bills to acknowledge female veterans, but none passed the Armed Services Committee.

For the Hello Girls, it felt like they were being forgotten. As Merle got older, she felt a growing sense of urgency. In the 1970s, when she was in her eighties, Merle wrote to Oregon congresswoman Edith Green: "I realize that time is short but I am a stubborn Irish gal (maiden name Egan) who would like to complete this job before I 'check in.'"[13]

Merle was so discouraged by Congress's inaction that she decided to reach out to the National Organization for Women (NOW), which was established in 1966. NOW is the largest organization of women's rights activists in the United States. Merle worked with Patricia Leeper, co-coordinator of a NOW task force on women in the military. Leeper knew that Merle's story would infuriate Americans, so she connected Merle with reporters. She also advised her to reach out to Arizona senator Barry Goldwater, who was an advocate for Women Airforce Service Pilots (WASPs) who served during World War II. The American Civil Liberties Union (ACLU) also got on board, and they used the Hello Girls' military uniforms as evidence in lawsuits that they were indeed soldiers.[14]

Merle was eighty-seven in 1977 when she finally received an invitation to testify before the Senate Committee on Veterans Affairs. She couldn't make it because of her health, but the blue coats, white blouses, and tan gloves sent by surviving Hello Girls to act as evidence told the story. In November 1977, Congress passed a bill recognizing these incredible women for their service. When President Jimmy Carter signed the bill, very few Hello Girls were still alive to receive their veterans' benefits. Grace Banker, their leader, had died of stomach cancer almost two decades earlier.

Thanks to their courageous service and Merle's perseverance, the Hello Girls were designated the first female veterans of the U.S. Army.[15]

It was a recognition more than five decades in the making. The operators had pushed the limits of what women could achieve in the army. They helped win World War I, and they opened the door for female soldiers to serve in World War II. And as we'll learn, these first female soldiers not only helped win the war, they also helped win the right to vote.

In 1978, when Merle finally received her discharge papers from the army, she reportedly held the sheet of paper to her lips and gave it a kiss.[16] It was the moment she had been fighting for, for most of her life.[17] Shortly before she got those papers she said, "If I do get a victory medal it should be for fighting the army all these years."

If I do get a victory medal it should be for fighting the army all these years.

—Merle Egan Anderson

Merle died in 1984, having accomplished what she set out to do.

A grateful nation is finally giving the Hello Girls their due. On December 23, 2024, President Joe Biden signed a bill that would honor them with the Congressional Gold Medal, the highest civilian honor awarded by the U.S. Congress.[18] I wish Merle could have been alive to see it.

23.

The Nineteenth Amendment: *The Vote*

The ratification of the Nineteenth Amendment in 1920 represented the culmination of over seven decades of struggle, sacrifice, and strategic evolution in the fight for women's political equality. What began with a revolutionary proposition at the 1848 Seneca Falls Convention had transformed by the early twentieth century into an unstoppable political force, propelled by the convergence of the Progressive Era reform movements, women's involvement in World War I, and a new generation of militant activists willing to endure imprisonment and violence for the cause.

The amendment's passage emerged from a unique historical moment when traditional arguments against women's suffrage—that women were too delicate for politics, belonged only in the domestic sphere, or lacked the intellect for civic participation—had been systematically dismantled by women's leadership in abolition, temperance, labor organizing, and wartime service.

Throughout U.S. history, women had served in every war (sometimes secretly), defended every ideal, and yet been denied the most basic freedoms—like voting, owning property, or seeking divorce. They risked everything for a country that often failed to return the favor or even grant them the freedoms promised in the Declaration of Independence. Public opinion didn't always support women's suffrage, but it began to shift in the early twentieth century—especially during World War I, when women took on critical roles supporting the war effort.

By 1917, the suffrage movement had largely evolved from polite petitioning into what was arguably political warfare, combining the lobbying of Carrie Chapman Catt's National American Woman Suffrage Association and the confrontational tactics of Alice Paul's National Woman's Party. The true test of their resolve would come in the crucible of militant protest and brutal government retaliation.

After suffragists were attacked during the famous 1913 march led by Inez Milholland, some women ramped up their efforts. In 1917, led by Alice Paul and the National Woman's Party, a dozen suffragists began standing silently outside the White House, holding banners demanding the right to vote.[1] The group grew to about two thousand and they called themselves the Silent Sentinels as they endured in all kinds of weather—freezing rain and sweltering heat.

Women suffragists representing different colleges picket outside the White House in February 1917 for the right to vote.

Their peaceful protest was met with hostility. Between June and November 1917, more than two hundred women were arrested on vague charges like "obstructing sidewalk traffic."[2] Ninety-seven of them were jailed—with sentences ranging from a few days to up to six months.[3] The conditions were appalling: Women were crammed into cold, filthy cells and fed food that was often infested with worms. When they protested by going on hunger strikes, the authorities retaliated by force-feeding them, a brutal and dangerous practice. Alice Paul was sentenced to seven months in jail, and when she began a hunger strike, she was force-fed raw eggs through a tube, which caused her to throw up. Another suffragist, Rose Winslow, wrote: "Miss Paul vomits much. I do too. . . . We think of the coming feeding all day. It is horrible."[4]

A woman who worked as a night guard at the Occoquan Workhouse in Virginia, where the suffragists were held, was fired for being too kind to them. When she left, she went straight to the headquarters of the National Woman's Party and told them what she had seen. She said that she knew of one woman who was "beaten until the blood had to be scrubbed from her clothing and from the floor."[5] When Illinois Senator J. Hamilton Lewis went to visit the suffragists in prison, he was appalled. "In all my years of criminal practice," he said, "I have never seen prisoners so badly treated, either before or after conviction."[6]

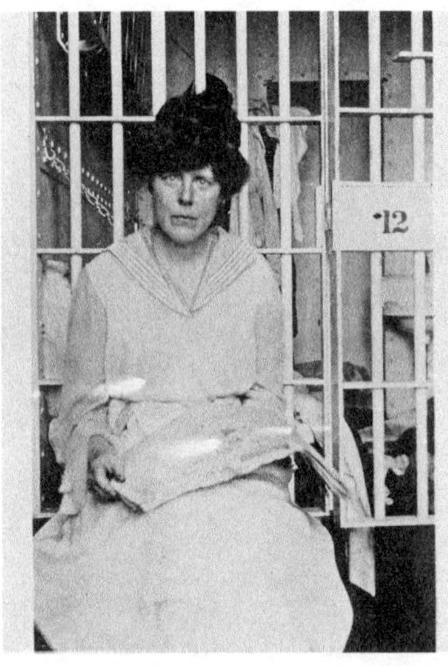

Lucy Burns, among the suffragists jailed for picketing, pictured at the Occoquan Workhouse in Virginia, where women endured brutal force-feeding and other torture

The worst of it came on the night of November 14, 1917—a night the press would later call the Night of Terror. That evening, thirty-three women were beaten, choked, and hurled against walls and iron beds by guards at the Occoquan Workhouse.[7] Dora Lewis was knocked unconscious, and her cellmate, Alice Cosu, suffered a heart attack, believing Lewis had been killed.[8] Lucy Burns was handcuffed with her arms above her head and left standing all night.[9] Dorothy Day, who would later go on to co-found the Catholic Worker Movement, was thrown violently over an iron bench.[10]

When news of the women's treatment reached the public, it sparked national outrage. The brutality they faced behind bars only strengthened public support for their cause. And in March 1918, the D.C. Court of Appeals ruled that their arrests had been unconstitutional.[11]

The women had endured arrests, hunger, and violence to secure the vote—and now the nation was finally paying attention.

Women's involvement in World War I also proved critically important to the cause.

In Congress, it took a woman to harness the shifting tide. Jeannette Rankin, elected in 1916 as a Republican from Montana, became the first woman ever to serve in the U.S. House of Representatives. Despite winning her race—many Western states had already granted women the right to vote—she had to wait nearly a month to be sworn in while Congress debated whether a woman could even hold federal office.[12] Once she took her seat, she wasted no time.

> ***I may be the first woman member of Congress. But I won't be the last.***
>
> ***—Congresswoman Jeannette Rankin***

Representative Rankin vowed to bring change to Washington. "I may be the first woman member of Congress," Congresswoman Rankin said. "But I won't be the last."[13] She knew that the more women who could vote, chances were the more women would be holding office.[14]

On January 10, 1918, Representative Rankin reopened debate on the Nineteenth Amendment, then called the Susan B. Anthony Amendment, which would prohibit states from denying citizens the right to vote based on sex. It had been forty years since the amendment was first introduced. There were only two women on the House floor the day of the vote: Congresswoman Rankin and May Offterdinger, the clerk of the Woman Suffrage Committee.

People for and against the amendment packed the House gallery to catch a glimpse of the debate. Suffragists came prepared with knitting needles and lunches, ready to wait all day. The night before the vote, President Wilson—who had long said suffrage was a state issue—announced his support for the amendment because it was "an act of right and justice."[15]

Representative Rankin gave a powerful speech, honoring Susan B. Anthony, Elizabeth Cady Stanton, and all the women who had fought before her. In wartime, she said, "as never before the Nation needs its women—needs the work of their hands and their hearts and their minds."[16]

Her final lines brought down the House: "Can we afford to allow these men and women to doubt for a single instant the sincerity of our protestations of democracy? How shall we answer their challenge, gentlemen; how shall we explain to them the meaning of democracy if the same Congress that voted for war to make the world safe for democracy refuses to give this small measure of democracy to the women of our country?"[17]

Representative Rankin's presence alone was proof that women were ready to lead. How strange, she argued, that she could serve in Congress, yet most American women still couldn't vote.

As a constitutional amendment, the resolution needed a two-thirds majority to pass the House, and it did, 274 to 136. That's the thinnest of margins. Now it was time for the Senate to follow suit. President Wilson's September 30, 1918, address to Congress marked a significant shift in the political climate surrounding women's suffrage, as his public endorsement lent presidential authority to the movement. In his speech, Wilson argued that women's wartime contributions had earned them the vote, asking, "We have made partners of the women in this war; shall we admit them only to a partnership of suffering and sacrifice and toil and not to a partnership of privilege and right?"[18]

However, the speech's immediate impact proved limited—the Senate defeated the amendment the next day. On October 1, it fell two votes short of the necessary two-thirds majority. Wilson's Democratic

Party would lose their majorities in both chambers weeks later in the midterm elections.

While Wilson's backing did not secure an instant legislative victory, it contributed to the mounting pressure.

It would take another Congress—and another year—before the Nineteenth Amendment finally passed in 1919.[19]

The road to ratification was even harder. Constitutional amendments require approval from three-fourths of the states. That road had been paved for decades by women of every kind—radicals and reformers, sisters and mothers, public speakers and quiet influencers who urged their sons and husbands to vote yes. The movement had formally begun at the Seneca Falls Convention in 1848, and now, more than seventy years later, it came down to one final vote.

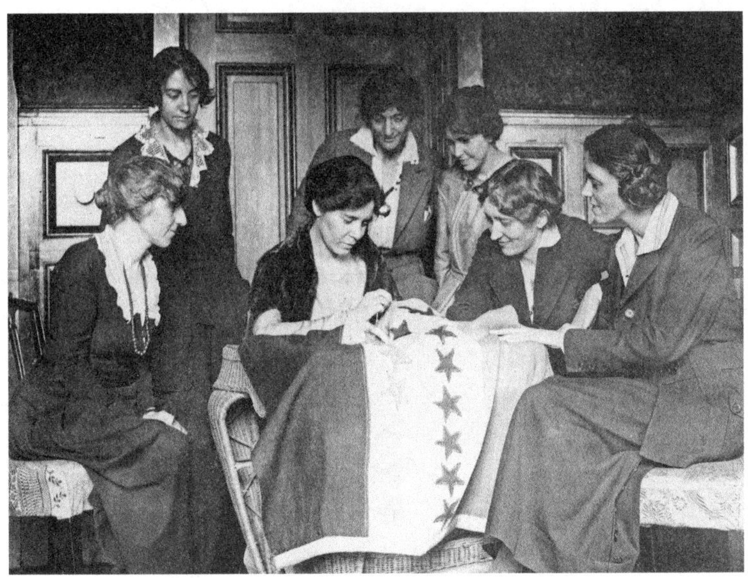

Alice Paul sews a star onto the National Woman's Party's Ratification Flag to represent another state ratifying the Nineteenth Amendment.

Thirty-five states had ratified the amendment. One more was needed. The last vote would come from Tennessee on August 18, 1920.

Harry Burn, a twenty-four-year-old state representative, arrived

Phoebe Ensminger Burn sent a seven-page letter to her son, Harry Burn, urging him to change his vote to support women's suffrage. His vote broke the tie in the Tennessee legislature, the final state needed to add the Nineteenth Amendment to the U.S. Constitution.

that day wearing a red rose—a symbol of his plan to vote no.[20] But in his pocket, he carried a letter from his mother, Phoebe Ensminger Burn, written in pencil after she ran out of ink.

It was three passages in the seven-page letter that convinced the Tennessee legislature's youngest member to vote aye:

"Hurrah, and vote for suffrage and don't keep them in doubt. . . . I've been watching to see how you stood but have not noticed anything yet." She told him to make suffragist leader Carrie Chapman Catt proud. In a way only a mother could, with a mix of humor, straight talk, and a subtle threat, she ended the note with this missive: "Be a good boy and help Mrs. 'Thomas Catt' with her rats. Is she the one that put 'rat' in ratification? Ha!"[21]

Harry Burn changed his vote. And with that, the Nineteenth Amendment was ratified. *It came down to a young man who was just listening to his mother.*

The Nineteenth Amendment was officially adopted on August 26,

1920. For Americans, it would mark the single greatest act of mass enfranchisement in history.

But real equality took time. Twenty-six million women finally had the right to vote after the Nineteenth Amendment was passed. But the new law of the land had limits. It made discrimination on the basis of sex against the law, but it did not address persistent discrimination faced by women of color, including Black, Asian, and Latina women who were kept out of the ballot box for decades after its passage.

> ***Hurrah, and vote for suffrage and don't keep them in doubt.***
>
> —*PHOEBE ENSMINGER BURN*

Women who came of age before the Nineteenth Amendment were less likely to vote than their daughters. It took until 1964 for women to outvote men for the first time—39.2 million women to 37.5 million men—and they've continued to outvote men ever since.[22]

Today, women don't just cast ballots—they decide elections. *That's what I call real power.*

24.

Agnes Meyer Driscoll: *The Codebreaker*

You've no doubt seen—or heard of—*Hidden Figures,* the inspiring film about three female African American mathematicians who worked at NASA in the 1960s during the space race. Katherine Johnson, Mary Jackson, and Dorothy Vaughan were "human computers" who performed complex mathematical calculations by hand, with life-or-death consequences, while breaking barriers of race and gender. I was moved by their perseverance and brilliance.

Katherine Johnson would later receive the Presidential Medal of Freedom from President Barack Obama for her trailblazing career that included calculating the flight path for America's first mission in space. In his remarks, the president noted that Johnson was asked to double-check the computers' math on John Glenn's orbit around the Earth. Turns out Katherine's computations were better than IBM's!

Her story led us to the discovery of another mathematician, Agnes Meyer Driscoll, whom I had never heard of, even though Agnes is known as the First Lady of Naval Cryptology. She too challenged that pernicious stereotype that girls can't do math.

Agnes was a pioneering American cryptanalyst who cracked multiple Japanese naval code systems, trained nearly all the male cryptanalysts in the military, and saved countless lives.[1]

"It is no exaggeration to say that she was a key, unsung reason why the U.S. won the Battle of Midway—one of the most famous sea battles of all time—and eventually, the Pacific War," wrote Liza Mundy, whose groundbreaking book *Code Girls* helped unearth Agnes's story plus those of many other female codebreakers.

"When I first came in contact with Mrs. Driscoll in 1925 in Washington, she was exceptionally capable, very capable," Lieutenant (later Captain) Joseph Rochefort said of Agnes. "I considered her sort of a teacher to me."[2] Years later, Rochefort helped crack a Japanese code that led U.S. forces to win the Battle of Midway in 1942.

It is no exaggeration to say that she was a key, unsung reason why the U.S. won the Battle of Midway.

—Liza Mundy

Captain Rochefort was just one of many prominent digital security experts who called Agnes their mentor, nicknamed "Madame X." She was a cryptologic prodigy whose career spanned World War I, World War II, and the beginning of the Cold War. Her genius at cracking codes was defined by tenacity and the ability to overcome challenges. Agnes Meyer Driscoll's life was nothing short of extraordinary.

Born in 1889 in Illinois, Agnes displayed her brilliance from an early age. As the third of eight children, she grew up in a strict family with an emphasis on education, studying mathematics, music, and physics. She was said to be proficient in five languages: German, French, Latin, Japanese, and English.[3]

After graduating from Ohio State University in 1911, Agnes initially worked as a teacher and chaired the math department at a high school in Amarillo, Texas. I grew up in San Antonio, Texas, and remember a truly humongous Texas history book we were required to read. I learned a lot about the Alamo but nothing about one of the greatest codebreakers of all time.

In 1917, following America's entry into World War I, the U.S. Navy allowed women to enlist, marking a major milestone for women in the military. (The Hello Girls represent the army's parallel effort to recruit women, although the female telephone operators were treated as contractors and not service members, like the women in the navy.)

One month before her twenty-ninth birthday, Agnes joined the Naval Reserve to become part of the historic group of women to first serve officially. More than eleven thousand women from all over the country volunteered, and they took over most of the clerical work to free up men for combat.[4] They were nicknamed "Yeomanettes," although their designation was actually Yeoman (F).

It was clear from the start that Agnes was not just another clerk. Her genius and natural talent in problem-solving led to a swift rise. In 1919, she was promoted to chief yeoman, which was the highest rank a woman could attain during World War I. She worked for the Director for Naval Communication in the Code and Signal Section in Washington, D.C. Because of a lack of opportunities for women, Agnes left the navy for a short period of time. But the service realized her value and, a few years later, recruited her back. She would become "one of the first Naval instructors in the field of cryptography."[5]

For years her official title was clerk/stenographer, but in 1929 she was finally promoted to cryptanalyst, according to her civilian personnel record.[6] By 1931, Agnes Meyer Driscoll was a highly skilled member of the U.S. Navy's small but crucial cryptanalysis team. At a time when codebreaking was a difficult, meticulous job done by hand, Agnes was one of the few who could decipher complex enemy communications using a pencil, graph paper, and her sharp mind. She often said, "Any man-made code could be broken by a woman."[7]

> ***Any man-made code could be broken by a woman.***
>
> —***Agnes Meyer Driscoll***

One of her most important contributions occurred during a routine workday. She noticed that her colleague was struggling to decipher a Japanese coded message in 1931. As Agnes looked over the shoulder of the officer in charge of the research desk, Captain Thomas Dyer, she immediately realized something was wrong. "This isn't the same code," she said, before taking the paper from his hands. "*This is a new code.*" In that moment, Agnes's quick thinking and expertise were crucial in preventing a potentially devastating setback. Dyer called her "absolutely brilliant."[8]

For the next three years, she led her colleagues on a mission to crack the new Japanese code, later known as the Blue Book code. Her perseverance, insight, and leadership allowed the team to break the new system, providing the United States with valuable intelligence about Japanese plans before World War II.

Using the Blue Book, she analyzed decrypted messages and discovered that the new Japanese battle cruiser *Nagato* had a top speed of twenty-six knots. That intelligence led commanders to redesign the new U.S. *North Carolina*–class battleships, increasing their speed and ultimately ensuring U.S. naval superiority. The discovery was important enough to justify the peacetime operating budget for the OP-20-G, the department where cryptanalysis was performed.[9]

In 1937, when Agnes was forty-eight years old, she was gravely injured in a car accident. She sustained severe facial injuries as well as a broken arm and leg. It took her almost a year to recover and she would walk with a cane for the rest of her life.[10]

But her work was her life, and she spent the next three decades trying to crack the most important codes. Leading up to America's entry into World War II, she was once again at the forefront of breaking Japan's complex naval codes.

Agnes was taking a Sunday drive with her family when she heard about the attack on Pearl Harbor on December 7, 1941. She was not entirely surprised that it happened; she had been following the Japanese military for a decade, and the country was a growing threat.

After she heard the news about the devastating attack, she drove by the Japanese embassy to see if embassy staff were burning codes, but she couldn't see anything. That was because the Japanese had already destroyed all but one copy of their codes.[11]

A year earlier, Agnes had been reassigned to focus on Germany, working on the Anglo-American Enigma project. The goal was to decrypt German naval communications critical for countering U-boat attacks on Allied convoys in the Atlantic. Here she was, an experienced American codebreaker who had been at the forefront decrypting Japanese messages since 1924 and cracking their codes since 1930. And yet she was reassigned from that job shortly before Pearl Harbor.[12] (There's no evidence that if Agnes hadn't been moved, the attack would have been prevented.)

Now serving a country at war, Agnes worked furiously to crack both German and Japanese codes. Her time was spent not only trying to break the hardest puzzles in the world; she was also teaching others how to do it too. Agnes "trained most of the Navy cryptanalysts who would become shining lights in, and after, World War II."[13]

At the end of her career, she shifted to the Cold War. She was transferred from naval intelligence to the Armed Forces Security Agency, later known as the National Security Agency (NSA), where she would remain until her retirement. During the 1950s, Agnes worked on decrypting Soviet intelligence as part of the Venona project, which exposed Soviet espionage in the United States.

In 1959, just before her retirement at age seventy, Agnes received her final assignment: to decode a set of "unreadable" messages that others in her section had found impossible to solve. Two weeks later, she figured it out. Of course she did!

"She was a kindly and brilliant-minded person, and while I was ignorant of her impressive background, she always treated me with respect and friendliness," said a co-worker at Fort Meade in Washington. "She performed research work, which some said would take only a fraction of the time if she would use and rely on machine support. But it was her apparent belief that there was no substitute for hard copy traffic, and she was supplied with endless boxes full of it to use for her analysis. She could often be seen with her huge magnifying glass, mounted on a special fixture, to scan each piece of traffic."[14]

Agnes Meyer Driscoll (far right) stands with Lieutenant General John A. Samford, U.S. Air Force, and her assistant, Helen Talley.

As a woman in a male-dominated world, Agnes faced what many women in leadership still face—unfair criticism and a lack of credit for her work. Some of her colleagues felt she was demanding, something that would likely have been rewarded if she were a man.

"I had been warned not to patronize 'Madame X,' as her colleagues sometimes referred to her, because she was sensitive to her role as a woman in a man's world," Rear Admiral Edwin Layton, who worked closely with Driscoll in navy intelligence, said. "While she could be warm and friendly, she usually affected an air of intense detachment," he added.

"It was surprising to hear Miss Aggie curse, which she frequently did—as fluently as any sailor whom I have ever heard," recalled Admiral Layton.[15]

Her biographer Kevin Wade Johnson called her "a giant" who

"lifted Navy cryptology up as high as anyone and rose high in the esteem of those she worked most closely with."

It was not until many years later, in 2000, that she would be inducted into the NSA's Cryptologic Hall of Fame, a small acknowledgment for a woman who for decades was known as the navy's best cryptologist. She is buried in Arlington National Cemetery.[16]

25.

Margaret Sanger and Katharine McCormick: *The Birth Control Pioneers*

To understand the urgency behind Margaret Sanger's and Katharine McCormick's work, we must first grasp the brutal reality facing women in the early twentieth century. In 1900, pregnancy and childbirth were among the leading causes of death for women of reproductive age. Healthcare for women was largely informal, prenatal visits were not standard, and most births took place at home assisted by midwives or family members. Simply put, being pregnant was extremely dangerous. There were about 850 maternal deaths per 100,000 births, a risk that has declined roughly 99 percent in the last century.[1] That is likely because family planning one hundred years ago was considered immoral and illegal *and* there have been advances in medicine.

The federal Comstock Act of 1873, along with similar laws in at least thirty states, made it a crime to distribute or even discuss birth control.[2] These laws reflected a society in which contraception was equated with "obscenity," and women's reproductive rights were virtually nonexistent. Without reliable birth control solutions, women faced repeated unplanned pregnancies, many miscarriages, and the very real prospect of infant deaths. At the beginning of the twentieth century, some U.S. cities saw 30 percent of babies die before their first birthday.[3] Margaret Sanger's own mother, who carried eighteen pregnancies, wasn't unusual—the number was not atypical for families of her era.

The abortion crisis was equally devastating. With contraception illegal and largely unavailable, desperate women turned to dangerous alternatives to manage the number of children they had. In 1930, abortion was listed as the official cause of death for almost 2,700 women—that's nearly a fifth of maternal deaths recorded that year. That meant that approximately one woman died every three hours from a botched illegal abortion.[4]

These statistics help explain why, in 1916, when Margaret Sanger, a nurse by trade, opened the first birth control clinic in the United States, in the Brownsville neighborhood of Brooklyn, New York, nearly 150 women lined up to receive care on the first day. They were fighting for their futures against a system that offered them no choice in reproduction.

People with baby carriages wait outside the Brownsville Clinic in Brooklyn, the first American birth control clinic.

Located in a working-class immigrant area, the clinic advertised discreetly in English, Hebrew, Russian, and Italian.[5] Although it distributed no physical contraceptives, the clinic offered verbal information about birth control methods, such as condoms, diaphragms, and sexual practices.[6]

The clinic proved extremely popular and desperately needed. But, just nine days after opening, the New York Police Department raided the clinic and arrested the staff. Margaret was convicted under the Comstock Act, which made it illegal to distribute materials deemed obscene—including contraceptive information.[7] She served thirty days in the Queens County Penitentiary. Her sister, Ethel Byrne, also a nurse, was sentenced to thirty days in the Blackwell's Island Workhouse on January 22, 1917, for distributing birth control information.

While serving her sentence, Ethel went on a hunger strike without food or water that lasted 185 hours.[8] Sanger feared her sister might die, and prison authorities responded by force-feeding her through a tube. According to historian Jill Lepore in *The Secret History of Wonder Woman,* Ethel became the first female prisoner in the United States to be subjected to force-feeding. Ethel declared that she was prepared to starve herself to death in support of the cause. Sanger supported her sister's decision, saying, "I didn't advise her to undertake this hunger strike, but I certainly would not tell her to end it now." Although the sisters later had a falling out, Byrne's ordeal attracted national attention and was one of the first of the "Sanger cases" to reach trial. Several women testified at the trial, sharing harrowing stories of dangerous abortions, maternal deaths, and the crushing burden of raising more children than they could afford.[9]

There was significant press coverage, with *New York Times* headlines like "Mrs. Sanger Defies Courts Before 3,000" and "Birth Control Crusader, Her Imprisonment Ended."[10]

Margaret appealed her conviction in what became a famous case. Though the New York Court of Appeals upheld the verdict, the ruling created an important legal loophole: Doctors were now permitted to prescribe contraceptives for the prevention or treatment of disease. This set the stage for future clinics and established a legal basis for privacy rights that would eventually inform landmark U.S. Supreme Court cases like *Griswold v. Connecticut* (1965)—which legalized contraception without a prescription for married couples nationwide. The right to contraception for unmarried couples would not be extended until the case of *Eisenstadt v. Baird* (1972).

Margaret's activism stemmed from her personal experience of watching her mother, an Irish immigrant, endure eighteen pregnancies—resulting in eleven children and seven miscarriages. Margaret believed that the strain of so many pregnancies led to her mother's death at just fifty years old. The official cause was tuberculosis, but Margaret nevertheless confronted her father at her mother's coffin and said, "You caused this. Mother is dead from having too many children."[11] *Can you imagine?*

Her family tragedy led her to work as a nurse on New York's Lower East Side, where she witnessed women suffering and dying from complications of childbirth or botched abortions. "I could bear it no longer," Margaret said, recalling a woman who died after begging for help to prevent another pregnancy. "I went to bed, knowing that no matter what it might cost, I was finished with palliatives and superficial cures; I was resolved to seek out the root of evil, to do something to change the destiny of mothers whose miseries were vast as the sky."[12]

Her grandson, Alex Sanger, later explained, "Woman after woman literally died in my grandmother's arms and she said enough, there's got to be something better we can do."[13]

In 1914, Margaret started a monthly newsletter called *The Woman Rebel,* in which she wrote, "Enforced motherhood is the most complete denial of a woman's right to life and liberty."[14] Her publication helped popularize the term *birth control,* and her attempts to mail copies of the newsletter got her arrested; that was the first time she would be jailed for violating the Comstock Act, three years before the clinic opened. In all, Margaret would be jailed eight times in her lifetime for her advocacy.[15] While she was awaiting trial, she wrote a sixteen-page pamphlet called "Family Limitation" that discussed marriage and sex and even chided husbands who fell asleep without bringing their wives to climax.[16] The pamphlet turned out to be wildly popular: More than one hundred thousand copies were printed in its first edition.[17]

Sanger was making a radical argument for her time: that control over reproduction was a fundamental human right, on par with the life, liberty, and pursuit of happiness promised in the Declaration of Independence. At a time when women couldn't vote, and sex was often framed solely in terms of reproduction, her advocacy challenged deeply entrenched norms.

President Theodore Roosevelt, in a 1905 address, condemned shrinking family sizes as a threat to national survival. He labeled women who avoided motherhood as "criminal against the race."[18] Margaret's response was that too many pregnancies endangered women's lives, strained families, and harmed children. She believed that family planning would strengthen marriages, improve public health, and liberate women.

> ***I was resolved to seek out the root of evil, to do something to change the destiny of mothers whose miseries were vast as the sky.***
>
> ***—Margaret Sanger***

In 1921, Margaret founded the American Birth Control League, which became Planned Parenthood in 1942.[19] She created a network of birth control clinics across the country that served hundreds of thousands of patients. During her lifetime she discouraged abortion, and the clinics never offered abortion services.[20] Margaret's ambition was to give women the option, for the first time, to make their own choices and have independence over their bodies.

The second major achievement of Margaret's life, and perhaps the most revolutionary, came decades later. For this accomplishment, she partnered with Katharine McCormick, a suffragist and biologist. Working together, they developed the birth control pill.

Katharine was one of the first women to graduate from the Massachusetts Institute of Technology (MIT), with a degree in biology. She married Stanley McCormick, heir to the International Harvester fortune. Not long after their wedding, Stanley was diagnosed with schizophrenia. Concerned about hereditary illness, Katharine chose not to have children—a decision that strengthened her belief that women must have the right to control their own bodies.

Margaret had been dreaming of a "magic pill" since 1912.[21] "No woman can call herself free until she can choose consciously whether she will or will not be a mother," she wrote.[22] Katharine McCormick and Margaret Sanger met in 1917, during the suffrage movement, but it would take decades before Katharine could support Margaret's dream for such a pill.[23] After her husband's death in 1947, Katharine inherited roughly $15 million (about $211 million today) and soon began directing her fortune toward women's health and birth control research.

With Margaret's encouragement, Katharine funded the work of Dr. Gregory Pincus, a scientist researching hormonal contraception. Katharine didn't just write checks—she moved from Santa Barbara, California, to Massachusetts to oversee the research personally. She pushed the scientists to accelerate their work and was a commanding presence. Dr. Pincus's wife recalled, "She carried herself like a ramrod. Little old woman she was not. She was a grenadier."[24]

By 1960, the pill was approved by the U.S. Food and Drug Administration (FDA)—forty-three years after Margaret's first clinic opened. Margaret gave Katharine a lot of the credit, writing to her, "You came along with your fine interest and enthusiasm and with your faith . . . and things began to happen."[25] Both women lived to see the culmination of their life's work. According to one story, after the pill became available, Katharine, in her eighties, walked into a pharmacy with a prescription just to see what it felt like to buy it. She didn't need it—she just wanted to experience the moment.[26]

Thanks to their perseverance and Katharine's financial support, about 80 percent of American women today aged fifteen to forty-nine have used a birth control pill at some point in their lives.[27] The medication empowered generations of women to control their futures.

When Katharine died on December 28, 1967, at age ninety-two, her death didn't even receive an obituary in a major newspaper. Despite having almost single-handedly funded the research that made the pill possible, she remained in Margaret's shadow.[28]

Margaret Sanger remains a towering and controversial figure. In addition to her work for reproductive rights, she was involved in the eugenics movement, a deplorable practice of "improving" the population's genetic quality. Proponents of eugenics sought to control the genetic quality of the population through sterilizing people deemed undesirable. That included women of color and those categorized as deficient in some way. It was deeply dehumanizing and cruel. In a 1921 article, "The Eugenic Value of Birth Control Propaganda," Margaret wrote that "the most urgent problem today is how to limit and discourage the over fertility of the mentally and physically defective."[29]

> ***No woman can call herself free until she can choose consciously whether she will or will not be a mother.***
>
> ***—Margaret Sanger***

In 2021, Planned Parenthood put out a statement acknowledging this disturbing link between their founder and eugenics. "Margaret Sanger was so intent on her mission to advocate for birth control that she chose to align herself with ideologies and organizations that were ableist and white supremacist."

This aspect of Sanger's legacy is shameful, yet her impact on women's autonomy is undeniable.

Together, these two women challenged the laws, the science, and the norms of their time. Their work laid the foundation for modern reproductive rights and changed the course of women's history forever.

PART IV

WARRIORS, REBELS, AND VISIONARIES: WOMEN AT WAR AT HOME AND ABROAD, 1926–1976

1926–1976

The fifty years between 1926 and 1976 marked one of the most transformative periods in American history. From the economic collapse of the Great Depression to the global turmoil of World War II, from the Civil Rights Movement to the Vietnam War and the passage of Title IX, the nation was in constant flux. Amid this upheaval, women advanced into new roles, claimed new rights, and helped redefine the meaning of American democracy.

During the Great Depression, while mass unemployment devastated traditional male-dominated industries like manufacturing and steel, women often became the glue holding families together. In many households, they were the only breadwinners. Ironically, because women worked largely in lower-paid service jobs—clerical work, teaching, nursing, and domestic labor—their employment rates actually rose during the Great Depression. One estimate suggests that women's employment increased by more than 20 percent during the 1930s.[1] Yet even with this new economic power, women continued to face wage disparities, job discrimination, and restrictive social expectations.

Still, there were leaders—both men and women—uniquely equipped to guide the nation through these challenges. Franklin Delano Roosevelt, elected to an unprecedented four terms, led the country through economic depression and world war. By his side, often acting as his moral and social conscience, was First Lady Eleanor Roosevelt. A self-described "agitator," she wielded her influence to help carry out some of the most significant social justice and civil rights reforms in our nation's history.

One of the architects behind those reforms was Frances Perkins, who became the first woman appointed to a U.S. Presidential Cabinet when President Roosevelt named her Secretary of Labor in 1933. A witness to the tragic Triangle Shirtwaist Factory fire in 1911, Frances insisted on securing a sweeping labor reform agenda before accepting the job. Her negotiations are legendary. In fact, many of the New Deal's hallmark achievements—Social Security, unemployment insurance, child labor laws—can be traced to Frances's vision and persistence. At the same time, Mary McLeod Bethune, the daughter of formerly enslaved parents who was born in a cotton field in South Carolina, rose to become one of President Roosevelt's most trusted advisors. A champion for Black education and civil rights, Mary founded the National Council of Negro Women (NCNW) and led FDR's informal Black Cabinet. Her efforts ensured that African American women served during World War II, paving the way for the historic 6888th Central Postal Directory Battalion, the only unit of Black women deployed overseas. The Six Triple Eight processed over seventeen million pieces of backlogged mail in record time, restoring morale by making sure soldiers and families could stay in touch.

I would not exchange my color for all the wealth in the world, for had I been born white I might not have been able to do all that I have done.

—Mary McLeod Bethune

"I would not exchange my color for all the wealth in the world," Mary wrote in her last will and testament. "For had I been born white I might not have been able to do all that I have done."

The presence of these two women in government simultaneously was not only remarkable but also ushered in policy changes. Women on the home front also answered the call during World War II, further increasing their participation in the workforce and gaining economic independence. With men at war, women filled roles in factories, shipyards, and transportation hubs, becoming welders, electricians, machinists, and streetcar operators. These wartime workers—later immortalized by Rosie the Riveter—helped fuel the Allied victory. The number of women in the workforce jumped from about twelve million in 1940 to nearly nineteen million by 1945, representing one-third of all workers.[2] According to the American Rosie the Riveter Association, these women helped produce nearly three hundred thousand aircraft, one hundred thousand tanks, and over forty-four billion rounds of ammunition.[3] They kept the economy humming at home, and they helped the Allies win the war overseas.

During this era, women were also building the legal framework of the Civil Rights Movement. Constance Baker Motley, a brilliant attorney with the NAACP Legal Defense Fund, helped draft the legal strategy behind *Brown v. Board of Education* (1954) and defended Dr. Martin Luther King, Jr., during pivotal protests. In 1966, she became the first Black woman appointed to the federal judiciary, paving the way for generations of women in the legal field, including future U.S. Supreme Court justices.

Not only was women's participation in the workforce changing, but also women's involvement with sports. Babe Didrikson Zaharias, arguably the greatest all-around female athlete of the twentieth century, dominated track and field, basketball, and later, professional golf. A two-time Olympic gold medalist, she became the first woman to compete in a men's PGA Tour tournament. She didn't just set a new standard for athletic excellence—she also expanded the boundaries of femininity in sports, especially when she went public about having a terminal illness during her career.

As women proved themselves indispensable in wartime, law, labor, and athletics, they were also laying the groundwork for a more equitable future. By the 1970s, that push reached a crescendo.

In 1973, Billie Jean King faced off against former Wimbledon champion Bobby Riggs in a match famously dubbed the Battle of the Sexes. It was blockbuster TV! An estimated fifty million Americans tuned in as Billie Jean beat Bobby in straight sets, while even more watched around the world. But her victory extended far beyond the court. A fierce advocate for gender equality in sports, she had lobbied Congress for the passage of Title IX, the 1972 law prohibiting sex-based discrimination in federally funded education.

"I just had to play," King said of the match. "Title IX had just passed and I . . . wanted to change the hearts and minds of people to match the legislation."[4]

The woman at the center of that fight to pass Title IX was Representative Patsy Mink of Hawaii, the first Asian American woman to serve in Congress. She had been denied entry to medical school, so she ended up being a lawyer, and today all of our daughters who play sports in school can thank Patsy for her groundbreaking efforts.

This fifty-year stretch witnessed the emergence of a powerful feminist movement that would fundamentally reshape American society. Betty Friedan's 1963 book, *The Feminine Mystique,* gave voice to the frustrations of countless women trapped in restrictive domestic roles, sparking what became known as the second wave of feminism. The movement gained momentum through the 1960s, culminating in the formation of the National Organization for Women (NOW) in 1966.

I just had to play. Title IX had just passed and I . . . wanted to change the hearts and minds of people to match the legislation.

—Billie Jean King

By the early 1970s, women were not only demanding workplace equality and educational opportunities—they were asserting control over their own bodies and reproductive choices. The Supreme Court's landmark decision in *Roe v. Wade* (1973) recognized a woman's constitutional right to an abortion, representing a seismic shift in how society viewed women's autonomy.

Simultaneously, women were translating activism into political power: In 1968, Shirley Chisholm became the first Black woman elected to Congress, and in 1972, the first to seek the Democratic presidential nomination, declaring, "If they don't give you a seat at the table, bring a folding chair." *This just happens to be one of my favorite quotes!*

These women exemplified a generation that refused to accept limitations—they demanded not just inclusion but the right to define their destinies. Their courage, persistence, and vision brought the country closer to fulfilling its founding promise—that all people, regardless of gender or race, are created equal and endowed with inalienable rights.

If they don't give you a seat at the table, bring a folding chair.

—SHIRLEY CHISHOLM

26.

Mary McLeod Bethune: *The First Lady of the Struggle*

On the eve of the 1922 mayoral elections, the Ku Klux Klan marched on Mary McLeod Bethune's boarding school for Black girls in Daytona, Florida. More than one hundred white-robed men, carrying banners declaring white supremacy, had come to intimidate, to terrorize, and to burn the place to the ground.[1]

Mary, the daughter of formerly enslaved parents, had been threatened before, but this time felt different. Her first thought was to protect the nearly three hundred students in her care.

"Get the students into the dormitory," she told the teachers. "Get them into bed, do not share what is happening right now."[2] The faculty spread out around the school to help stand watch.

At the center of the quadrangle, Mary stood alone, arms folded, head held high, daring the Klansmen to come closer.[3] They didn't. After a few tense minutes, the Klansmen moved on. Some say they were tipped off that a group of armed Black residents were prepared to defend the school if violence erupted. But I also imagine her standing her ground, intimidating the men with her strength of will alone.

Mary knew why the KKK had come to her school. She was a threat to their political power. They hated her not only because she was educating Black girls but also because she was registering so many new Black voters. In fact, new Black voters in Daytona were outnumbering new white voters.[4]

This was two years after the passage of the Nineteenth Amendment, which gave women the right to vote. But Mary recognized that in the Jim Crow South, barriers like literacy tests and poll taxes continued to suppress Black voters. Mary understood the power of the ballot box and knew that Black people could only seize political power if they registered in record numbers.

There was a lot to fight for in this election, including whether to establish a local high school for Black students. Undeterred by the threat of violence and the Klansmen's march on her school, Mary showed up to the polls with more than a hundred people, but they were forced to wait all day to vote.[5]

In the end, Mary's political efforts were successful, and Daytona's first Black high school would become a reality.

One hundred years later, in 2022, Mary became the first Black person represented in the National Statuary Hall with a state-sponsored statue in the U.S. Capitol. Each state picks the two people they want to commemorate and represent their state. Mary's statue replaced one of Confederate general Edmund Kirby Smith.[6]

> ***Invest in the human soul. Who knows, it might be a diamond in the rough.***
>
> ***—Mary McLeod Bethune***

The statue weighs three tons and measures eleven feet tall. It is made of Carrara marble that came from the same Tuscan quarry used by Michelangelo to carve *David.*[7]

The three bands on each sleeve of Mary's robe indicate doctoral status and show how incredibly respected she was as a teacher and as an intellectual. She was awarded *nine honorary doctorates* in her lifetime. The quote engraved on the base of Mary's statue reads, "Invest in the human soul. Who knows, it might be a diamond in the rough." It aptly summarizes Mary's central belief that learning, especially literacy, was key to a better life for Black Americans.

If you look at the white marble statue today you will notice that in her left hand, she is holding a rose made from black marble. Mary first saw a Black Velvet rose in a Swiss garden, growing with roses of other colors. She would later refer to her students in college as "black roses."

It was her belief that "loving thy neighbor" as described in the Bible also meant there could be interracial harmony.[8]

In her right hand is a walking stick once owned by President Franklin Delano Roosevelt. Mary collected walking sticks, and Eleanor Roosevelt sent one of the president's canes to her after his death. The inclusion of that cane was a nod to Mary's role as the leader of FDR's Black Cabinet, an informal network of more than one hundred African American government employees who were part of the Federal Council on Negro Affairs. Mary was the only Black woman to hold an influential post in the administration, giving her access to not only the president and the First Lady, but also to a radio audience of millions.

In 1939, two years before America's entrance into World War II, she joined a discussion on NBC's weekly public affairs radio broadcast, *America's Town Meeting of the Air.* The central question for the panel was: "What does American democracy mean to me?"[9]

When I heard that address, I was moved by her booming and authoritative voice. *She sounds like a female FDR!*

Like many of the women we've profiled in this book, Mary made the case that America was not living up to the ideals promised in the Declaration of Independence: Black Americans had always been willing to die for American democracy but were shut out from its promise of freedom. Here's how she put it in that 1939 radio panel discussion:

> Democracy is for me, and for 12 million Black Americans, a goal towards which our nation is marching. It is a dream and an ideal in whose ultimate realization we have a deep and abiding faith. For me, it is based on Christianity, in which we confidently entrust our destiny as a people. Under God's guidance in this great democracy, we are rising out of the darkness of slavery into the light of freedom. Here my race has been afforded [the] opportunity to advance from a people 80 percent illiterate to a people 80 percent literate; from abject poverty to the ownership and operation of a million farms and 750,000 homes; from total disfranchisement to participation in government; from the

> status of chattels to recognized contributors to the American culture.
>
> As we have been extended a measure of democracy, we have brought to the nation rich gifts. We have helped to build America with our labor, strengthened it with our faith and enriched it with our song. We have given you Paul Lawrence Dunbar, Booker T. Washington, Marian Anderson and George Washington Carver. But even these are only the first fruits of a rich harvest, which will be reaped when new and wider fields are opened to us.
>
> The democratic doors of equal opportunity have not been opened wide to Negroes.[10]

Mary's lifelong work was to open wide those democratic doors. It earned her the nickname "First Lady of the Struggle" during the New Deal era. And because of her influence on President Roosevelt and civil rights issues, she left behind a legacy as one of the most influential women of her generation.[11] And yet many people today are unfamiliar with her accomplishments.

Mary McLeod Bethune was born in the humblest of beginnings on July 10, 1875, in South Carolina, the fifteenth of seventeen children. Entering the world a decade after abolition and the passing of the Thirteenth Amendment in 1865, Mary was the first in her family not born into slavery.

Her parents, Patsy and Samuel, owned a five-acre parcel of land, and her mother continued to work for the family that had once enslaved her.

In an interview later in her life, she described a key moment when she was about ten years old, while visiting that family with her mom. Mary was invited into the playhouse and picked up a book. She was quickly admonished by a white girl.

"When she said to me, 'You can't read that—put that down,' it just did something to my pride and to my heart that made me feel that someday I would read just as she was reading," Mary recalled. "I went away from there determined to learn how to read."[12]

One day when the family was out in the field picking cotton, a teacher came by and told Mary's parents that the Presbyterian church had established a mission where Black children could get an education. Mary was one of the first to enroll.[13]

"That morning on my way to school I kept the thought uppermost 'Put that down—you can't read,'" she said. "It was one of the incentives that fired me in my determination to read."[14]

Years later, she was asked if she had told her mother about what happened in the playhouse. Her reply made me emotional as I thought about her mother, Patsy, having been enslaved, having seventeen children, and yet filling Mary's head and heart with confidence.

"When I told her, that instant, you know, she said to me—'Oh, never mind, my child, your time will come. You will learn some day.' My mother had a great philosophy of life. She came down from one of the great royalties of Africa. She could not be discouraged."[15]

Patsy aimed to instill confidence in her daughter. "No matter what kind of plight we found ourselves in, she always believed there was, through prayer and work, a way out. And it was one of the greatest things she stimulated life with . . . that determination that there was a way out if we put forth effort ourselves."[16]

The first school that Mary attended was in Mayesville, South Carolina, a one-room Black schoolhouse called Trinity Mission School.[17] It was five miles from her cabin, and she walked there and back every day.[18] Her schoolteacher, Emma Jane Wilson, helped her receive a scholarship to attend Scotia Seminary in Concord, North Carolina, a new college prep school for Black women.[19] She then applied and was admitted in 1894 to the Moody Bible Institute, where she was the only Black student. It was there that she dreamed of becoming a missionary.[20]

In 1898, she married Albertus Bethune and gave birth to their only child, a son, a year later.

Mary McLeod Bethune leads a line of students from her Daytona Educational and Industrial Training School for Negro Girls.

In a way, she did become a sort of missionary, preaching the gospel of *education.* Mary started her school in 1904 and called it the Daytona Educational and Industrial Training School for Negro Girls.[21] She did it with $1.50 and five young girls as her first students. Money was so tight that she used charred wood to make pencils and old crates as desks and seating areas.[22] A couple of years later there were 250 students. She discovered that Black people were desperate for the opportunity to give their children access to education, even as other people would do anything in their power to stop it.[23] Mary was prepared to stand up to hate—like that of the KKK—and devoted her life to expanding her young students' minds.

In 1923, Bethune successfully negotiated the merger of her school in Daytona, Florida, with the Cookman Institute in Jacksonville, Florida. She helped establish the coeducational four-year school that is known today as Bethune-Cookman College, now a Historically Black College and University (HBCU). The school became the first institution of higher education for Black students in Florida and one of the few below the Mason-Dixon Line where Black Americans could continue their education after high school.[24] Mary served as its first president for nearly two decades.

As she aimed to open doors for Black people in America, she opened the doors to the Mary McLeod Hospital and Training School for Nurses, the only school of its kind for Black women on the East Coast.

Mary worked diligently on the national stage for a better America, but she always made herself "readily accessible to average men and women and the college students that she mothered and mentored."[25] Her friendship with Eleanor Roosevelt led the first lady to visit the university four times, staying in Mary's home.[26]

Mary McLeod Bethune would carry the determination instilled by her mother all the way to the White House, inspiring a historic friendship with both First Lady Eleanor Roosevelt and President Franklin D. Roosevelt. Her alliance with the most powerful couple in the country—and the world at large—desegregated the White House.

Eleanor and Mary first met in December 1927, in New York City, at a luncheon hosted by Sara Delano Roosevelt. Sara was the overbearing mother of Franklin Delano Roosevelt, who was then running for governor.

The event was organized by the National Council of Women, and Mary was the eighth national president of the National Association of Colored Women at the time. She was the only Black woman at the lunch and none of the other delegates wanted to sit with her. Sara was appalled and took her "arm-in-arm" to the table with her daughter-in-law, Eleanor, so they could eat together.[27]

The two women immediately hit it off, and that moment began a lifelong friendship and partnership that would change the course of American history. Mary would become a trusted advisor to the Roosevelts on issues impacting Black Americans.[28]

Mary McLeod Bethune seated in her office at Bethune-Cookman College

Shortly after they met, the stock market crashed, ushering in the Great Depression. President Roosevelt was elected in the midst of immense poverty and high unemployment rates. His New Deal was a series of domestic programs aimed at easing the suffering experienced by the American people. His administration created the National Youth Administration (NYA) in 1935 as part of the Works Progress

Administration (WPA). The mission of the program was to help young people aged sixteen to twenty-four through educational aid, job training skills, and employment opportunities.

In 1935, President Roosevelt asked Mary to serve as a special advisor to the NYA. The next year he named her its Director of Negro Affairs, making her the first Black woman to head a federal agency.[29] At the time, Mary was the highest-paid Black American in the federal government—with a $5,000 salary (more than $100,000 in today's dollars).

As the Great Depression raged on, Mary came up with programs to employ thousands of Black women. Through her work at the NYA, she helped create work-study programs for Black college students and helped girls who could not afford college tuition train for other jobs, including as secretaries and nursery school teachers. It was the first time that the federal government established programs to help Black youth and young adults. Unlike other New Deal work programs, the NYA paid Black and white students equal wages for their projects.[30] *Mary undoubtedly had influence on that decision.*

When the economy improved in 1944, the NYA was discontinued. But it was considered a huge success, assisting close to three hundred thousand Black youth over the years to gain opportunities in the job market.

Mary worked with the Roosevelt administration for almost a decade, from 1936 until Roosevelt's death in 1945. But even though she was the highest-ranking Black female advisor, she still faced frequent discrimination as a visitor to the White House. "Dr. Bethune was on the elevator in the White House and the elevator operator said, 'I can't take you up.' Dr. Bethune said, 'That's okay, darling, I will take you up!' "[31]

As the leader of Roosevelt's Black Cabinet, she advised him on pressing issues in the Black community like lynching, poll taxes, and job creation. These efforts are credited with laying the groundwork for the modern Civil Rights Movement.

Mary influenced policy not only with her relationships but by inspiring community organizations. In 1935, she founded the National Council of Negro Women (NCNW) to empower Black women. It was the single most powerful national women's organization during the Civil Rights Movement. It had an astounding 850,000 members, including Martin Luther King, Jr.'s wife, Coretta Scott King.[32]

One of Mary's most underappreciated accomplishments was her hard-fought work to integrate the U.S. military during World War II. As an advisor to the Women's Army Corps (WAC), Mary personally recruited the first forty Black women to serve—paving the way for more than 6,500 to enlist overseas.[33] For her work, she would later be named an honorary general of the Women's Army for National Defense.[34]

Mary's fight came at a time when women's military service faced deep resistance. Earlier efforts to authorize a women's corps had failed in Congress, even after Pearl Harbor. One Democratic congressman declared that it would be "humiliation" if women did the "duty of men." "The thing is so revolting to me, to my sense of decency," New York congressman Andrew Lawrence Somers said. "I just cannot discuss it."[35]

Mary's influence extended beyond the WAC. She helped found the United Negro College Fund and lobbied for aviation training at historically Black colleges, leading to the creation of the Tuskegee Airmen.[36] When the NCNW was excluded from a War Department conference in 1941, Mary wrote directly to Secretary of War Henry Stimson, insisting that Black women refused to be treated as "apart from Our American democracy."[37] The War Department reversed its decision and invited the NCNW to participate.[38]

> ***I LEAVE YOU LOVE. Love builds. It is positive and helpful. It is more beneficial than hate.***
>
> ***—Mary McLeod Bethune***

At a time when Black women were virtually shut out of military service,

Mary's leadership helped recruit Charity Adams, who would become the highest-ranking Black army officer during World War II.[39]

As a lifelong educator and civil rights pioneer, Mary was beside herself with joy when the Supreme Court's *Brown v. Board of Education* (1954) decision made racial segregation in public schools unconstitutional. It was the culmination of her life's work as a public servant, teacher, and school founder. During remarks in Detroit, she said, "When first I heard of the Supreme Court decision, I lifted my voice to utter the first inspiration of my heart—and I said, 'Let the people praise Thee, O God! Let ALL the people praise thee.'. . . All of our people are free or none are free."[40]

Mary McLeod Bethune passed away at her home on the campus of Bethune-Cookman University in Daytona Beach on May 18, 1955. She was seventy-nine years old.

Her last will and testament is one of the most beautiful essays I have ever read. Mary left us with this: "I LEAVE YOU LOVE. Love builds. It is positive and helpful. It is more beneficial than hate. . . . 'Love thy neighbor' is a precept which could transform the world if it were universally practiced."[41]

"Despite many crushing burdens and handicaps," she wrote, "I have risen from the cotton fields of South Carolina to found a college, administer it during its years of growth, become a public servant in the government of our country and a leader of women. I would not exchange my color for all the wealth in the world, for had I been born white I might not have been able to do all that I have done or yet hope to do."

I have risen from the cotton fields of South Carolina to found a college, administer it during its years of growth, become a public servant in the government of our country and a leader of women.

—Mary McLeod Bethune

To this day, she continues to especially inspire Black women. Former Florida representative Val Demings explained how it felt to know that Mary would have a statue in the U.S. Capitol: “Mary McLeod Bethune was the most powerful woman I can remember as a child. She has been an inspiration throughout my whole life.”[42]

Eleanor Roosevelt outlived Mary by seven years. She dedicated her popular syndicated column “My Day” to her friend two days after Mary died. In it she pledged to always “cherish the spirit she lived by and try to promote the causes she believed in, in loving memory of a very wonderful life.”[43]

27.

Eleanor Roosevelt: *The Great "Agitator"*

On Christmas Day in 1942, Eleanor Roosevelt was visiting wounded soldiers at Walter Reed General Hospital. It was something she did frequently during World War II.[1] She stopped at the bedside of Private Hardie Robbins, a high school music teacher from California whose hands had been badly burned when his army transport, the USS *Bliss,* was torpedoed off the coast of North Africa.[2]

Eleanor asked him what he wanted to do once his bandages were removed. Private Robbins told her he wanted to play the piano again. Weeks later, she wrote to his commanding officer to tell Robbins that if he would like to practice on the piano at the White House, he was free to do so. Robbins said, "This was the beginning of a friendship."[3] After seventeen months in the hospital, Robbins became a regular at the White House, playing Beethoven and Tchaikovsky on the Steinway concert grand piano and attending luncheons of wild duck gifted by the king of Egypt.[4]

This little-known story was classic Eleanor. Known as ER to her friends, Eleanor knew how to make everyone feel important. She saw the best in people. As Private Robbins put it, "Great people do not intend to be great. They simply have that inherent integrity that unfolds and strengthens with adversity."[5]

She took to calling herself "the agitator" and her husband "the politician." She understood her own power and refused to stay quiet about controversial issues of the time like civil rights and women's rights, constantly pushing for social change when others expected First Ladies to remain decorative and silent.

She wielded her power through her media platforms—her newspaper column reached millions, her radio shows brought her voice into homes nationwide, and her travels would let her spotlight injustices firsthand. Rather than relying on formal authority, she built coalitions by connecting activists with policymakers and used persistent, strategic pressure across multiple channels.

Beyond trusting in her own abilities to enact change, she believed that women were powerful. Her self-confidence would help propel women forward by pushing notable policy changes. "You gain strength, courage and confidence by every experience in which you really stop to look fear in the face," she said. "You are able to say to yourself, 'I have lived through this horror. I can take the next thing that comes along.' "[6]

She felt that as wives and caretakers, women could be especially effective activists for human rights and social reforms.[7] For as much as she did in public, it's her work uplifting women and people of color behind the scenes that intrigues me most. "Women are by nature progressives," she told *The New York Times.*[8] Arguably, with her influence, those feminine ideals would become the philosophical underpinning of the entire Roosevelt presidency. In the White House, Eleanor was

You gain strength, courage and confidence by every experience in which you really stop to look fear in the face. You are able to say to yourself, "I have lived through this horror. I can take the next thing that comes along."

—Eleanor Roosevelt

often her husband's conscience and America's moral compass during a time when the world was at the brink of destruction during World War II.

Beyond her influence, her advocacy and prolific travels at home and abroad would help change the way the world *viewed* women in power. Eleanor was the longest-serving First Lady in American history, holding the position for twelve years. In all, she would spend more than fifty years in public life, and she was among the most well-known women in the world. After Eleanor, there was no doubt that women could create their own playbook and wield substantial political power.

Anna Eleanor Roosevelt was born on October 11, 1884, in New York City, into an aristocratic family that was the namesake of two future U.S. presidents. But despite her wealth and status, her childhood was marked by loneliness and loss.

Her mother, Anna Hall Roosevelt, was a celebrated beauty who often mocked Eleanor's looks and serious nature. Eleanor would later recall standing in the parlor doorway at home as a child, "often with my finger in my mouth," and hearing her mother tell visitors: "She is such a funny child, so old-fashioned that we always call her Granny." *Can you imagine?* Poor Eleanor never forgot it. "I wanted to sink through the floor in shame."[9]

When Eleanor was just eight years old, her mother died of diphtheria. Her father, Elliott Roosevelt, the younger brother of President Theodore Roosevelt, struggled with alcoholism and died two years later. Eleanor was an orphan and went to live with her maternal grandmother, who was reportedly a stern disciplinarian.[10]

A turning point in her life came at age fifteen when her grandmother sent her to Allenswood Academy, an exclusive all-girls boarding school outside London. There, Eleanor was mentored by the headmistress, Marie Souvestre, a fiercely independent educator who instilled in her confidence, intellectual curiosity, and a passion for social justice. Years later, Eleanor reflected on this influence, writing, "I think I came to feel that the underdog was always the one to be championed."[11]

Souvestre introduced Eleanor to progressive European ideas about class, justice, and civic responsibility.[12] When Eleanor returned home to New York, she put these lessons into practice by joining the Junior League and teaching immigrant girls at a settlement house on the Lower East Side, making a deliberate effort to understand the struggles of working-class women.

These early experiences—combined with her natural empathy and growing social awareness—would shape the rest of her life.

At eighteen years old, Eleanor reconnected with Franklin Delano Roosevelt, her father's fifth cousin once removed. They married a few years later in 1905, with her uncle, President Theodore Roosevelt, walking her down the aisle. The president's attendance made it front-page news in *The New York Times* and other newspapers. When asked for his thoughts on the Roosevelt-Roosevelt union, the president said, "It is a good thing to keep the name in the family."[13] She and Franklin had six children: Anna (1906), James (1907), Franklin, Jr. (1909, who died as an infant), Elliott (1910), Franklin, Jr. II (1914), and John (1916).

In 1913, FDR was nominated to be Assistant Secretary of the Navy, a position that introduced Eleanor to the inner workings of government. During World War I, Eleanor visited Arlington National Cemetery daily to attend the burials of American soldiers who were killed in the war. She also visited St. Elizabeth Hospital, where hundreds of shell-shocked navy men were being treated. Appalled by the hospital's conditions, she pushed a friend in government to investigate. A formal inquiry confirmed her concerns, and as a result, funding was increased to improve care for the veterans. This was one of Eleanor's first experiences in using influence to effect change—earning her the nickname "the agitator."

During this period, she also endured a deep personal betrayal. In 1918, while unpacking her husband's things, Eleanor discovered a bundle of love letters from Lucy Mercer, her social secretary and longtime trusted aide.[14] Devastated, she offered him a divorce, but it was decided that a separation would ruin his political career, so they stayed married.

After an unsuccessful run for vice president, Franklin contracted polio at thirty-nine years old, leaving him permanently paralyzed from the waist down. When he withdrew from public life in 1921 to Hyde Park to focus on rehabilitation, Eleanor played a crucial role in assisting in his bathing and shaving, and tending to him day and night. FDR's mother wanted him to retire from politics, but Eleanor was intent on keeping his political career alive. She encouraged him to remain engaged, gathered family and political allies to support his recovery, and stepped into public life on his behalf.[15]

His absence let her capture the spotlight and build her own political identity. She represented her husband at public events, rallied Democratic women in New York, and campaigned for party candidates while championing social reform and women's rights. She joined the League of Women Voters and the Women's Trade Union League, and with friends Nancy Cook and Marion Dickerman built Val-Kill Cottage on the Roosevelt estate—a retreat that later became her personal residence and political hub. She also bought the Todhunter School, a private girls' school in New York City, where she taught part-time until entering the White House in 1933. Her growing public role not only kept FDR's name alive in politics but cemented her own as a force to be reckoned with.

Though their romantic relationship never fully recovered, they became political partners. Eleanor was partly responsible for Franklin's rise to power, helping him get elected as governor of New York in 1928 and then as president in 1932.

Their marriage evolved into what one White House usher later described as "the most separate relationship I have ever seen between man and wife—and the most equal."[16]

While the president maintained a quiet but ongoing relationship with Lucy Mercer, Eleanor found emotional (and possibly intimate) kinship in close friendships, particularly with journalist Lorena Hickok and political confidant Joseph Lash, who slept in a small blue bedroom on the second floor, across from FDR's study.[17]

When Eleanor became First Lady in 1933, she used her unique role as her husband's political partner to transform the ceremonial position into a powerful platform. There was no one like her before, and some might argue no one like her since. In 1939, *Time*'s cover story on Eleanor called her "the world's foremost female political force," crediting her "unequaled influence in the world" to "thousands of small activities."[18]

To truly appreciate Eleanor Roosevelt's impact, you must consider the world in which she lived. A 1936 Gallup poll found that four-fifths of Americans believed that married women should not work, and between 1932 and 1937, the federal government dismissed 1,600 women from jobs simply because they were married.[19]

Not long after she became First Lady, Eleanor sent letters to the many government departments requesting names of women who worked there. Then she invited these women to dinners and receptions at the White House—events they had previously been excluded from—to ask them what they were seeing in their departments. She later began hosting annual spring garden parties for them at the White House. She valued what these educated women had to say and how hard they had worked to get where they were. Many told her they had never been invited to the White House before.

Eleanor was the first First Lady to travel by airplane across the Atlantic and the first to visit soldiers in the Pacific. She was the first First Lady to speak at a party convention and to write newspaper articles. Her "My Day" column was so popular that it appeared in nearly one hundred newspapers almost every day for twenty-seven years.[20] In her spare time, she was a radio commentator. *Truly remarkable.*

She was also the first wife of a president to hold her own press conferences designed specifically for female reporters, who had been excluded from the White House press corps. Her first White House press conference was on March 6, 1933—just two days after FDR's inauguration. Her last was on April 12, 1945, several hours before her husband died. Over her twelve years as First Lady, she held 348 press conferences—amounting to one per week while she was in Washington.[21]

She wrote her own speeches and spoke publicly without seeking the approval of her husband's West Wing aides, and her independence irritated some of them. FDR's Secretary of the Interior, Harold Ickes, was particularly unnerved by Eleanor's outspokenness, once complaining, "I wish Mrs. R would stick to her knitting."

For decades Eleanor pushed FDR to be more forceful on the issue of civil rights, though she was not always successful. In 1934, she joined the NAACP and worked with its leader, Walter White, on a federal anti-lynching bill. However, FDR refused to support the bill publicly, fearing it would alienate Southern Democrats, whose votes he needed for his New Deal legislation.

Undeterred, Eleanor arranged for White to meet with the president, and she attended the NAACP's exhibition that graphically depicted white mobs attacking Black Americans. She continued advocating for anti-lynching legislation until her death. (Shockingly, a bill designating lynching as a federal hate crime was not signed into law until 2022.)[22]

In 1939, the Daughters of the American Revolution (DAR) refused to allow Black opera singer Marian Anderson to perform at the organization's Constitution Hall in Washington, D.C., because of their "whites-only" policy. In protest, Eleanor resigned from the organization.

"I am afraid I have never been a very useful member of the Daughters of the American Revolution, so I know it will make very little difference to you whether I resign," she wrote tongue-in-cheek in a nationally published letter. "However, I am in complete disagreement with the attitude taken in refusing Constitution Hall to a great artist. . . . You had an opportunity to lead in an enlightened way and it seems to me that your organization failed."[23]

Marian wouldn't perform at Constitution Hall but instead found a bigger stage: on the National Mall—on the steps of the monument to the president who signed the Emancipation Proclamation. The historic Easter Sunday concert was arranged by the Roosevelts at the Lincoln Memorial, where seventy-five thousand people gathered to hear her sing "My Country, 'Tis of Thee." Eleanor was not present, perhaps to ensure that the spotlight remained on Anderson, but her influence in making the event possible was undeniable.[24]

Eleanor's actions were not just symbolic—they were a public, courageous stand for justice, racial equality, and women's dignity. Because of that, Eleanor endured blistering attacks from powerful critics, including Federal Bureau of Investigation (FBI) Director J. Edgar Hoover, who spread rumors that she had "Black blood"[25] and accused her of being a communist. Because of her work with liberal groups, the FBI compiled a three-thousand-page file on her—one of the largest files ever assembled by the agency on a single person.[26] In the 1950s, the Ku Klux Klan even placed a $25,000 bounty on her head. Yet she never wavered in her convictions. She famously gave the advice "Do what you feel in your heart to be right—for you'll be criticized anyway."[27]

> ***Do what you feel in your heart to be right—for you'll be criticized anyway.***
>
> —*ELEANOR ROOSEVELT*

One of her most courageous stands came after the attack on Pearl Harbor, when 120,000 Japanese Americans living on the West Coast were forcibly relocated to military internment camps surrounded by barbed wire and guard towers. Many lost their homes and businesses. Military leaders claimed that these Japanese Americans posed a security threat, even though the United States never uncovered a single case of a Japanese American acting as a spy or engaging in sabotage during World War II.[28]

Just days after the attack, Eleanor spoke out, writing in her December 16, 1941, "My Day" column, "This is, perhaps, the greatest test this country has ever met. Perhaps it is the test which is going to show whether the United States can furnish a pattern for the rest of the world for the future."

In April 1943, she visited an internment camp and was concerned by what she saw. She called for the camps to be closed and for Japanese Americans to be released.[29] Though the camps remained open until 1946, it was Eleanor Roosevelt's words that helped shift public opinion.

World War II projected Eleanor's image across the globe in a new and profound way. During the war, Eleanor's global travel was so extensive, flying thousands of miles and visiting countless wounded soldiers and sailors, that the Secret Service gave her the code name "Rover."

She was at her best when she was talking to soldiers and nurses, making them feel so comfortable that they could tell her anything. In those moments, she was just like any other mother, worrying about her four sons—Jimmy; Elliott; Franklin, Jr.; and John—who were serving in the war.

In the fall of 1942, less than a year after the United States had entered the war, Eleanor traveled to Great Britain at the invitation of Queen Elizabeth II.[30] The main goals of the First Lady's wartime diplomatic mission were to visit American troops and study how British civilians, especially women, were contributing to the war effort. She spent a month visiting factories, shipyards, hospitals, schools, bomb shelters, Red Cross clubs, and military installations across the British Isles. She was tireless, reportedly keeping a rigorous schedule that began early in the morning and ended late at night. The press coverage captured the exhausting pace she maintained, with one reporter famously writing, "She walked 50 miles through factories, clubs and hospitals. She walked me off my feet."

Eleanor was no sedentary stateswoman; she wore out the soles of her shoes during her travels. When the chief usher of the White House heard about her deteriorating footwear, he sent her another pair.[31]

Much of what she learned she shared in her "My Day" column, always keeping a direct line to the American public and often leaving them with words of wisdom like "With the new day comes new strength."[32]

During her visit to Rainbow Corner, the American Red Cross club in London, she met with American GIs who were stationed in Britain. There she learned that the soldiers were developing blisters on their feet from wearing cotton socks. The next day, she spoke with General Dwight Eisenhower, Supreme Commander of the Allied Forces in Europe. A half million pairs of wool socks were distributed almost immediately.[33] *The agitator got things done!*

By the time she left, British prime minister Winston Churchill wrote her a handwritten note that read, "You certainly have left golden footprints behind you."[34]

Chalmers Roberts, a press aide for the U.S. Office of War Informa-

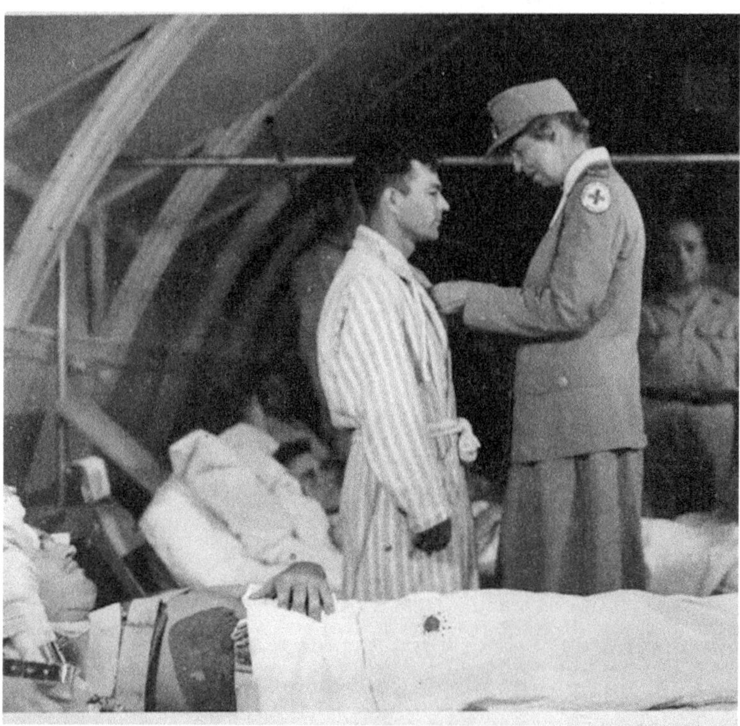

First Lady Eleanor Roosevelt pins a medal onto an injured service member at a field hospital in the South Pacific.

tion and later an influential journalist, reflected on the First Lady's immense power and influence. "Mrs. Roosevelt has done more to bring real understanding of the spirit of the United States to the people of Great Britain than any other single American who has ever visited these islands," he said.[35]

I marvel at Eleanor Roosevelt's confidence, stamina, and what almost seems like an innate ability to become—*dare I say—the shadow commander in chief?* The president was partially paralyzed and unable to travel the globe. It was Eleanor who stepped in to do what was necessary to fill in for the hardest job in the world—leader of the free world.

For five weeks, starting in August 1943, she traveled to the Pacific theater to visit troops stationed in Australia, New Zealand, and the tiny islands in the South Pacific that had seen intense combat.[36] At the advice of one of her sons, she would wake early to have breakfast with the enlisted soldiers. In the afternoons, she would visit hospitals, hoping to console the gravely wounded.

"Over and over again on this trip I wished that I could be changed in some magic way into the mother or the sweetheart or the wife or sister that these men longed to see," she wrote. She was not there as entertainment, like Bob Hope, Betty Grable, or Lana Turner; she was giving these exhausted, scared soldiers a sense of home. And the reassurance that their country was behind them.

"Over here she was something none of us had seen in over a year, an American mother," one soldier said after her visit.

An American mother.

As I learned about this extraordinary mission, risking her life to visit soldiers, it conjured up images of an epic Oscar-winning movie. Eleanor lost thirty pounds on this five-week journey,[37] leaving in secret from San Francisco and traveling nearly twenty-six thousand miles—that's about equal to the Earth's circumference—to seventeen islands and nations, including Australia, New Zealand, and military installations in Hawaii, Guadalcanal, New Caledonia, and other tiny islands.[38] In the end, it was estimated she had seen four hundred thousand troops in different hospitals and camps.[39] If Eleanor's journey was taught in

First Lady Eleanor Roosevelt visits U.S. troops on a trip to Central and South America.

school, I wonder if more Americans would be able to envision a *female* commander in chief.

On April 12, 1945, Eleanor was in Washington when she received the news that her husband of forty years had died in Warm Springs, Georgia. Lucy Mercer (now Rutherfurd) had been with him at the time.[40]

Less than a month after Franklin's death, World War II ended in Europe. On August 15, 1945, Japan surrendered after the atomic bombing of Hiroshima and Nagasaki. Reflecting on the war's toll, Eleanor wrote in "My Day" that "the weight of suffering which has engulfed the world during so many years could not so quickly be wiped out."[41]

Although Eleanor was no longer First Lady, her life in public service did not end with the White House. At President Harry Truman's request, she joined the first U.S. delegation to the United Nations in

1946. The U.N. had been created by dozens of countries to ensure that another world war would never happen.

She became chair of the U.N. Commission on Human Rights and was instrumental in drafting the Universal Declaration of Human Rights, which was adopted on December 10, 1948—the landmark document asserting fundamental human rights worldwide. President Harry Truman called her "the First Lady of the World."

Eleanor's influence was so profound that some speculated she could be President Truman's running mate in 1948. Conservative politician Clare Boothe Luce remarked that she was "the only person in the Democratic Party who could take back from Mr. [Henry] Wallace the Negro vote, the labor vote, the underdog minority vote, and, as the mother of four boys in the service, the Pacific vote."[42] But Eleanor had no interest in elected office; instead, she remained devoted to her activism and humanitarian work.

Eleanor Roosevelt passed away from aplastic anemia, tuberculosis, and heart failure on November 7, 1962, at age seventy-eight.[43] Her funeral in Hyde Park, New York, was a celebration of her remarkable life. The guest list was akin to that for a state funeral: President John F. Kennedy, Jacqueline Kennedy, former Presidents Harry Truman and Dwight Eisenhower, Supreme Court justices, and world dignitaries were all there to pay their respects, along with thousands of admirers.

Though she never sought power for herself alone, Eleanor Roosevelt reshaped the role of First Lady, championed civil rights, and left an enduring mark on global human rights. Perhaps she was never fully comfortable admitting her influence, but history has regarded her for what she was: one of the most important women of the twentieth century.

28.

Frances Perkins: *The Cabinet Member*

On March 25, 1911, Frances Perkins was having tea with friends in New York City's Washington Square when she heard fire engines approaching. Rushing to the scene of an inferno at a nearby garment sweatshop, she witnessed more than fifty workers—mostly young Italian and Jewish immigrant women—jumping to their deaths to escape engulfing flames on the eighth, ninth, and tenth floors of a building in Greenwich Village.[1]

The building's sole fire escape collapsed, leaving workers with a terrible choice: burn to death, jump, or be trampled as they rushed toward locked doors and exits that opened inward, trapping them inside. (The doors were locked to keep the workers from stealing.) That day, 146 workers died, many of them teenage girls, at the Triangle Shirtwaist Factory.

It remains one of the deadliest workplace disasters in U.S. history. Frances never forgot the horror, recalling, "People who had their clothes afire would jump. It was a most horrid spectacle. . . . There was no place to go."[2] The tragedy defined the rest of her life. "Something must be done," she later reflected. "We've got to turn this into some kind of victory, some kind of constructive action."[3]

The Triangle Shirtwaist owners were indicted on charges of manslaughter but were found not guilty. Civil suits against the building's owners resulted in settlements averaging just $75 per victim's family. The public outcry, however, led to a series of reforms, and it inspired Frances to embark on a career as a reformer. The Triangle Shirtwaist

Factory fire, Frances later declared, was "the day the New Deal was born."

Within a few months, the Committee on Safety was created, and former President Theodore Roosevelt recommended that Frances become the executive secretary. One of the committee's first actions was establishing a commission to examine worker health and safety conditions in New York factories.[4]

Between 1911 and 1915, Frances helped drive a sweeping transformation of labor law in New York. As a key member of the New York State Factory Commission, she helped push through thirty-six groundbreaking laws—establishing the strongest workplace safety protections in the country.[5] Her strategy was as bold as it was effective: She dragged lawmakers out of their offices and into the sweltering, hazardous factories where workers toiled in unsafe conditions. She would have them gather at 4 a.m. at factory gates so the commissioners could watch children file out of the factories after their grueling nighttime shifts.[6]

These visceral encounters forced the political elite to confront the human cost of inaction. As Frances later put it, the Triangle Shirtwaist fire had become "a torch that lighted up the industrial scene," and the laws that followed were a national turning point in how Americans viewed the responsibility of government to protect workers.[7]

The governor's race in 1918 was the first in which women in New York had the right to vote in statewide elections. Frances campaigned hard for the man she had served on the safety commission with, her friend and ally Al Smith. After his election, Governor Smith appointed her to a vacant seat on the New York State Industrial Commission; she became the first woman to hold an administrative position in the state government, with a salary of $8,000. At the time, she was the highest-paid woman in public office in the United States.[8]

When Governor Smith lost his bid for president in 1928, New York's new governor, Franklin Delano Roosevelt, asked Frances to become the state's Industrial Commissioner—a prestigious post with oversight of the entire labor department. This meant Frances Perkins was now the most prominent state labor official in the nation. What's incredible to realize is that her rise to power was only just the beginning.

The close working relationship Frances formed with Roosevelt during his time as New York's governor led him to call on her again when he became president in 1933. As the nation reeled from the Great Depression, with unemployment at nearly 25 percent and families losing jobs, savings, and homes, President Roosevelt asked Frances to serve as Secretary of Labor. In her bestselling memoir, *The Roosevelt I Knew*, she recalled bringing a list of proposed reforms to their meeting: unemployment insurance, a minimum wage, a forty-hour workweek, abolition of child labor, and pensions among them. When the president gave her his full support, she agreed to serve—becoming the first woman in U.S. history to hold a Cabinet post. The list became a blueprint for much of President Roosevelt's domestic agenda. Nearly every item would eventually become law, woven into the fabric of the New Deal. The only major goal she did not achieve was universal health insurance.

Secretary of Labor Frances Perkins enters a mine in Oklahoma to look at working conditions.

At the time, Frances got a lot of credit for the bold new social reforms that helped lift the country out of the Great Depression. She appeared on the cover of *Time* magazine on August 14, 1933. *Collier's* magazine recognized her profound impact on policy by stating her accomplishment: "What the country has been operating under . . . is not so much the Roosevelt New Deal as it is the Perkins New Deal."[9] *Wow.*

Her work, ultimately, was about protecting human rights.

With war breaking out in Europe, Frances also pushed to make the United States a haven for Jewish refugees, despite the lack of public support. As Labor Secretary, she oversaw the Immigration and Naturalization Service, but it was the State Department that reviewed immigration applications. Frances persuaded President Roosevelt to extend temporary visas so that some 12,000–15,000 German Jews already in the United States on temporary tourist visas could stay in the country indefinitely. She later wrote, "Immigration matters have to be decided in a few days. They involve human lives. There can be no delaying." It should be noted that while she convinced President Roosevelt to extend some visas, Frances could not significantly expand Jewish immigration to the United States, as she had hoped.[10]

Because she was a woman, her time in power did not come easy, but her grit—and humor—were admirable. She famously once said, "Being a woman has only bothered me in climbing trees." When she

Secretary Frances Perkins attends a meeting of President Franklin D. Roosevelt's Cabinet. She is the only woman in the room.

was young, her mother told her she wasn't a natural beauty and that she couldn't rely on looks to achieve her lofty goals—so Frances always wore a three-cornered hat, which became a symbol of her fight for the working people.[11]

Being a woman has only bothered me in climbing trees.

—Frances Perkins

Frances recalled, "I was apprehensive and on guard at the first official Cabinet meeting. As the only woman member, I did not want my colleagues to get the impression that I was too talkative. I resolved not to speak unless asked to do so. . . . My colleagues looked at me with tense curiosity. I think some weren't sure I could speak."[12]

At one point, President Roosevelt turned to her and asked, "Now what's on your mind?"

"I just replied as briefly and clearly as I could," she recalled. When the meeting was over, Vice President John Nance Garner came over to her, slapped her on the back, and exclaimed, "You're all right; you've got something on your mind. You said it and then you stopped."

In retrospect, she said, "I guess he feared I would be a vague woman—not quite sure of anything. Really, I don't believe men would long tolerate vague women in public office."[13]

Even her mentor Al Smith, the longtime New York powerbroker, was skeptical about how it would work. He didn't think that men could handle a woman in a leadership position. "Men will take advice from a woman," he said, "but it is hard for them to take orders from a woman."[14] And to be sure, Frances suffered the indignities of being a "first." When FDR gave a speech at the Gridiron Club dinner, Frances was the only member of his Cabinet left off the guest list because women were not invited. Eleanor held a party for her at the White House that evening for women only.[15]

In fact, Eleanor had played a crucial role in Frances's appointment. She and Molly Dewson, head of the Women's Division of the Democratic National Committee, championed the inclusion of more women in top government positions.[16] At a dinner honoring Frances, Eleanor dismissed any notion that she was merely a "fluttery feminine do-gooder" and asserted that Frances was chosen not because she was a woman but because "the particular place which she occupies could be better filled by her than by anyone else, man or woman, with whom the President was acquainted."[17]

When Frances faced criticism, Eleanor stood by her side. She understood the challenges of being a woman in power. "She and Miss Perkins had a lot of huddles," one of Eleanor's friends recalled. When Frances confided to the First Lady about a particular issue at the Labor Department, Eleanor replied, "How men hate a woman in a position of real power!"[18]

I don't believe men would long tolerate vague women in public office.

—*Frances Perkins*

After Franklin Roosevelt's sudden death in office in 1945, Harry Truman became president and replaced Frances with his longtime Senate colleague Lewis B. Schwellenbach, making the Cabinet all-male once again. Frances had become the longest-serving Labor Secretary in U.S. history and one of only two Cabinet members to serve throughout Roosevelt's entire twelve-year presidency.

Before leaving the Department of Labor that June, she stood in the department's auditorium, shaking the hand of every one of the department's 1,800 employees while an orchestra played—a final gesture of gratitude.[19]

Even in retirement, Frances remained dedicated to labor issues, becoming a lecturer at Cornell University's School of Industrial and Labor Relations. Decades after the Triangle Shirtwaist Factory fire, she reflected on how the tragedy inspired her life's mission: "We all felt that we had been wrong, that something was wrong with that building. . . . moved by this sense of stricken guilt, we banded ourselves together to find a way by law to prevent this kind of disaster. . . . It was the beginning of a new and important drive to bring the humanities to the life of the brothers and sisters we all had in the working groups of these United States."[20]

Frances Perkins suffered a stroke and passed away on May 14, 1965, at age eighty-five. Upon her death, then Secretary of Labor Willard Wirtz paid tribute to her legacy: "Every man and woman in America who works at a living wage, under safe conditions, for reasonable hours, or who is protected by unemployment insurance or social security is her debtor."[21]

> ***If anybody opens a door, one should always go through.***
> —*Frances Perkins*

Her impact was so profound that, in 1980, President Jimmy Carter honored her by renaming the U.S. Department of Labor headquarters in Washington, D.C., the Frances Perkins Building—ensuring that her legacy as a champion of American workers would never be forgotten.

Frances understood the historic significance of being the first woman in a presidential Cabinet—the literal first to have a seat at the table!

"The overwhelming argument and thought which made me do it in the end in spite of personal difficulties was the realization that the door might not be opened to a woman again for a long, long time," she said. "I had a kind of duty to other women to walk in and sit down on the chair that was offered, and so establish the right of others long hence and far distant in geography to sit in the high seats."[22]

When she was asked if she ever regretted taking the job, she recalled her grandmother's wisdom: "If anybody opens a door," she said, "one should always go through. Opportunity comes that way."[23]

29.

The Six Triple Eight: *The Soldiers*

A visit to the Normandy American Cemetery in Colleville-sur-Mer, France, is a profoundly moving experience. The white marble headstones, including crosses and Stars of David, stand in perfect rows on lush green lawns overlooking Omaha Beach and the English Channel. Of the approximately 9,400 graves, only four are those of women: Mary Bankston, Mary Barlow, Dolores Browne, and Elizabeth Richardson. Their graves serve as a reminder of the often-overlooked roles American women, especially Black women, played overseas during World War II. They crossed oceans and broke barriers to become members of the greatest generation.

Bankston and Barlow, both privates, and Browne, a sergeant, were together called the Three B's. They were part of the 6888th Central Postal Directory Battalion (the Six Triple Eight), the only all-female battalion of Black women in the Women's Army Corps (WAC) during World War II.

In early 1945, the Six Triple Eight was deployed to Europe with an urgent mission: Clear the massive backlog of mail sitting in warehouses since D-Day. At the time, letters and packages were the primary way for service members to communicate with loved ones back home, and the delays were affecting morale.

"Just think about how many times a day you look at your phone or expect a phone call," said retired Army Colonel Edna W. Cummings, who spent a decade working to secure recognition for the unit. "Once that final communication with loved ones is interrupted, troop morale plummets."[1]

The battalion, composed of 855 enlisted Black women and officers, was tasked with clearing seventeen million pieces of mail in just six months. Cummings believed the women were set up to fail because the assignment was nearly impossible.

One of two buildings in France housing an overflow of unsorted mail en route to American troops fighting in World War II

During World War II, there was a shortage of soldiers, yet Black women still had to fight for the right to serve. (Black men had their own struggles within the military.) More than one million Black men and women were in the military during World War II, serving in every branch of the U.S. Armed Forces.[2] It took a powerful partnership to make it happen. Civil rights activist Mary McLeod Bethune persuaded First Lady Eleanor Roosevelt to push for a role for women overseas. When her National Council of Negro Women was excluded from a

1941 War Department conference about women in the military, she wrote a letter to Secretary of War Henry L. Stimson, stating: "We are anxious for you to know that we want to be and insist upon being considered a part of Our American democracy, not something apart from it. . . . We are incensed!" The War Department reversed its decision, and Mary McLeod Bethune's National Council of Negro Women was invited to come to the conference.[3]

By the end of the war, less than 5 percent of the members of the Women's Army Corps were Black.[4] But if it hadn't been for Mary McLeod Bethune, there would have been no Black women serving overseas.

Major Charity Adams inspects the 6888th Central Postal Directory Battalion upon their arrival in England in February 1945.

The Six Triple Eight arrived in England around Valentine's Day in 1945 after a harrowing two-week voyage across the Nazi U-boat-infested Atlantic Ocean. In Birmingham, they worked in facilities once used as a private school that had been taken over by the British Ministry of Defense. What they discovered there was shocking—they found letters stacked to the ceilings spread across multiple airplane hangars, some having sat there for two years.

Many letters had incorrect addresses, making delivery even more challenging since the seven million U.S. service members stationed in Europe at the time were constantly on the move.[5]

Their motto was simple: *No Mail, Low Morale.*

They worked seven days a week, sifting through mountains of undeliverable mail. Their conditions were harsh: Rats had gnawed through some of the letters and packages, and the hangars had to be kept dark so that they wouldn't become enemy targets.

The women created an innovative tracking system to tackle the massive mail backlog. They didn't have the high-tech machines we have today, so they invented a comprehensive indexing system with over seven million individual cards to track people with similar names, using military serial numbers to identify the correct recipient. *It was ingenious!* All of the work had to be done manually.[6] They were so efficient—processing almost two hundred thousand pieces of mail every day—that they completed the job in half the time expected. They had cleared the backlog, even with inadequate supplies, and in the face of discrimination not only at home but in the army. "They did not send us because they thought we could do it. We are here because they are sure we cannot," said Major Charity Adams Earley, who commanded the battalion and is portrayed by Kerry Washington in the 2024 Netflix film *The Six Triple Eight.*

> ***We are anxious for you to know that we want to be and insist upon being considered a part of Our American democracy, not something apart from it.***
>
> **—Mary McLeod Bethune**

Major Adams, who had joined the army in 1942, became the first Black woman to receive a commission. In her memoir, *One Woman's Army,* she recounted a 1945 encounter with a general who visited her troops. She had instructed the women to continue working while only some of the off-duty personnel lined up for inspection.

The general was displeased: "Adams, where are the other personnel of this unit? It certainly does not look like a battalion to me."

The major explained that some of her troops were missing because they were resting. The unit worked around the clock, in three eight-hour shifts, to ensure that the mail was processed as quickly as possible.

> ***They did not send us because they thought we could do it. We are here because they are sure we cannot.***
>
> —***Major Charity Adams Earley***

The general was unimpressed and issued a threat.

"I'm going to send a white first lieutenant down here to show you how to run this unit," he shouted.

Major Adams didn't hold back. Her reaction was swift and fearless: "Over my dead body, sir."

The general walked away, saying, "You'll hear from me, Adams."[7]

He put Major Adams up for a court-martial but later dropped it. He would ultimately apologize.[8]

Not only was she not punished, she was promoted to lieutenant colonel in 1945, making her the highest-ranking Black woman in the army by the end of World War II.

The Six Triple Eight was so efficient in England that in May 1945 the unit was sent on another critical assignment, this time in France. One of the women assigned to the mission recalled, "The mail had been held up for months. . . . There was mail that was two or three years old."[9] Once again, they completed the assignment ahead of schedule, this time in just five months! As Margaret Thatcher famously said, "If you want something done, ask a woman."

Despite their invaluable contributions, the Six Triple Eight received no public recognition upon their return to the United States.

"We served our country proudly, and we did a good job," said 6888th member Mary Crawford Ragland. "When we came back, though, there were no parades, there were no speeches. . . . They gave us our papers discharging us and sent us on our way." (Just like the Hello Girls in World War I.)

As Six Triple Eight member Anna Tarryk put it: "We had to fight the war on three fronts: first we had to fight segregation, second was the war, and third were the men."[10]

It wasn't until April 29, 2025, when the 6888th Central Postal Directory Battalion was awarded the Congressional Gold Medal, the nation's highest civilian honor, that the women finally got their due. Sadly, only two members of the battalion were still alive at the time.

We had to fight the war on three fronts: first we had to fight segregation, second was the war, and third were the men.

—Anna Tarryk

In a moving ceremony at Emancipation Hall in the U.S. Capitol, Speaker of the House Mike Johnson described the honor as "reserved for those whose courage and service shaped our country and our nation's story," calling the battalion "valiant members of our Greatest Generation" who were "loyal to a nation that, for far too long, failed to return that favor."[11]

Representative Gwen Moore, who co-sponsored the bill to award the Congressional Gold Medal, called the women "unsung sheroes" who "did it because they were patriotic, not because they thought that they would ever get any recognition." She quoted a *New York Times* reporter: "The Six Triple Eight was an experiment—a pass-fail test to determine the value Black women brought to the military."

There's no doubt they passed with flying colors, and at long last, the nation has remembered. The women of the Six Triple Eight delivered more than mail—they delivered morale, hope, and a reminder of what it means to blaze a trail with courage and conviction.

30.

The New Orleans Four: *The Barrier Breakers*

It was not until eleventh grade that Tessie Prevost Williams discovered that her first day of first grade was an event with national implications and that she had been part of something bigger than her personal experience. Her history teacher assigned everyone a subject to study, and hers was *Brown v. Board of Education* (1954). It was only then that she realized that she was in the history books.

When she told her teacher that she had come across her own name, he was not surprised. "I know who you are," he told her. "Every teacher in this school knows who you are, and we know what you did." That day, she went home and asked her parents what her teacher meant. They showed her letters from Eleanor Roosevelt and pictures of the family with Thurgood Marshall, the lawyer who argued *Brown v. Board of Education* before the Supreme Court.[1]

What Tessie learned was that in 1960, she was one of four six-year-old girls, called the New Orleans Four, who helped force desegregation. Leona Tate, Gail Etienne, and Tessie Prevost desegregated McDonogh 19 Elementary School, while Ruby Bridges desegregated William Frantz Elementary School a few blocks away. Together, they made history.

Although segregation was declared illegal in public schools in 1954, many states in the Deep South lived by Jim Crow laws and had no intention of complying with federal law. The White Citizens' Council was one of the most powerful local segregationist groups created in the South after *Brown v. Board of Education.* The council presented a petition signed by fifteen thousand people to the Orleans Parish Board, warning of the consequences of school integration.[2]

The White Citizens' Council was described by Martin Luther King, Jr., as "a modern Ku Klux Klan."[3] There were hundreds of chapters and thousands of members throughout the South. "They must be held responsible for all of the terror, the mob rule, and brutal murders that have encompassed the South over the last several years," King said in 1956.[4]

That same year—1956—New Orleans schools were ordered by a federal court to desegregate "with all deliberate speed." But time passed, and nothing changed. When desegregation was finally set to begin in 1960, the school board required kindergartners to undergo psychological and academic testing to determine if they could "qualify" to attend all-white schools. Out of about 135 tested, only six met the board's criteria and four of them enrolled at white schools.[5] Tessie was one of the few selected.

On the morning of November 14, 1960, the girls were escorted by federal marshals into the all-white schools. They were forced to walk past protesters chanting "Five, six, seven, eight, we don't want to integrate." Gail Etienne remembered thinking the protesters would kill her if they could.

Tessie Prevost Williams, pictured at six years old, when she became one of four Black students to integrate New Orleans's public schools

"My daddy told me in the car he said, 'Look straight ahead, take my hand, and I'm here,'" Tessie Prevost Williams recalled. "For some reason, I just wasn't afraid."[6]

By 9:25 a.m., the first two public elementary schools in New Orleans were integrated. However, every single white student left McDonogh 19. For the rest of the year, there were only three students in the entire school—Tessie, Gail, and Leona.

Protesters continued to gather outside even when there were no white students there. For security, brown paper covered classroom windows, preventing outsiders from peering in. Instead of recess on the playground, the girls had to stay indoors and play under a stairwell—it was too dangerous to be outside.[7]

The way we were prepared was not to do anything alone. Whatever we did, we had to do it with the three of us.

—Leona Tate

Dorothy Prevost, Tessie's mother, recalled the mornings when marshals would pick up her young daughter to go to school.

"I'd be crying," she said. "My oldest child. Scared . . . I used to pray every morning when that baby would leave." One of the marshals, seeing her fear, reassured her. "This child is in my hands. Nothing will happen to this child." He advised Tessie to look straight ahead as she walked into the school. "Don't care what they say. Just go ahead on."[8]

Tessie Prevost Williams fondly remembered her first-grade teacher, Mrs. Meyers. "She was sweet, with a wonderful spirit," she recalled. "She made us feel safe and comfortable. She taught us our schoolwork and she taught us about love. I can't imagine how difficult that time was for her, a white woman raised in New Orleans, teaching Black children. At the end of each day, I went back to my family and community where everyone supported me. What about Mrs. Meyers? What kind of support did she have?"[9]

These girls were so young that at first, they had no idea why everyone was angry at them. "I was excited because I was coming to a new school," Leona Tate said, remembering that first day. "I was a little upset because just seeing that crowd out there, seeing the police on horseback holding the crowd back, I thought a Mardi Gras parade was coming. I knew a parade usually passed there and didn't know why I had to go to school when everyone else was at the parade."[10]

Thankfully, perhaps, the six-year-olds didn't internalize the harsh reality of the institutional racism they were facing. "I didn't pick up on the anger," Leona said of those first few days at McDonogh 19. "I'm kind of thinking I saw it and then I didn't see it. My mom had already told me to sit in the back of the seat of the car and don't put my face in the window."[11] But the girls drew strength from one another. "The way we were prepared was not to do anything alone," Leona recalled.

Leona Tate (front) and Gail Etienne are escorted by U.S. marshals out of McDonogh 19 Elementary School.

"Whatever we did, we had to do it with the three of us."[12] The three women called one another "sisters for life."

When they got to McDonogh 19, the three girls were told to bring their own food for lunch and their own water bottles. Eating school lunch and drinking water served in the cafeteria was simply too dangerous. What if an upset teacher or parent tried to poison their food or water? They also couldn't go near the windows because the angry mob could throw something and break the glass. Gail remembered how the adults outside looked at her. It looked, she said, "like they wanted to kill us."[13]

At home things were only marginally better. Police were stationed outside their houses. At night officers walked around the perimeter of their homes and shined lights in their yards so that no one would try to break in. Once the police pulled someone over who kept driving by Gail Etienne's house. They found a gun in the trunk.[14]

Two years after starting at McDonogh, the three girls were transferred to T. J. Semmes School in a predominantly white neighborhood. The marshals no longer escorted them to school, and with that, the treatment by their peers and teachers got worse.

"The white teachers and students did not want us there," Tessie said. "Every day there were beatings and cursing. They spat on us and ripped off our clothes."[15]

After sixth grade, Tessie told her father she'd had enough and wanted to leave her predominantly white school. When she finally left, she said, "I was like a bird set out of a cage."[16]

It's important to learn the history of the three girls who desegregated McDonogh 19 Elementary School because their bravery has been overlooked for too long. Most people only know one student from this era, if they know the story at all—Ruby Bridges.

People are familiar with Ruby Bridges's story because of Norman Rockwell's 1964 painting *The Problem We All Live With.* The artwork depicts a small girl dressed in all white, escorted by four deputy U.S. marshals as violent protests rage around her. The racial slur "nigger" and the letters *KKK* are written on the wall behind her. It's a powerful work of art that became iconic.

Ruby was all alone when she arrived at William Frantz Elementary, another school in New Orleans's Ninth Ward. Ruby vividly remembers her first day at that school, when she was escorted by U.S. marshals. Once she got past the crowd of angry white protesters, she was led straight to the principal's office. "The crowd that was outside, they immediately rushed in behind me," she recalled. "They started to run into every class, and they took every child out of school. So, by the end of that day, 500 kids . . . were taken out."[17] She spent her first day alone in the principal's office. *How incredibly sad.* But these little girls, and their parents, felt a higher calling.

Recognizing Leona Tate, Tessie Prevost, and Gail Etienne alongside Ruby Bridges is crucial for telling the complete and accurate story of New Orleans school desegregation. "People seem to have forgotten that it was the New Orleans Four and I'm glad that is finally coming out. It's taken 61 years to do it, but thank God the whole story will be told; the good and the bad," Gail said.[18]

Their collective experience demonstrates that this historic moment was because of the bravery of four six-year-olds who together broke down the barriers of segregation. Acknowledging all four ensures that history reflects the full scope of courage required and honors each child who risked her safety to advance civil rights for future students.

The New Orleans Four were the tip of the spear. By 1970, just a decade after they entered McDonogh 19 Elementary and William Frantz Elementary, more than 70 percent of public school students in New Orleans were Black. That's partially because the Black population in New Orleans grew and many middle-class white families left for the suburbs.[19] But what these four girls did had a ripple effect and helped the South become much more integrated. In fact, by 1988, 44 percent of Black students in the South went to schools that were predominantly white.[20] (The number of Black students who attend schools with a mostly white student body has dropped significantly since then, however.)

On the sixtieth anniversary of school desegregation, Alanah Odoms Hebert, executive director of the American Civil Liberties Union of Louisiana, said, "Black girls and black women have always shouldered the immense responsibility of perfecting our democracy. The New Orleans Four were emissaries of justice and freedom, turning the tide of hate in this nation and calling us towards the liberties enshrined in the United States Constitution."[21]

It opened up doors, opportunities for other people. Somebody had to make the sacrifice.

—Gail Etienne

November 14 is now New Orleans Four Day in the city. When asked if they would endure that fear and violence again, all three women who went to McDonogh said they would. "It opened up doors, opportunities for other people," said Gail Etienne. "Somebody had to make the sacrifice."[22]

Ruby Bridges and her family made a tremendous sacrifice. Her mother, Lucille, lost her job, and when her father, Abon, also lost his job, he was warned by the NAACP that it might be too risky for him to look for a new one right away. "I'm the oldest of eight, and at that point he was no longer able to provide for his family," Ruby recalled, "so they were solely dependent on donations and people that would help them."[23] Her parents eventually separated under the emotional and financial strain. But even as she faced many hard times in her life, Ruby remained triumphant. By the time she went to high school, her school had been desegregated for a little less than a decade. After she graduated, she left Louisiana and traveled the world for several years.

She returned to Louisiana and helped raise her brother's four daughters after he was murdered in New Orleans in 1993. Her nieces joined her own large family; she and her husband had four sons. She never stopped being a civil rights activist. In 1999 she set up her own anti-racism foundation with proceeds from a book written about her life. Incredibly, Ruby's nieces went to William Frantz Elementary. When she saw that the school didn't have after-school programs in the arts, she worked to bring programs there herself, a full-circle moment. The place that had once made her feel so alone was now the recipient of her beneficence.

After Hurricane Katrina damaged the school, plans were put in place to demolish it. Ruby would not let that happen. The school symbolized the fight for desegregation. She made sure that William Frantz Elementary was placed on the National Register of Historic Places so that it could be restored and preserved. She's written several books about her life experience, and she's become an icon in American history.

The McDonogh three have also thrived. And, like Ruby, they've helped the school they desegregated survive. After Hurricane Katrina, Leona Tate's foundation bought McDonogh 19 Elementary and transformed the building into an educational center. They named it the TEP Center—after the first initial of each girl's last name. The school opened in 2022 and teaches people about the Civil Rights Movement. The classroom where these girls made history exists today and is a testament to the loneliness they faced and the courage they showed the world.

When they got older, Tessa, Gail, and Leona shared their experience through speaking engagements. After one presentation in Baton Rouge, a white man approached them and confessed, "I was one of the students who taunted you. I spat on you and called you names." He continued, "Can you forgive me and shake my hand?"

The women responded in unison: "No. We won't give you a handshake, but we will give you a hug." *That's true grace.*

In July 2024, more than sixty years after she bravely walked into a schoolhouse as a young girl, Tessie Prevost Williams was honored in death with the dignity she had been denied. Her flag-draped casket lay in state at Gallier Hall, where mourners gathered to pay tribute to her. In a poignant echo of 1960, the U.S. marshals—the agency which had once shielded her and the other girls from angry mobs—again escorted her in a ceremonial procession. This final act was more than a funeral; it was a symbolic recognition that Tessie's courage had helped move the nation closer to its promise of equality.

Just six weeks later, at the Democratic National Convention, Oprah Winfrey paid tribute, calling it the "grace and guts" of women like Tessie Prevost Williams that helped pave the way for Vice President Kamala Harris. As a young girl, Harris became part of the second class to integrate Berkeley public schools in California.

Tessie's story is a reminder that she, together with Leona Tate, Gail Etienne, and Ruby Bridges, proved that in standing tall, even little girls can help bend the arc of history.

31.

Romana Acosta Bañuelos: *The Treasurer*

Romana Bañuelos's life embodied the promise of the American dream, as well as the overwhelming challenges many people overcome to achieve it. There is nothing in Romana's early life story to indicate that one day she would be sitting in the Oval Office with the president of the United States. Quite the opposite. Born in 1925 to Mexican immigrant parents in a dusty Arizona mining town, Romana was just seven when, in the midst of the Great Depression, U.S. authorities deported her family, even though she was an American citizen.[1]

Yet in 1971, President Richard Nixon appointed Romana as U.S. Treasurer—making her the first Latina to hold a senior U.S. government post. President Nixon later told her that she was "one of the finest appointments" that he made.[2] Her signature appeared on every bill printed during her tenure, joining the faces of America's founders on the very currency that fuels our economy.

After being deported, Romana's family moved to Sonora, Mexico, where her parents worked on a ranch. In Mexico, Romana helped sell her mother's empanadas to local bakeries and restaurants to make extra money.[3] "My mother was the type of woman that taught us how to live in any place and work with what we have," Romana later said.[4]

Romana only had a middle school education, but when she returned to the United States—a young, divorced mother with two children and little more than determination—she built a successful tortilla business from her modest $400 savings.[5] That humble operation grew into Ramona's Mexican Food Products, a multimillion-dollar enterprise that still thrives today.[6]

When a group of businessmen asked her husband if he wanted to help create a bank specifically to help the Latino community, he told them to talk to his wife. She was the more business-minded of the two. But the men were reluctant to do business with a woman. "You don't know my wife," he said. "Once you meet her, you will forget I ever existed."[7] That led Romana to become one of the co-founders of the Pan American National Bank in East Los Angeles, designed to serve a Latino community often shut out of mainstream banking.

As they set out to open the bank, the founders faced pushback. A representative of the Federal Deposit Insurance Corporation (FDIC) doubted the project, saying, "Be sure to recommend to those people that want to build a bank to build it more or less like a supermarket because they're not going to last even six months."[8]

By 1969, Romana was chairperson of the bank's board of directors. By 1979, the bank had deposits of almost $40 million.[9]

Romana encouraged Mexican Americans to make deposits, apply for loans, and trust the financial system—opening doors to home ownership and business creation. It was the oldest Latino-owned bank in California until it was sold in 2016.[10]

Her work at the bank caught the attention of Washington. By the time she was nominated as U.S. Treasurer, Romana was known as a gifted entrepreneur and a shrewd businesswoman, inspiring a generation of Latinas to envision themselves in positions of leadership.

President Nixon had other reasons for wanting her in the job. He had performed poorly with Latino voters in the 1968 election and saw the nomination of a Latina as a way to strengthen his chances in 1972.[11] He also wanted to appeal to women voters; 1970 marked the fiftieth anniversary of the Nineteenth Amendment, and he had already appointed 105 women to important government posts during his first term.[12]

When asked to submit her name, Romana hesitated. She didn't know the job and doubted her chances. In fact, she thought it was a joke, telling her husband: "Alejandro, maybe these guys are kidding. Maybe they need a loan."[13] He encouraged her to try—and after weeks of phone calls with staff at the White House, President Nixon chose her out of dozens of other women he was considering.

The honor came at a cost. Just after she was nominated, her business was raided by U.S. immigration agents, who found undocumented immigrants on the payroll. The raid made national news. At her confirmation hearing, Senate Finance Committee Chairman Russell B. Long called the case "unfortunate" and noted it had drawn an unusually high number of letters—most opposing her.[14] Romana testified that she did not know that the workers were undocumented and that it was an "attempt by Democrats to block my nomination."[15] A Senate investigation later concluded she had been caught up in a broader effort to embarrass the Nixon administration. Nevertheless, on December 17, 1971, she was sworn in as treasurer, becoming the highest-ranking Mexican American in government.

The treasurer of the United States is the second-oldest post in the U.S. government, right behind the president of the United States; it is older than the Treasury Department itself.[16] The job was created to help fund the Revolutionary War, and the treasurer today reports to the treasury secretary and oversees the Bureau of Engraving and Printing, which produces bills, and the U.S. Mint, which makes coins. They are also a key liaison with the Federal Reserve.[17] This is one of the rare positions in government traditionally held by a woman: Between 1949 and 2025, seventeen women have served in the role.[18] The treasurer's signature is on the currency, which must have been validating for Romana, who has been described as an "enthusiastic numismatist"—someone who collects currency.[19]

Romana's success is even more striking given the barriers Latina women face. They are a vital part of the workforce yet remain underrepresented in leadership roles and high-paying fields. The wage gap for Latinas is among the widest of any demographic, and Latinas are promoted to management far less often than men.[20] Though Latinas make up 8 percent of the U.S. population, they hold just a fraction of jobs in fields like engineering, science, and medicine—proof of the systemic hurdles Romana had to overcome.[21]

Romana Acosta Bañuelos meets with President Richard Nixon and Treasury Secretary John Connally in the Oval Office on the day she was announced as the nominee for United States Treasurer.

Even in the nation's capital, Romana was constantly underestimated. Shortly after she was named treasurer, during a White House budget meeting, a man asked for a calculation. Romana quickly gave the answer—but none of the men in the room believed she could possibly be correct. They didn't even look her way. An economist pulled out a calculator, ran the numbers, and finally announced, "Mrs. Acosta Bañuelos is right." Everyone was stunned. Afterward, her boss, Treasury Secretary John Connally, asked how she had done it so fast without a calculator. Romana, who hadn't gone to school beyond sixth grade, replied simply: "In Mexico, we learned to do numbers in our head."[22]

During her tenure as U.S. Treasurer, she was outraged to find applications from minorities that had been pushed to the bottom of the résumé pile. She tried to create a more diverse workforce. Romana worked hard and she drove her staff hard too. Some of her assistants complained to Secretary Connally about her work style. He joked, "By God, you mean to tell me she's actually working?"[23] She was trying to run the place efficiently like a business, something Washington wasn't known for.

In 1974, she left her post as treasurer and went back to running Ramona's Mexican Food Products. The company she founded is still in her family and does millions of dollars in business every year.[24]

Her family gave back to the country they loved. Romana established a scholarship program to help Mexican American high school graduates pursue a college education. Both of her sons served in the Los Angeles County Sheriff's Department. One son, Carlos A. Torres, was a Marine in Vietnam and was honored with a Purple Heart for his service.[25]

Romana not only built financial security for her family, but she also created an environment in which an immigrant with limited education could succeed in multiple arenas. In 1976, the American Bicentennial Research Institute included her in the Library of Human Resources because of her historic contribution to the country. Romana passed away on January 15, 2018, when she was ninety-two years old. She left behind a daughter, a son, and twelve grandchildren.[26]

After her passing, her family honored her memory: "She was a tough taskmaster, demanding the best and then more from us. She made us better people, she forced people to grow beyond their own expectations. She had a wicked sense of humor that ambushed you just when you thought she wasn't human."[27]

Thirty-five years later, Rosa "Rosie" Rios would pick up that mantle. Nominated by President Barack Obama in 2009, Rios became the first Latina treasurer appointed by a Democratic president. Her signature appears on an astounding $1.8 trillion worth of U.S. currency. Rosie is the chair of America250, the nonpartisan group working to mark the country's semiquincentennial.

President Donald Trump's nomination, during his first term, of Jovita Carranza for U.S. Treasurer, continued a decades-long tradition, begun in the Nixon era, of presidents appointing Latinas to this historic post. Carranza became the fourth Latina in a row—and the seventh overall—to serve as treasurer, following a line that started with Romana Acosta Bañuelos (Nixon) and continued with Katherine Dávalos Ortega (Reagan and George H. W. Bush), Catalina Vasquez Villalpando (George H. W. Bush), Rosario Marin (George W. Bush), Anna Escobedo Cabral (George W. Bush), and Rosa Gumataotao Rios (Obama). Each of their signatures has appeared on U.S. currency, a visible mark of Latina leadership at the heart of the nation's financial system—and a reminder that for more than half a century, Latinas have helped safeguard the nation's money.

As America marks 250 years since the Declaration of Independence, the stories of Bañuelos, Rios, and their fellow Latina treasurers challenge us to ensure that the story of America includes every face that helped build it.

32.

Babe Didrikson: *"The Greatest Athlete Who Ever Lived"*

In the early 1930s, a New York newspaper reporter had an innocent question for Babe Didrikson. At least that was what they thought. Babe was only nineteen years old at the time, but she was already famous—and outspoken. She was known around the country as a championship basketball player and as a double gold and silver medalist in track and field at the 1932 Los Angeles Olympics. "I'm told you also swim, shoot, ride, row, box, and play tennis, golf, basketball, football, polo and billiards," the reporter said. "Is there anything at all you don't play?" Babe cut to the chase. "Yeah," she replied, "dolls."[1]

> ***The formula for success is simple. Practice and concentration, then more practice and more concentration.***
>
> —***Babe Didrikson***

It was quintessential Babe: bold, some might even say brash. Babe hadn't gotten the nickname "Wonder Girl" for nothing. Known for her unmatched confidence and Texas-sized ego, she would stride into a locker room and announce, "What'd y'all show up for? See who's gonna finish second?"[2] To Babe, any game worth playing was a game worth winning.

Thanks in large part to Babe, the idea of women excelling in sports is now widely accepted. But when she was growing up in southeastern Texas, Babe was an aberration. When she was a young teenager she would declare to anyone who would listen that she would one day be known as "the greatest athlete of all time."[3] She didn't qualify it as the greatest "female" athlete, because even as a young girl she understood that she had the talent to break barriers. She could beat the boys, if they'd only let her try.

Mildred Ella "Babe" Didrikson was born in 1911 and grew up in Beaumont, Texas. One of seven children, she was sporty from the start. She left high school to work for a company with a basketball team.[4] (Yes, a company had a nationally competitive basketball team. Employers Casualty Insurance's team was called the Golden Cyclones.)

When she read about the 1928 Olympics, she set her sights on competing in track and field at the next games. She practiced every day with her sister by jumping hedges in their town.[5] And sure enough, she made it. "The formula for success is simple," she said. "Practice and concentration, then more practice and more concentration."[6]

Babe Didrikson shoots a basketball with other members of the Brooklyn Yankees.

She qualified for five Olympic events, but because of regulations limiting women to only compete in three, she had to choose.[7] At the 1932 Los Angeles Olympics, Babe shattered records with an unprecedented medal haul.

Babe Didrikson pitches for the minor league New Orleans Pelicans against the Cleveland Indians.

Her dominance remains unmatched. Following the Olympics, she toured with the Babe Didrikson All-Stars basketball team and even pitched in three Major League Baseball exhibition games.

She acted as her own publicist from the start of her career. Long before Muhammad Ali declared "I am the greatest!" Babe was building her own legend, intimidating rivals, and captivating the press. She exaggerated certain details of her life, claiming, for instance, that she earned the nickname Babe after hitting five home runs in a single baseball game as a child. It is true that her Norwegian parents called her "bebe" during her early years, but the nickname Babe stuck, linking her forever to Babe Ruth.[8]

When I wanta really bust one, I just loosen my girdle and let 'er fly.

—Babe Didrikson

While many people may not know her name, America's top athletes certainly do. Jackie Joyner-Kersee, named *Sports Illustrated*'s greatest female athlete of the twentieth century, was inspired by Babe. "She was able to show that if she wanted to be a superstar in basketball, she could. If she wanted to be a superstar in golf,

Babe Didrikson competes in the Women's National Track Championships in Jersey City.

she was. If she wanted to be a superstar in track and field, it didn't matter."[9]

In 1935, she found her true calling: golf. She competed in and won her first tournament. She loved to tease onlookers, saying, "When I wanta really bust one, I just loosen my girdle and let 'er fly."[10]

A few years later, she became the first woman to compete in a PGA Tour tournament. Babe went on to become the most accomplished female golfer of her time. She was the first person—man or woman, just as she had predicted—to win thirteen consecutive tournaments. The Associated Press named her Female Athlete of the Year six times between 1932 and 1954.[11]

She made it possible for other female golfers to make money as professional athletes—even though her intended goal was mostly about making money for herself.[12] She teamed up with golfer Patty Berg to co-found the Ladies Professional Golf Association (LPGA). Except for that first year, when Patty was president, Babe was the president for the rest of her life. In her last years as a professional athlete, she was said to be making $100,000 a year from tournaments and endorsement deals. That's equal to more than a million dollars today.

Incredibly, in 1950, she completed the Grand Slam by winning all three major women's golf championships, the same year she co-founded the LPGA.[13]

As ESPN once put it, Babe Didrikson was a "woman ahead of her time," but she was not without her critics.

Sportswriter Joe Williams once remarked, "It would be much better if she and her ilk stayed at home, got themselves prettied up and waited for the phone to ring." Commentators frequently criticized her appearance, describing her as "mannish."[14]

Babe embraced her athletic persona but also tried to conform to societal expectations. In her 1955 memoir, *This Life I've Led,* she wrote about boyfriends, cooking, and sewing to perhaps appear more acceptable—though much of this was exaggerated or untrue. She understood that her muscular build and competitive swagger challenged

Babe Didrikson competes in her first major tournament against men at the 1936 "$1500 Southern California Open Golf Tournament."

conventional femininity.[15] Babe and the famous wrestler George Zaharias were frequent golf partners, and they got married in 1938. Their marriage was far from happy, but Babe felt societal pressure to present herself as a married woman. She often insisted on being referred to as Mrs. Zaharias, even though she was famous in her own right well before then.

The elite golf community was initially reluctant to embrace her, but her jaw-dropping talent forced them to acknowledge her impact. In 1947, the *Saturday Evening Post* declared, "Not much has been made of the undeniable fact that the Babe has revolutionized the feminine approach to golf." Another writer wrote, "Babe Zaharias created big-time women's golf. . . . Her booming power game lowered scores and forced others to imitate her."[16]

By 1950, she had won every major title available to women. In 1953, when she was still competing, she was diagnosed with colon cancer. At a time when cancer was considered taboo, she was the first prominent U.S. athlete to openly discuss her diagnosis. Babe spoke often about her illness, raising money for medical research and helping to reduce the stigma surrounding the disease. Despite surgery to remove a tumor, she made a remarkable return to golf, winning the U.S. Women's Open in 1954 by twelve strokes, while wearing a colostomy bag. *I am in awe of her grit.*

"I've had over 15,000 letters from people, and this victory is an answer to them," she said after she won. "It will show a lot of people that they need not be afraid of an operation and can go on and live a normal life."[17]

Throughout her battle with cancer, Babe was supported by her close friend and fellow golfer Betty Dodd. Although Babe rarely mentioned Betty in her memoir, perhaps because of rumors about their relationship, those who knew them recognized their deep bond. Whether their relationship was romantic remains unknown, but their connection was undeniable.[18]

Despite her great comeback, her cancer had spread, and Babe

Didrikson Zaharias passed away in Galveston, Texas, in 1956 at just forty-five years old.

President Dwight D. Eisenhower paid tribute to her at a press conference, saying, "She was a woman who, in her athletic career, certainly won the admiration of every person in the United States, all sports people all over the world, and in her gallant fight against cancer, she put up one of the kind of fights that inspired us all. . . . I think that every one of us feels sad that finally she had to lose this last one of all her battles."[19]

33.

Patsy Mink: *The Mother of Title IX*

Kathrine Switzer was a twenty-year-old Syracuse University junior when she showed up to run the Boston Marathon in 1967. Women were not allowed to officially run the marathon, so when Kathrine registered, she used her initials, K. V. Switzer, so as not to raise any alarm bells. All was fine until mile four, Kathrine recalled, when she heard horns honking and someone yelling, "Get over, runners move to your right!" A large flatbed truck pulled up next to the runners and forced them over to the side of the road. Behind the truck was a press bus crammed with cameramen trying to get photos. The photographers had no idea what an astounding moment they were about to witness.

Suddenly, out of nowhere, Jock Semple, a Boston Marathon official, jumped off the truck. He ran up to Kathrine, wagging his finger at her. Then he grabbed her shoulder and yelled—with a menacing scowl on his face—"Get the hell out of my race and give me those numbers!" He held on to the back of her sweatshirt and tried grabbing at the numbers on the front of her shirt. Kathrine was terrified. "The physical power and swiftness of the attack stunned me," she recalled. Luckily her boyfriend, who was also running the marathon, pushed Semple hard, and Kathrine managed to finish the race. It wasn't until she saw the story everywhere in the news that she knew it was a turning point in her life.[1]

Five years later, women were officially allowed to run in the Boston Marathon. The experience turned Kathrine into a fighter on behalf

A Boston Marathon race official confronted Kathrine Switzer and tried to remove her from the race in April 1967. She got away and became the first woman to officially run the world's oldest annual marathon.

of female runners. She says her biggest "life victory" was her part in getting the women's marathon added to the Olympic Games in 1984.[2]

Women like Kathrine Switzer and Babe Didrikson would not have had to fight so hard if Title IX—the federal law ensuring equal access to sports for women in schools receiving federal funding—had existed earlier. The law had broad implications. It completely changed the limitations placed on women in sports while expanding women's access to scholarships and providing a crucial framework for reporting sexual harassment and violence on campus.

Title IX was championed by the remarkable Representative Patsy Mink. The congresswoman played such a pivotal role in the legislation that when she passed away in 2002, the law was renamed the Patsy T. Mink Equal Opportunity in Education Act in her honor. She was posthumously awarded the Presidential Medal of Freedom for her groundbreaking work.

Patsy Matsu Takemoto Mink was a pioneer from the start, making history as the first woman of color and the first Asian American woman to serve in the U.S. Congress. During her career, she became a fierce advocate for gender and racial equality.

"I realized that . . . because women were not in politics, and because there were only eight women at the time who were members of Congress, that I had a special burden to bear to speak for them," she reflected. "They didn't have people who could express their concerns for them adequately."[3]

Born in Paia, Hawaii, in 1927—before Hawaii became a U.S. state—Patsy demonstrated leadership early, winning the election for high school class president. She was pre-med at the University of Hawaii, graduating in 1948. However, she was denied entry into medical school, and some of the schools explicitly told her it was because she was a woman![4]

She pivoted to law, earning her degree from the University of Chicago in 1951 as one of two women in her class. Later she would reflect on the irony of her admission: "I got into my law school on the grounds that they considered me a foreigner." Of course, she had lived in U.S. territory for her entire life.[5] Her family, of Japanese background, had lived on Maui for three generations. Their path to citizenship had been a difficult one. Patsy was fourteen years old when the Japanese bombed Pearl Harbor. Not long after that, her father, a civil engineer, was held overnight and questioned, as were many other Japanese Americans. She never forgot the sight of him burning Japanese family heirlooms when he returned.

"It made me realize that one could not take citizenship and the promise of the U.S. Constitution for granted," she said later.[6] What did it mean to be an American citizen? What kind of protections did it offer? Patsy's grandparents had been classified as "aliens ineligible for citizenship." It wasn't until 1952 that Japanese and other Asian immigrants were permitted to become U.S. citizens. Though

Mink herself was a citizen by birth, she carried the weight of those exclusionary policies throughout her career. She knew what it felt like to be an outsider. After law school, she married and had a child but struggled to find employment; law firms assumed that she couldn't handle the stress and long hours. Undeterred, she became the first Japanese American woman to practice law in Hawaii.

> ***Our country is now in a position where it can no longer afford to rely on the antediluvian notion that men should rule the world. We need women; their abilities and talents must be fully utilized.***
>
> ***—Patsy Mink***

When Hawaii achieved statehood in 1959, Mink ran for Congress but lost. She didn't give up, remaining active in politics. In 1964, she made history by winning a seat in the U.S. House of Representatives. In 1972, she ran for president, making her the first Asian American woman to run for the highest office in the country. She lost but used her campaign to bring attention to the anti–Vietnam War movement. She would also lose a race for the U.S. Senate but would return to the House, where she cemented her legacy. She dedicated her twelve terms in Congress to advancing racial and gender equality, particularly in education.

In the 1940s and 1950s, societal expectations largely limited women's career options to narrow roles, including secretaries, nurses, or teachers. Patsy considered these limitations unfair, not just to women but to the entire country. She argued, "Our country is now in a position where it can no longer afford to rely on the antediluvian notion that men should rule the world. We need women; their abilities and talents must be fully utilized."[7] It was her strong and persistent advocacy that led to the passage of Title IX, which President Richard Nixon signed into law on June 23, 1972.

Prior to Title IX, fewer than 300,000 girls played high school sports, accounting for just 7 percent of all high school athletes.[8] By the 2024 school year, that number had surged to 3.5 million, or 42.8 percent of all high school athletes.[9] This isn't surprising; my mom told me she never had the chance to play sports like basketball, and that was why she made sure my sister and I took advantage of school athletics.

Patsy was also a strong supporter of the Equal Rights Amendment (ERA), a proposed constitutional amendment that would eliminate sex discrimination. First introduced in Congress in 1923 by Susan B. Anthony's nephew, Daniel Read Anthony, Jr., the ERA languished in obscurity until the 1970s, when more women entered politics.[10]

When Patsy was in Washington, very few women served in Congress—and in many cases they banded together. Recognizing the importance of collective action, Patsy worked alongside Representatives Shirley Chisholm and Martha Griffiths to push the ERA forward. It passed Congress in 1972 but failed to meet the required state ratifications before the imposed deadline. The amendment has never been added to the Constitution.

Of the 535 lawmakers in the House of Representatives and the U.S. Senate, only thirteen members of the 89th Congress (1965–1967) were women. Twelve of them are pictured here, including Patsy Mink (back row, fourth from the left).

Women's political views are as diverse as men's, and the battle over the ERA underscored these divisions. Conservative activist and lawyer Phyllis Schlafly led the STOP ERA campaign, arguing that the amendment would eliminate protective laws for women and pave the way for unrestricted abortion access.

"The Equal Rights Amendment is a 'terminal case,'" Schlafly declared in 1973. "The only question remaining is whether its sponsors will let it die peacefully, and with dignity, or whether they will engage in massive bloodletting in a vain attempt to save their offspring."[11]

Despite widespread public support—including endorsements from current, former, and future First Ladies Patricia Nixon, Lady Bird Johnson, Betty Ford, and Rosalynn Carter—the ERA ultimately failed to overcome Schlafly's determined opposition.[12]

However, a young lawyer named Ruth Bader Ginsburg saw another path forward. Before becoming a Supreme Court justice and feminist icon, Ginsburg represented Sally Reed in the landmark Supreme Court case *Reed v. Reed* (1971). The case challenged an Idaho law that automatically granted men preference over women in estate administration. Sally Reed was a divorced single mother who said that she should be able to administer her dead son's estate and not her ex-husband. The Court ruled unanimously in Sally Reed's favor, marking the first time the Equal Protection Clause of the Fourteenth Amendment was applied to gender discrimination. The decision laid the foundation for future gender rulings.

She taught me change might be slow, but change is going to happen.

—Wendy Mink

"Sally Reed thought that this law was not just, and, this is the most remarkable thing, she had faith in the legal system of the United States to right the wrong that she thought had been done to her," Ginsburg wrote in her brief on behalf of her client. "So, when this case was going to the trial court, the appeals court, the Supreme Court in the state of Idaho, people were noticing it, and thinking, 'This is the case that will

Congresswoman Patsy Mink (D-HI) speaks at a press conference introducing legislation on gender equity in education.

enable the Supreme Court to understand the pernicious effects of making laws on the assumption that women are this way and men are that way.' And that prediction proved correct."[13]

The debate over the ERA continues today, and there's no doubt in my mind that Patsy would want the battle to persist.

After a thirteen-year break from Congress, when she pursued higher office, Patsy was re-elected to the U.S. House of Representatives in 1990. "I am astonished to find that," she said, "we are still debating the question of what equality really means in this country."[14]

In September 2002, Patsy Mink passed away in her beloved Honolulu, Hawaii. Because the next congressional election was just two months later, there was no time to change the ballots. She won by a landslide! Her longtime colleague Norman Mineta called her "an American hero, a leader and a trailblazer who made an irreplaceable mark in the fabric of our country."[15]

Patsy's daughter, Wendy, reflected on her mother's legacy: "I am the child of someone who made a huge difference for women and girls in education. She taught me change might be slow, but change is going to happen."[16]

34.

Pat Schroeder: *The Legislator*

When Representative Pat Schroeder joined the Armed Services Committee after she was elected to Congress in 1972, chairman F. Edward Hébert refused to acknowledge her appointment, insisting she share a chair with Representative Ron Dellums of California, the lone African American on the important committee.

"This is the worst thing that's ever happened. It's not even worth running for Congress anymore," Chairman Hébert screamed. "However, I still have the power to determine how many seats are at the dais, and these two people are only worth half of the rest of my Members, so they're getting one chair."[1] *Can you imagine?* The lone female and only Black member had to share a seat.

In the early 1970s, Pat was one of only fourteen women serving in the House of Representatives, and Dellums was one of fifteen Black members.[2] They were told to vote as one member. She later recalled they sat "cheek to cheek" through the meeting.

Pat Schroeder finally got her own chair on the Armed Services Committee dais. It was a seat she kept for all twenty-four years of her congressional career—long after Hébert had been forced out. He lost his chairmanship "in a revolt against seniority made possible by the votes of reform-minded freshman elected in the aftermath of Watergate."[3] She would use her record-breaking tenure as a woman in Congress to become the leading feminist legislator of her time, setting the standard for women who followed her into American politics.

Hébert's savage rudeness is only one example of the boys'-club an-

Representative Patricia Schroeder (D-CO)

tics Pat encountered in Congress. She found male members sunbathing pantsless on the Speaker's porch.[4] Another time, she heard some of the men joking with one another in the cloakroom: "Well, how about the abortion bill?" one congressman asked. "Yeah, I paid mine," said the other.[5]

My first job as a reporter was covering Congress for the newspaper *Roll Call.* At twenty-five years old, I would roam the halls of Congress and see firsthand how few women were serving and how none were in leadership roles. Pat had recently retired, but I immediately was captivated by the stories about this woman who embodied the famous Shirley Chisholm line: "If they don't give you a seat at the table, bring a folding chair." Her influence could still be felt as I walked the halls, especially when a women's restroom was installed in the House, something she joked was her greatest triumph.[6] She brought the statues of suffragists Lucretia Mott, Susan B. Anthony, and Elizabeth Cady Stanton out of the Capitol basement. When told the statues were "too ugly," she joked: "Look, if it's about ugliness, we're going to clear the Statue Hall out here. It's really bad."[7]

Interrogated many times on how she would balance motherhood and a career, she repeated her now-famous line: "I have a brain and a uterus and I use both."

With intelligence, humor, and moral clarity, she exposed hypocrisy and demanded change even as she faced unrelenting judgment about her dual roles as mother and congresswoman. "One of the problems with being a working mother, whether you're a Congresswoman or a stenographer or whatever, is that everybody feels perfectly free to come and tell you what they think: 'I think what you're doing to your children is terrible.' 'I think you should be home.' They don't do that to men."[8] *It is so true.*

Forty years later, a senior male at CBS News would ask me in a job interview, "How are you going to cover the White House as a reporter with three young children at home?" I could feel the blood rush up my neck into my face and I quickly shot back, "Do you ask men that question?"

I have a brain and a uterus and I use both.

—Pat Schroeder

Pat Schroeder was dubbed the "tart-tongued maverick" by *The Washington Post.*[9] She was first to call President Ronald Reagan the "Teflon president" because scandals never stuck to him. Of Vice President Dan Quayle, she quipped that he thought "Roe versus Wade are two ways to cross the Potomac."[10] When Colonel Oliver North listed her among the "25 most dangerous liberals," she wore it as a badge of honor: "I love the image of this big, strong Marine being terrified of me."[11]

She used humor in politics, but her work was no joke. Schroeder's over two-decades-long congressional career (1973–1997) transformed American policy on family issues, women's health research, and military family support. Her legislative priorities evolved from anti-war activism to comprehensive family policy reform, culminating in landmark achievements like the Family and Medical Leave Act of 1993, which became the first major legislation signed by President Bill Clinton. *If you've ever taken parental leave, you can thank Pat Schroeder.*

Born Patricia Nell Scott on July 30, 1940, in Portland, Oregon, Schroeder was raised to be fearless. Her pilot father taught her to "never frown at your enemies, always smile. It scares the hell out of them."[12] *I really love that.* She earned her pilot's license at age fifteen—and then used it to finance her education.

At the University of Minnesota, she operated her own flying service, working as an insurance claims adjuster and flying out to assess damage at airplane crash sites. *What a maverick!* Plus, she graduated magna cum laude and Phi Beta Kappa in just three years with a triple major in philosophy, history, and political science. She continued her aviation work to pay her way through Harvard Law School.

At Harvard (1961–1964), she was one of only fifteen women among over five hundred men in an environment she later described as "submerged in sexism." On her first day, the male student assigned to sit beside her refused, saying he'd "never gone to school with a girl and did not plan to start now." Professors instituted humiliating "Ladies' Days" to embarrass female students with cases designed to make them uncomfortable.

Another vivid example was a dinner thrown by the law school dean, Erwin Griswold, where all the women were called upon, one by one, to answer the dean's question, "Why are you at Harvard Law School, taking the place of a man?"[13] Pat was furious but not intimidated. Before she had a chance to answer, her classmate Ann Cronkhite Goldblatt said she'd come to Harvard because Yale turned her down. "It broke all the tension," Pat recalled, "but I thought, 'Why in the world are we playing this game?' "[14]

She married James Schroeder, a fellow law student who was supportive of her ambitions, during her second year. It was a bold choice when most people expected women to abandon careers upon marriage. Their relationship required navigating not just academic pressures but legal ones: They had to smuggle birth control pills into Massachusetts because contraceptives were illegal in the state.[15]

Never frown at your enemies, always smile. It scares the hell out of them.

—Pat Schroeder's Father

If Pat had been convicted of bringing contraception across state lines, she would not have been able to practice law. It was not until three years later that the Supreme Court ruled in *Griswold v. Connecticut* (1965) that married couples had the right to obtain contraceptives. "When I tell young women that story today," Pat wrote in her memoir, "they look at me like I rode to school on a pterodactyl."

After graduating from law school in 1964, the Schroeders moved to Denver, where she worked for the National Labor Relations Board and provided pro bono legal services to Planned Parenthood. When she had children (Scott in 1966, Jamie in 1970), no maternity leave was available, and she had to quit her job—a forced choice that would later drive her authorship of the Family and Medical Leave Act.

In 1972, at age thirty-two with two small children (ages two and six), she made the audacious decision to run for Congress as an anti-war Democrat. "Denver Housewife Announces for Congress" was the headline of a local newspaper.[16] Prominent feminist Gloria Steinem campaigned for Pat, but she had no party support. She ran her campaign from her basement and defeated a Republican incumbent in Nixon's landslide year—a political miracle that surprised even her.

Her inaugural legislative success was the Child Abuse Prevention and Treatment Act of 1974, which laid the foundation for her decades-long advocacy for children and families. Working alongside Senator Walter Mondale, Pat helped establish the National Center on Child Abuse and Neglect and secured federal funding for prevention programs.

Pat was also a co-founder of the Congressional Caucus for Women's Issues, a bipartisan coalition that fundamentally reshaped the policy landscape for women. Under her leadership, the caucus championed critical issues like economic equity, access to childcare, breast and cervical cancer research, and reproductive health. The caucus also worked to eliminate gender disparities in medical research at both the National Institutes of Health and the Department of Defense. It was Pat's leadership that led to the mandating of federally funded medical research on women.

While not the primary sponsor, Schroeder played a key advocacy role in the passage of the 1978 Pregnancy Discrimination Act, which amended Title VII of the Civil Rights Act to prohibit discrimination on the basis of pregnancy. She brought her voice, experience, and organizing power to help pass legislation that directly responded to the Supreme Court's *General Electric v. Gilbert* (1976) decision, which had allowed employers to deny disability benefits for pregnancy.

Pat Schroeder understood that women's rights weren't abstract policy debates—they were life-or-death issues. She was a fierce and consistent advocate for abortion rights and women's reproductive health, having nearly died in childbirth herself. One of her final bills before retirement was the Safe Motherhood Act—the first legislation to propose a national plan to reduce maternal mortality in the United States. Among the many bills she sponsored or championed were the Economic Equity Act, the Violence Against Women Act, and the Women's Health Equity Act. She was instrumental in the decision to allow women to fly combat missions in the military. Each of these victories came through relentless advocacy within an institution not designed for her or for the people she represented.

> ***I think women still should never kid themselves that they're going to come [to Congress] and be part of the team. And you ought to come here with a very clear definition of what it is you want to do, and that you will not be deterred.***
>
> —***Pat Schroeder***

Politically, Congresswoman Schroeder was a catalytic force. In 1991, she led the march of women members of Congress to the Senate chamber demanding that Anita Hill be allowed to testify in the Clarence Thomas confirmation hearings. That moment sparked public outrage, and the next year a record number of women were elected to Congress. Through it all, she endured frequent condescension and being called "Little Patsy." Sometimes her fellow congressmen just didn't get it. Pat remembered one pulling her aside in the cloakroom and saying, "If you take men out of this, I'll back you, but I want to tell you, don't leave men in here because the next thing you know my wife is going to want me to babysit."[17] Pat informed him that when a woman does it, it's called parenting, not babysitting.

In 1987, Pat had a moment when it felt as if she might get much further than her predecessors. Indeed, it felt as if she could upend the conventional wisdom and transform not just her party but her nation. After Gary Hart's presidential campaign collapsed, Pat Schroeder's exploratory campaign caught fire. Polls quickly identified her as one of the top contenders in the first primary of New Hampshire and the first caucus of Iowa—and a national survey for *Time* magazine eventually put her in third place.

But on September 29, 1987, Pat announced she would not seek the Democratic nomination because "winning would take a lot more preparation, time, and money than I had."[18]

"I cannot run a campaign that would let you down," she told several thousand supporters, many of whom were shocked by the deci-

Congresswoman Patricia Schroeder (D-CO) gets choked up as she announces she will not seek the 1988 Democratic presidential nomination. Her tears made headlines and upset some women who said that her crying set women back.

sion. When she explained that "I could not figure out how to run," she paused, overcome by emotion and unable to finish the sentence.

The media frenzy that followed illustrated the tricky terrain for female candidates who show emotion. "Women across the country reacted with embarrassment, sympathy and disgust," a reporter wrote in the *Chicago Tribune*, a week after the incident. Those seventeen seconds of tears would haunt her for decades. Many women activists charged that her emotional outburst seriously set back women's efforts to run for political office and compete on a par with men.

Pat titled a chapter in her autobiography "The Presidential Weep-Stakes," writing: "I went on with my speech, but it was my tears, not my words, that got the headlines. Those 17 seconds were treated like a total breakdown." She believed that emotion was not a liability but part of authentic leadership. "Of course I wept," she wrote. "There's no law against crying."

Pat Schroeder was a pioneer, retiring in 1996 as the longest-serving woman in the House at that time. She refused to accept incremental progress as sufficient. When the Year of the Woman in 1992 brought a record number of women to Congress, she noted that women still weren't even 10 percent of the House. She told the Library of Congress that at the current rate, it would take three hundred years for women to reach equality in Congress—a prediction that sadly seems prescient.

"She was the coach, the leader, the strategist," Representative Carolyn Maloney, a Democrat from New York, told *The Washington Post.* "She was, by far, the greatest feminist of my time."

On March 13, 2023, Schroeder died from complications of a stroke at a hospital in Celebration, Florida, at age eighty-two. She asked that a brick be made from her cremated remains to hold doors open for other women.[19] Even in death, she wanted to pave the way for those who would follow.

Her final advice to women entering politics captured her fierce spirit: "I think women still should never kid themselves that they're going to come here and be part of the team. And you ought to come here with a very clear definition of what it is you want to do, and that you will not be deterred."[20]

Pat Schroeder proved that women could fight, lead, and change the world, even when forced to do it from half a chair. Her legacy isn't just in the laws she passed or the barriers she broke but in the fierce example she set: Never apologize for taking up space, never stop fighting for what's right, and never feel ashamed to use both your brain and your uterus.

35.

Constance Baker Motley: *The Judge*

Many are familiar with Thurgood Marshall, the first Black U.S. Supreme Court justice. But far fewer have heard of Constance Baker Motley, a civil rights titan who worked with Marshall and changed the course of American history.

In 1963, as Martin Luther King, Jr., delivered his iconic "I Have a Dream" speech from the steps of the Lincoln Memorial, Constance sat on the platform beside him, calling it "the twentieth century's finest hour."[1] It was no accident that Constance was there on that historic day; just months earlier she had been with him as his lawyer in Birmingham, Alabama, the city that had become the center of the civil rights struggle.

Jailed after the Good Friday march, Dr. King would spend eight days behind bars and write his famous "Letter from Birmingham Jail." Constance served as the defense counsel at King's trial. The hearing turned into a spectacle. The courtroom was packed with Black people from "all over the state who came to watch the Columbia University–trained woman lawyer."[2] Most of the courthouse employees were white women and they also wanted to witness something they'd never seen before.[3]

When a prosecutor pointed a finger at Constance and dismissively called her "she," Constance replied, "If you can't address me as 'Mrs. Motley,' don't address me at all."[4] Despite the strength of her argument, the judge ruled that Dr. King was in contempt of court for holding a protest, and Dr. King was jailed for another five days.

Constance Baker Motley stands with her client, Reverend Martin Luther King, Jr., and fellow attorney William Kunstler, in Albany, Georgia, in 1962.

With concern mounting that the movement was losing momentum, a decision was made to ramp up the demonstrations and recruit young adults. On May 2 and 3, children left class across Birmingham and gathered at the Sixteenth Street Baptist Church to begin a march, singing hymns like "We Shall Overcome."[5] The protests would become known as the Children's Crusade, and "images of police hosing down and clubbing the youngsters horrified a global audience."[6] Bull Connor, Birmingham's racist commissioner, arrested hundreds of schoolchildren. When the city's school superintendent expelled the more than one thousand students who'd joined in the marches, parents and kids were upset with Dr. King. Constance stepped in.

With her legal pen as her weapon, Constance filed a lawsuit in federal court, arguing that the school board's actions violated the students' rights. In her autobiography, Constance points out that there was little time to get the kids reinstated because some of the students were just a week away from graduation![7] The case went all the way to the U.S. Court of Appeals, and she won. The children could not be legally punished for protesting segregation and would not be expelled.

It was just one of many extraordinary cases in which Constance prevailed. These cases would help focus the nation's attention on the evils of segregation and, in the end, create the political will to pass the Civil Rights Act of 1964.[8]

Constance Juanita Baker was born in 1921 in New Haven, Connecticut, the ninth of twelve children.[9] Her mother was a civil rights activist, and her father was a chef at Yale University who emigrated from the Caribbean island of Nevis.[10]

Her mom thought Constance would become a hairdresser.

"She had no conception of a woman wanting to be a lawyer," Constance said.[11] When Constance was a senior in high school, her father asked why she had already decided to pursue a legal career. Her simple answer: "Law is difficult, and I want to do something difficult."[12] *I love that quote.*

Constance knew the injustices she fought to change because she lived them. In 1941, on her way to Fisk University in Nashville, she was forced to sit in a separate section of the train when crossing the state line into Kentucky.

Law is difficult, and I want to do something difficult.

—Constance Baker Motley

"Although I had known this would happen, I was both frightened and humiliated," she recalled in her memoir.[13] After transferring to New York University, she later attended Columbia Law School, becoming only the second Black woman to graduate from the prestigious school, in 1946.[14]

She joined the NAACP Legal Defense Fund (LDF) while still a student. "When she got ahold of a case, pity the lawyer on the other side," said her LDF colleague Jack Greenberg.[15]

In 1948, Constance experienced again the ugliness of Jim Crow segregation firsthand. When she visited the U.S. Supreme Court for the first time, Constance was forced to stay in segregated housing in

Washington, D.C., and eat in segregated restaurants. This was all happening as she was devoting her life's work to overturning Jim Crow laws. Fifteen years later she would become the first woman of color to argue before the highest court in the land.

There were times when she felt unsafe. In 1949, she and her colleague became the first Black lawyers since Reconstruction to present a case in a Mississippi courtroom. She was representing Black teachers who were paid much less than their white colleagues. Just as Constance had been dismissed as "she" in the courtroom in Birmingham, she was called "that Motley woman" in Mississippi.[16] But no one could diminish her power, no matter what they called her.

Her influence on the Civil Rights Movement was so profound that President Lyndon B. Johnson invited her—along with Dr. King and Thurgood Marshall—to the U.S. Capitol in August 1965 for the ceremonial signing of the Voting Rights Act, one of the most monumental laws in the history of America.

"Today is a triumph for freedom as huge as any victory that has ever been won on any battlefield," the president declared from the Capitol Rotunda.[17]

That landmark victory and many more would not have occurred without Constance Baker Motley.

She began her legal career as a protégé of Thurgood Marshall in 1945 when she became his law clerk during her second year at Columbia Law School.[18] She would spend many years working for the NAACP Legal Defense Fund as its only female lawyer.

She was at the LDF for what seemed like every pivotal moment of the civil rights era, helping to write the brief for the landmark *Brown v. Board of Education* (1954) case. For the next ten years after that desegregation decision, she traveled around the Deep South working to enforce the high court's ruling, in total winning over two hundred legal cases.

She helped litigate every major campaign of the fight, contributing to the victories in the Montgomery bus boycott (1955), the lunch counter sit-ins (1959), the Freedom Rides (1961), and Dr. King's Albany, Georgia, and Birmingham, Alabama, desegregation efforts. She helped integrate the Universities of Georgia, Alabama, and Mississippi. She called the legal war she waged to get James Meredith, a Black student, enrolled in the University of Mississippi in 1962 "the last battle of the Civil War."[19]

In addition to all of her state work, she was the first Black woman to argue a case before the U.S. Supreme Court. She would go on to argue ten cases before the highest court in the land, and she won all of them except one.[20] The only case she lost was overturned in 1986 "on grounds that had been largely asserted by Constance."[21]

Her victories would earn her the nickname "Civil Rights Queen," but it would not shield her from sexism and being passed over for key opportunities, including replacing Thurgood Marshall as director-counsel of the LDF when he became a judge in 1961.[22] When Georgetown law professor Sheryll Cashin asked Marshall directly why he chose Jack Greenberg instead, Marshall quickly became defensive and said he thought Greenberg was "the best man for the job."[23]

Well, I guess he was literally being honest. What about the best *person* for the job?

"I think it was just beyond his imagination then to put a woman in charge," said Cashin, who had clerked for Justice Marshall on the Supreme Court.

But with one door closed, a bigger one opened for Constance.

After two decades with the NAACP, she become the first Black woman to be elected to the New York State Senate and the first female borough president of Manhattan. In 1966, President Johnson appointed her to become a judge on a federal trial court, and with her confirmation, Constance became the first Black woman to serve on the federal bench.[24] For generations, women—especially Black women—have considered Judge Motley a role model. Former Vice President Kamala Harris called Constance "a personal hero of mine."[25]

Justice Ruth Bader Ginsburg said of Constance's legacy: "She taught me and others of my generation that law and courts could become positive forces in achieving our nation's high aspiration—as carved above the entrance to the U.S. Supreme Court—Equal Justice under Law."[26]

Justice Ketanji Brown Jackson, the first Black woman on the U.S. Supreme Court, vividly recalls in her memoir, *Lovely One*, reading about Constance in a magazine as a teenager and feeling like her story was a "beacon of hope, showing me that I could dare to imagine making history too." So not only did Constance's groundbreaking work shape the course of civil rights law, but she also inspired women to pursue careers in law and politics.

Today, women make up almost 40 percent of the full-time active Article III judges, the lifetime-appointed judges nominated by the president and confirmed by the U.S. Senate.[27]

Constance faced the same doubts many women, especially women of color, encountered. She was told she could never reach her dreams. Yet she shattered every barrier and pulled others up with her.

Her dedication to empowering other women was legendary. Constance gave her clerks challenging work, believing that they too could rise to greatness. "The trust she gave her clerks was mind-boggling, but it taught me I could do this work," said Chief Judge Laura Taylor Swain, a former law clerk for Motley. "If she believes I can do this, I must be able to do this."[28] And she did.

To fully appreciate Judge Motley's extraordinary accomplishments, consider this: For the first two hundred years of American history, women could not even serve on juries in many states. The Civil Rights Act of 1957 allowed women to serve on federal juries, but it was not until 1973 that every state allowed women to serve on juries.[29] By then Motley had been a judge for seven years.

Judge Motley was wise, and it seems to me that she had an uncanny ability to see into the future. In her 1965 autobiography, *Equal Justice Under Law*, she wrote, "Sexism, like racism, goes with us into the next century, but I see class warfare as overshadowing both. What to do about those of all racial and ethnic groups left behind by our latest economic revolution will challenge us all."[30]

Today we look back on Judge Motley's work as a triumphant story, but it's important to recognize the systemic racism and sexism that she battled to get there. In fact, as a federal judge, she presided over some landmark cases.

In the mid-1970s, she was assigned to adjudicate *Blank v. Sullivan & Cromwell*, a gender-discrimination class action against several of New York's most prestigious law firms. It was one of the first cases to test the Civil Rights Act of 1964.[31]

Sexism, like racism, goes with us into the next century, but I see class warfare as overshadowing both. What to do about those of all racial and ethnic groups left behind by our latest economic revolution will challenge us all.

—Constance Baker Motley

Diane Blank and other law school graduates sued, claiming they were rejected from associate positions because of their sex. Judge Motley was asked by defense counsel to recuse herself because she was a woman. She not only refused to do so, but in her ruling, she made it clear that if she needed to recuse herself . . . every other judge needed to too.

"If background or sex or race of each judge were, by definition, sufficient grounds for removal, no judge on this court could hear this case, or many others, by virtue of the fact that all of them were attorneys, of a sex, often with distinguished law firm or public service backgrounds."[32]

Her biographer Tomiko Brown-Nagin points out that while Constance endorsed greater representation of women and minorities in the legal field, she "did not view herself as a representative of her race or her gender."[33] All she wanted was equal justice for all.

When *Sports Illustrated* reporter Melissa Ludtke was banned from going into teams' locker rooms at the 1977 World Series between the New York Yankees and the Los Angeles Dodgers, Constance was the judge in Ludtke's groundbreaking case against Major League Baseball and Commissioner Bowie Kuhn.

In her book *Locker Room Talk: A Woman's Struggle to Get Inside*, Ludtke explained the ruling and its far-reaching consequences. "When Judge Motley, who was the only woman judge on the Southern District Court in Manhattan, ruled in my favor in September 1978, she based her order on Kuhn's infringement of my Constitutional equal protection and due process rights to perform my job as the men performed theirs. After her ruling, girls realized they could perform jobs in sports media that previously had seemed out of reach. Since then, tens of thousands of women have worked in sports media, leading to many firsts for women as in-booth broadcasters in baseball, football, basketball, hockey and soccer, to name a few."[34]

Judge Motley's career was nothing short of extraordinary. She was driven by her goals and her sense of mission and propelled by her incredible work ethic. She worked as a senior judge until her death at age eighty-four in 2005. She had assumed senior status in 1986 and was alive to receive the Presidential Citizens Medal from President Bill Clinton, who called her a key legal strategist who won landmark victories that dismantled segregation in America. "Her pursuit of equal justice under the law," Clinton said, "has widened the circle of opportunity in America."[35]

PART V

MY LIFETIME: WOMEN'S PROGRESS IN AMERICA, 1976–TODAY

1976–Today

Writing about the last fifty years of women's progress in America feels different from chronicling earlier eras because this history coincides almost exactly with my own lifetime. As a fifty-two-year-old, I bring not just research to these years but personal witness. I have experienced the transformation of this period, benefited from it, and watched it unfold in real time, and yet I remain profoundly frustrated by the challenges that still persist.

Women still hold very few of the top positions across politics and business. And of course, while women have been running for the presidency since Belva Lockwood in 1884, no one has cracked the highest and hardest glass ceiling. Sometimes the inequities that still exist today can be depressing. But the benefit of studying our past heroines is learning that, again and again, women have confronted and overcome barriers that seemed insurmountable. What is abundantly clear to me is that we all stand on the shoulders of the women in the last two centuries of American history, and that their success will help us reach new heights.

"It has not been easy for our country to make 'We, the people' mean all the people," former Secretary of State Condoleezza Rice declared in front of millions at the Republican National Convention in 2000. "Democracy in America is a work in progress, not a finished masterpiece."[1]

The idea that democracy is not a finished masterpiece is why I've titled this book *We the Women.* American women have been demanding freedoms and denouncing double standards since the Revolutionary era—like Abigail Adams imploring her husband to "remember the ladies" and poet Phillis Wheatley shaping the ideals of American freedom and independence. What's changed in the last fifty years is that women are no longer asking to be remembered. They've become impossible to ignore.

From the courtroom to the boardroom, from the laboratory to the battlefield, from the concert stage to representation in media, women are no longer supporting actors but protagonists of America's continuing story. That transformation—from margin to center, from inclusion to influence, from breakthrough to normalcy—represents the greatest democratization of power in American history. And as the stories in this book demonstrate, it's only just the beginning.

It has been one of the most challenging and rewarding experiences of my career to write this book. It has taken 250 years to recognize and celebrate the roles that women have played in shaping American history. (The dearth of historical research and scholarship about women was eye-opening.) It would be impossible to conclude this book with a series of profiles of trailblazers from the past fifty years because we would inevitably leave someone out who deserves recognition. Plus, their work is not done! Women's achievements have been exponential, but it is still a "work in progress," as Secretary Rice has said.

However, it is worth taking a moment to look at the gains that have been made since the late twentieth century in the areas of education, law, medicine, business, sports, and culture.

One of the most important lessons of this last half century is that the expansion of women's legal rights in the 1970s represents a striking fulfillment of many of the demands laid out more than a century earlier in the 1848 Declaration of Sentiments. Drafted for the Seneca Falls Convention by Elizabeth Cady Stanton and others, the declaration, as we detailed earlier, was a bold and revolutionary document that enumerated the injustices women faced in American society. It included denial of the right to vote, lack of legal status in marriage and divorce, unequal access to education, limited employment opportunities, and the inability to control property or earnings. The grievances they outlined formed *a blueprint for gender equality*, and although some progress occurred in the decades that followed, many of the goals remained unrealized until the seventies.

In fact, the 1970s became a turning point. Through landmark legislation and court cases, many of the declaration's foundational demands were finally addressed. The passage of Title IX of the Education Amendments Act of 1972 was a watershed moment, mandating equal access to educational programs and funding regardless of sex. It not only opened the doors of classrooms and athletic fields to girls and women but also affirmed education as a key pathway to equality.

In the workplace, laws such as the Equal Employment Opportunity Act (1972) and court decisions expanding the scope of Title VII of the Civil Rights Act of 1964 strengthened protections against sex-based discrimination, bringing the nation closer to honoring the declaration's call for equal employment and economic independence. Legal reforms also advanced women's rights in marriage, divorce, and property ownership. States began to recognize no-fault divorce and uphold women's rights to control their earnings and jointly acquired assets.

These changes signaled a shift toward legal recognition of women as autonomous individuals—an idea at the heart of the Seneca Falls resolutions.

And though reproductive rights were not explicitly mentioned in the 1848 document, the decade's strides in this area—most notably the *Roe v. Wade* (1973) decision—can be seen as a modern extension of the demand for personal and legal liberties. But the overturning of that decision with *Dobbs v. Jackson Women's Health Organization* (2022) indicates the current conservative-leaning Supreme Court believes women's reproductive rights are not guaranteed by the Constitution.

This period of transformation was part of what is now known as the second wave of feminism, which swept through the United States from the 1960s through the 1980s. While the first wave had focused primarily on suffrage, the second wave took aim at a broader range of structural inequalities—in education, employment, family law, and reproductive rights.

Leaders like Gloria Steinem became powerful voices for this movement, creating and using platforms like *Ms.* magazine to illuminate sexism in everyday life and galvanize a generation of women. Alongside Gloria were activists, lawyers, legislators, and everyday women organizing for equal rights, often drawing a direct line from the injustices outlined in the Declaration of Sentiments to the unfinished business of the twentieth century.

This slow progress toward equality is not just abstract or theoretical—it is personal. I was born in 1974, the same year Congress passed the Equal Credit Opportunity Act (ECOA), which made it illegal for banks to deny a woman credit simply because of her sex or marital status. Before then, women routinely needed a male co-signer—often a husband or father—to obtain a mortgage, a car loan, or even a credit card. *Can you imagine?* I know it's difficult to fathom today, but that kind of systemic economic discrimination was common and legal until the mid-1970s.

It's worth noting that the ECOA was championed by a Republican: Congresswoman Margaret Heckler, one of just twelve women in Congress when she was first elected in 1967.[2] Heckler worked with bank executives to push through the legislation, while her colleague Congresswoman Lindy Boggs, a Democrat from Louisiana, famously added language barring sex and marital-status discrimination during the committee markup—without telling her (male) colleagues in advance. When Boggs presented the altered version, she told them she was "sure" the exclusion of women "was just an omission"—and the committee approved it unanimously.[3] It was a masterful and necessary correction of injustice.

Representation played a crucial role in driving these changes. Prior to the 1970s, women made up less than 4 percent of Congress, often far less.[4] It wasn't until that decade and the one that followed that the number of female legislators began to inch upward, setting the stage for the broader transformations of the 1990s and beyond.

Congresswoman Heckler also co-sponsored Title IX and was an early proponent of the Equal Rights Amendment, proving that even a small number of determined, and bipartisan, women in government could make a profound impact. Their work helped move the nation closer to the vision of full citizenship demanded at Seneca Falls, proving that even the most revolutionary demands of the past can, over time, become the law of the land.

Yet they also remind us that the fight for equality is never fully complete—it evolves with each generation.

STANDING ON THE SHOULDERS OF GIANTS

The legal victories of the 1970s that shaped my generation also make me think about the woman whose courage made my own opportunities possible. Sometimes I wonder what my Irish grandmother, Mary Teresa Monaghan of Belfast, who boldly crossed the Atlantic all alone at age twenty-three in 1930, would think if she could see the world today. After she arrived at Ellis Island on the SS *California,* my grandmother got a job in Queens, New York, at a psychiatric hospital as an attendant, working twelve-hour shifts.

Could this woman—who arrived with twenty dollars and an eighth-grade education—have imagined that her granddaughter would grow up in a world where women could become Supreme Court justices, CEOs of Fortune 500 companies, four-star generals, and billionaire entrepreneurs? Could my grandmother have envisioned a time when the highest-grossing concert tour in history would be performed by a woman, or when the biggest movie of the year would center on a doll that taught girls that they didn't need to shrink themselves to fit the world's expectations?

I am overcome with emotion wondering what my grandmother would think knowing that her namesake, my younger sister, Mary Teresa, is the chief of colon and rectal surgery at one of our country's most prestigious hospitals. No doubt she would be incredibly proud and in awe of the transformation of what's possible for women in America today. True, less than one in four surgeons in America is female, but the next decades will see exponential growth, as women now make up the majority of medical school students.[5]

My grandmother passed away many years ago, but her name is immortalized on microfilm in Washington in the National Archives. This past year, I went to search for it and found my grandmother's name on a ship manifest. Mary Teresa Monaghan listed her occupation as hemstitcher. I think of my grandmother every time I have a hard day. As the Irish poet William Butler Yeats wrote, "Joy is of the will which labours, which overcomes obstacles, which knows triumph."

That pioneering spirit—that bravery that brought her alone across the Atlantic—is the bravery that lives in her granddaughters, who have a hopeful heart about the ability not only to change their own life and create their own destiny but to change the course of history itself. It is that same spirit that American women can draw on as they face the challenges that still lie ahead.

LEGAL EQUALITY AND EDUCATIONAL ACCESS

The legal revolution driven by women created a domino effect across American institutions. Trailblazers like Constance Baker Motley, Pauli Murray, Sarah Weddington, and Ruth Bader Ginsburg shaped outcomes in some of the most significant Supreme Court cases in the last half century.

In the 1970s, Ruth Bader Ginsburg (known as RBG) argued six major gender-discrimination cases before the Supreme Court, winning five of them.[6] There were no women on the Court, but she brilliantly persuaded the male justices to apply the Equal Protection Clause of the Fourteenth Amendment to laws that discriminated on the basis of gender, fundamentally changing constitutional doctrine. What's remarkable is that Justice Ginsburg's legal strategy rested on the assumption that gender discrimination hurts everyone. She argued many of her cases on behalf of male plaintiffs.

"She, case by case, brought the all-male Supreme Court along by educating them about how laws predicated on gender stereotypes do not just hold women back; they also hold men back," said UC Berkeley law professor Amanda Tyler, who clerked for Justice Ginsburg.[7]

Never before had the Supreme Court ruled that women have the same rights as men. RBG changed that.

Once the Supreme Court established that women deserved equal protection under the law, the educational barriers began to crumble. Women didn't just gain access to law schools—they transformed them.

We've come a long way from when former Representative Pat Schroeder and former Senator Elizabeth Dole were among just a handful of women at Harvard Law School in the 1960s. Today, women make up 56.2 percent of law students and are the majority of law firm associates and federal government general lawyers.[8]

The transformation extends far beyond law. Women during my lifetime have crashed through the educational glass ceiling and now make up the majority of both college and graduate students in the United States.[9] The shift is reflected in enrollment, degree attainment, and completion rates across nearly every demographic group, marking a profound change in the landscape of higher education.

But perhaps the most dramatic shift has been in the Supreme Court itself. From zero women when RBG argued her first case to nearly half the Court today, the transformation has been remarkable. Six women have now served on the Supreme Court, each bringing unique perspectives and breaking new ground.

Sandra Day O'Connor, appointed in 1981 by President Ronald Reagan, became the first woman on the Supreme Court. A pragmatic conservative from Arizona, she was often the swing vote on crucial cases and faced down doubters with characteristic grace. She was confirmed unanimously—a testament to her qualifications and the recognition that it was simply time.[10] Justice O'Connor would serve as the only woman on the nation's highest court for more than two decades.

Ruth Bader Ginsburg, appointed in 1993, brought the weight of decades of gender equality litigation to the bench. Her fiery dissents and unwavering logic made her a cultural icon—"the Notorious RBG"—and her judicial philosophy continued the work she had begun as a lawyer arguing before the Court.

Sonia Sotomayor, appointed in 2009, was the first Latina justice. Raised in a Bronx housing project by a single mother, she brought an unflinching focus on justice for marginalized communities. She once described herself as a "wise Latina" shaped by her experiences, and that wisdom has informed her jurisprudence.[11]

Elena Kagan, a former Harvard Law School dean and U.S. solicitor general, joined the Court in 2010. Known for her sharp wit and incisive questions during oral arguments, she's helped shape major decisions on healthcare, free speech, and federal power.

Amy Coney Barrett, confirmed in 2020, is a former Notre Dame law professor with a judicial philosophy rooted in textualism and originalism. Her presence solidified the Court's conservative majority, and legal scholars describe her as "the most interesting justice on the court" due to her nuanced approach and willingness to diverge from ideological expectations.[12] When she joined the Court to replace Justice Ginsburg, she was the fifth vote to overturn *Roe v. Wade* (1973), the decision that held that the Constitution protects a woman's right to an abortion.

Ketanji Brown Jackson, appointed in 2022, holds the historic distinction of being the first Black woman to serve on the Court. Her story traces directly back to her childhood inspiration reading about Judge Constance Baker Motley, the civil rights trailblazer who never made it to the Supreme Court herself but sparked a vision that helped put Justice Jackson there. When Jackson was almost twelve years old, she discovered that she and Judge Motley shared the same birthday. "I sat up abruptly, my mind racing," she would later write. "A cascade of new possibilities crashing inside me. . . . The image of Judge Motley smiling enigmatically in front of her bookcase of law journals burned itself into my mind."[13]

She was a former public defender and trial judge. At her swearing-in, she placed her hand on two Bibles: one from her family and one donated by Justice John Marshall Harlan, the lone dissenter in *Plessy v. Ferguson* (1896).[14]

"I have a seat at the table now," Jackson said. "And I'm ready to work."[15] She quickly became the most prolific questioner on the bench and one of its most frequent opinion writers.

Together, these four women—Sotomayor, Kagan, Barrett, and Jackson—make up nearly half the Court, an unimaginable scenario just decades ago. Their presence represents not just individual achievement but a fundamental shift in how America's highest court reflects the nation it serves.

ECONOMIC AND CULTURAL POWER

With legal equality established and educational pipelines flowing, women began translating knowledge into economic and cultural power on an unprecedented scale.

The financial revolution has been particularly striking. Women now control over half of the wealth in America, a figure expected to rise significantly as the "great wealth transfer" unfolds. Approximately $54 trillion will pass to younger generations in the next two decades, and no group will benefit more than women.[16] The shift is not only increasing the number of female billionaires—who now account for about 12 percent of the world's billionaires—but they're reaching this milestone at a younger average age than men, transforming how wealth impacts society.[17]

Over the last five decades, a new generation of women has emerged at the forefront of entrepreneurship, reshaping industries and gaining remarkable financial power. Sara Blakely, for example, launched Spanx with just $5,000 in savings and went on to be named the youngest self-made female billionaire in 2012, revolutionizing women's shapewear. Jamie Kern Lima started IT Cosmetics in her living room and, through grit and innovation, sold it to L'Oréal for $1.2 billion, becoming the company's first-ever female CEO. Diane Hendricks built her fortune by co-founding and leading ABC Supply, now the largest distributor of roofing materials in North America. Judy Faulkner founded Epic Systems, breaking ground as a self-made billionaire in the healthcare technology sector. In the fast-food industry, Marian Ilitch co-founded Little Caesars Pizza.

These pioneers illustrate how women today are defining economic power and entrepreneurial success in new ways. They are breaking barriers, as exemplified by Mellody Hobson, now co-CEO of Ariel Investments, a nearly $15 billion money management firm.[18] Raised by a single mother in Chicago, Mellody experienced the weight of unpaid bills and school tuition her family couldn't afford. But those hard lessons became her driving force. "I was desperate to understand money. Not to make it, to understand it," she said.[19]

That understanding propelled her from intern to president at Ariel Investments by age thirty-one and eventually to co-CEO.[20] Mellody also made history as the first Black woman to serve as chair of the board of a Fortune 500 company when she was elected to lead Starbucks's board in 2021.[21] Her career embodies the principle she lives by: "You have dues now. You have dues later"—an ethos that drives her to approach every task with care and focus.[22]

Mellody is doing more than leading; she is investing in the future. Through Project Black, she is working to scale up minority-owned businesses. She speaks candidly about stereotypes, biases, and being "lumped together by narrowed expectations," even as she pushes past them.[23] And perhaps most important, she is reminding young women and girls—especially those of color—that they belong. A residential college at Princeton now bears her name, the first building at the university named after a Black person. "My hope," Hobson says, "is that my name will remind future generations of students—especially those who are Black and brown and the 'firsts' in their families—that they too belong."[24]

Mellody's story connects to a lineage of financial pioneers. In 1903,

Maggie Lena Walker became the first Black woman in the United States to charter and lead a bank. At a time when both her race and gender were seen as barriers, she built the St. Luke Penny Savings Bank to empower the Black community of Richmond, Virginia. Her motto: "Let us have a bank that will take the nickels and turn them into dollars." Her pioneering leadership laid the foundation for women to be seen not just as participants in the economy but as leaders of it.

More than a century later, in 2021, Jane Fraser became the first woman to lead a major Wall Street bank as CEO of Citigroup, shattering a long-standing barrier in one of the most male-dominated sectors.[25]

Women now lead 11 percent of Fortune 500 companies—a record high.[26] But that number should be much higher. Leaders like Karen Lynch, who led CVS Health (formerly the highest-ranked company ever run by a woman), demonstrate the impact of female leadership at the highest levels.

The title of Lynch's memoir, *Taking Up Space,* captures the generational shift perfectly. Early in her career, a male colleague told her to "sit in the back of the room, not at the table, because women just take up space."[27] When she became CEO, she wore a T-shirt reading "Taking Up Space"—a bold reclamation of what was once meant as a dismissal. "Don't let others dim your light," she told me in an interview. "Take up space and invite others to join you."

From Maggie Lena Walker's ledger book to Mellody Hobson's investment firm to Jane Fraser's Wall Street office, the arc of women's progress in business demonstrates how individual breakthroughs create pathways for systemic change and more women in positions of financial power. But despite all the progress, women are still earning less than their male colleagues. Women in the United States are paid eighty-three cents for every dollar paid to men, and the current data indicates it will take more than 130 years to reach parity.[28] That's insane! And the wage gap is even worse for women of color.

Women are also at the center of a cultural transformation. I can remember my mom saying the biggest concert she went to growing up was the Beatles. The biggest live shows I've attended are Taylor Swift concerts, where seventy-thousand-plus people pack NFL stadiums night after night. Taylor's *Eras* tour grossed more than $2 billion in ticket sales, making it the highest-grossing concert tour of all time (in fact, that's double the gross ticket sales of any other concert tour).[29]

But it's not just about the receipts—it's about the respect Taylor Swift demands in her lyrics and public remarks. At the 2019 Billboard Women in Music event, she declared: Women in music "are held at a higher, sometimes impossible-feeling standard. . . . It seems like the pressure that could have crushed us made us into diamonds instead."[30] She insisted, "What didn't kill us actually did make us stronger."

The highest-grossing film of 2023, *Barbie,* delivered a similar message to global audiences. The movie's cultural watershed moment came through America Ferrera's monologue: "It is literally impossible to be a woman. You are so beautiful, and so smart, and it kills me that you don't think you're good enough."[31] That message resonated powerfully for me because it echoed themes from more than 175 years earlier in the Declaration of Sentiments, which stated: "He has endeavored, in every way that he could to destroy her confidence in her own powers, to lessen her self-respect."[32]

The movie's director, Greta Gerwig, became the first solo female director to produce a billion-dollar-grossing film, shattering another barrier in Hollywood.[33] From Swift's record-breaking tours to Gerwig's box office triumph, women aren't just participating in American culture—they're defining it.

Sports have seen a remarkable transformation, building on the foundation Billie Jean King established when she defeated Bobby Riggs, a former world number one tennis player, in the Battle of the Sexes in 1973. Watched by ninety million people worldwide, King's victory wasn't just a tennis match—it was a cultural earthquake.[34]

"I thought it would set us back 50 years if I didn't win," she later said. "It would ruin the women's tour and affect all women's self-esteem."[35]

The match was more than sport—it was theater. Billie Jean entered like Cleopatra, carried aloft in a feathered chair. Riggs arrived in a rickshaw pulled by models wearing shirts that said *Sugar Daddy.* Despite the circus, she won decisively (6–4, 6–3, 6–3) and proved, in real time, that women could compete, and win, on their own terms.[36]

> ***It is not unladylike to be assertive.***
>
> ***—Billie Jean King***

"She was a crusader fighting a battle for all of us," said tennis legend Martina Navratilova. "She was carrying the flag; it was all right to be a jock."[37]

Billie Jean didn't watch the match again until twenty-five years later.[38] What stood out? The way she was described. Howard Cosell, the legendary sportscaster, focused on her looks: "A very attractive young lady, and sometimes you get the feeling that if she ever let her hair grow down to her shoulders, and took her glasses off, you'd have somebody vying for a Hollywood screen test."[39] Billie Jean later said, "Only my looks. He talked about Bobby's—you know, what he'd done, like Hall of Famer, all his accomplishments, right?"[40]

The cultural resistance she faced was blatant. When she testified before Congress in 1973 on the need for equal athletic opportunities for girls, she declared, "It is not unladylike to be assertive."[41] But even progressive senator Walter Mondale introduced her by saying, "Our first witness today, even though she is a woman, became one of the world's most successful and respected athletes."[42]

When she won Wimbledon in 1968, she received £750. The men's champion, Rod Laver, earned £2,000. "My heart sank when I got that check," Billie Jean later said.[43] "Just like, oh no. Now, I have to fight for this." And fight she did.

In 1970, she and eight other women put their careers on the line to form their own tournament—the Virginia Slims Circuit—signing symbolic $1 contracts.[44] It was a defiant act of protest and vision. Three years later, Billie Jean founded the Women's Tennis Association. In 1973, the U.S. Open became the first major tournament to offer equal prize money to men and women.[45] That was a huge accomplishment! Since 2007, women in tennis receive equal prize money to men at all Grand Slam tournaments, but not in many other professional tournaments throughout the year.[46]

Her bold activism and public platform paved the way for future generations. Tennis stars like Venus and Serena Williams, Chris Evert, Monica Seles, Lindsay Davenport, and Mary Joe Fernandez have all credited Billie Jean King with opening the door. She didn't just elevate the sport—she created opportunities, fought for fair pay, and showed what leadership could look like. Without her, the path to the top would have been steeper for countless women who followed.

In a 2023 interview, Billie Jean was asked why she first got into tennis. Her answer caught me off guard—not because it was unfamiliar but because it framed the story in a way I hadn't heard before.

"At 12, I was playing at the Los Angeles Tennis Club. All the big tournaments were there. And I was sitting in the stands and kind of daydreaming," she said. "It was kind of late in the afternoon. And I started realizing everyone wore white shoes, white clothes, played with white balls, everybody who played was white. And I asked myself, where is everybody else? Where's everybody else? That was the moment I decided I would champion equality the rest of my life. But I knew tennis would allow me to have that opportunity if I could be good enough."[47]

That realization didn't just change the trajectory of her life—it shaped her mission. Tennis would become her job, but the fight for inclusion and equal pay would become her purpose.

Today's explosion in women's sports proves that Billie Jean's vision wasn't just bold—it was right.

The 2023 NCAA women's basketball championship game between Louisiana State University (LSU) and the University of Iowa was a watershed moment, drawing nearly ten million viewers—a 103 percent increase from the previous year.[48] It became the most-watched women's college basketball game in history. LSU, with its star player, forward Angel Reese, won the game 102–85. Angel Reese's rivalry with Iowa's star guard, Caitlin Clark, drew much of the attention.

Over her collegiate career, Clark electrified audiences with her long-range three-point shooting and competitiveness. She quickly became a household name and a catalyst for the sport's meteoric rise. Dubbed the "Caitlin Clark effect," her presence helped Iowa shatter attendance records, including drawing 55,646 fans to an outdoor exhibition game at Kinnick Stadium—home to the school's football team. Clark's and Reese's popularity helped the WNBA to break a single-attendance record in 2025.[49]

Beyond the headlines, participation numbers also tell the story. The 2023–2024 academic year saw an all-time high of 235,735 student athletes competing in NCAA women's sports. Compare that to the 1920s, around the time of golfer Babe Didrikson (who did not go to college), when only 22 percent of American universities even had intercollegiate sports for women.[50]

The number of female athletic directors is also on the rise—with a 23 percent increase over the past decade.[51] This is progress, but it's also a signal: Women are not just playing the game. They're leading it.

Billie Jean King didn't just break barriers—she built a new arena. One where, as she likes to say, "Pressure is a privilege."

TRANSFORMING MILITARY, MEDICINE, AND BEYOND

Armed with legal equality, educational credentials, economic influence, and cultural power, women began reshaping institutions that had excluded them for centuries.

The military transformation has been particularly striking. Admiral Lisa Franchetti's rise to become the first woman to lead the U.S. Navy and serve on the Joint Chiefs of Staff in 2023 reflects a much larger shift. When she first entered the navy in 1985, women couldn't serve on combat ships—only seventeen women were allowed to serve on ships as officers each year, and there was just one female admiral in the entire navy.[52]

Policy, culture, and ambition evolved together. In 1993, Congress lifted the ban on women serving on combat ships and flying combat missions, thanks to lawmakers like Congresswoman Pat Schroeder. By 2015, the final barriers fell when the U.S. military opened all combat roles to women. Admiral Franchetti's own career mirrored these changes as she commanded destroyers and aircraft carriers, led operations across the globe, and became only the second woman in navy history to earn four-star rank.

The numbers tell the story: Women now make up 17.7 percent of the active-duty force and 21.9 percent of the National Guard and reserves.[53] Nearly ten thousand women signed up for active duty in the U.S. Army in 2024—an 18 percent increase from the previous year, helping the army meet its recruiting goals.[54] More than one hundred women have completed the army's grueling Ranger School, and over three hundred thousand women have served in Iraq and Afghanistan since 9/11.[55]

In 2023, I interviewed all four of the nation's female four-star generals and admirals serving at the time—Admiral Franchetti, Army General Laura Richardson, Air Force General Jacqueline Van Ovost, and Coast Guard Commandant Linda Fagan. Each had served for more than three decades, navigating Cold War tensions, the aftermath of 9/11, and rising threats from China and Russia. Their combined experience represents over a century of military leadership at the highest levels. It is important to note that though America has had hundreds of four-star generals and admirals, only ten have been women. As of 2025, there were no four-star female officers actively serving because of retirements and high-profile firings by the Trump administration.

"I can't wait till we're not talking about the first," Admiral Fagan told me. "I can't wait to celebrate who's next." That sentiment captures the broader transformation: Women are moving from breakthrough to normalcy across traditional male bastions.

In science and medicine, the revolution is equally profound. Today, women make up more than one-third of all active physicians in the United States and the majority in key specialties like pediatrics (66 percent), obstetrics and gynecology (62 percent), and dermatology

(53 percent).[56] Since 2004, the number of active female physicians has grown by 97 percent.[57]

Increased enrollment in graduate school programs is making waves throughout the professions. Women are now the majority of medical school students—54.6 percent as of the 2023–2024 academic year—and multiple studies show that having a female physician leads to better outcomes for patients. Research also reveals that hospitalized patients are less likely to die or be readmitted when treated by female surgeons.[58] *Simply put, women's increased participation is saving lives.*

Young women today are celebrating that remarkable achievement. Every February 3, you'll see all over social media women physicians gathering around birthday cakes in hospitals and clinics to celebrate National Women Physicians Day, honoring Elizabeth Blackwell's 1849 achievement as the first woman to earn a medical degree in the United States.

If you do what scares you, you might just find how much you're capable of.

—Christina Koch

The broader STEM (science, technology, engineering, and mathematics) transformation is equally impressive. Women now make up 34 percent of the STEM workforce, according to data from the U.S. Census Bureau.[59] In veterinary medicine, they've surged ahead entirely: Women now comprise 69 percent of all veterinarians.[60]

Scientific breakthroughs are being led by pioneers like Frances H. Arnold, winner of the 2018 Nobel Prize in Chemistry for her work on directed evolution. "If you're going to change the world," Arnold says, "you've got to be fearless."[61]

That fearlessness extends to space exploration. While NASA has selected only 61 women among its 360 astronaut candidates in history, the trajectory is clear.[62] Sally Ride broke the barrier in 1983, Christina Koch and Jessica Meir completed the first all-female space walk in 2019, and Peggy Whitson has logged more time in space than any other American. As Christina Koch told me: "If you do what scares you, you might just find how much you're capable of."[63]

THE NEXT GENERATION

After writing this book and reflecting on these five decades that I have lived through, I've come to realize that we're witnessing something unprecedented in American history: the normalization of female leadership across every sector of society. The last five decades of my lifetime have witnessed not just incremental progress, but a fundamental shift in American power structures.

We're moving from celebrating "firsts" to expecting excellence from women in positions of power—exactly the shift Oprah Winfrey envisioned in 2018 when, as the first Black woman to receive the Cecil B. DeMille Award, she declared, "I want all the girls watching here and now to know that a new day is on the horizon!"[64] Her message wasn't just about breaking barriers, but about ensuring that the women who follow are no longer exceptions—they are the expectation.

That "new day" was made possible by the legal foundation laid by female lawmakers and lawyers like Ruth Bader Ginsburg, who transformed equality from an aspiration into a constitutional principle. Their work ensured that opportunity would no longer depend on gender, paving the way for a generation of women whose success is not defined by being the first, but by leading with excellence. From the individual profiles chronicled throughout this book to the broader patterns examined in this concluding chapter, the trajectory is unmistakable: Women have moved from breakthrough to normalcy across American society. The title *We the Women* reflects this evolution: from a time when women had to ask to be remembered to an era when they are writing about the very future of American democracy. That experience—from my grandmother's $20 and a suitcase to today's women leading Fortune 500 companies and space missions—represents more than individual success stories. But the race is far from over. The women who fought for the right to vote have now passed the metaphorical baton to the women fighting today for full equality.

Our shared journey, and that of our mothers, represents the progress toward the fulfillment of America's founding promise that talent and determination, not gender or circumstance, should decide one's destiny. As America's Declaration of Independence, 250 years ago, so boldly declared, each of us is created equal and endowed with certain inalienable rights, including "Life, Liberty and the Pursuit of Happiness."

Acknowledgments

We started this three-year journey with a mission. We wanted to celebrate the lives of extraordinary American women on the 250th anniversary of the founding of our country. We especially wanted to shine a light on the women whose stories are not well-known but whose contributions to the great American experiment were pivotal.

This tremendous undertaking would not have been possible without an incredible team, including my co-author, Kate Andersen Brower, whose skill and experience in writing many previous bestselling books was invaluable. I am also indebted to Julie Morse, who compiled the painstaking research and was a fantastic thought partner throughout the editing process.

A heartfelt thank you to Mary Reynics, who is the best editor in publishing and guided this project with enthusiasm and excellence. The Ballantine and Random House teams, including Susan Corcoran, Karen Fink, and Ivanka Perez, were helpful every step of the way.

As always, I appreciate working with Keith Urbahn, Matt Latimer, and Robin Sproul at Javelin, who helped me develop the idea for this ambitious book. And a big thanks to my longtime agent, Jay Sures of UTA, who is an endless source of encouragement and good advice in all of my projects.

I also want to thank CBS News for allowing me to continue my journalistic work while tackling this historic project and for promoting this work. To Gayle King, whose guidance and friendship have helped me immeasurably. To Susan, Adam, Julie, Callie, Keith, Roxanne, Isabel, Maurcell, Ally, Olivia R., Margaret, Olivia G., Lauren, Sheena, Cheryl, and Brandy, who have always been my best collaborators and colleagues at work.

To my "Texas Peeps"—my best friends since elementary school in San Antonio—for the decades-long friendship and motivation. And to Mellody, Dasha, and Margot for reminding me of the power and potential of women.

I also want to acknowledge my family. To my mother and father, whose love of books, biography, and women's stories inspires me. My husband, Geoff Tracy, brought me lots of coffee when he found me most mornings already at work, writing away. My children, Grace, Henry, and Riley, provided endless encouragement when I would regale them with stories of these incredible women.

In the process, we spoke with historians who have devoted their careers to uncovering these hidden figures. That included authors like Mary Beth Norton, a pioneering historian who was the first woman to join Cornell University's history faculty. Her book *Liberty's Daughters: The Revolutionary Experience of American Women, 1750–1800* helped shape the earliest chapters of *We the Women*. Norton created the field of colonial women's history. It's hard to believe, but just a few decades ago women's history was not even its own area of study at most universities.

My fellow journalist, the late Cokie Roberts, set the stage for *We the Women*. Her books *Founding Mothers: The Women Who Raised Our Nation* and *Ladies of Liberty: The Women Who Shaped Our Nation* are required reading for anyone interested in American history.

We stand on the shoulders of historians whose lifework is to study and research the past: Shelly Lowe, who served as chair of the National Endowment for the Humanities; Professor Laurel Thatcher Ulrich; historian Nancy Isenberg; Dr. Maria Rosario Jackson, former chair of the National Endowment for the Arts; Dr. Susan Sleeper-Smith; scholar Holly Guise; David Waldstreicher, an author and professor at the Graduate Center of the City University of New York; Catherine Kelly, executive director of the Omohundro Institute of Early American History & Culture and professor of history at William & Mary; Holly Mayer, professor emerita of history at Duquesne University in Pittsburgh and an expert on women during the American Revolution.

A very special thank-you to my friend Lonnie Bunch, secretary of the Smithsonian Institution and the founding director of the Smithsonian's National Museum of African American History and Culture, for his priceless guidance. The Smithsonian is an amazing resource, and we've worked with several people across a number of their museums and disciplines, including Angela Tate, Mary Elliott, and Ellie Reynolds.

The work of the following authors provided the background to get started on this project: Janice Nimura, author of *The Doctors Blackwell: How Two Pioneering Sisters Brought Medicine to Women—and Women to Medicine;* Megan Marshall, author of *Margaret Fuller: A New American Life;* Annette Gordon-Reed, author of award-winning books about Sally Hemings and her family, including *The Hemingses of Monticello: An American Family;* Mae Ngai, professor of Asian American studies and professor of history at Columbia University and author of *The Lucky Ones: One Family and the Extraordinary Invention of Chinese America;* Kerri K. Greenidge, author of *The Grimkes: The Legacy of Slavery in an American Family;* Lynne Olson, author of *Freedom's Daughters: The Unsung Heroines of the Civil Rights Movement from 1830 to 1970;* Rosemarie Zagarri, author of *A Woman's Dilemma: Mercy Otis Warren and the American Revolution;* and Tomiko Brown-Nagin, dean of Harvard Radcliffe Institute and author of *Civil Rights Queen: Constance Baker Motley and the Struggle for Equality.*

I am also grateful to Matthew Skic, curator of exhibitions at the Museum of the American Revolution, who helped inform our research on Charlotte Forten Grimké; Elizabeth Novara, a specialist in American women's history at the Library of Congress Manuscript Division; Jenny Sweeny, a specialist for records related to women's history at the National Archives; Patrice Green, curator for African American and African diasporic collections at Harvard's Schlesinger Library on the History of Women in America; and Martha King, whose work on the early American printer Mary Katherine Goddard was incredibly important to our research. A special thanks to Harry Haskell for not just his fascinating podcast about his step-grandmother, Katharine Wright, but for answering our questions; and Joel Wilson Motley III for helping us find pictures of his incredible mother.

The Gilder Lehrman Institute of American History is a tremendous resource for anyone interested in our country's inspiring—and complicated—history.

Through this process we've gotten to know the wonderful people working at the National Women's History Museum as they aim to celebrate women's contributions to the United States. A special thank-you to NWHM's president, Frédérique Irwin, and former chief communications officer, Jennifer Herrera, for championing our work. Their She Is Not a Footnote* campaign energized us.

The Women's Bureau at the Department of Labor was established in 1920 to improve working conditions for women. We discovered this hidden federal treasure of data and information while working on this book and are thankful to Gretchen Livingston, Monica Vereen, and Tiffany Boiman for their help, which would make Frances Perkins proud.

I am always amazed at the depth of knowledge among the researchers at our presidential libraries. Thank you especially to Emma Sperry at the FDR Presidential Library & Museum and the team at the Nixon Library.

Thank you to David Lei, a board member of the Chinese Historical Society of America, and to the Berkeley Architectural Heritage Association for their help in teaching us more about the Tape family.

A special word for these authors and their incredible books: Christine Stansell's *The Feminist Promise: 1792 to the Present;* Linda Kerber's *Women of the Republic: Intellect and Ideology in Revolutionary America;* Catherine Allgor's *Parlor Politics: In Which the Ladies of Washington Help Build a City and a Government;* and Cathleen Cahill's *Recasting the Vote: How Women of Color Transformed the Suffrage Movement.*

While working on this book I thought back to conversations I've had over the course of my career with thought leaders, politicians, entrepreneurs, and athletes. My interviews with Billie Jean King and Mellody Hobson have made me feel optimistic about the future. Women have certainly come a long way, but there is much work left to be done.

Photo Credits

1. The New York Public Library, Manuscripts and Archives Division
2. Library of Congress, Rare Book and Special Collections Division
3. Museum of Fine Arts, Boston, Mrs. James Warren (Mercy Otis) by John Singleton Copley
4. The New York Public Library, The Miriam and Ira D. Wallach Division of Art, Prints and Photographs: Print Collection
5. Massachusetts Judicial Archives
6. Massachusetts Historical Society
7. Library of Congress, Prints and Photographs Division
8. Library of Congress, Prints and Photographs Division
9. Library of Congress, Elizabeth Cady Stanton Papers, Manuscript Division
10. Library of Congress, Prints and Photographs Division
11. Library of Congress, Prints and Photographs Division
12. Library of Congress, Prints and Photographs Division
13. The New York Public Library, Schomburg Center for Research in Black Culture, Photographs and Prints Division
14. Library of Congress, Rare Book and Special Collections Division
15. Library of Congress, Blackwell Family Papers, Manuscript Division
16. New York Academy of Medicine, Carte de Visite Collection
17. Bettmann/Getty Images
18. National Archives and Records Administration, Brady's National Portrait Gallery
19. National Archives and Records Administration, National Archives at St. Louis
20. Nebraska State Historical Society, Photograph Collections
21. Smithsonian Institution, National Portrait Gallery
22. Library of Congress, Prints and Photographs Division, Brady's National Portrait Gallery

23. Library of Congress, Prints and Photographs Division, Brady-Handy Collection
24. Oakland Museum of California
25. Brooklyn Museum, Gift of Paul Roebling, Portrait of Emily Warren Roebling by Charles-Émile-Auguste Carolus-Duran
26. Wright State University Libraries' Special Collections and Archives
27. Library of Congress, Prints and Photographs Division, George Grantham Bain Collection
28. Library of Congress, Prints and Photographs Division, George Grantham Bain Collection
29. Library of Congress, Prints and Photographs Division
30. U.S. National Park Service, Maggie L. Walker Papers
31. U.S. National Park Service
32. Smithsonian Institution, National Museum of American History, Mina Turner
33. National Archives and Records Administration
34. Library of Congress, National Woman's Party Records, Manuscript Division
35. Library of Congress, National Woman's Party Records, Manuscript Division
36. Library of Congress, National Woman's Party Records, Manuscript Division
37. Knox County Public Library, Harry T. Burn Papers, McClung Historical Collection
38. National Cryptologic Museum
39. Library of Congress, Prints and Photographs Division, Social Press Association
40. State Archives of Florida, Florida Memory
41. Library of Congress Prints and Photographs Division, photo by Gordon Parks
42. Franklin D. Roosevelt Presidential Library & Museum
43. Franklin D. Roosevelt Presidential Library & Museum
44. Columbia University Rare Book & Manuscript Library, Frances Perkins Papers
45. National Park Service, Harry S. Truman Library & Museum, Abbie Rowe
46. National Archives and Records Administration, Photographs of American Military Activities Series
47. National Archives and Records Administration, Photographs of American Military Activities Series
48. Don Cravens/Getty Images
49. Photo by Rolls Press/Popperfoto/Getty Images
50. The Richard Nixon Presidential Library and Museum
51. Bettmann/Getty Images
52. Associated Press
53. Bettmann/Getty Images
54. Associated Press

55. Paul Connell/*The Boston Globe* via Getty Images
56. National Archives at College Park
57. Library of Congress, R. Michael Jenkins
58. Library of Congress, U.S. News & World Report Magazine Photograph Collection, Marion S Trikosko
59. Aaron E. Tomlinson/Associated Press
60. Bettmann/Getty Images

Notes

INTRODUCTION

1. New York Public Library, "Reading the Original Declaration of Independence, in Philadelphia, July 4, 1876," New York Public Library Digital Collections, https://digitalcollections.nypl.org/items/2dacec80-c533-012f-99ae-58d385a7bc34.
2. Elizabeth Cady Stanton, *Eighty Years and More: Reminiscences 1815–1897* (Fisher Unwin, 1898), 144.
3. Stanton, *Eighty Years and More,* 144.
4. Stanton, *Eighty Years and More,* 144.
5. Stanton, *Eighty Years and More,* 144.
6. Susan B. Anthony, Matilda Joslyn Gage, and Elizabeth Cady Stanton, "Declaration of Rights of the Women of the United States—July 4, 1876," National Woman Suffrage Association, https://www.loc.gov/resource/rbpe.16000300/?sp=1.
7. John F. Kennedy, "Address Before the Irish Parliament," speech, Dublin, Ireland, June 28, 1963.
8. Elizabeth Stone, "The Woman Who Saved the Statue of Liberty," *Smithsonian Magazine,* May 4, 2023, https://www.smithsonianmag.com/history/the-woman-who-saved-the-statue-of-liberty-180982100/.
9. "Theodore Parker and the 'Moral Universe,'" *All Things Considered,* podcast, hosted by Melissa Block, NPR, September 2, 2010, https://www.npr.org/2010/09/02/129609461/theodore-parker-and-the-moral-universe.

CHAPTER 1

1. Martha J. King, "Mary Katherine Goddard Petitions the President," *Women Who Made History,* Gilder Lehrman Collection, accessed August 9, 2025, https://

www.gilderlehrman.org/sites/default/files/2022-05/GLI_Goddard_by%20 King%20%281%29.pdf.

2. *Journals of the Continental Congress,* vol. 7, "1777: January 1–May 21" (U.S. Government Printing Office, 1907).
3. *Journals of the Continental Congress,* vol. 6, "1776: October 9–December 31" (U.S. Government Printing Office, 1907).
4. Harvard Declaration Resources Project, "March Highlight: Mary Katherine Goddard," *Course of Human Events,* March 4, 2016, https://declaration.fas.harvard.edu/blog/march-goddard.
5. Harvard Declaration Resources Project, "March Highlight."
6. New York Public Library, "Broadside of the Declaration of Independence," *NYPL Beginnings Exhibition,* accessed August 9, 2025, https://www.nypl.org/events/exhibitions/galleries/beginnings/item/3570.
7. National Park Service, "Richard Stockton," last modified July 4, 2004, in *Signers of the Declaration: Historic Places Commemorating the Signing of the Declaration of Independence,* rev. ed., ed. Robert G. Ferris (U.S. Department of the Interior, 1975), https://www.nps.gov/parkhistory/online_books/declaration/bio46.htm.
8. Alexis de Tocqueville, *Democracy in America,* ed. J. P. Mayer, trans. George Lawrence (Doubleday, 1969).
9. Erick Trickey, "Mary Katharine Goddard, the Woman Whose Name Appears on the Declaration of Independence," *Smithsonian Magazine*, November 14, 2018, https://www.smithsonianmag.com/history/mary-katharine-goddard-woman-whose-name-appears-declaration-independence-180970816.
10. Trickey, "Mary Katharine Goddard."
11. King, "Goddard Petitions the President."
12. "The Revolutionary Role Mail Played in America's Fight for Independence," *Smithsonian Magazine,* September 6, 2022, https://www.smithsonianmag.com/smithsonian-institution/the-revolutionary-role-mail-played-in-americas-fight-for-independence-180980687/.
13. King, "Goddard Petitions the President."
14. Gilder Lehrman Institute, "To Samuel Osgood, Postmaster General of New York, November 12, 1789," https://www.gilderlehrman.org/sites/default/files/2022-05/09756.04_OS.pdf.
15. Christopher J. Young, "Mary K. Goddard: A Classical Republican in the Age of Revolution," *Maryland Historical Magazine* 96, no. 1 (Spring 2001): 23, fn. 27.
16. Young, "Mary K. Goddard."
17. "Mary Katherine Goddard to George Washington, December 23, 1789," letter,

Founders Online, National Archives, https://founders.archives.gov/documents/Washington/05-04-02-0302.

18. Trickey, "Mary Katharine Goddard."

CHAPTER 2

1. Phillis Wheatley, "To the Right Honourable William, Earl of Dartmouth," 1772, in *Poems on Various Subjects, Religious and Moral* (Aldgate, 1773), Gilder Lehrman Institute, GLC06154.
2. Wheatley, "To the Right Honourable William."
3. James G. Basker, "Phillis Wheatley: Poet Laureate of the American Revolution," *History Now: The Journal*, no. 60 (Summer 2021), Gilder Lehrman Institute of American History, https://www.gilderlehrman.org/history-resources/essays/phillis-wheatley-poet-laureate-american-revolution.
4. George W. Boudreau and Charlene M. Boyer Lewis, *Women in George Washington's World* (University of Virginia Press, 2022).
5. David Waldstreicher, *The Odyssey of Phillis Wheatley* (Farrar, Straus and Giroux, 2023).
6. Vincent Carretta, *Phillis Wheatley: Biography of a Genius in Bondage* (University of Georgia Press, 2011).
7. Library of Congress, "Today in History—September 1," Digital Collections, accessed August 9, 2025, https://www.loc.gov/item/today-in-history/september-01/.
8. Waldstreicher, *Odyssey of Phillis Wheatley.*
9. Waldstreicher, *Odyssey of Phillis Wheatley.*
10. Phillis Wheatley, *Poems on Various Subjects, Religious and Moral,* Project Gutenberg, accessed August 9, 2025, https://www.gutenberg.org/ebooks/409.
11. Jennifer Benedetto Beals, "Library Owns Signed Phillis Wheatley First Edition," University of Tennessee Knoxville, February 10, 2021, https://volumes.lib.utk.edu/features/library-owns-signed-phillis-wheatley-first-edition/.
12. Westminster College, "Phillis Wheatley and the Countess of Huntingdon," *Westminster College Blog,* October 2019, https://www.westminster.cam.ac.uk/wp-content/uploads/2019/10/2019-10-BLOG-Phillis-Wheatley-in-the-Cheshunt-Archives.pdf.
13. Wheatley, *Poems on Various Subjects.*
14. Stephanie Sheridan, "Phillis Wheatley: Her Life, Poetry, and Legacy," National Portrait Gallery, Smithsonian Institution, accessed August 9, 2025, https://npg.si.edu/blog/phillis-wheatley-her-life-poetry-and-legacy.

15. Betsy Erkkila, "Provocation: Phillis Wheatley on the Streets of Revolutionary Boston and in the Atlantic World," *Early American Literature* 56, no. 2 (2021): 351–372, https://dx.doi.org/10.1353/eal.2021.0034.
16. "Enclosure: Poem by Phillis Wheatley, 26 October 1775," in *The Papers of George Washington,* Revolutionary War Series, vol. 2, *16 September 1775–31 December 1775,* ed. Philander D. Chase (University of Virginia Press, 1987), 242–244, Founders Online, National Archives, https://founders.archives.gov/documents/Washington/03-02-02-0222-0002.
17. "From George Washington to Phillis Wheatley, 28 February 1776," letter, in *The Papers of George Washington,* Revolutionary War Series, vol. 3, *1 January 1776–31 March 1776,* ed. Philander D. Chase (University of Virginia Press, 1988), 387, Founders Online, National Archives, https://founders.archives.gov/documents/Washington/03-03-02-0281.
18. "George Washington to Phillis Wheatley, 28 February 1776," 387.
19. James G. Basker, "Phillis Wheatley: Poet Laureate of the American Revolution," *History Now: The Journal,* no. 60 (Summer 2021), Gilder Lehrman Institute of American History, https://www.gilderlehrman.org/history-resources/essays/phillis-wheatley-poet-laureate-american-revolution.
20. Basker, "Phillis Wheatley."
21. M. A. Isani and Phillis Wheatley, "On the Death of General Wooster: An Unpublished Poem by Phillis Wheatley," *Modern Philology* 77, no. 3 (1980): 306–309.
22. Nicholas Mosvick, "Forgotten Founders: Phillis Wheatley, African-American Poet of the Revolution," National Constitution Center, February 17, 2022, https://constitutioncenter.org/blog/forgotten-founders-phillis-wheatley-african-american-poet-of-the-revolution.
23. Henry Louis Gates, Jr., *The Trials of Phillis Wheatley: America's First Black Poet and Her Encounters with the Founding Fathers* (Basic Books, 2009).
24. Amanda Gorman (@TheAmandaGorman), "Whenever I feel unable to write, I remember that Thomas Jefferson singled out young black poetess Phillis Wheatley with shallow disdain," X (formerly Twitter), February 1, 2021, https://x.com/TheAmandaGorman/status/1356346736915095553.
25. Sheridan, "Phillis Wheatley."
26. "Wheatley, Phillis (1753–1784) Newspaper Notice of Her Passing," Swann Auction Galleries, accessed July 9, 2025, https://www.swanngalleries.com/auction-lot/wheatley-phillis-1753-1784-newspaper-notice-of-he_65B4EFBA67.
27. Carretta, *Phillis Wheatley.*

CHAPTER 3

1. "From John Adams to Elbridge Gerry, 17 April 1813," letter, Founders Online, National Archives, https://founders.archives.gov/documents/Adams/99-02-02-6000.
2. "From John Adams to James Warren, 18 March 1780," letter, Founders Online, National Archives, https://founders.archives.gov/documents/Adams/06-09-02-0043, original source: *Papers of John Adams,* vol. 9, *March 1780–July 1780,* ed. Gregg L. Lint and Richard Alan Ryerson (Belknap Press, 1996), 63–64.
3. Rosemarie Zagarri, *A Woman's Dilemma: Mercy Otis Warren and the American Revolution,* 2nd ed. (Wiley-Blackwell, 2015).
4. "Mercy Otis Warren, *Observations on the New Constitution,* 1788," National Constitution Center, Historic Document Library, https://constitutioncenter.org/the-constitution/historic-document-library/detail/mercy-otis-warren-observations-on-the-new-constitution-1788.
5. Mercy Otis Warren, *History of the Rise, Progress and Termination of the American Revolution,* vol. 3 (Manning and Loring, 1805), 675–676.
6. Rosemarie Zagarri, "Mercy Otis Warren," transcript, *We the People,* podcast, National Constitution Center, August 18, 2021, https://constitutioncenter.org/media/files/2021-08-18_Mercy_Otis_Warren.pdf.
7. "To John Adams from Mercy Otis Warren, 27 August 1807," Founders Online, National Archives, https://founders.archives.gov/documents/Adams/99-02-02-5210.
8. Barnstable County, "Who Was the First Lady of the American Revolution?" July 12, 2023, https://www.capecod.gov/2023/07/12/who-was-the-first-lady-of-the-american-revolution.
9. Danielle Herring, "Mercy Otis Warren: The Secret Muse of the Bill of Rights," *In Custodia Legis: Law Librarians of Congress,* Library of Congress Blogs, December 15, 2022, https://blogs.loc.gov/law/2022/12/mercy-otis-warren-the-secret-muse-of-the-bill-of-rights/.
10. Rosemarie Zagarri, *A Woman's Dilemma: Mercy Otis Warren and the American Revolution,* 2nd ed. (Wiley-Blackwell, 2015).
11. Zagarri, *A Woman's Dilemma.*
12. Zagarri, *A Woman's Dilemma.*
13. Jillian LaRue Viar, "Political Aspirations of Colonial Women: The Correspondence of Mercy Otis Warren and Abigail Smith Adams," master's thesis, Eastern Illinois University, 2012.
14. Mary Grace Day, "Liberty and Justice for All? Female Portraiture in the Age of the Early American Republic," *Art Journal,* no. 1 (2019): article 3.

15. Zagarri, *A Woman's Dilemma.*
16. Erick Trickey, "The Woman Whose Words Inflamed the American Revolution," *Smithsonian Magazine,* June 20, 2017, https://www.smithsonianmag.com/history/woman-whose-words-inflamed-american-revolution-180963765/.
17. Ray Raphael, "The Righteous Revolution of Mercy Otis Warren," *History Now: The Journal,* no. 21 (Fall 2009), Gilder Lehrman Institute of American History, https://www.gilderlehrman.org/history-resources/essays/righteous-revolution-mercy-otis-warren.
18. Mercy Otis Warren, *Poems, Dramatic and Miscellaneous,* Evans Early American Imprint Collection, University of Michigan, https://name.umdl.umich.edu/n17785.0001.001.
19. American Battlefield Trust, "The Jeffersonian Party," March 25, 2020, https://www.battlefields.org/learn/articles/jeffersonian-party.
20. Massachusetts Historical Society, "The Ratification of the U.S. Constitution in Massachusetts," 2002, https://www.masshist.org/objects/cabinet/february2003/february2003.htm.
21. Trickey, "Woman Whose Words Inflamed."
22. The Papers of Thomas Jefferson, vol. 33, 17 February–30 April 1801, ed. Barbara B. Oberg. Princeton: Princeton University Press, 2006, pp. 398–399. Founders Online, National Archives.
23. The Papers of Alexander Hamilton, vol. 8, February 1791–July 1791, ed. Harold C. Syrett, New York: Columbia University Press, 1965, pp. 522–523. Founders Online, National Archives.
24. "From Thomas Jefferson to James Warren, 21 March 1801," letter, Founders Online, National Archives, https://founders.archives.gov/documents/Jefferson/01-33-02-0339, original source: *The Papers of Thomas Jefferson,* vol. 33, *17 February–30 April 1801,* ed. Barbara B. Oberg (Princeton University Press, 2006), 398–399.
25. "From Alexander Hamilton to Mercy Warren, 1 July 1791," letter, Founders Online, National Archives, https://founders.archives.gov/documents/Hamilton/01-08-02-0465, original source: *The Papers of Alexander Hamilton,* vol. 8, *February 1791–July 1791,* ed. Harold C. Syrett (Columbia University Press, 1965), 522–523.
26. Elizabeth F. Ellet, *The Women of the American Revolution,* vol. 1 (Baker and Scribner, 1848).

CHAPTER 4

1. "Elizabeth Fries Ellet," *The New York Times,* June 4, 1877.
2. "A Look Back at Women's Studies Since the 1970s," *Tell Me More,* NPR,

March 17, 2010, https://www.npr.org/2010/03/17/124775888/a-look-back-at-women-s-studies-since-the-1970s.

3. Elizabeth F. Ellet, *The Women of the American Revolution*, vol. 1 (Baker and Scribner, 1848), xi.
4. Elizabeth F. Ellet, *The Women of the American Revolution*, vol. 2 (Baker and Scribner, 1849).
5. Gretchen Ferris Schoel, "In Pursuit of Possibility: Elizabeth Ellet and the Women of the American Revolution," master's thesis, College of William & Mary, 1992.
6. Carol Mattingly, "Elizabeth Fries Lummis Ellet (1818–1877)," *Legacy* 18, no. 1 (2001): 101–106.
7. Michigan State University, "Ellet, E. F. (Elizabeth Fries), 1818–1877," https://d.lib.msu.edu/msul:43.
8. Mary Kelley, *Private Woman, Public Stage* (University of North Carolina Press, 1984), cited in Schoel, "In Pursuit of Possibility."
9. Library Company of Philadelphia, "Elizabeth F. Ellet (1818–1877)," Portraits of American Writers That Appeared in Print Before 1861, accessed August 10, 2025, https://www.librarycompany.org/women/portraits/ellet.htm.
10. Michigan State University, "Ellet, E. F."
11. Christine Stansell, *City of Women: Sex and Class in New York, 1789–1860* (Knopf, 1986).
12. Schoel, "In Pursuit of Possibility."
13. Schoel, "In Pursuit of Possibility."
14. Northern Illinois University Libraries, "Ellet, Elizabeth F.," The House of Beadle & Adams and Its Dime and Nickel Novels, accessed August 10, 2025, https://ulib.niu.edu/badndp/ellet_elizabeth.html.
15. Schoel, "In Pursuit of Possibility."
16. Ellet, *Women of the American Revolution*, vol. 2.
17. Andrew Davis, "South Carolina State House | Let's Go!," *Let's Go!* (South Carolina ETV, July 4, 2022), South Carolina ETV, https://www.scetv.org/stories/2022/south-carolina-state-house-lets-go.
18. Mattingly, "Elizabeth Fries Lummis Ellet."
19. "Review of *Women of the American Revolution*, by Elizabeth F. Ellet (New York, 1848)," *North American Review*, April 1849, cited in Schoel, "In Pursuit of Possibility."
20. Elizabeth F. Ellet, *The Practical Housekeeper: A Cyclopaedia of Domestic Economy* (Keeler and Kirkpatrick, 1898).

CHAPTER 5

1. Massachusetts Historical Society, *The Object of History,* podcast, season 1, episode 4, "A Miniature Portrait of Elizabeth Freeman," accessed August 9, 2025, https://www.masshist.org/podcast/season-1-episode-4-miniature-portrait-elizabeth-freeman.
2. "Life Story: Elizabeth Freeman (ca. 1744–1829)," Women & the American Story, The New York Historical, accessed August 9, 2025, https://wams.nyhistory.org/settler-colonialism-and-revolution/the-american-revolution/elizabeth-freeman/.
3. "Life Story: Elizabeth Freeman."
4. Jim Miller, archivist, Sheffield Historical Society, personal communication, April 7, 2025.
5. Catharine Maria Sedgwick, "Slavery in New England," manuscript draft, 1853, Massachusetts Historical Society, accessed August 9, 2025, https://www.masshist.org/database/547.
6. Sedgwick, "Slavery in New England."
7. Nancy Eve Cohen, "How an Enslaved Woman Sued and Won Her Freedom in 18th-Century Massachusetts," WBUR News, January 27, 2020, https://www.wbur.org/news/2020/01/27/elizabeth-freeman-sheffield-slave-ashley-sedgwick.
8. Harriet Martineau, *Retrospect of Western Travel,* vol. 2 (Saunders and Otley, 1838).
9. Massachusetts Constitution, Article I.
10. Sedgwick, "Slavery in New England."
11. Cohen, "How an Enslaved Woman Sued"; Sedgwick, "Slavery in New England."
12. Sedgwick, "Slavery in New England."
13. Sari Edelstein, "'Good Mother, Farewell': Elizabeth Freeman's Silence and the Stories of Mumbet," *New England Quarterly* 92, no. 4 (2019): 584–614.
14. Edelstein, "'Good Mother, Farewell.'"
15. Suzanne Geissler Bowles, "Tapping Reeve and Mumbet: Abolishing Slavery in Massachusetts," Princeton & Slavery Project, accessed August 9, 2025, https://slavery.princeton.edu/stories/tapping-reeve#ref-4.
16. Geissler Bowles, "Tapping Reeve and Mumbet."
17. Massachusetts Historical Society, "The Legal End of Slavery in Massachusetts," *African Americans and the End of Slavery in Massachusetts*, Massachusetts Historical Society, https://www.masshist.org/features/endofslavery/end_MA.
18. Geissler Bowles, "Tapping Reeve and Mumbet."

19. Geissler Bowles, "Tapping Reeve and Mumbet."
20. Massachusetts Historical Society, "Legal End of Slavery."
21. John Stauffer, *Boston's Crusade Against Slavery,* online exhibition, Harvard University, accessed August 9, 2025, https://library.harvard.edu/sites/default/files/static/onlineexhibits/emancipation/index.html.
22. "The Story of Elizabeth Freeman and How Slavery Ended in Massachusetts," GBH News, updated August 28, 2023, https://www.wgbh.org/news/2022-02-25/the-story-of-elizabeth-freeman-and-how-slavery-ended-in-massachusetts.
23. "Life Story: Elizabeth Freeman."
24. Sedgwick, "Slavery in New England."
25. Catharine Maria Sedgwick, *The Power of Her Sympathy: The Autobiography and Journal of Catharine Maria Sedgwick,* ed. Mary Kelley (Northeastern University Press, 1993).
26. "Life Story: Elizabeth Freeman."
27. Edelstein, "'Good Mother, Farewell.'"
28. Edelstein, "'Good Mother, Farewell.'"
29. Nancy Eve Cohen, "How an Enslaved Woman Sued."
30. Edelstein, "'Good Mother, Farewell.'"
31. Edelstein, "'Good Mother, Farewell.'"

CHAPTER 6

1. Jessie Serfilippi, "Deborah Sampson," in *The Digital Encyclopedia of George Washington,* ed. Zoie Horecny and Alexandra Montgomery (Mount Vernon Ladies' Association, 2012–), https://www.mountvernon.org/library/digitalhistory/digital-encyclopedia/article/deborah-sampson.
2. Serfilippi, "Deborah Sampson."
3. Elizabeth F. Ellet, *The Women of the American Revolution,* vol. 2 (Baker and Scribner, 1850).
4. Ellet, *Women of the American Revolution.*
5. Alfred F. Young, *Masquerade: The Life and Times of Deborah Sampson, Continental Soldier* (Knopf, 2004).
6. Ellet, *Women of the American Revolution.*
7. Young, *Masquerade.*
8. Young, *Masquerade.*
9. Young, *Masquerade.*
10. Carol Mattingly, "Elizabeth Fries Lummis Ellet (1818–1877)," *Legacy* 18, no. 1 (2001): 101–106.
11. Ellet, *Women of the American Revolution.*

12. Secretary of the Commonwealth of Massachusetts, "Deborah Sampson," accessed August 9, 2025, https://www.sec.state.ma.us/divisions/state-house-tours/did-you-know/Deborah-Sampson.htm.
13. Young, *Masquerade.*
14. Young, *Masquerade.*
15. Jennifer Schuessler, "The Woman Who Sneaked into George Washington's Army," *The New York Times,* July 2, 2019, https://www.nytimes.com/2019/07/02/arts/design/the-woman-who-sneaked-into-george-washingtons-army.html.
16. Fairchild Air Force Base, "Remembering a Women's Rights Pioneer: Deborah Sampson," https://web.archive.org/web/20250131102150/ https://www.fairchild.af.mil/News/Commentaries/Display/Article/496443/remembering-a-womens-rights-pioneer-deborah-sampson/.
17. Young, *Masquerade.*
18. Herman Mann, *The Female Review: Life of Deborah Sampson, the Female Soldier in the War of Revolution,* ed. John Adams Vinton (J. K. Wiggin & W. P. Lunt, 1866), 188–189, https://www.loc.gov/item/06016552/.
19. Mann, *Female Review,* 188–189.
20. Young, *Masquerade.*
21. Serfilippi, "Deborah Sampson."
22. "Letter from Paul Revere to William Eustis, 20 February 1804," letter, Massachusetts Historical Society, https://www.masshist.org/database/326.
23. Serfilippi, "Deborah Sampson."
24. Commonwealth of Massachusetts, "Deborah Sampson: American Revolutionary War Hero," accessed August 9, 2025, https://www.mass.gov/info-details/deborah-sampson-american-revolutionary-war-hero.
25. Serfilippi, "Deborah Sampson."

CHAPTER 7

1. Charles Coleman Sellers, *Patience Wright: American Artist and Spy in George III's London* (Wesleyan University Press, 1976).
2. NWSSA Staff, "Women as Sculptors," Northwest Stone Sculptors Association, March 22, 2018, https://carvestone.org/women-as-sculptors/.
3. Sellers, *Patience Wright,* 67.
4. "Patience Wright, Wax Modeller," *Journal of the Friends Historical Society* 20 (1923): 95, https://journals.sas.ac.uk/fhs/article/view/3811.
5. Sellers, *Patience Wright.*
6. Sellers, *Patience Wright,* 35–36.

7. Angela Serratore, "The Madame Tussaud of the American Colonies Was a Founding Fathers Stalker," *Smithsonian Magazine*, December 23, 2013, https://www.smithsonianmag.com/history/the-madame-tussaud-of-the-american-colonies-was-a-founding-fathers-stalker-180948610/.
8. "George Washington to Patience Wright, 30 January 1785," letter, Founders Online, National Archives, https://founders.archives.gov/documents/Washington/04-02-02-0218.
9. Sellers, *Patience Wright*, 4.
10. "Harlequin, No. XX," *London Magazine*, February 1775, p. 53, https://babel.hathitrust.org/cgi/pt?id=mdp.39015021284677&seq=65&q1=wright.
11. "William Pitt and Family," Westminster Abbey, accessed August 9, 2025, https://www.westminster-abbey.org/abbey-commemorations/commemorations/william-pitt-and-family.
12. Sellers, *Patience Wright*, 56.
13. Sellers, *Patience Wright.*
14. Sellers, *Patience Wright*, 84.
15. Sellers, *Patience Wright*, 84.
16. Reginald Victor Jones, "Benjamin Franklin," *Notes and Records of the Royal Society of London* 31, no. 2 (January 1977): 201–225.
17. "Petition of Rachel Wells, May 18, 1786," Papers of the Continental Congress, M-247, roll 56, item 42: VIII, 354–355, accessed at "A Petition by Rachel Lovell Wells, 1786," New Jersey Women's History, https://njwomenshistory.org/learn/topics/petition-rachel-lovell-wells/; Serratore, "Madame Tussaud of the American Colonies."
18. Sellers, *Patience Wright*, 84.
19. Robert Edge Pine, *Patience Lovell Wright*, c. 1782, oil on canvas, 49½ × 39 7/16 in. (125.7 × 100.2 cm), National Portrait Gallery, Smithsonian Institution, Washington, D.C., https://www.si.edu/object/patience-lovell-wright%3Anpg_NPG.86.168.
20. Sellers, *Patience Wright*, 220.
21. Rachel Wells to Benjamin Franklin, December 16, 1785, letter, The Papers of Benjamin Franklin, https://franklinpapers.org/yale?vol=43&page=593.
22. "Patience Wright to Thomas Jefferson, 14 August 1785," letter, in *The Papers of Thomas Jefferson* 8 (Princeton University Press, 1953), 380–381, Founders Online, National Archives, https://founders.archives.gov/documents/Jefferson/01-08-02-0303.
23. Joel Barlow, *The Columbiad: A Poem*, 1809, Project Gutenberg, accessed August 9, 2025, https://www.gutenberg.org/files/8683/8683-h/8683-h.htm.

PART II

1. Elizabeth Cady Stanton, *Eighty Years and More: Reminiscences 1815–1897* (Fisher Unwin, 1898), 148.
2. J. David Hacker, "A Census-Based Count of the Civil War Dead," *Civil War History* 57, no. 4 (2011): 306–347.
3. Christine Stansell, *The Feminist Promise: 1792 to the Present* (Modern Library, 2010).
4. Jennie Miller, "Meet Anna Dickinson: Trailblazing Orator and Political Firebrand," Smithsonian National Museum of American History, August 31, 2021, https://americanhistory.si.edu/blog/anna-dickinson.
5. David M. Schizer, "RBG: Nonprofit Entrepreneur," *Columbia Law Review* 121 (2021): 633, https://scholarship.law.columbia.edu/faculty_scholarship/2755.
6. Mariana Brandman, "Victoria Woodhull," National Women's History Museum, 2022, http://www.womenshistory.org/education-resources/biographies/victoria-woodhull.
7. Amara Huddleston, "Happy 200th Birthday to Eunice Foote, Hidden Climate Science Pioneer," NOAA Climate.gov, July 17, 2019, https://www.climate.gov/news-features/features/happy-200th-birthday-eunice-foote-hidden-climate-science-pioneer.
8. "Eunice Foote: The Nearly-Forgotten 'Mother of Climate Science,'" Hidden Voices (NYC Schools), April 22, 2025, https://www.schools.nyc.gov/learning/subjects/social-studies/hidden-voices/contentdetails/hidden-voices/2025/04/22/eunice-foote-the-nearly-forgotten-mother-of-climate-science.
9. John Schwartz, "Overlooked No More: Eunice Foote, Climate Scientist Lost to History," *The New York Times,* April 21, 2020, https://www.nytimes.com/2020/04/21/obituaries/eunice-foote-overlooked.html.

CHAPTER 8

1. Kerri K. Greenidge, *The Grimkes: The Legacy of Slavery in an American Family* (Norton, 2023); Theodore D. Weld, Angelina Grimké, and Sarah Grimké, *American Slavery as It Is: Testimony of a Thousand Witnesses* (American Anti-Slavery Society, 1839), 53–54.
2. National Park Service, "Grimke Sisters," National Historical Park New York, accessed August 10, 2025, https://www.nps.gov/wori/learn/historyculture/grimke-sisters.htm.
3. Weld, Grimké, and Grimké, *American Slavery as It Is,* 53–54.
4. Gerda Lerner, *The Grimké Sisters from South Carolina: Pioneers for Woman's Rights and Abolition* (Schocken Books, 1971).

5. Angelina Grimké, diary entry, June 4, 1829, in Mary Louise Wilbanks, *Walking by Faith: The Diary of Angelina Grimké* (University of South Carolina Press, 2003), 79.
6. Lerner, *Grimké Sisters from South Carolina*; Mark Perry, *Lift Up Thy Voice: The Grimké Family's Journey from Slaveholders to Civil Rights Leaders* (Penguin Books, 2003), 2.
7. Christine Stansell, *The Feminist Promise: 1792 to the Present* (Modern Library, 2010).
8. Gerda Lerner, "The Grimké Sisters and the Struggle Against Race Prejudice," *Journal of Negro History* 48, no. 4 (1963): 277–291.
9. Erin K. Gillett, "'This Is a Cause Worth Dying For': Sarah and Angelina Grimké and the Development of a Political Identity," master's thesis, James Madison University, 2013, https://commons.lib.jmu.edu/cgi/viewcontent.cgi?article=1234&context=master201019.
10. Angelina Emily Grimké, *Appeal to the Christian Women of the South* (American Anti-Slavery Society, 1836), http://nationalhumanitiescenter.org/ows/seminarsflvs/religionabolition/grimkechristianwomen.pdf.
11. Grimké, *Appeal to the Christian Women,* 56.
12. Library of Congress, "African American Perspectives: Materials Selected from the Rare Book Collection—Women Authors," https://www.loc.gov/collections/african-american-perspectives-rare-books/articles-and-essays/women-authors/.
13. "Pastoral Letter: The General Association of Massachusetts to Churches Under Their Care," July 1837, reprinted in Kathryn Kish Sklar, *Women's Rights Emerges Within the Antislavery Movement, 1830–1870* (Palgrave Macmillan, 2000), 119–121.
14. Sarah Grimké, *Letters on the Equality of the Sexes, and the Condition of Woman. Addressed to Mary S. Parker* (Knapp, 1838), letter III.
15. Grimké, *Equality of the Sexes,* letter II.
16. U.S. Supreme Court, *Sharron A. Frontiero and Joseph Frontiero v. Melvin R. Laird et al.,* transcript, No. 71-1694, January 17, 1973, 20, https://www.supremecourt.gov/pdfs/transcripts/1972/71-1694_01-17-1973.pdf.
17. Stansell, *The Feminist Promise.*
18. Stansell, *The Feminist Promise.*
19. Beverly Tomek, "Grimke-Weld Wedding," *Universal Emancipation* (blog), accessed September 30, 2025, https://universalemancipation.wordpress.com/major-abolition-events/grimke-weld-wedding/.
20. PBS, "Pennsylvania Hall: 1838," *Africans in America,* Resource Bank, accessed September 30, 2025, https://www.pbs.org/wgbh/aia/part4/4p2938.html.
21. Stansell, *The Feminist Promise.*

22. Angelina Grimké Weld, "Address to the Massachusetts Legislature—Feb. 21, 1838," Archives of Women's Political Communication, Carrie Chapman Catt Center for Women and Politics, Iowa State University, https://awpc.cattcenter.iastate.edu/2022/02/23/address-to-the-massachusetts-legislature-feb-21-1838/.
23. Greenidge, *The Grimkes.*
24. Patrice Gattozzi and Peter Brown, "1870 Women's March and Vote," Hyde Park Historical Society, accessed August 10, 2025, https://www.hydeparkhistoricalsociety.org/1870-womens-march-and-vote/.

CHAPTER 9

1. PBS, "Charlotte Forten (1837–1914)," *Only a Teacher,* accessed August 10, 2025, https://www.pbs.org/onlyateacher/charlotte.html.
2. Museum of the American Revolution, "Black Founders Big Idea 6: Elder James Forten's World," accessed August 10, 2025, https://www.amrevmuseum.org/big-idea-6-elder-james-forten-s-world.
3. National Humanities Center, *Journal of Charlotte Forten, Free Woman of Color: Selections from 1854 to 1859*, in National Humanities Center Resource Toolbox, *The Making of African American Identity, vol. 1, 1500–1865*, PDF, https://nationalhumanitiescenter.org/pds/maai/identity/text3/charlottefortenjournal.pdf.
4. Charlotte Forten Grimké, *The Journals of Charlotte Forten Grimké,* ed. Brenda Stevenson (Oxford University Press, 1988).
5. Grimké, *Journals of Charlotte Forten Grimké,* 140.
6. National Archives, "Dred Scott v. Sandford (1857)," Milestone Documents, accessed August 10, 2025, https://www.archives.gov/milestone-documents/dred-scott-v-sandford.
7. American Antiquarian Society, "Publishing God: Printing, Preaching, and Reading in Eighteenth-Century America," *The Book,* no. 64 (November 2004), https://www.americanantiquarian.org/pdfs/thebook/Nov2004.pdf; National Park Service, "Crispus Attucks," Boston National Historical Park, accessed August 10, 2025, https://www.nps.gov/people/crispus-attucks.htm.
8. National Park Service, "Education During the Port Royal Experiment," Reconstruction Era National Historical Park, accessed August 10, 2025, https://www.nps.gov/articles/000/education-during-the-port-royal-experiment.htm.
9. Akiko Ochiai, "The Port Royal Experiment Revisited: Northern Visions of Reconstruction and the Land Question," *New England Quarterly* 74, no. 1 (2001): 94–117.
10. Augusta Strong, "Negro Women in Freedom's Battles," *Freedomways* 7, no. 4 (Winter 1967): 94–117, https://jstor.org/stable/community.28037001.

11. Grimké, *Journals of Charlotte Forten Grimké.*
12. Jeffrey Goldberg, "Illuminating the Whole American Idea: Introducing 'Inheritance,'" *The Atlantic,* March 2021, https://www.theatlantic.com/magazine/archive/2021/03/the-atlantic-and-black-history/617784/.
13. Kerri K. Greenidge, *The Grimkes: The Legacy of Slavery in an American Family* (Norton, 2023).
14. Matthew Pinsker, "Emancipation Among Black Troops in South Carolina," House Divided Project, Dickinson College, accessed August 10, 2025, https://housedivided.dickinson.edu/sites/emancipation/2012/11/06/emancipation-among-black-troops-in-south-carolina/; Louis P. Masur, ed., *"The Real War Will Never Get in the Books": Selections from Writers During the Civil War* (Oxford University Press, 1993), 151.
15. Kelly Concini and Marcelle Maureen Thomas, "Charlotte Forten Grimké," Pennsylvania Center for the Book, Spring 2021, https://pabook.libraries.psu.edu/literary-cultural-heritage-map-pa/bios/grimke__charlotte_forten.
16. Greenidge, *The Grimkes.*
17. Howard University, "One Phase of the Race Distinction," Manuscripts for the Grimke Book, 40, accessed August 10, 2025, https://dh.howard.edu/ajc_grimke_manuscripts/40/.
18. Howard University, "One Phase."

CHAPTER 10

1. Elizabeth Cady Stanton, *Eighty Years and More: Reminiscences 1815–1897* (Fisher Unwin, 1898).
2. Jennifer Chapin Harris, "Celebrating Women's Herstory: The Story of Seneca Falls," *Off Our Backs* 28, no. 7 (1998): 9.
3. Library of Congress, "Today in History—July 19," Digital Collections, accessed August 9, 2025, https://www.loc.gov/item/today-in-history/july-19/.
4. Library of Congress, "July 19."
5. Veronica Chambers, "How Negro History Week Became Black History Month," *The New York Times,* January 31, 2025.
6. Sally G. McMillen, "A Second Declaration of Independence: The 1848 Declaration of Sentiments," *History Now: The Journal,* no. 63 (Summer 2022), Gilder Lehrman Institute of American History, https://www.gilderlehrman.org/history-resources/essays/second-declaration-independence-1848-declaration-sentiments.
7. Judith Wellman, *The Road to Seneca Falls: Elizabeth Cady Stanton and the First Woman's Rights Convention,* Urbana: University of Illinois Press, 2004.

8. Elizabeth Cady Stanton et al., "Declaration of Sentiments," Seneca Falls Convention, July 19–20, 1848, National Park Service, https://www.nps.gov/wori/learn/historyculture/declaration-of-sentiments.htm.
9. Lucretia Mott, "Discourse on Woman," lecture, December 17, 1849, Philadelphia, Pennsylvania, Library of Congress, https://www.loc.gov/item/09002748/.
10. Wesleyan University, "Black Women & The Suffrage Movement: 1848–1923," accessed August 10, 2025, https://www.wesleyan.edu/mlk/posters/suffrage.html.
11. Arlene Balkansky, "Sojourner Truth's Most Famous Speech," April 7, 2021, Headlines & Heroes, Library of Congress, https://blogs.loc.gov/headlinesandheroes/2021/04/sojourner-truths-most-famous-speech/.
12. Balkansky, "Sojourner Truth's Most Famous Speech."
13. Kat Eschner, "Only One Woman Who Was at the Seneca Falls Women's Rights Convention Lived to See Women Win the Vote," *Smithsonian Magazine*, July 17, 2017, https://www.smithsonianmag.com/smart-news/only-one-woman-who-was-seneca-falls-lived-see-women-win-vote-180964044/.

CHAPTER 11

1. Michael Fuller, "Woman Attends Medical School," May and June 2003, Hobart and William Smith Colleges, https://www.hws.edu/about/history/elizabeth-blackwell/woman-attends-medical-school.aspx.
2. Elizabeth Blackwell, *Pioneer Work in Opening the Medical Profession to Women: Autobiographical Sketches, 1821–1910* (Longmans, Green, 1895), University of Pennsylvania Digital Library, https://digital.library.upenn.edu/women/blackwell/pioneer/pioneer.html.
3. Janice P. Nimura, *The Doctors Blackwell: How Two Pioneering Sisters Brought Medicine to Women and Women to Medicine*, New York: W. W. Norton & Company, 2021.
4. Blackwell, *Pioneer Work.*
5. Fuller, "Woman Attends Medical School."
6. Blackwell, *Pioneer Work.*
7. Blackwell, *Pioneer Work.*
8. Blackwell, *Pioneer Work.*
9. Casey Cep, "The Blackwell Sisters and the Harrowing History of Modern Medicine," *New Yorker*, January 25, 2020, https://www.newyorker.com/magazine/2021/02/01/the-blackwell-sisters-and-the-harrowing-history-of-modern-medicine.
10. Cep, "Blackwell Sisters."

11. Samuel Sanes, "Elizabeth Blackwell: Her First Medical Publication," *Bulletin of the History of Medicine* 16, no. 1 (1944): 83–88.
12. Sanes, "Elizabeth Blackwell."
13. Stacy Weiner, "A Brief Timeline of Women in Medicine," Association of American Medical Colleges, March 5, 2024, https://www.aamc.org/news/brief-timeline-women-medicine.
14. National Library of Medicine, "Dr. Emily Blackwell," Changing the Face of Medicine, last updated June 3, 2015, https://cfmedicine.nlm.nih.gov/physicians/biography_36.html.
15. George Szasz, "Elizabeth Blackwell, Remembering a Pioneering MD," *BCMJ Blog*, January 21, 2022, *British Columbia Medical Journal*, https://bcmj.org/blog/elizabeth-blackwell-remembering-pioneering-md.
16. Beth Weinhouse, "How the Blackwell Sisters Paved the Way for Women Physicians," *Columbia Magazine*, Spring/Summer 2021, https://magazine.columbia.edu/article/review-doctors-blackwell.
17. Eve Heyn, "It Happened Here: Dr. Elizabeth Blackwell," *Health Matters*, February 3, 2020, NewYork-Presbyterian, https://healthmatters.nyp.org/happened-dr-elizabeth-blackwell/.
18. National Library of Medicine, "Dr. Emily Blackwell."
19. National Library of Medicine, "Dr. Emily Blackwell."
20. National Library of Medicine, "Dr. Emily Blackwell."
21. Cep, "Blackwell Sisters."
22. National Library of Medicine. "Elizabeth Blackwell: 'That Girl There Is Doctor in Medicine' Part II," *Circulating Now*, March 25, 2021. https://circulatingnow.nlm.nih.gov/2021/03/25/elizabeth-blackwell-that-girl-there-is-doctor-in-medicine-part-ii.
23. Heyn, "It Happened Here."
24. Weinhouse, "How the Blackwell Sisters."
25. Association of American Medical Colleges, *The State of Women in Academic Medicine 2023–2024: Progressing Toward Equity*, July 2024, https://www.aamc.org/data-reports/data/state-women-academic-medicine-2023-2024-progressing-toward-equity.
26. Bernard Little, "National Women Physicians Day: In the Footsteps of Dr. Elizabeth Blackwell," January 31, 2023, U.S. Department of the Navy, Bureau of Medicine and Surgery, https://www.med.navy.mil/Media/News/Article/3284714/national-women-physicians-day-in-the-footsteps-of-dr-elizabeth-blackwell/.
27. "Room for the Ladies!," *British Medical Journal* 1, no. 119 (April 9, 1859): 292–294.

CHAPTER 12

1. Alexis Coe, "Mary Walker's Quest to Be Appointed as a Union Doctor in the Civil War," *The Atlantic*, February 7, 2013, https://www.theatlantic.com/sexes/archive/2013/02/mary-walkers-quest-to-be-appointed-as-a-union-doctor-in-the-civil-war/272909/.
2. Webb Garrison, *Amazing Women of the Civil War: Fascinating True Stories of Women Who Made a Difference* (Nashville: Thomas Nelson, 1999).
3. Columbia University Irving Medical Center, Department of Surgery, "History of Medicine: Woman of Honor," Columbia Surgery, May 21, 2015. https://columbiasurgery.org/news/2015/05/21/history-medicine-woman-honor.
4. Kentucky National Guard, "Dr. Mary Edwards Walker—The Only Woman to Ever Receive the Medal of Honor," March 7, 2014, https://ky.ng.mil/News/Article/2616159/dr-mary-edwards-walker-the-only-woman-to-ever-receive-the-medal-of-honor/.
5. Salima Appiah-Duffell, "A Temple of the Useful Arts: Highlights from the History of the Patent Office Building," *Smithsonian Libraries and Archives Blog*, May 11, 2018, https://blog.library.si.edu/blog/2018/05/11/a-temple-of-the-useful-arts-highlights-from-the-history-of-the-patent-office-building/.
6. Coe, "Mary Walker's Quest."
7. Sara L. Latta, *I Could Not Do Otherwise: The Remarkable Life of Dr. Mary Edwards Walker* (Zest Books, 2022).
8. Latta, *I Could Not Do Otherwise.*
9. Coe, "Mary Walker's Quest."
10. Gilder Lehrman Institute of American History, "The Service Medal of Honor Recipient Dr. Mary Walker, 1864," History Resources, accessed August 10, 2025, https://www.gilderlehrman.org/history-resources/spotlight-primary-source/service-medal-honor-recipient-dr-mary-walker-1864.
11. Latta, *I Could Not Do Otherwise.*
12. Women's Armed Services Integration Act, S. 1641, 80th Cong (1948) (enacted).
13. Congressional Medal of Honor Society, "Mary Edwards Walker," Stories of Sacrifice, accessed August 10, 2025, https://www.cmohs.org/recipients/mary-e-walker.
14. Lorraine Boissoneault, "Amelia Bloomer Didn't Mean to Start a Fashion Revolution, but Her Name Became Synonymous With Trousers," *Smithsonian Magazine*, May 24, 2018, https://www.smithsonianmag.com/history/amelia-bloomer-didnt-mean-start-fashion-revolution-her-name-became-synonymous-trousers-180969164.
15. Jessie Aucoin, "Dr. Mary Edwards Walker Recognized on New U.S. Quarter,"

Smithsonian American Women's History Museum, June 4, 2024, https://womenshistory.si.edu/blog/dr-mary-edwards-walker-recognized-new-us-quarter.

16. Randy Pellis, "Town of Oswego Commemorates Dr. Mary Walker, the Only Woman Awarded the Medal of Honor," *NNY360*, March 30, 2022, https://www.nny360.com/artsandlife/localhistory/town-of-oswego-commemorates-dr-mary-walker-the-only-woman-awarded-the-medal-of-honor/article_03cef76c-319c-509a-8245-bbdd692fd809.html.
17. Sharon M. Harris, *Dr. Mary Walker: An American Radical, 1832–1919* (Rutgers University Press, 2009).
18. Kerri Lee Alexander and Emma Z. Rothberg, "Mary Edwards Walker," 2023, National Women's History Museum, https://www.womenshistory.org/education-resources/biographies/mary-edwards-walker.
19. Mary E. Walker, *Hit: Essays on Women's Rights* (American News Company, 1871).
20. Adam C. Haeselbarth, ed., "Dr. Mary Walker," *Rockland County Journal*, vol. 40, May 3, 1890, p. 2.
21. U.S. Congress, *Women's Suffrage Hearings Before the House Committee on the Judiciary, February 14, 1912* (U.S. Government Printing Office, 1912).

CHAPTER 13

1. "Declaration of Independence: A Transcription," America's Founding Documents, U.S. National Archives and Records Administration, last modified August 7, 2025, https://www.archives.gov/founding-docs/declaration-transcript.
2. National Library of Medicine, "Dr. Susan La Flesche Picotte," Changing the Face of Medicine, accessed August 10, 2025, https://cfmedicine.nlm.nih.gov/physicians/biography_253.html.
3. Matt Herbison, "Native American Heritage Month: Dr. Susan La Flesche Picotte and Dr. Lillie Rosa Minoka-Hill," Drexel University College of Medicine, November 24, 2020, https://drexel.edu/medicine/about/community-health-and-inclusive-excellence/ochie-blog/native-american-heritage-month-dr-la-flesche-picotte-and-dr-minoka-hill/.
4. Ellen Terry Johnson, *Historical Sketch of the Connecticut Indian Association from 1881 to 1888* (Fowler and Miller, 1888).
5. Patricia Morris Buckley, *Susan La Flesche Picotte: An Arrow of the Future* (Core Knowledge Foundation, 2023), 25, https://www.coreknowledge.org/wp-content/uploads/2023/11/CKBios_G5_SusanLaFleschePicotte_W1.pdf.
6. Valeria Sherer Mathes, "Susan LaFlesche Picotte, M.D.: Nineteenth-Century Physician and Reformer," *Great Plains Quarterly* 13, no. 3 (Summer 1993): 172–186.
7. National Library of Medicine, "Susan La Flesche Picotte."

8. National Library of Medicine, "Susan La Flesche Picotte."
9. Mathes, "Susan LaFlesche Picotte."
10. Mathes, "Susan LaFlesche Picotte."
11. Susan La Flesche Picotte to Commissioner of Indian Affairs Francis E. Leupp, November 15, 1907, Office of Indian Affairs, Letters Received, File 162, no. 90863, courtesy National Archives and Records Administration, https://www.nlm.nih.gov/exhibition/if_you_knew/ifyouknew_12.html.
12. Sarah Ross Pripas-Kapit, "'We Have Lived on Broken Promises': Charles A. Eastman, Susan La Flesche Picotte, and the Politics of American Indian Assimilation during the Progressive Era," *Great Plains Quarterly* 35, no. 1 (2015): 51–78, http://www.jstor.org/stable/24465561.
13. Pripas-Kapit, "'We Have Lived on Broken Promises."
14. Iowa State University, "Susette La Flesche Tibbles," Carrie Chapman Catt Center for Women and Politics, accessed August 10, 2025, https://awpc.cattcenter.iastate.edu/directory/susette-la-flesche-tibbles/.
15. Susette La Flesche Tibbles, "Bright Eyes," Smithsonian Institution, National Museum of the American Indian Archives Transcription Center, December 30, 1880, https://transcription.si.edu/project/8132.
16. National Archives, "The Dawes Act (1887)," Milestone Documents, accessed August 10, 2025, https://www.archives.gov/milestone-documents/dawes-act.
17. Carson Vaughan, "The Incredible Legacy of Susan La Flesche, the First Native American to Earn a Medical Degree," *Smithsonian Magazine,* March 1, 2017, https://www.smithsonianmag.com/history/incredible-legacy-susan-la-flesche-first-native-american-earn-medical-degree-180962332/.
18. John Yang and Winston Wilde, "How Susan La Flesche Picotte Became the First Native American Medical Doctor," *PBS NewsHour,* November 5, 2023, https://www.pbs.org/newshour/show/how-susan-la-flesche-picotte-became-the-1st-native-american-medical-doctor.

CHAPTER 14

1. Anna Dickinson, "Southern Outrage," *The Liberator,* vol. 26, no. 8, February 22, 1856, p. 4.
2. James Harvey Young, "Anna Elizabeth Dickinson and the Civil War: For and Against Lincoln," *Journal of American History* 31, no. 1 (June 1944): 59–80.
3. Ginia Bellafante, "The Civil War's Oratorical Wunderkind," *The New York Times,* May 21, 2013, https://archive.nytimes.com/opinionator.blogs.nytimes.com/2013/05/21/the-civil-wars-oratorical-wunderkind/.
4. Anna Dickinson, "Perils of the Hour," speech, U.S. House of Representa-

tives, January 16, 1864, House Divided Project, Dickinson College, accessed Augus 10, 2025, https://housedivided.dickinson.edu/sites/teagle/texts/anna-dickinson-perils-of-the-hour-1864/.

5. Young, "Anna Elizabeth Dickinson."
6. Young, "Anna Elizabeth Dickinson."
7. Young, "Anna Elizabeth Dickinson"; Jennie Miller, "Meet Anna Dickinson: Trailblazing Orator and Political Firebrand," Smithsonian National Museum of American History, August 31, 2021, https://americanhistory.si.edu/explore/stories/meet-anna-dickinson-trailblazing-orator-and-political-firebrand.
8. Angela G. Ray, "What Hath She Wrought? Woman's Rights and the Nineteenth-Century Lyceum," *Rhetoric and Public Affairs* 9, no. 2 (Summer 2006): 183–213; Paulette Beete, "Five Questions on the National Portrait Gallery Exhibit 'Votes for Women: A Portrait of Persistence,'" National Endowment for the Arts, August 13, 2019, https://www.arts.gov/stories/blog/2019/five-questions-national-portrait-gallery-exhibit-votes-women-portrait-persistence.
9. Ray, "What Hath She Wrought?"
10. Library of Congress, "Timeline," Anna E. Dickinson Papers, accessed August 10, 2025, https://www.loc.gov/collections/anna-e-dickinson-papers/articles-and-essays/timeline/.
11. J. Matthew Gallman, *America's Joan of Arc: The Life of Anna Elizabeth Dickinson* (Oxford University Press, 2006).
12. Anna E. Dickinson, "Whited Sepulchres," speech, Anna E. Dickinson Papers: Speeches and Writings File, Library of Congress, https://tile.loc.gov/storage-services/service/gdc/gdccrowd/mss/mss18424/mss18424-017/mss18424-017_0575_0602.txt.

CHAPTER 15

1. Melinda Evans, "Belva Lockwood: The 'Nerviest Woman in the United States,' Who Became the Latter-day Saints' Irrepressible Advocate and Friend," *BYU Studies Quarterly* 59, no. 3 (2020): 123–149.
2. Ruth Bader Ginsburg, "Foreword," in Jill Norgren, *Belva Lockwood: The Woman Who Would Be President* (New York University Press, 2007), ix–xii.
3. "A Woman Pioneer," *Farmington (MO) Times,* August 3, 1917, p. 7, col. 5, Chronicling America, Library of Congress, https://chroniclingamerica.loc.gov/lccn/sn89066996/1917-08-03/ed-1/seq-7/.
4. Julia Hull Winner, "That Extraordinary Woman," *Wisconsin Magazine of History* 39, no. 4 (October 1958): 321–340.
5. Amber Paranick, "Belva Lockwood: Suffragist, Lawyer, and Presidential Candi-

date," September 28, 2020, Headlines & Heroes, Library of Congress, https://blogs.loc.gov/headlinesandheroes/2020/09/belva-lockwood-suffragist-lawyer-and-presidential-candidate/.

6. Ruth Steinhardt, "In Her Own Words: The First Female Candidate for President," *GW Today,* November 7, 2016, George Washington University, https://gwtoday.gwu.edu/her-own-words-first-female-candidate-president.
7. Jill Norgren, "Belva Lockwood: Blazing the Trail for Women in Law," *Prologue* 37, no. 1 (Spring 2005), National Archives, https://www.archives.gov/publications/prologue/2005/spring/belva-lockwood-1.
8. "A Woman Pioneer."
9. Norgren, "Belva Lockwood."
10. Supreme Court of the United States, "In Re Lady Lawyers: The Rise of Women Attorneys and the Supreme Court," Exhibitions, accessed August 10, 2025, https://www.supremecourt.gov/visiting/exhibitions/LadyLawyers/Default.aspx.
11. "A Woman Case in the Supreme Court," *Evening Star* (Washington, D.C.), December 2, 1880, p. 1, col. 3, Chronicling America, Library of Congress, https://chroniclingamerica.loc.gov/lccn/sn83045462/1880-12-02/ed-1/seq-1/.
12. Supreme Court of the United States, "In Re Lady Lawyers."
13. "Mrs. Belva A. Lockwood," *Frank Leslie's Illustrated Newspaper,* April 5, 1879.
14. Adam Liptak, "The Supreme Court's Gender Gap," *The New York Times,* January 17, 2022, https://www.nytimes.com/2022/01/17/us/supreme-court-gender-gap.html.
15. Steinhardt, "In Her Own Words."
16. Steve Cichon, "Belva Lockwood, Niagara County Native and America's First Female Presidential Candidate," *Buffalo News,* October 24, 2016, https://buffalonews.com/news/local/history/belva-lockwood-niagara-county-native-and-america-s-first-female-presidential-candidate/article_e8f76927-caf1-545f-a917-ab95c910dc05.html.
17. Winner, "That Extraordinary Woman."
18. Norgren, "Belva Lockwood."
19. Norgren, "Belva Lockwood"; Joseph Stromberg, "'Bicycle Face': A 19th-Century Health Problem Made Up to Scare Women Away from Biking," *Vox Almanac,* March 24, 2015, https://www.vox.com/2014/7/8/5880931/the-19th-century-health-scare-that-told-women-to-worry-about-bicycle.
20. *The Daytona Daily News,* Daytona Beach, FL, February 24, 1913, https://www.loc.gov/item/sn93063916/1913-02-24/ed-1.
21. Steinhardt, "In Her Own Words."

22. *Casper (WY) Daily Tribune,* January 25, 1917, p. 5, col. 2, Chronicling America, Library of Congress, https://chroniclingamerica.loc.gov/lccn/sn86072160/1917-01-25/ed-1/seq-5/.
23. Jill Norgren, *Belva Lockwood: The Woman Who Would Be President* (New York University Press, 2007).

PART III

1. Ruth Bordin, *Woman and Temperance: The Quest for Power and Liberty, 1873–1900* (Temple University Press, 1981).
2. Ida B. Wells, *The Light of Truth: Writings of an Anti-Lynching Crusader,* ed. Mia Bay and Henry Louis Gates, Jr., (Penguin Classics, 2014).
3. American Fuel & Petrochemical Manufacturers, "The Women Who Made the Future Possible," *AFPM Communications,* March 8, 2022, https://www.afpm.org/newsroom/blog/women-who-made-future-possible.
4. B. Zorina Khan, "'Not for Ornament': Patenting Activity by Nineteenth-Century Women Inventors," *Journal of Interdisciplinary History* 31, no. 2 (2000): 159–195.
5. "A Lady Inventor," *Newton (NC) Enterprise,* May 31, 1888, https://www.newspapers.com/article/the-newton-enterprise-a-lady-inventor/90479179/.
6. Frederick N. Rasmussen, "She Took the Pain out of the Train Innovator: One of the First Women to Earn a Cornell Engineering Degree, Olive Dennis Helped Make Rail Travel Less Complicated and More Comfortable," *Baltimore Sun,* November 23, 1997, https://www.baltimoresun.com/1997/11/23/she-took-the-pain-out-of-the-train-innovator-one-of-the-first-women-to-earn-a-cornell-engineering-degree-olive-dennis-helped-make-rail-travel-less-complicated-and-more-comfortable/.
7. Chris Enss, *Iron Women: The Ladies Who Helped Build the Railroad* (TwoDot, 2021).
8. Enss, *Iron Women.*
9. Enss, *Iron Women.*
10. Enss, *Iron Women.*
11. National Inventors Hall of Fame, "Josephine Garis Cochran," inductee profile, https://www.invent.org/inductees/josephine-garis-cochran.
12. Lynn Weinstein, "Honoring African Americans: Historic Women Trailblazers and Advocacy Organizations," *Inside Adams* (blog of the Library of Congress), March 8, 2021, https://blogs.loc.gov/inside_adams/2021/03/historic-women-trailblazers.
13. National Park Service, "Memorable Quotes from Maggie L. Walker," speech to the Negro Young People's Christian and Educational Congress, Washington,

D.C., August 5, 1906, National Historic Site Virginia, https://www.nps.gov/mawa/learn/historyculture/memorable-quotes-from-maggie-l-walker.htm.

14. Hollie Pich, "Various, Beautiful, and Terrible: The Life and Legacy of Ida B. Wells-Barnett," *Australasian Journal of American Studies* 34, no. 2 (December 2015): 59–74.
15. Fannie Barrier Williams, "The Woman's Part in a Man's Business," *Voice of the Negro* 1 (1904): 544.
16. Austin Allen, "Emma Lazarus: 'The New Colossus,'" Poetry Foundation, November 22, 2017, https://www.poetryfoundation.org/articles/144956/emma-lazarus-the-new-colossus.
17. National Park Service, "Emma Lazarus," accessed August 10, 2025, https://www.nps.gov/stli/learn/historyculture/emma-lazarus.htm.
18. Elizabeth Stone, "The Woman Who Saved the Statue of Liberty," *Smithsonian Magazine,* May 4, 2023, https://www.smithsonianmag.com/history/the-woman-who-saved-the-statue-of-liberty-180982100/.
19. Lila Thulin, "The Thorny Road to the 19th Amendment," *Smithsonian Magazine,* March 18, 2020, https://www.smithsonianmag.com/history/thorny-road-19th-amendment-180974438/.
20. "Women's Suffrage in the U.S. by State," Rutgers University, Center for American Women and Politics, August 2014, https://tag.rutgers.edu/wp-content/uploads/2014/05/suffrage-by-state.pdf.
21. Elizabeth Cobbs, *The Hello Girls: America's First Women Soldiers* (Harvard University Press, 2019).
22. Tyler L. Boyd, *Tennessee Statesman Harry T. Burn: Woman Suffrage, Free Elections and a Life of Service* (Arcadia, 2019).

CHAPTER 16

1. Jessica Bennett, "Emily Warren Roebling, 1843–1903," Overlooked, *The New York Times,* March 8, 2018, interactive feature on overlooked women's obituaries, https://www.nytimes.com/interactive/2018/obituaries/overlooked-emily-warren-roebling.html.
2. W. P. Butler, "Caisson Disease During the Construction of the Eads and Brooklyn Bridges: A Review," *Undersea and Hyperbaric Medicine* 31, no. 4 (Winter 2004): 445–459.
3. Butler, "Caisson Disease."
4. Bennett, "Emily Warren Roebling."
5. Marian Betancourt, *Heroes of New York Harbor: Tales from the City's Port* (Globe Pequot, 2005), 74.

6. "Mrs. Roebling's Skill," *The New York Times,* May 23, 1883.
7. Bennett, "Emily Warren Roebling."
8. Ruth Oldenziel, *Making Technology Masculine: Men, Women, and Modern Machines in America, 1870–1945* (Amsterdam University Press, 1999).
9. "A Majority for Roebling," *The New York Times,* September 12, 1882.
10. "A Majority for Roebling."
11. "Mrs. Roebling's Skill."
12. John A. Stuart, "The Confluence of Allegory and Technology in Gendered Public Space: Emily Roebling and the Construction of the Brooklyn Bridge," PhD diss., Florida International University, 1996.
13. Betancourt, *Heroes of New York Harbor,* 74.
14. Charles-Émile-Auguste Carolus-Duran, *Portrait of Emily Warren Roebling,* 1896, oil on canvas, 89 × 47½ in. (226.1 × 120.7 cm), Brooklyn Museum, Brooklyn, New York, https://www.brooklynmuseum.org/objects/4960.
15. Betancourt, *Heroes of New York Harbor,* 74.
16. New York Historical, "Life Story: Emily Warren Roebling, 1843–1903," Women and the American Story, accessed August 10, 2025, https://wams.nyhistory.org/industry-and-empire/labor-and-industry/emily-warren-roebling/.
17. Emily Warren Roebling, "A Wife's Disabilities," *Albany Law Journal,* no. 59 (April 15, 1899): 342.
18. "The Builders of the Bridge Dedicated to the Memory of Emily Warren Roebling," Columbia University Libraries, Digital Library Collections, https://dlc.library.columbia.edu/catalog/cul:prr4xgxd3s.
19. Hannah Kliger, "Honoring the Legacy of Emily Warren Roebling, Who Helped Build the Brooklyn Bridge," CBS News, March 17, 2025, https://www.cbsnews.com/newyork/news/honoring-the-legacy-of-emily-warren-roebling-who-helped-build-the-brooklyn-bridge.

CHAPTER 17

1. Oberlin College, "The Wright Sister," accessed August 10, 2025, https://isis2.cc.oberlin.edu/175/didyouknow-kwright.html.
2. Harry Haskell, *In Her Own Wright,* podcast (3 episode series), episode 1, "Part 1: Introducing the Wright Sister," February 6, 2022, Apple Podcasts, https://podcasts.apple.com/us/podcast/in-her-own-wright/id1607384836.
3. Katherine Crawford-Lackey, "Places of Women in Aviation," National Park Service, accessed August 10, 2025, https://www.nps.gov/articles/000/places-of-women-in-aviation.htm.
4. National Park Service, "Orville Wright's Life Story," Dayton Aviation Heritage

National Historical Park, https://www.nps.gov/daav/learn/historyculture/orvillewrightslifestory.htm.

5. *Scrapbooks: January—December 1909,* Wilbur Wright and Orville Wright Papers, 1809–1979, Library of Congress, https://www.loc.gov/item/wright002800/.
6. R. Maurer, *The Wright Sister: Katharine Wright and Her Famous Brothers* (Roaring Brook Press, 2003).
7. Airman 1st Class Michael Merrell, 7th Contracting Squadron, "The Contract That Started It All," January 13, 2015, Air Combat Command, https://www.acc.af.mil/News/Commentaries/Display/Article/661822/the-contract-that-started-it-all/.
8. Milena Evtimova, "Forever and Always Wright," *Oberlin Review,* September 15, 2006, https://www2.oberlin.edu/stupub/ocreview/2006/09/15/features/Forever_and_Always_Wright.html.
9. Wright State University, "Katharine Wright's First Time Flying," photograph, February 15, 1909, Wright Brothers Photographs, https://corescholar.libraries.wright.edu/special_ms1_photographs/402/.
10. Haskell, *In Her Own Wright,* episode 2, "Part 2: Katie and 'The Boys,'" February 13, 2022.
11. Wright State University, "Katharine Wright Haskell Papers, MS-700," Special Collections, https://wright.libraryhost.com/repositories/2/resources/1730.
12. Haskell, *In Her Own Wright,* episode 1.
13. 35 Stat. 1627 (1909).
14. "Nation Honors Wright Boys," *Daily Star* (Fredericksburg, VA), vol. 16, no. 302, June 11, 1909, p. 1, col. 4.
15. Katherine Ruffing and Dorothy Cochrane, "Katharine Wright: The Wright Sister," National Air and Space Museum, March 31, 2023, https://airandspace.si.edu/stories/editorial/katharine-wright-wright-sister.
16. Colleen Kilday, "A Trailblazer in Her Own Wright," March 14, 2024, Federal Aviation Administration, https://www.faa.gov/media/77006.
17. Katharine Wright [Haskell] to Harry [Henry J. Haskell], letter, November 11, 1924, https://corescholar.libraries.wright.edu/special_ms700_correspondence/34/.
18. Katharine Wright [Haskell] to Harry [Henry J. Haskell], letter, November 6, 1924, https://corescholar.libraries.wright.edu/special_ms700_correspondence/33/.
19. National Park Service, *Hawthorn Hill Historic Furnishings Report* (Dayton Aviation Heritage National Historical Park, 2010), https://www.nps.gov/parkhistory/online_books/daav/hawthorn_hill_hfr.pdf.

20. Haskell, *In Her Own Wright*, episode 3, "Part 3: 'The Hazards of Love,'" February 20, 2022.
21. Haskell, *In Her Own Wright*, episode 3.

CHAPTER 18

1. Meredith Mendelsohn, "She Was More Than Just the 'Most Beautiful Suffragist,'" *The New York Times*, August 19, 2020, https://www.nytimes.com/2020/08/19/arts/design/inez-milholland-suffragist.html.
2. Jill Lepore, "The Surprising Origin Story of Wonder Woman," *Smithsonian Magazine*, October 2014, https://www.smithsonianmag.com/arts-culture/origin-story-wonder-woman-180952710/.
3. Linda J. Lumsden, "The Woman on the White Horse: The Forgotten Fighter Who Led the Way for Women's Suffrage," *Talking Points Memo*, December 1, 2016, https://talkingpointsmemo.com/feature/the-woman-on-the-white-horse-inez-milholland.
4. Allison K. Lange and Cara Bennet, "Parading for Progress," March 1, 2018, National Women's History Museum, https://www.womenshistory.org/exhibits/parading-progress.
5. National Park Service, "1913 Woman Suffrage Procession," May 18, 2025, https://www.nps.gov/articles/woman-suffrage-procession1913.htm.
6. Rachel Wallach, "Video Screenings Explore the 1913 March on Washington for Women's Suffrage and Its Fallout," *Johns Hopkins University Hub*, April 27, 2020, https://hub.jhu.edu/2020/04/27/screenings-explore-womens-suffrage-march/.
7. National Park Service, "1913 Woman Suffrage Procession," last updated May 18, 2025, https://www.nps.gov/articles/woman-suffrage-procession1913.htm.
8. National Park Service, "1913 Woman Suffrage Procession."
9. Sharon McMahon, *The Small and the Mighty: Twelve Unsung Americans Who Changed the Course of History* (Penguin Publishing Group, 2024).
10. Diane Bernard, "She Was the Glamorous Face of Suffrage. Then She Became Its Martyr," *The Washington Post*, August 7, 2020, https://www.washingtonpost.com/graphics/2020/local/history/inez-milholland-suffrage-parade-womens-rights/.
11. Linda J. Lumsden, *Inez: The Life and Time of Inez Milholland* (Indiana University Press, 2004).
12. National Museum of American History, "Report of the Senate Hearing on the 1913 Woman Suffrage Parade," accessed October 3, 2025, https://americanhistory.si.edu/collections/object/nmah_1065355.

13. Lumsden, *Inez.*
14. U.S. Congress, *Senate's Suffrage Parade: Report of the Committee on the District of Columbia,* 63rd Cong., 1st sess., Report no. 53 (May 29, 1913).
15. "Along the Color Line," *The Crisis* 5, no. 6 (April 1913): 267, https://edan.si.edu/slideshow/viewer/?damspath=/Public_Sets/NMAAHC/NMAAHC_Slideshows/2015_97_14_6.
16. Cathleen D. Cahill, *Recasting the Vote: How Women of Color Transformed the Suffrage Movement* (University of North Carolina Press, 2020).
17. "Illinois Women Feature Parade: Delegation from This State Wins High Praise by Order in Marching," *Chicago Daily Tribune,* March 4, 1913, p. 3.
18. "Illinois Women Participate in Suffrage Parade; This State Was Well Represented," *Chicago Daily Tribune,* March 5, 1913, p. 5.
19. National Park Service, "Inez Milholland," accessed August 10, 2025, https://www.nps.gov/people/inez-milholland.htm.
20. Lowell Milken Center for Unsung Heroes, "Meet the Hero: Inez Milholland," accessed August 10, 2025, https://www.lowellmilkencenter.org/programs/projects/view/inez-milholland/hero.
21. Bernard, "Glamorous Face of Suffrage."
22. Mendelsohn, "'Most Beautiful Suffragist.'"
23. Mendelsohn, "'Most Beautiful Suffragist.'"
24. Lumsden, *Inez.*

CHAPTER 19

1. National Park Service "The St. Luke Penny Savings Bank," February 7, 2023, https://www.nps.gov/mawa/the-st-luke-penny-savings-bank.htm.
2. John Mullin, "Maggie Lena Walker: How the Daughter of a Former Slave Became a Banking Pioneer," *Econ Focus* (Federal Reserve Bank of Richmond), Fourth Quarter 2022, https://www.richmondfed.org/publications/research/econ_focus/2022/q4_economic_history.
3. PBS Learning Media, "Our Inspiration: The Story of Maggie Lena Walker," PBS Wisconsin, accessed August 10, 2025, https://www.pbslearningmedia.org/resource/a9dedf68-e383-4d04-85a0-0a5ac0ed2eac/our-inspiration-the-story-of-maggie-lena-walker/.
4. National Park Service, "Maggie Lena Walker," Maggie L. Walker National Historic Site, last modified June 7, 2025, https://www.nps.gov/mawa/learn/historyculture/maggie-lena-walker.htm.
5. National Park Service, "St. Luke Penny Savings."
6. Crystal Marie Moten, "Pennies and Nickels Add Up to Success: Maggie Lena

Walker," February 27, 2020, National Museum of American History, Smithsonian Institution, https://americanhistory.si.edu/explore/stories/pennies-and-nickels-add-success-maggie-lena-walker.

7. Elsa Barkley Brown, "Constructing a Life and a Community: A Partial Story of Maggie Lena Walker," *OAH Magazine of History* 7, no. 4 (1993): 28–31.
8. Crystal Moten, "How Maggie Lena Walker Became the First Black Woman to Run a Bank in the Segregated South," *Smithsonian Magazine,* February 17, 2021, https://www.smithsonianmag.com/blogs/national-museum-american-history/2021/02/17/maggie-lena-walker/.
9. Moten, "How Maggie Lena Walker."
10. Moten, "How Maggie Lena Walker."
11. Charles Willis Simmons, "Maggie Lena Walker and the Consolidated Bank and Trust Company," *Negro History Bulletin* 38, no. 2 (February/March 1975): 345–349.
12. National Park Service, "The St. Luke Herald—The Trumpet of Progress," last updated January 4, 2017, https://www.nps.gov/mawa/learn/historyculture/st-luke-herald.htm.
13. David T. Beito, "To Advance the 'Practice of Thrift and Economy': Fraternal Societies and Social Capital, 1890–1920," *Journal of Interdisciplinary History* 29, no. 4 (Spring 1999): 585–612.
14. National Park Service, "Upholstered Wheel Chair and Writing Table," Maggie L. Walker National Historic Site, last modified June 7, 2025, https://www.nps.gov/museum/exhibits/maggie_walker/exb/life%20at%20home/b%20work%20at%20home/mawa00000527_g.html.
15. National Museum of African American History and Culture, "Independent Order of St. Luke," accessed October 5, 2025, https://www.searchablemuseum.com/independent-order-of-st-luke/.
16. Celia Jackson Suggs and Maggie L. Walker, "Commemorating the Twentieth Anniversary of the Association of Black Women Historians 1979–1999," *Negro History Bulletin* 63, no. 1/4 (January–December 2000): 39–44.
17. PBS Learning Media, *Our Inspiration.*
18. Maggie L. Walker, ed., *Memoirs: Independent Order of St. Luke P.R.W. Grand Chiefs, 1881–1931,* 1931, p. 53, National Park Service, A-2333 (Subcollection XII, IOSL Records, box 15, folder 8).
19. Rhonda L. Crenshaw, "Maggie Lena Walker: America's National Treasure in Banking," Federal Deposit Insurance Corporation (FDIC), last modified April 10, 2025, https://www.fdic.gov/minority-depository-institutions-program/maggie-lena-walker-americas-national-treasure-banking.

CHAPTER 20

1. Heather Thomas, "Before *Brown v. Board of Education,* There Was *Tape v. Hurley,*" May 5, 2021, Headlines and Heroes, Library of Congress, https://blogs.loc.gov/headlinesandheroes/2021/05/before-brown-v-education-there-was-tape-v-hurley/.
2. Charmaine Lam, "Disentangling and Interpreting the Mui Tsai Experience," New York University, accessed August 10, 2025, https://digitalhumanities.nyu.edu/projects/g2023lam/.
3. Karen Yuen, "Theorizing the Chinese: The Mui Tsai Controversy and Constructions of Transnational Chineseness in Hong Kong and British Malaya," *New Zealand Journal of Asian Studies* 6, no. 2 (December 2004): 95–110.
4. Edward Wong, "Broken Blossoms: A Struggle from Servitude to Freedom," *Prologue* 48, no. 1 (Spring 2016), National Archives, https://www.archives.gov/publications/prologue/2016/spring/broken-blossoms.
5. Judy Yung, *Unbound Feet: A Social History of Chinese Women in San Francisco* (University of California Press, 1995).
6. Mae Ngai, *The Lucky Ones: An Extraordinary Invention by the Chinese* (Norton, 2006).
7. Ngai, *The Lucky Ones.*
8. National Park Service, "Mary Tape," accessed August 10, 2025, https://www.nps.gov/people/mary-tape.htm.
9. National Park Service, "Mary Tape."
10. Thomas, "Before *Brown v. Board of Education.*"
11. Thomas, "Before *Brown v. Board of Education.*"
12. Mary Tape, "An Indignant Mother," *New North-West* (Deer Lodge, MT), vol. 16, no. 47, May 22, 1885, p. 1, col. 3, Library of Congress, https://blogs.loc.gov/headlinesandheroes/2021/05/before-brown-v-education-there-was-tape-v-hurley/.
13. Leland Gamble, "What a Chinese Girl Did: An Expert Photographer and Telegrapher," *Morning Call* (San Francisco, CA), vol. 72, no. 176, November 23, 1892, p. 12, col. 1–3, Library of Congress, https://www.loc.gov/item/sn94052989/1892-11-23/ed-1/.

CHAPTER 21

1. Cathleen D. Cahill, *Recasting the Vote: How Women of Color Transformed the Suffrage Movement* (University of North Carolina Press, 2020).
2. Tadeusz Lewandowski, *Red Bird, Red Power: The Life and Legacy of Zitkala-Ša,*

American Indian Literature and Critical Studies 67 (University of Oklahoma Press, 2016).

3. Lewandowski, *Red Bird, Red Power.*
4. Zitkala-Ša, *American Indian Stories, Legends, and Other Writings,* Kindle edition, ed. Cathy N. Davidson and Ada Norris (Penguin Classics, 2003).
5. Cahill, *Women of Color Transformed.*
6. Wolfgang Mieder, "'The Only Good Indian Is a Dead Indian': History and Meaning of a Proverbial Stereotype," *Journal of American Folklore* 106, no. 419 (Winter 1993): 38–60.
7. National Park Service, "The Dawes Act," Badlands National Park, last modified July 9, 2021, https://www.nps.gov/articles/000/dawes-act.htm.
8. Zitkala-Ša, "The School Days of an Indian Girl," *The Atlantic,* February 1900, https://www.theatlantic.com/magazine/archive/1900/02/the-school-days-of-an-indian-girl/636476/.
9. Zitkala-Ša, "School Days."
10. Cahill, *Women of Color Transformed.*
11. Nicole McNew Chen, "Zitkála-Šá: On Creativity, Copyright, and Cultural Empowerment," March 31, 2021, Library of Congress, https://blogs.loc.gov/copyright/2021/03/zitkla-on-creativity-copyright-and-cultural-empowerment/.
12. Franklin Welles Calkins, "Zitkala-Sa the Red Bird of the Sioux," *Evening Star* (Washington, D.C.), September 23, 1906, Library of Congress, https://chroniclingamerica.loc.gov/lccn/sn83045462/1906-09-23/ed-1/seq-28.
13. Zitkala-Ša, *American Indian Stories* (Hayworth, 1921).
14. Lewandowski, *Red Bird, Red Power.*
15. Gertrude Bonnin, "Address by Mrs. Gertrude Bonnin," *American Indian* 7, no. 3 (1919), speech delivered at the Annual Convention of the Society of American Indians, October 2–4, 1919.
16. Jessica Enoch, "Resisting the Script of Indian Education: Zitkala-Ša and the Carlisle Indian School," *College English* 65, no. 2 (November 2002): 117–141.
17. Lewandowski, *Red Bird, Red Power,* 150–151.
18. Cahill, *Women of Color Transformed.*
19. Cahill, *Women of Color Transformed.*

CHAPTER 22

1. Elizabeth Cobbs, *The Hello Girls: America's First Women Soldiers* (Harvard University Press, 2019).

2. Military Times, "Grace Banker," Hall of Valor, accessed August 10, 2025, https://valor.militarytimes.com/recipient/recipient-17234/.
3. Carolyn Timbie, "100 Years Ago: Hello Girl Grace Banker Receives Distinguished Service Medal," United States World War One Centennial Commission, accessed August 10, 2025, https://www.worldwar1centennial.org/index.php/communicate/press-media/wwi-centennial-news/6250-100-years-ago-hello-girl-grace-banker-receives-distinguished-service-medal.html.
4. PBS, *The Hello Girls,* November 11, 2023, https://www.pbs.org/video/the-hello-girls-smfkeu/.
5. Grace Banker Paddock, "I Was a 'Hello Girl,'" *Congressional Record—Senate,* April 28, 1977, https://www.govinfo.gov/content/pkg/GPO-CRECB-1977-pt11/pdf/GPO-CRECB-1977-pt11-1-2.pdf.
6. Delaney Brewer, "Grace Banker Paddock," National Museum of the United States Army, accessed August 10, 2025, https://www.thenmusa.org/biographies/grace-banker/.
7. Library of Congress, "Hello Girls: Topics in Chronicling America," Research Guides, accessed August 10, 2025, https://guides.loc.gov/chronicling-america-hello-girls.
8. National Archives, "The Meuse-Argonne Offensive," Military Records, April 5, 2023, https://www.archives.gov/research/military/ww1/meuse-argonne.
9. Cobbs, *The Hello Girls.*
10. U.S. Department of Veterans Affairs, "'Hello Girls' of World War I Quest for Veteran Recognition: Telephone Operators 60-Year Struggle for Benefits After the Great War," accessed August 10, 2025, https://department.va.gov/history/featured-stories/hello-girls/.
11. PBS, *The Hello Girls.*
12. Annie Hanshew, "Merle Egan Anderson: Montana's 'Hello Girl,'" *Montana Women's History,* November 11, 2014, https://montanawomenshistory.org/merle-egan-anderson-montanas-hello-girl.
13. Cobbs, *The Hello Girls.*
14. Cobbs, *The Hello Girls.*
15. National Archives, "The Hello Girls Finally Get Paid," Pieces of History, June 24, 2015, https://prologue.blogs.archives.gov/2015/06/24/the-hello-girls-finally-get-paid/.
16. PBS, *The Hello Girls.*
17. Megan Garcia, "Nevertheless, She Persisted: Fort Benning Officer Honors the Hello Girls," U.S. Army, March 15, 2018, https://www.army.mil/article

/202309/nevertheless_she_persisted_fort_benning_officer_honors_the_hello _girls.

18. H.R. 5009—To Authorize Appropriations for Fiscal Year 2025 for Military Activities of the Department of Defense, for Military Construction, and for Defense Activities of the Department of Energy, to Prescribe Military Personnel Strengths for Such Fiscal Year, and for Other Purposes, 118th Cong. (2023–2024).

CHAPTER 23

1. Lee Anne Spear, "Silent Sentinels and Scandalous Radicals: Suffragettes Take D.C.," *Evolution D.C.,* exhibition, George Washington University Museum, May 18, 2023, https://evolutiondc.museum.gwu.edu/suffragettes -in-dc/.
2. Smithsonian, "Suffragists arrested for picketing outside the White House—the first group to protest there—could face six months in jail," Facebook, August 26, 2020, https://www.facebook.com/Smithsonian/photos/a.57737704573 /10158942749394574/?type=3; Liza Mundy, "The Long Battle for Women's Suffrage," *Smithsonian Magazine,* April 2019, https://www.smithsonianmag.com /smithsonian-institution/long-battle-womens-suffrage-180971637/.
3. Library of Congress, "Today in History—August 28," Library of Congress, last modified August 28, 2025, https://www.loc.gov/item/today-in-history/august -28/.
4. Doris Stevens, *Jailed for Freedom* (Liveright, 1920).
5. Stevens, *Jailed for Freedom.*
6. Stevens, *Jailed for Freedom.*
7. Terrence McArdle, " 'Night of Terror': The Suffragists Who Were Beaten and Tortured for Seeking the Vote," *The Washington Post,* November 10, 2017, https://www.washingtonpost.com/news/retropolis/wp/2017/11/10/night-of -terror-the-suffragists-who-were-beaten-and-tortured-for-seeking-the-vote/.
8. McArdle, " 'Night of Terror.' "
9. National Park Service, "Lucy Burns," last updated August 7, 2024, https://www .nps.gov/people/lucy-burns.htm.
10. Stevens, *Jailed for Freedom.*
11. McArdle, "'Night of Terror.'"
12. United States Senate, "The Nineteenth Amendment: A Vertical Timeline," https://www.senate.gov/about/women-of-the-senate/nineteenth-amendment -vertical-timeline.htm.

13. History, Art & Archives, U.S. House of Representatives. "Edition for Educators—Celebrating Women's History Month." March 18, 2014. https://history.house.gov/Blog/2014/March/3-18-Educators-Womens-History.
14. National Constitution Center, "On This Day, Jeannette Rankin's History-Making Moment," April 2, 2024, https://constitutioncenter.org/blog/on-this-day-jeanette-rankins-history-making-moment.
15. U.S. House of Representatives, "About Women's Suffrage," History, Art & Archives, accessed August 11, 2025, https://history.house.gov/Education/Primary-Sources/Primary-Source-Sets/Womens-Suffrage/About-Womens-Suffrage.
16. U.S. House of Representatives, "Rankin, Jeannette," History, Art & Archives, accessed August 11, 2025, https://history.house.gov/People/Listing/R/RANKIN,-Jeannette-(R000055).
17. U.S. House of Representatives, "Suffrage Committee," January 10, 2018, History, Art & Archives, https://history.house.gov/Blog/2018/January/1-10-Suffrage-Committee.
18. "Address to the Senate on the Nineteenth Amendment," September 30, 1918, American Presidency Project, https://www.presidency.ucsb.edu/documents/address-the-senate-the-nineteenth-amendment.
19. U.S. House of Representatives, "The House's 1918 Passage of a Constitutional Amendment Granting Women the Right to Vote," January 10, 1918, History, Art & Archives, https://history.house.gov/Historical-Highlights/1901-1950/The-House-s-1918-passage-of-a-constitutional-amendment-granting-women-the-right-to-vote/.
20. Tyler L. Boyd, *Tennessee Statesman Harry T. Burn: Woman Suffrage, Free Elections and a Life of Service* (Arcadia, 2019).
21. Tyler L. Boyd, *Tennessee Statesman Harry T. Burn*.
22. Center for American Women and Politics, "Gender Differences in Voter Turnout," Eagleton Institute of Politics, Rutgers University, 2025, https://cawp.rutgers.edu/facts/voters/gender-differences-voter-turnout.

CHAPTER 24

1. Wendy E. Arevalo, "Agnes Meyer Driscoll: The First Lady of Naval Cryptology," Naval History and Heritage Command, accessed July 14, 2025, https://www.history.navy.mil/content/history/nhhc/browse-by-topic/wars-conflicts-and-operations/cold-war/agnes-meyer-driscoll-the-first-lady-of-naval-cryptology.html.
2. Kevin Wade Johnson, *The Neglected Giant: Agnes Meyer Driscoll,* Center for Crypto-

logic History Special Series 10 (Center for Cryptologic History, National Security Agency, 2015).

3. Lou Leto and Jen Wilcox, "Pioneering Women in Cryptology," Smithsonian National Air and Space Museum, March 29, 2018, https://airandspace.si.edu/stories/editorial/pioneering-women-cryptology.
4. Regina T. Akers, "Historical Overview of Yeomen (F)," Naval History and Heritage Command, accessed July 14, 2025, https://www.history.navy.mil/content/history/nhhc/browse-by-topic/wars-conflicts-and-operations/world-war-i/people/historical-overview-of-yeomen-f.html.
5. "Agnes Meyer Driscoll," Center of Excellence for Women & Technology, Indiana University, accessed July 14, 2025, https://womenandtech.indiana.edu/programs/cybersecurity/profiles-cybersecurity-women/driscoll.html.
6. Arevalo, "Agnes Meyer Driscoll."
7. Liza Mundy, "'Any Man-Made Code Can Be Broken by a Woman': The Groundbreaking Female Naval Cryptographer Who Helped Change the Course of World War II," National Cryptologic Foundation, October 11, 2017, https://cryptologicfoundation.org/news-events/blog/blog-archive.html/article/2017/10/11/-any-man-made-code-can-be-broken-by-a-woman-the-groundbreaking-female-naval-cryptographer-who-helped-change-the-course-of-world-war-ii-.
8. Johnson, *The Neglected Giant.*
9. Arevalo, "Agnes Meyer Driscoll."
10. Arevalo, "Agnes Meyer Driscoll."
11. Johnson, *The Neglected Giant.*
12. Johnson, *The Neglected Giant.*
13. Johnson, *The Neglected Giant.*
14. Johnson, *The Neglected Giant.*
15. Johnson, *The Neglected Giant.*
16. "Agnes Meyer Driscoll," NSA Historical Figures, National Security Agency, accessed July 14, 2025, https://www.nsa.gov/History/Cryptologic-History/Historical-Figures/Historical-Figures-View/Article/1623020/agnes-meyer-driscoll/.

CHAPTER 25

1. R. L. Goldenberg and E. M. McClure, "Maternal Mortality," *American Journal of Obstetrics and Gynecology* 205, no. 4 (October 2011): 293–295.
2. Rainey Horwitz, "First American Birth Control Clinic (The Brownsville Clinic), 1916," October 11, 2019, Embryo Project Encyclopedia, Arizona State

University, https://embryo.asu.edu/pages/first-american-birth-control-clinic-brownsville-clinic-1916.

3. "Achievements in Public Health, 1900–1999: Healthier Mothers and Babies," *MMWR Weekly* 48, no. 38 (October 1, 1999): 849–858, https://www.cdc.gov/mmwr/preview/mmwrhtml/mm4838a2.htm.
4. Rachel Benson Gold and Guttmacher Institute, "Lessons from Before Roe: Will Past Be Prologue?," *Guttmacher Policy Review* 6, no. 1 (March 1, 2003), https://www.guttmacher.org/gpr/2003/03/lessons-roe-will-past-be-prologue.
5. Horwitz, "First American Birth Control Clinic."
6. Howard Merkel, "How This New York Clinic Helped Transform Reproductive Health Care," PBS, October 20, 2022, https://www.pbs.org/newshour/nation/how-this-new-york-clinic-helped-transform-reproductive-health-care.
7. 8 U.S.C. § 1461.
8. "Sanger on Trial: The Brownsville Clinic Testimony," Newsletter #25 (Fall 2000), The Margaret Sanger Papers Project, New York University, https://sanger.hosting.nyu.edu/articles/sanger_on_trial/.
9. Horwitz, "First American Birth Control Clinic."
10. *New York Times*, January 30, 1917, p. 4; March 7, 1917, p. 13.
11. "Margaret Sanger (1879–1966)," American Experience, PBS/WGBH Educational Foundation, accessed October 5, 2025, https://www.pbs.org/wgbh/americanexperience/features/pill-margaret-sanger-1879-1966/.
12. "Roots of the Pill," American Experience, PBS/WGBH Educational Foundation, accessed July 14, 2025, https://www.pbs.org/wgbh/americanexperience/features/roots-pill/.
13. "Roots of the Pill."
14. Anya Jabour, "Abortion and Birth-Control Restrictions Curtail Women's Citizenship," *The Washington Post*, Outlook, June 26, 2022, https://www.washingtonpost.com/outlook/2022/06/26/abortion-birth-control-restrictions-curtail-womens-citizenship/.
15. Lesley Hoyt Croft, "Margaret Sanger," 2021, EBSCO, https://www.ebsco.com/research-starters/history/margaret-sanger.
16. Jean H. Baker, *Margaret Sanger: A Life of Passion* (Hill and Wang, 2011), 85–87.
17. D. Wardell, "Margaret Sanger: Birth Control's Successful Revolutionary," *American Journal of Public Health* 70, no. 7 (1980): 736.
18. Linda Gordon, *Woman's Body, Woman's Right* (New York: Grossman, 1974, 1976), 156–57.
19. "Seventy-Fifth Anniversary of the Brownsville Clinic," Newsletter #2 (Winter

1991), The Margaret Sanger Papers Project, New York University, https://sanger.hosting.nyu.edu/articles/seventieth_anniversary_of_brownsville.

20. Margaret Sanger, *Margaret Sanger: An Autobiography* (Norton, 1938).
21. "Margaret Sanger (1879–1966)," American Experience, PBS/WGBH Educational Foundation, accessed October 5, 2025, https://www.pbs.org/wgbh/americanexperience/features/pill-margaret-sanger-1879-1966.
22. Margaret Sanger, *Woman and the New Race* (Truth, 1920).
23. "Katharine Dexter McCormick."
24. "Katharine Dexter McCormick."
25. James Reed, *The Birth Control Movement and American Society: From Private Vice to Public Virtue* (Basic Books, 1978; repr. Princeton University Press, 2014).
26. Terry Gross, host, "The Great Bluff That Led to a 'Magical' Pill and a Sexual Revolution," *Fresh Air* podcast, transcript, NPR, October 7, 2014, https://www.npr.org/transcripts/354103536.
27. Kimberly Daniels and Joyce C. Abma, *Contraceptive Methods Women Have Ever Used: United States, 2015–2019,* National Health Statistics Reports, no. 195, National Center for Health Statistics, December 14, 2023, https://www.cdc.gov/nchs/data/nhsr/nhsr195.pdf.
28. "Katharine Dexter McCormick."
29. Margaret Sanger, "The Eugenic Value of Birth Control Propaganda," *The Birth Control Review* 5, no. 10 (October 1921): 5.

PART IV

1. Andriana Bellou and Emanuela Cardia, "The Great Depression and the Rise of Female Employment: A New Hypothesis," *Explorations in Economic History* 80 (2021): 101383; Jessica Pierce Rotondi, "Underpaid, But Employed: How the Great Depression Affected Working Women," History.com, March 11, 2019, https://www.history.com/news/working-women-great-depression.
2. *Employment of Women in War Production,* Social Security Administration Bulletin, July 1942, https://www.ssa.gov/policy/docs/ssb/v5n7/v5n7p4.pdf; "'Rosie the Riveter' Coveralls," Wisconsin Historical Society, August 16, 2007, https://www.wisconsinhistory.org/Records/Article/CS2676.
3. Julie Zauzmer Weil, "Real-Life 'Rosie the Riveter' Women Share Their Stories and Philosophy," *The Washington Post,* August 10, 2014.
4. Barbara Winslow, "The Impact of Title IX," Gilder Lehrman Institute of American History, accessed August 11, 2025, https://www.gilderlehrman.org/history-resources/essays/impact-title-ix.

CHAPTER 26

1. Martha S. Jones, "Mary McLeod Bethune Was at the Vanguard of More Than 50 Years of Black Progress," *Smithsonian Magazine,* July 2020, https://www.smithsonianmag.com/history/mary-mcleod-bethune-vanguard-more-than-50-years-black-progress-180975202/.
2. Jones, "Mary McLeod Bethune."
3. Jones, "Mary McLeod Bethune."
4. Jones, "Mary McLeod Bethune."
5. Martha S. Jones, *Vanguard: How Black Women Broke Barriers, Won the Vote, and Insisted on Equality for All* (Basic Books, 2020).
6. April Rubin, "Statue of Black Educator Replaces Confederate General in U.S. Capitol," *The New York Times,* July 13, 2022, https://www.nytimes.com/2022/07/13/us/bethune-statue-confederate-capitol.htm.
7. Florida Arts & Culture, "Interview with Nilda Comas," video, *Culture Builds Florida* (blog), April 27, 2021, https://culturebuildsflorida.org/2021/04/27/interview-nilda-comas/.
8. "Mary McLeod Bethune," statue, Architect of the Capitol, accessed August 11, 2025, https://www.aoc.gov/explore-capitol-campus/art/mary-mcleod-bethune-statue.
9. Mary McLeod Bethune, "What Does American Democracy Mean to Me?," *America's Town Meeting of the Air,* NBC, radio broadcast, November 23, 1939, American Public Media, http://americanradioworks.publicradio.org/features/sayitplain/mmbethune.html.
10. Bethune, "What Does American Democracy Mean to Me?"
11. Bethune, "What Does American Democracy Mean to Me?"
12. Mary McLeod Bethune, interview by Charles S. Johnson, Florida Memory Project, accessed August 11, 2025, https://www.floridamemory.com/learn/classroom/learning-units/mary-mcleod-bethune/lessonplans/sets/interview/.
13. Bethune, interview by Charles S. Johnson.
14. Bethune, interview by Charles S. Johnson.
15. Bethune, interview by Charles S. Johnson.
16. Bethune, interview by Charles S. Johnson.
17. National Park Service, "Mary McLeod Bethune," accessed August 11, 2025, https://www.nps.gov/mamc/learn/historyculture/mary-mcleod-bethune.htm.
18. Bethune, interview by Charles S. Johnson.
19. "About Barber-Scotia College," Barber-Scotia College, accessed August 11, 2025, https://b-sc.edu/our-history/.

20. Yahya Jongintaba, "Mary McLeod Bethune at Moody," Moody Bible Institute, February 26, 2020, https://www.moody.edu/stories/undergrad/2020/bethune/.
21. Jones, "Mary McLeod Bethune."
22. Tim Walters, "Mary McLeod Bethune: Born the Daughter of Slaves, Died a Retired College President," *USA Today Network*, February 25, 2025.
23. "Dr. Mary McLeod Bethune," Bethune-Cookman University, accessed August 11, 2025, https://www.cookman.edu/history/our-founder.html.
24. Walters, "Mary McLeod Bethune"; National Park Service, "Mary McLeod Bethune."
25. "2012 Hall of Fame Roster: Mary McLeod Bethune," Bethune-Cookman Wildcats, accessed August 11, 2025, https://bcuathletics.com/sports/hall-of-fame/roster/mary-mcleod-bethune/1554.
26. Mark Harper, "What Can Be Learned from the Friendship of Eleanor Roosevelt and Mary McLeod Bethune?," *Daytona Beach News-Journal,* February 7, 2020.
27. Jill Watts, *The Black Cabinet: The Untold Story of African Americans and Politics During the Age of Roosevelt,* illustrated ed. (Grove Press, 2020).
28. Theodore Rosenof, "Roosevelt House: Saving a National Treasure for a New Generation, 1943–2023," Public Policy Institute at Hunter College, accessed August 11, 2025, https://www.roosevelthouse.hunter.cuny.edu/exhibits/roosevelt-house-saving-national-treasure-new-generation/.
29. Smithsonian American Women's History Museum, Mary McLeod Bethune and Roosevelt's "Black Cabinet," https://womenshistory.si.edu/exhibitions/mary-mcleod-bethune-and-roosevelts-black-cabinet%3Aevent-exhib-4309.
30. Jametta Davis, "Providing a New Deal for Young Black Women: Mary McLeod Bethune and the Negro Affairs Division of the NYA," Rediscovering Black History, National Archives, March 25, 2014, https://rediscovering-black-history.blogs.archives.gov/2014/03/25/providing-a-new-deal-for-young-black-women/.
31. Jeannette F. Ford, *Head, Heart, Hand: Mary McLeod Bethune and Bethune-Cookman College 1904–2004,* April, 2004. https://www.cookman.edu/oral-history/_files/its-about-time-article.pdf
32. "National Council of Negro Women (NCNW)," Martin Luther King, Jr., Research and Education Institute, Stanford University, accessed August 11, 2025, https://kinginstitute.stanford.edu/national-council-negro-women-ncnw.
33. Katie Lange, "All-Black Female WWII Unit to Receive Congressional Gold Medal," DOD News, U.S. Department of Defense, March 18, 2022, https://www.defense.gov/News/Feature-Stories/story/Article/2971608/all-black-female-wwii-unit-to-receive-congressional-gold-medal/.

34. National Park Service, "The 6888th Central Postal Directory Battalion," accessed August 11, 2025, https://www.nps.gov/mamc/the-6888th-central-postal-directory-battalion.htm.
35. Jennifer Nichol Stewart, "Wacky Times: An Analysis of the WAC in World War II and Its Effects on Women," *International Social Science Review* 75, nos. 1–2 (2000): 26–37.
36. Linda Welz, "Three Women to Thank for Tuskegee Airmen Existence," March Air Reserve Base, February 10, 2012, https://www.march.afrc.af.mil/News/Article-Display/Article/167712/three-women-to-thank-for-tuskegee-airmen-existence/.
37. Mary McLeod Bethune Council House National Historic Site, "In 1941, an incident occurred that allowed organized Negro women to participate in government programs," Facebook post, November 11, 2014, https://www.facebook.com/NPS.MAMC/photos/a.222769104439532/744675075582263/?type=3.
38. Melissa Thaxton and Jennifer Dubina, "A Different Kind of Victory: The 6888th Central Postal Directory Battalion," National Museum of the United States Army, accessed August 11, 2025, https://www.thenmusa.org/articles/a-different-kind-of-victory-the-6888th-central-postal-directory-battalion/.
39. Thaxton and Dubina, "Different Kind of Victory."
40. D. W. Houck and D. E. Dixon, eds., *Women and the Civil Rights Movement, 1954–1965* (University Press of Mississippi, 2009).
41. "Dr. Bethune's Last Will & Testament," Bethune-Cookman University, accessed August 11, 2025, https://www.cookman.edu/history/last-will-testament.html.
42. Jones, "Mary McLeod Bethune."
43. Eleanor Roosevelt, "My Day," May 20, 1955, Eleanor Roosevelt Papers Project, George Washington University, https://www2.gwu.edu/~erpapers/myday/displaydoc.cfm?_y=1955&_f=md003174.

CHAPTER 27

1. Eleanor Roosevelt, "My Day," December 26, 1942, White House Historical Association, https://www.whitehousehistory.org/eleanor-roosevelts-my-day-12-26-1942.
2. Hardie Robbins, "My First Lady," Franklin D. Roosevelt Presidential Library and Museum.
3. Hardie Robbins, "My First Lady."
4. "U.S. At War: At the White House Steinway," *Time Magazine,* March 1, 1943.
5. Robbins, "My First Lady."

6. Eleanor Roosevelt, *You Learn by Living: Eleven Keys for a More Fulfilling Life* (Harper-Perennial Modern Classics, 2011).
7. Fran Burke, "Eleanor Roosevelt, October 11, 1884–November 7, 1962—She Made a Difference," *Public Administration Review* 44, no. 5 (September–October 1984): 365–372.
8. Blanche Wiesen Cook, *Eleanor Roosevelt*, vol. 1, *1884–1933* (Viking Press, 1992), 341.
9. "Women: She Was Eleanor," *Time*, November 16, 1962.
10. "Women: She Was Eleanor."
11. "Marie Souvestre (1830–1905)," Eleanor Roosevelt Papers Project, Columbian College of Arts & Sciences, George Washington University accessed October 5, 2025, https://erpapers.columbian.gwu.edu/marie-souvestre-1830-1905.
12. "Marie Souvestre."
13. Barbara Maranzani, "10 Things You May Not Know About the Roosevelts," History, last updated May 28, 2025, https://www.history.com/articles/10-things-you-may-not-know-about-the-roosevelts.
14. Deirdre Carmody, "Letters by Eleanor Roosevelt Detail Friendship with Lorena Hickok," *The New York Times*, October 21, 1979.
15. Amy Berish, "FDR and Polio," Franklin D. Roosevelt Presidential Library and Museum, accessed August 11, 2025, https://www.fdrlibrary.org/polio.
16. Laura Shapiro, "The First Kitchen: Eleanor Roosevelt's Austerity Drive," *New Yorker*, November 14, 2010.
17. Susan Quinn, *Eleanor and Hick: The Love Affair that Shaped a First Lady* (Penguin Press, 2016).
18. "Women: Oracle," TIME, April 17, 1939, https://time.com/archive/6760367/women-oracle.
19. Lydia Saad, "Gallup Vault: A Sea Change in Support for Working Women," Gallup, July 20, 2017, https://news.gallup.com/vault/214328/gallup-vault-sea-change-support-working-women.aspx.
20. "My Day," Eleanor Roosevelt Papers Project, Columbian College of Arts & Sciences, George Washington University. https://erpapers.columbian.gwu.edu/my-day.
21. Frances M. Seeber, "Eleanor Roosevelt and Women in the New Deal: A Network of Friends," *Presidential Studies Quarterly* 20, no. 4 (Fall 1990): 707–717.
22. "Joe Biden Signs Anti-Lynching Bill in Historic First," BBC, March 29, 2022, https://www.bbc.com/news/world-us-canada-60679930.
23. Paul M. Sparrow, "Forward with Roosevelt: It's Time to Put Eleanor Roosevelt on the $10 Bill," Franklin D. Roosevelt Presidential Library and Museum, Octo-

ber 8, 2015, https://fdr.blogs.archives.gov/2015/10/08/its-time-to-put-eleanor-roosevelt-on-the-10-bill/.

24. "Eleanor Roosevelt and Marian Anderson," Franklin D. Roosevelt Presidential Library and Museum, accessed August 11, 2025, https://www.fdrlibrary.org/anderson.
25. "Eleanor Roosevelt's Battle to End Lynching," Franklin D. Roosevelt Presidential Library and Museum, February 12, 2016, https://fdr.blogs.archives.gov/2016/02/12/eleanor-roosevelts-battle-to-end-lynching/.
26. "FBI Files on Eleanor Roosevelt," American Experience, PBS/WGBH Educational Foundation, accessed July 14, 2025, https://www.pbs.org/wgbh/americanexperience/features/eleanor-fbi/.
27. Dale Carnegie, *How to Stop Worrying and Start Living: Time-Tested Methods for Conquering Worry* (Simon and Schuster, 1948; rev. ed., Gallery Books, 2004).
28. U.S. Central Intelligence Agency. U.S. Knew of Japanese-American Spies. CIA-RDP90-00552R000202030026-8. Washington, D.C., May 31, 1983. https://www.cia.gov/readingroom/docs/CIA-RDP90-00552R000202030026-8.pdf
29. National Park Service, "Eleanor Roosevelt: Undo the Mistake of Internment," U.S. Department of the Interior, June 29, 2018, https://www.nps.gov/articles/erooseveltinternment.htm.
30. "Touring the British Homefront (1942)," Eleanor Roosevelt Papers Project, Columbian College of Arts & Sciences, George Washington University, accessed August 11, 2025, https://erpapers.columbian.gwu.edu/touring-british-homefront-1942.
31. Eleanor Roosevelt, *Autobiography of Eleanor Roosevelt* (Harper and Brothers, 1961).
32. Eleanor Roosevelt, "My Day," January 8, 1936, Eleanor Roosevelt Papers Project, Columbian College of Arts & Sciences, George Washington University, https://www2.gwu.edu/~erpapers/myday/displaydoc.cfm?_y=1936&_f=md054227.
33. "Touring the British Homefront."
34. "Touring the British Homefront."
35. "Touring the British Homefront."
36. "First Lady on the Front Lines: Eleanor Roosevelt's Tour of the South Pacific—August & September 1943," Franklin D. Roosevelt Presidential Library and Museum, August 25, 2016, https://fdr.blogs.archives.gov/2016/08/25/a-first-lady-on-the-front-lines/.
37. "First Lady on the Front Lines."
38. *Unsung History*, podcast, "Eleanor Roosevelt's Visit to the Pacific Theatre Dur-

ing World War II," March 25, 2024, https://www.unsunghistorypodcast.com/eleanor-roosevelt/.

39. *Unsung History,* "Eleanor Roosevelt's Visit."
40. National Park Service, "Lucy Mercer Rutherfurd," accessed August 11, 2025, https://www.nps.gov/people/lucy-mercer-rutherfurd.htm.
41. Eleanor Roosevelt, "My Day," August 15, 1945, Eleanor Roosevelt Papers Project, Columbian College of Arts & Sciences, George Washington University, https://www2.gwu.edu/~erpapers/myday/displaydoc.cfm?_y=1945&_f=md000103.
42. Frederic J. Frommer, "Truman's Secret Plea to Eisenhower: Take My Job," *Politico,* March 26, 2023, https://www.politico.com/news/magazine/2023/03/26/truman-asked-eisenhower-to-replace-him-as-nominee-00086435.
43. "Eleanor Roosevelt Facts," Franklin D. Roosevelt Presidential Library and Museum, accessed August 11, 2025, https://www.fdrlibrary.org/er-facts.

CHAPTER 28

1. "The Triangle Shirtwaist Factory Fire," Occupational Safety and Health Administration, U.S. Department of Labor, https://www.osha.gov/aboutosha/40-years/trianglefactoryfire.
2. Columbia University Libraries Oral History Research Office, "Oral History Interview with Frances Perkins, 1955," transcript, part 1, 126, accessed August 12, 2025, https://dlc.library.columbia.edu/catalog/cul:3xsj3txc7v.
3. Frances Perkins, "Lecture by Frances Perkins," excerpt from lecture given September 30, 1964, Cornell University, School of Industrial and Labor Relations.
4. U.S. Department of Labor, "The New York Factory Investigating Commission," accessed August 12, 2025, https://www.dol.gov/general/aboutdol/history/mono-regsafepart07.
5. Gordon Berg, "Frances Perkins and the Flowering of Economic and Social Policies," *Monthly Labor Review* 112, no. 6 (1989): 28–32.
6. Berg, "Frances Perkins."
7. U.S. Department of Labor, "Factory Investigating Commission."
8. Frances Perkins Center, "1918–1928: Industrial Commission and Gov. Al Smith," accessed August 12, 2025, https://francesperkinscenter.org/learn/her-life/#smith.
9. Adam S. Cohen, "Frances Perkins," *Harvard Magazine,* January–February 2009, https://www.harvardmagazine.com/2009/01/frances-perkins.
10. "Americans and the Holocaust: Immigration and Refugees, a Case Study on the Wagner-Rogers Bill," United States Holocaust Memorial Museum, ac-

cessed October 6, 2025, https://www.ushmm.org/m/pdfs/USHMM-wagner-rogers-presentation.pdf.

11. Kirstin Downey, *The Woman Behind the New Deal: The Life of Frances Perkins, FDR's Secretary of Labor and His Moral Conscience* (Random House, 2009).
12. Frances Perkins, *The Roosevelt I Knew* (Viking Press, 1946), 152.
13. "Frances Perkins, the First Woman in Cabinet, Is Dead," *The New York Times,* May 15, 1965.
14. "Frances Perkins Born in Boston," MassMoments, Massachusetts Foundation for the Humanities, accessed August 12, 2025, https://www.massmoments.org/moment-details/frances-perkins-born-in-boston.html.
15. "The Presidency: The Roosevelt Week, May 8, 1933," *Time,* May 8, 1933, https://time.com/archive/6750994/the-presidency-the-roosevelt-week-may-8-1933/.
16. Debra Michals, "Eleanor Roosevelt," National Women's History Museum, accessed August 12, 2025, https://www.womenshistory.org/education-resources/biographies/eleanor-roosevelt.
17. Frances M. Seeber, "Eleanor Roosevelt and Women in the New Deal: A Network of Friends," *Presidential Studies Quarterly* 20, no. 4 (Fall 1990): 707–717.
18. Seeber, "Eleanor Roosevelt and Women."
19. Frances Perkins Center, "The Woman Behind the New Deal," accessed August 12, 2025, https://francesperkinscenter.org/learn/her-life/.
20. Douglas O. Linder, "The Triangle Shirtwaist Factory Trial," 2002, UMKC School of Law, https://law2.umkc.edu/faculty/projects/ftrials/triangle/triangle account.html.
21. Willard Wirtz, quoted in Joseph R. Biden, Jr., "Proclamation 10873: Establishment of the Frances Perkins National Monument," American Presidency Project, December 16, 2024, https://www.presidency.ucsb.edu/documents/proclamation-10873-establishment-the-frances-perkins-national-monument.
22. Susan Ware, "Letter to the Editor," *The New York Times,* July 22, 1984, p. 130, https://timesmachine.nytimes.com/timesmachine/1984/07/22/082250.html?pageNumber=130.
23. Frances Perkins Center, "Awards & Honorees." Frances Perkins Center, https://francesperkinscenter.org/programs-events/awards-honorees.

CHAPTER 29

1. Phillip Walter Wellman, "4 Women Are Buried Among Several Thousand Men at the U.S. D-Day Cemetery. These Are Their Stories," *Stars & Stripes,* June 4, 2024.

2. "African Americans Fought for Freedom at Home and Abroad during World War II," The National WWII Museum, New Orleans, February 1, 2020.
3. Melissa Thaxton and Jennifer Dubina, "A Different Kind of Victory: The 6888th Central Postal Directory Battalion," National Museum of the United States Army, accessed August 11, 2025, https://www.thenmusa.org/articles/a-different-kind-of-victory-the-6888th-central-postal-directory-battalion/.
4. Sandy Bolzenius, "Black Women Pushed the U.S. Army to Become More Inclusive and Equal," *The Washington Post,* October 20, 2021.
5. Nathan Cross, "6888th Central Postal Directory Battalion: A Guide to First-Person Narratives in the Veterans History Project," Library of Congress, January 10, 2023, https://guides.loc.gov/6888th-central-postal-directory-battalion/introduction.
6. National Park Service, "Charity Adams Earley," accessed August 12, 2025, https://www.nps.gov/people/charityadams.htm.
7. Charity Adams Earley, *One Woman's Army: A Black Officer Remembers the WAC* (Texas A&M University Press, 1995).
8. Avis Thomas-Lester, "Neither Rain, Nor Racial Bias," *The Washington Post,* February 26, 2009.
9. Thaxton and Dubina, "Different Kind of Victory."
10. Cross, "6888th Central Postal Directory Battalion."
11. "Speaker Johnson Presents Congressional Gold Medal to the Six Triple Eight," U.S. Congressman Mike Johnson, April 30, 2025, https://mikejohnson.house.gov/news/documentsingle.aspx?DocumentID=1586.

CHAPTER 30

1. "Hero Among Us: The Civil Rights Movement Through the Eyes of a Child," LSU Health New Orleans School of Dentistry, February 2011, https://www.lsusd.lsuhsc.edu/news/NewsTessieWilliams.html.
2. Alan Wieder, "The New Orleans School Crisis of 1960: Causes and Consequences," *Phylon* 48, no. 2 (2nd Quarter 1987): 122–131.
3. "White Citizens' Councils (WCC)," Martin Luther King, Jr., Research and Education Institute, Stanford University, accessed September 1, 2025, https://kinginstitute.stanford.edu/white-citizens-councils-wcc.
4. Martin Luther King, Jr., " 'Desegregation and the Future': Address Delivered at the Annual Luncheon of the National Committee for Rural Schools," December 15, 1956, New York, New York, Stanford University, https://kinginstitute.stanford.edu/king-papers/documents/desegregation-and-future-address-delivered-annual-luncheon-national-committee.

5. Tim Morris, "The Little Girls Who Desegregated New Orleans Schools," NOLA.com, May 17, 2019, https://www.nola.com/opinions/the-little-girls-who-desegregated-new-orleans-schools/article_b082d384-0e9d-52a9-ba82-cdf2c242f117.html.
6. Jamie Wax and Analisa Novak, "Meet 3 Unsung Civil Rights Pioneers Who Helped Desegregate Schools in New Orleans," CBS News, February 14, 2023, https://www.cbsnews.com/news/the-mcdonogh-three-civil-rights-pioneers-desegregate-schools-new-orleans-louisiana-leona-tate-gail-etienne-tessie-prevost/.
7. Debbie Elliott, "Tessie Prevost, Pioneer of Deep South School Desegregation, Dies at 69," NPR, July 9, 2024, https://www.npr.org/2024/07/09/nx-s1-5034337/tessie-prevost-new-orleans-school-desegregation-dies.
8. Dorothy Prevost, "New Orleans School Desegregation: Through a Mother's Eyes," Voices of the Civil Rights Movement, NBC, accessed August 12, 2025, https://voicesofthecivilrightsmovement.com/video-collection/2022/1/30/new-orleans-school-desegregation-through-a-mothers-eyes.
9. "Hero Among Us."
10. Dwayne Fatherree, "Formerly Segregated Louisiana School Transformed into Civil Rights Center," Southern Poverty Law Center, February 16, 2024, https://www.splcenter.org/resources/stories/formerly-segregated-louisiana-school-transformed-civil-rights-center/.
11. Fatherree, "Formerly Segregated Louisiana School."
12. Elliott, "Tessie Prevost, Pioneer."
13. Bailey Breuhl, "The Light Within the Dark: Lasting Successes of the New Orleans Public School Integration in 1960," thesis, Louisiana State University, April 2020, https://repository.lsu.edu/cgi/viewcontent.cgi?article=1207&context=honors_etd.
14. Breuhl, "Light Within the Dark."
15. "Hero Among Us."
16. "Resilience and Hope 60 Years After New Orleans School Desegregation," Voices of the Civil Rights Movement, NBC, accessed October 7, 2025, https://voicesofthecivilrightsmovement.com/articles/new-orleans-4.
17. Shay Dawson, "Ruby Bridges," National Women's History Museum, accessed August 12, 2025, https://www.womenshistory.org/education-resources/biographies/ruby-bridges.
18. Christina Watkins, "'New Orleans Four' Reflect on Making History, Desegregating Public Elementary Schools 61 Years Ago," WDSU News, February 18, 2022, https://www.wdsu.com/article/new-orleans-four-reflect-on-making-history-desegregating-public-elementary-schools-61-years-ago/38289250.

19. "Ruby Bridges and Integration of New Orleans Schools," American Experience, PBS, accessed August 12, 2025, https://www.pbs.org/wgbh/american experience/features/neworleans-ruby-bridges-and-integration-new-orleans -schools/.
20. Christina A. Samuels, "Racial Segregation Grows as Southern Communities Splinter into New Districts," Education Week, September 4, 2019, https://www .edweek.org/leadership/racial-segregation-grows-as-southern-communities -splinter-into-new-districts/2019/09.
21. "The New Orleans Four," Herstory, New Orleans Legacy Project, accessed August 12, 2025, https://www.neworleanslegacyproject.org/herstory.
22. Jamie Wax and Analisa Novak, "Meet 3 Unsung Civil Rights Pioneers Who Helped Desegregate Schools in New Orleans," CBS News, February 14, 2023, https://www.cbsnews.com/news/the-mcdonogh-three-civil-rights-pioneers -desegregate-schools-new-orleans-louisiana-leona-tate-gail-etienne-tessie -prevost.
23. Dawson, "Ruby Bridges."

CHAPTER 31

1. Becky May, "Emulating Mrs. B," *Hispanic Executive,* March 1, 2018, https:// hispanicexecutive.com/emulating-mrs-b-ramonas-food-group.
2. "Oral History Interview with Romana Bañuelos, 1971–2006," Box 3, A Few Good Women Oral History Collection, 00001, Eberly Family Special Collections Library, https://archives.libraries.psu.edu/repositories/3/archival_objects /1186313.
3. "Interview with Romana Bañuelos."
4. Ronie-Richele Garcia-Johnson, "Romana Acosta Bañuelos," In *Notable Hispanic American Women,* vol. 1, ed. Diane Telgen and Jim Kamp (Gale Research, 1993), 49–51.
5. Garcia-Johnson, "Romana Acosta Bañuelos."
6. Garcia-Johnson, "Romana Acosta Bañuelos."
7. Alejandra Reyes-Velarde, "Romana Acosta Bañuelos, First Latina U.S. Treasurer and Mexican American Pioneer, Dies at 92," *Los Angeles Times,* January 22, 2018, https://www.latimes.com/local/obituaries/la-me-romana-acosta-banuelos -20180119-story.html.
8. "Interview with Romana Bañuelos."
9. Christine Marin, "Romana Acosta Bañuelos: United States Treasurer," Arizona Memory Project, Arizona State Library, Archives and Public Records, April 2009, https://azmemory.azlibrary.gov/nodes/view/159268.

10. E. Scott Reckard, "East L.A.'s Pan American Bank Gets $6-Million Bailout from Other Banks," *Los Angeles Times,* July 23, 2014, https://www.latimes.com/business/la-fi-pan-american-bank-saved-20140723-story.html.
11. Adeel Hassan, "Romana Acosta Bañuelos, U.S. Treasurer Under Nixon, Dies at 92," *The New York Times,* February 5, 2018, https://www.nytimes.com/2018/02/05/obituaries/romana-acosta-banuelos-us-treasurer-under-nixon-dies-at-92.html.
12. Elisabeth Griffith, *Formidable: American Women and the Fight for Equality, 1920–2020* (New York: Pegasus Books, 2022).
13. "Interview with Romana Bañuelos."
14. *Nomination of Romana Acosta Bañuelos to Be Treasurer of the United States,* Hearing before the Committee on Finance, United States Senate, Ninety-Second Congress (U.S. Government Printing Office, November 29, 1971).
15. "Magazine Links Tip to Bañuelos Raid," *The New York Times,* October 11, 1971, p. 39, https://www.nytimes.com/1971/10/11/archives/magazine-links-tip-to-banuelos-raid.html.
16. USAGov, "Treasurer of the United States—Career Spotlight," YouTube video, 2:24, posted March 15, 2011, https://www.youtube.com/watch?v=0M0b6bcgI_0.
17. "Treasurer of the United States," U.S. Department of the Treasury, accessed October 7, 2025, https://home.treasury.gov/about/offices/treasurer.
18. Lenika Cruz, "Why Have All the U.S. Treasurers Since 1949 Been Women?," *The Atlantic,* August 13, 2014, https://www.theatlantic.com/business/archive/2014/08/why-all-of-the-us-treasurers-since-1949-have-been-women/376004/.
19. Thomas V. Haney, "New Signature on Paper Currency," *The New York Times,* January 23, 1972, https://www.nytimes.com/1972/01/23/archives/new-signature-on-paper-currency.html.
20. "Latinas Aren't Paid Fairly—and That's Just the Tip of the Iceberg," Lean In, accessed October 7, 2025, https://leanin.org/data-about-the-gender-pay-gap-for-latinas.
21. Angela Byars-Winston, Nadya Fouad, and Yao Wen, "Race/Ethnicity and Sex in U.S. Occupations, 1970–2010: Implications for Research, Practice, and Policy," *Journal of Vocational Behavior* 87 (April 2015): 54–70.
22. Reyes-Velarde, "Romana Acosta Bañuelos."
23. Reyes-Velarde, "Romana Acosta Bañuelos."
24. "Most Influential Family Owned Businesses 2019: Ramona's Food Group LLC / Ramona's Restaurant Group LLC," *Los Angeles Business Journal,* October 29,

2019, https://labusinessjournal.com/advertorials/most-influential-family-owned-businesses-2019-ramo/.

25. *Nomination of Romana Acosta Bañuelos.*
26. Reyes-Velarde, "Romana Acosta Bañuelos."
27. Ramona's Food Group, "My grandmother, Romana Acosta Bañuelos passed on 1/15/18. She was unwittingly a pioneer while pursuing her dream of financial security for her and her family," Facebook post, January 17, 2018, https://www.facebook.com/photo.php?fbid=1844364645596136&id=143312305701387&set=a.228406407191976.

CHAPTER 32

1. Susan E. Cayleff, "The 'Texas Tomboy': The Life and Legend of Babe Didrikson Zaharias," *OAH Magazine of History* 7, no. 1 (Summer 1992): 28–33.
2. Cayleff, "The 'Texas Tomboy.'"
3. "Remembering a 'Babe' Sports Fans Shouldn't Forget" (interview with Don Van Natta, Jr.), *All Things Considered,* NPR, June 26, 2011, https://www.npr.org/2011/06/26/137319975/remembering-a-babe-sports-fans-shouldnt-forget.
4. "Remembering a 'Babe.'
5. Debra Michals, ed., "Mildred 'Babe' Didrikson Zaharias," National Women's History Museum, 2015, https://www.womenshistory.org/education-resources/biographies/mildred-zaharias.
6. "Daily Almanac," *Columbus Dispatch,* June 26, 2011, https://www.dispatch.com/story/lifestyle/2011/06/26/daily-almanac/24151119007/.
7. "The Legend of Babe Didrikson," Olympics.com, August 3, 2019, https://olympics.com/en/news/the-legend-of-babe-didrikson.
8. "The Legend of Babe Didrikson."
9. Larry Schwartz, "Didrikson Was a Woman Ahead of Her Time," ESPN, accessed August 12, 2025, https://www.espn.com/classic/biography/s/Didrikson_babe.html.
10. Susan E. Cayleff, *Babe: The Life and Legend of Babe Didrikson Zaharia* (University of Illinois Press, 1996).
11. "Legend of Babe Didrikson."
12. Rory Jiwani, "Moments Paving the Way for Gender Equality in Sport," Olympics.com, March 7, 2024, https://www.olympics.com/en/news/top-10-moments-gender-equality-in-sport-intl-equal-pay-day.
13. "Babe Didrikson Zaharias," LPGA Hall of Fame, https://www.lpga.com/lpga-hall-of-fame/babe-didrikson-zaharias.
14. Cayleff, *Babe.*

15. Cayleff, "The 'Texas Tomboy.'"
16. Cayleff, *Babe.*
17. "Zaharias Opened Eyes with Battle Against Cancer," *Washington Times,* July 5, 2004.
18. Cayleff, "The 'Texas Tomboy.'"
19. Thomas V. Haney, "Babe Zaharias Dies; Athlete Had Cancer," *The New York Times,* September 28, 1956.

CHAPTER 33

1. Kathrine Switzer, *Marathon Woman: Running the Race to Revolutionize Women's Sports* (Da Capo Press, 2009).
2. Kathrine Switzer, *Marathon Woman: FAQ*, KathrineSwitzer.com. accessed August 12, 2025, https://kathrineswitzer.com/kathrine-switzer-faqs/.
3. "A Principled Politician: The Story of Patsy Mink, the First Woman of Color Elected to Congress," *UChicago News,* March 8, 2024, University of Chicago, https://news.uchicago.edu/story/principled-politician-story-patsy-mink-first-woman-color-elected-congress.
4. Judy Tzu-Chun Wu and Gwendolyn Mink, "How Patsy Takemoto Mink, the First Woman of Color in Congress, Helped Craft Title IX," *Time,* June 1, 2022.
5. "Conversation on Women's Rights," C-SPAN, November 26, 1974, https://www.c-span.org/video/?455213-1/conversation-womens-rights.
6. "A Principled Politician."
7. Patsy T. Mink, "Testimony by Representative Patsy T. Mink," June 24, 1970, During Special Subcommittee on Education, U.S. House Committee on Education and Labor, Hearings on Discrimination Against Women in Higher Education," Library of Congress, accessed August 12, 2025, https://www.loc.gov/resource/mss84957.00102/?sp=1.
8. National Coalition for Women and Girls in Education (NCWGE), *Title IX at 40: Working to Ensure Gender Equity in Education* (NCWGE, 2012).
9. National Federation of State High School Associations, "2024–25 NFHS High School Athletics Participation Survey," September 9, 2025, https://nfhs.org/stories/participation-in-high-school-sports-hits-record-high-with-sizable-increase-in-2024-25.
10. U.S. House of Representatives, "Daniel Read Anthony Jr.," *House Collection,* History, Art & Archives, https://history.house.gov/Collection/Listing/2005/2005-216-003/.
11. Nick Thimmesch, "Will Nine More States Approve? The Sexual Equality Amendment," *The New York Times,* June 24, 1973, p. 8.

12. Karen M. Kedrowski, "Guest Column: A Look at First Ladies' Influence on the ERA 100 Years Later," *East Wing Magazine,* October 18, 2023.
13. "Historic U.S. Court Case Inspired Equal Rights for Both Genders," *Voice of America,* November 29, 2011, https://www.voanews.com/a/historic-case-inspired-equal-rights-for-both-genders-134757348/163295.html.
14. "User Clip: Patsy Mink," C-SPAN, October 23, 1990, https://www.c-span.org/clip/news-conference/user-clip-patsy-mink/4533545.
15. "Patsy Takemoto Mink," History, Art & Archives, U.S. House of Representatives, accessed October 7, 2025, https://history.house.gov/People/detail/18329?fbclid=IwAR1vziaOLp0U8j2zo-dxghbuogqLioY9cjZcXMHMyzfYLSITqC-2DJuiV8o.
16. "MINK!," directed by Ben Proudfoot, produced by Breakwater Studios and *The New York Times* Op-Docs, 22 min., 2022.

CHAPTER 34

1. "The Honorable Patricia Scott Schroeder Oral History Interview," conducted June 3, 2015, Office of the Historian, U.S. House of Representatives.
2. Katharine Q. Seelye, "Patricia Schroeder, Feminist Force in Congress, Dies at 82," *New York Times,* March 14, 2023, https://www.nytimes.com/2023/03/14/obituaries/pat-schroeder-dead.html; Ida A. Brudnick and Jennifer E. Manning, *African American Members of the U.S. Congress: 1870–2020*, CRS Report RL30378, Congressional Research Service, December 15, 2020, https://www.congress.gov/crs-product/RL30378.
3. Martin Weil, "Former Rep. F. Edward Hébert Dies," *The Washington Post,* December 29, 1979, https://www.washingtonpost.com/archive/local/1979/12/30/former-rep-f-edward-hebert-dies/c7557a7d-afdc-4f2c-b70d-ed76b5e5b857/.
4. Patricia S. Schroeder, *24 Years of House Work . . . and the Place Is Still a Mess: My Life in Politics* (Andrews McMeel, 1998).
5. Susan B. Glasser, host, *The Global Politico,* podcast, episode featuring Pat Schroeder and Deborah James, November 7, 2017, https://www.politico.com/magazine/story/2017/11/07/pat-schroeder-and-deborah-james-the-full-transcript-215793/.
6. Shaun Boyd, "Friends and Colleagues Remember Colorado's First Congresswoman Pat Schroeder as Iconic Feminist," CBS News, March 14, 2023, https://www.cbsnews.com/colorado/news/friends-and-colleagues-remember-colorados-first-congresswoman-pat-schroeder-iconic-feminist/.
7. Patricia S. Schroeder, "Remarks (Annual Meeting of the American Historical Association, Washington, D.C., January 4, 2008)," oral presentation as partici-

pant in the roundtable "The People's House: Roundtable on Robert V. Remini's *The House: The History of the House of Representatives,*" January 4, 2008.

8. Marilyn Gardner, "A One-Woman, Pro-Family Lobby," *Christian Science Monitor,* March 15, 1989, https://www.csmonitor.com/1989/0315/ppat.html.
9. Lloyd Grove, "Laying Down Her Quip for Rep. Pat Schroeder, a Hard-Hitting Decision," *The Washington Post,* November 30, 1995, https://www.washingtonpost.com/archive/lifestyle/1995/12/01/laying-down-her-quip/ac48bf34-d056-430a-a585-8076b62dbe14/.
10. Seelye, "Patricia Schroeder, Feminist Force."
11. Grove, "Laying Down Her Quip."
12. Marjorie Williams, "Pat Schroeder: The Agony of Decision," *The Washington Post,* September 24, 1987, https://www.washingtonpost.com/archive/lifestyle/1987/09/25/pat-schroeder-the-agony-of-decision/fc703ac3-5164-44cb-94e7-44e4e7a90185/.
13. Judith Richards Hope, *Pinstripes & Pearls: The Women of the Harvard Law Class of '64 Who Forged an Old-Girl Network and Paved the Way for Future Generations* (Scribner, 2003).
14. Margie Kelley, "When I'm '64," *Harvard Law Bulletin,* Alumni Focus, July 1, 2003, Harvard Law School, https://hls.harvard.edu/today/im-64/.
15. Schroeder, *24 Years of House Work.*
16. "Honorable Patricia Scott Schroeder."
17. Schroeder, "Remarks."
18. Schroeder, *24 Years of House Work.*
19. Olivia Prentzel, "Pat Schroeder Remembered for Her 'Creative, Unorthodox, Energetic' Personality During 24 Years in Congress," *Colorado Sun,* April 28, 2023, https://www.coloradosun.com/2023/04/28/pat-schroeder-memorial-history-colorado/.
20. Melissa Healy, "Patricia Schroeder: Fighting for 24 Years to Expand Women's Role in Government," *Los Angeles Times,* December 1, 1996.

CHAPTER 35

1. Constance Baker Motley, *Equal Justice Under Law: An Autobiography* (Farrar, Straus and Giroux, 1998), 160.
2. Tomiko Brown-Nagin, "Constance Baker Motley Taught the Nation How to Win Justice," *Smithsonian Magazine,* March 2022, https://www.smithsonianmag.com/history/constance-baker-motley-how-to-win-justice-180979527/.
3. Brown-Nagin, "Constance Baker Motley Taught."
4. Brown-Nagin, "Constance Baker Motley Taught."
5. Tomiko Brown-Nagin, "Rescuing the Civil Rights Movement—and Children

of Birmingham," *Harvard Gazette*, January 13, 2022, https://news.harvard.edu/gazette/story/2022/01/rescuing-the-civil-rights-movement-and-children-of-birmingham/.

6. Brown-Nagin, "Constance Baker Motley Taught."
7. Motley, *Equal Justice Under Law.*
8. "Celebrating the Life of Constance Baker Motley '46," Columbia Law School, March 31, 2023, https://www.law.columbia.edu/news/archive/celebrating-life-constance-baker-motley-46.
9. Anna Quindlen, "Case History: Judge v. Life," *New York Times,* August 25, 1977, p. 48.
10. Ketanji Brown Jackson, *Lovely One: A Memoir* (Random House, 2024).
11. Joe Holley, "Constance Motley Dies," *The Washington Post,* September 28, 2005; Jeffrey Cole and Joseph A. Greenaway, "Judge Constance Baker Motley and the Struggle for Equal Justice," *Litigation* 29, no. 4 (2003): 6–16.
12. "Work if You Can Pay the Maid, Says Woman Judge to Women," *Hartford Courant,* January 27, 1966.
13. Motley, *Equal Justice Under Law.*
14. "Celebrating the Life."
15. "Celebrating the Life."
16. Tomiko Brown-Nagin, "Constance Baker Motley and the Struggle for Equality," *Literary Hub,* January 26, 2022.
17. LBJ Library (@LBJLibrary), "Fifty-three years ago today, on Aug. 6, 1965, President Johnson signed the Voting Rights Act," X (formerly Twitter), August 16, 2018, https://x.com/LBJLibrary/status/1026450040280244225.
18. NAACP Legal Defense Fund, "The Life and Legacy of Constance Baker Motley," accessed August 12, 2025, https://www.naacpldf.org/naacp-publications/ldf-blog/cbm-100/.
19. "Constance Baker Motley: A Forgotten Connecticut Icon," *Connecticut Public Radio,* March 1, 2018, https://www.ctpublic.org/arts-and-culture/2018-03-01/constance-baker-motley-a-forgotten-connecticut-icon.
20. "Constance Baker Motley: Judiciary's Unsung Rights Hero," United States Courts, February 20, 2020, https://www.uscourts.gov/data-news/judiciary-news/2020/02/20/constance-baker-motley-judiciarys-unsung-rights-hero.
21. H.R. 497, Recognizing and Honoring the Life and Achievements of Constance Baker Motley, Judge, U.S. District Court, S.D.N.Y., 109th Cong, 2005.
22. "Celebrating the Life."
23. Brett Milano and HLS Correspondent, "Constance Baker Motley," *Harvard Law Today,* February 15, 2022.

24. NAACP Legal Defense Fund, "Life and Legacy."
25. Kamala Harris (Vice President Kamala Harris Archived), "I want to tell you about a personal hero of mine—Constance Baker Motley," Facebook, September 14, 2021, https://www.facebook.com/VP46archive/posts/i-want-to-tell-you-about-a-personal-hero-of-mineconstance-baker-motley-today-on-/260818172667504/.
26. Ruth Bader Ginsburg, "Human Rights Hero: Tribute to Constance Baker Motley," *American Bar Association Journal* 32, no. 4 (Fall 2005): 26.
27. "Women Judges Reflect on Constance Baker Motley's Legacy," United States Courts, March 1, 2023, https://www.uscourts.gov/data-news/judiciary-news/2023/03/01/women-judges-reflect-constance-baker-motleys-legacy.
28. "Constance Baker Motley: Judiciary's Unsung Rights Hero."
29. "History Made When Women Were Allowed to Serve on Jury," Associated Press, November 16, 2018, https://apnews.com/article/50fb651b7fb84221887f8a7534a87fff.
30. Motley, *Equal Justice Under Law.*
31. Tomiko Brown-Nagin, "Identity Matters: The Case of Judge Constance Baker Motley," *Columbia Law Review* 117, no. 7 (2017).
32. *Blank v. Sullivan & Cromwell,* 418 F. Supp. 1, 4 (S.D.N.Y. 1975).
33. Brown-Nagin, "Identity Matters."
34. Melissa Ludtke, *Locker Room Talk: A Woman's Struggle to Get Inside* (Rutgers University Press, 2024).
35. "President Clinton Awards the Presidential Citizens Medals," The White House, January 8, 2001, https://clintonwhitehouse5.archives.gov/WH/new/html/Mon_Jan_8_141714_2001.html.

PART V

1. Condoleezza Rice, "Remarks at the 2000 Republican National Convention—Aug. 1, 2000," Archives of Women's Political Communication, Catt Center, Iowa State University, March 9, 2017, https://awpc.cattcenter.iastate.edu/2017/03/09/remarks-at-the-2000-rnc-aug-1-2000/.
2. Ida A. Brudnick and Jennifer E. Manning, "Women in Congress, 1917–2022: Service Dates and Committee Assignments by Member, and Lists by State and Congress," CRS Report RL30261, Congressional Research Service, July 2, 2024, https://www.congress.gov/crs-product/RL30261.
3. Cokie Roberts, "An Afternoon with Cokie Roberts," transcript, oral history interview, May 25, 2017, Office of the Historian, U.S. House of Representatives, July 14, 2025, https://history.house.gov/Oral-History/Women/Cokie-Roberts/.

4. "History of Women in the U.S. Congress," Center for American Women and Politics, Eagleton Institute of Politics, Rutgers University, accessed August 12, 2025, https://cawp.rutgers.edu/facts/levels-office/congress/history-women-us-congress.
5. Patrick Boyle, Michael Dill, Rosalie Kelly, and Zakia Nouri, "Women Are Changing the Face of Medicine in America," *AAMCNews,* May 28, 2024, Association of American Medical Colleges, https://www.aamc.org/news/women-are-changing-face-medicine-america.
6. National Archives and Records Administration, "U.S. Supreme Court Cases: Ruth Bader Ginsburg," overview of major sex-discrimination cases before the U.S. Supreme Court, accessed August 12, 2025, https://www.archives.gov/files/women/ginsburg-cases.pdf.
7. Melissa Block, "Pathmarking the Way: Ruth Bader Ginsburg's Lifelong Fight for Gender Equality," NPR, September 24, 2020, https://www.npr.org/2020/09/24/916377135/pathmarking-the-way-ruth-bader-ginsburgs-lifelong-fight-for-gender-equality.
8. American Bar Association, "Women in the Legal Profession," ABA News & Insights, accessed August 12, 2025, https://www.americanbar.org/news/profile-legal-profession/women/.
9. Kiley Hurst, "U.S. Women Are Outpacing Men in College Completion, Including in Every Major Racial and Ethnic Group," Pew Research Center, November 18, 2024, https://www.pewresearch.org/short-reads/2024/11/18/us-women-are-outpacing-men-in-college-completion-including-in-every-major-racial-and-ethnic-group/; Mark J. Perry, "Women Earned the Majority of Doctoral Degrees in 2020 for the 12th Straight Year and Outnumber Men in Grad School 148 to 100," *Carpe Diem* (blog), American Enterprise Institute, October 14, 2021, https://www.aei.org/carpe-diem/women-earned-the-majority-of-doctoral-degrees-in-2020-for-the-12th-straight-year-and-outnumber-men-in-grad-school-148-to-100/.
10. Supreme Court of the United States, "Sandra Day O'Connor: First Woman on the Supreme Court—Appointment to the Supreme Court," Exhibitions, accessed August 12, 2025, https://www.supremecourt.gov/visiting/exhibitions/SOCExhibit/Section3.aspx.
11. "Sotomayor Explains 'Wise Latina' Comment," CBS News, July 14, 2009, https://www.cbsnews.com/news/sotomayor-explains-wise-latina-comment/.
12. David Lat, "Amy Coney Barrett Is the Most Interesting Justice on the Court," *U.S. Law Week,* Bloomberg Law, July 2, 2025, https://news.bloomberglaw.com/us-law-week/amy-coney-barrett-is-the-most-interesting-justice-on-the-court.

13. Ketanji Brown Jackson, *Lovely One: A Memoir* (Random House, 2024), 66–67.
14. Melissa Quinn, "Ketanji Brown Jackson Sworn in as Supreme Court Justice," CBS News, June 30, 2022, https://www.cbsnews.com/live-updates/ketanji-brown-jackson-sworn-in-supreme-court-watch-live-stream-today-2022-06-30/.
15. Mark Sherman, "Justice Jackson Says She Has 'a Seat at the Table,'" Associated Press, September 30, 2022, https://apnews.com/article/ketanji-brown-jackson-biden-us-supreme-court-race-and-ethnicity-merrick-garland-3fb126a5a457958a2a6a1d0d4e8b00ce.
16. Cerulli Associates, "$54 Trillion Will Transfer to Widows Through 2048; More Than 95 Percent Will Go to Women," press release, January 22, 2025, https://www.cerulli.com/press-releases/54-trillion-will-transfer-to-widows-through-2048-more-than-95-will-go-to-women.
17. Susan Chira, "Why Aren't There More Female Billionaires?," *The New York Times,* December 30, 2016, https://www.nytimes.com/2016/12/30/business/why-arent-there-more-female-billionaires.html.
18. Sheryl Estrada, "How Mellody Hobson's Journey to Co-CEO at $14.9 Billion Ariel Investments Began with a Payphone Call from a Basement at Princeton," *Fortune,* March 6, 2024, https://fortune.com/2024/03/06/mellody-hobson-co-ceo-14-9-billion-ariel-investments-princeton/.
19. Moira Forbes, "Mellody Hobson on the Power of Paying Your Dues," *Forbes,* December 19, 2019, https://www.forbes.com/sites/moiraforbes/2019/12/19/mellody-hobson-on-the-power-of-paying-your-dues/.
20. Mellody Hobson, "Own Who You Are," chap. 12 in *Lean In: For Graduates,* ed. Sheryl Sandberg and Nell Scovell (Knopf, 2014).
21. Ally Marotti, "Mellody Hobson to Chair Economic Club of Chicago, First Black Woman in Post," *Chicago Tribune,* May 2, 2017, https://www.chicagotribune.com/2017/05/02/mellody-hobson-to-chair-economic-club-of-chicago-first-black-woman-in-post/.
22. *Forbes,* "Power of Paying Your Dues."
23. Hobson, "Own Who You Are."
24. Elisabeth H. Daugherty, "Oct. 13: College Named for Mellody Hobson '91; Annamie Paul '01 Leads in Canada," *Princeton Alumni Weekly,* October 13, 2020, https://paw.princeton.edu/article/oct-13-college-named-mellody-hobson-91-annamie-paul-01-leads-canada.
25. Emily Flitter, "Citigroup's Fraser to Be First Woman to Lead a Big Wall Street Bank," *The New York Times,* September 10, 2020, https://www.nytimes.com/2020/09/10/business/citigroup-ceo-jane-fraser.html.

26. Nina Ajemian, "Women Run 11 Percent of Fortune 500 Companies in 2025," *Fortune*, June 2, 2025, https://fortune.com/2025/06/02/fortune-500-companies-run-by-female-ceos-women-2025/.
27. Karen S. Lynch, *Taking Up Space: Get Heard, Deliver Results, and Make a Difference* (McGraw-Hill, 2024), xi.
28. Ashir Coillberg, "A Window into the Wage Gap: What's Behind It and How to Close It," National Women's Law Center, February 2025, https://nwlc.org/wp-content/uploads/2024/01/2025-Window-Into-the-Wage-Gap-Factsheet.pdf; Jonas Helth Lønborg, "134 Years to Go? The Data Behind Achieving Gender Equality This International Women's Day," *World Bank Data Blog*, March 8, 2025, https://blogs.worldbank.org/en/opendata/134-years-to-go--the-data-behind-achieving-gender-equality-this-.
29. Ben Sisario, "Taylor Swift's Eras Tour Grand Total: A Record $2 Billion," *The New York Times*, December 9, 2024, https://www.nytimes.com/2024/12/09/arts/music/taylor-swift-eras-tour-ticket-sales.html.
30. Taylor Swift, "Woman of the Decade Speech," *Billboard*, December 13, 2019, https://www.billboard.com/music/awards/taylor-swift-woman-of-the-decade-speech-billboard-women-in-music-8546156/.
31. America Ferrera, "Monologue from *Barbie* (2023)," quoted in Yvonne Villarreal, "Read the Stirring Monologue About Womanhood America Ferrera Delivers in *Barbie*," *Los Angeles Times*, July 23, 2023, https://www.latimes.com/entertainment-arts/movies/story/2023-07-23/barbie-america-ferrera-monologue.
32. Elizabeth Cady Stanton et al., "Declaration of Sentiments," Seneca Falls Convention, July 19–20, 1848, National Park Service, https://www.nps.gov/wori/learn/historyculture/declaration-of-sentiments.htm.
33. Margaret Osborne, "'Barbie' Makes History, Becoming First Billion-Dollar Movie Directed Solely by a Woman," *Smithsonian Magazine*, August 9, 2023, https://www.smithsonianmag.com/smart-news/barbie-first-billion-dollar-movie-directed-by-a-woman-180982672/.
34. Eric W. Jentsch, "Beyond the Court: Billie Jean King's Triumph in the Battle of the Sexes," Smithsonian American Women's History Museum, September 14, 2023, https://womenshistory.si.edu/blog/beyond-court-billie-jean-kings-triumph-battle-sexes.
35. Larry Schwartz, "Billie Jean Won for All Women," ESPN.com, accessed August 12, 2025, https://www.espn.com/sportscentury/features/00016060.html.
36. "Battle of the Sexes," BillieJeanKing.com, accessed August 12, 2025, https://www.billiejeanking.com/battle-of-the-sexes/.

37. Schwartz, "Billie Jean Won."
38. Billie Jean King, *Being . . . Billie Jean King,* interview transcript, segment 3, CNN, December 10, 2023, https://transcripts.cnn.com/show/se/date/2023-12-10/segment/03.
39. King, *Being . . . Billie Jean King.*
40. King, *Being . . . Billie Jean King.*
41. Subcommittee on Education, *Women's Educational Equity Act of 1973: Hearings Before the Subcommittee on Education of the Committee on Labor and Public Welfare, United States Senate, Ninety-Third Congress, First Session, on S. 2518, October 17 and November 9, 1973* (U.S. Government Printing Office, 1973).
42. Subcommittee on Education, *Women's Educational Equity Act of 1973.*
43. King, *Being . . . Billie Jean King.*
44. Joel Drucker, "The Original Nine: The Beginning of Women's Pro Tennis," US Open, March 9, 2020, https://www.usopen.org/en_US/news/articles/2020-03-09/2020-03-09_2020-03-09_the_original_nine_the_beginning_of_womens_pro_tennis.html.
45. "The WTA Story: 50 Years and Rising," Women's Tennis Association, accessed August 12, 2025, https://www.wtatennis.com/wta-history.
46. Joel Drucker, "Milestones in Equality: A Long Climb to Equal Prize Money at the Four Grand Slams," US Open, March 30, 2023, https://www.usopen.org/en_US/news/articles/2023-03-30/milestones_in_equality_a_long_climb_to_equal_prize_money_at_the_four_grand_slams.html.
47. King, *Being . . . Billie Jean King.*
48. Corbin McGuire, "The Caitlin Clark Effect," NCAA.org, February 15, 2024, https://www.ncaa.org/news/2024/2/15/media-center-the-caitlin-clark-effect.aspx.
49. WNBA Communications, "WNBA sets an all-time attendance record with 2,501,609 fans as of 8/20/25. In 2002, the record was set with 16 teams across 256 games. This season, the WNBA broke the record with 13 teams and just 226 games," X (formerly Twitter), August 21, 2025, 11:00 a.m., https://x.com/WNBAComms/status/1958544705915846669.
50. Nancy Theriot, "Towards a New Sporting Ideal: The Women's Division of the National Amateur Athletic Federation," *Frontiers: A Journal of Women Studies* 3, no. 1 (1978): 1–7.
51. Corbin McGuire, "Celebrating Progress: Women's Representation in NCAA Sports, Leadership Roles," NCAA.org, March 1, 2025, https://www.ncaa.org/news/2025/3/1/media-center-celebrating-progress-womens-representation-in-ncaa-sports-leadership-roles.aspx.

52. Lisa Franchetti, "Navigating the Seas with Admiral Lisa Franchetti, Chief of Naval Operations of the U.S. Navy," interview by Dr. Kathleen McInnis, *Smart Women, Smart Power,* podcast transcript, April 23, 2024, https://www.csis.org/events/navigating-seas-admiral-lisa-franchetti-chief-naval-operations-us-navy.
53. U.S. Department of Defense and Office of the Deputy Assistant Secretary of Defense for Military Community and Family Policy, *2023 Demographics Profile of the Military Community* (U.S. Government Printing Office, 2023), https://download.militaryonesource.mil/12038/MOS/Reports/2023-demographics-report.pdf.
54. Steve Beynon, "Surge of Female Enlistments Helped Drive Army Success in Reaching 2024 Recruiting Goal," Military.com, January 9, 2025, https://www.military.com/daily-news/2025/01/09/surge-of-female-enlistments-helped-drive-army-success-reaching-2024-recruiting-goal.html.
55. Danielle DeSimone, "Over 200 Years of Service: The History of Women in the U.S. Military," USO.org, February 28, 2023, https://www.uso.org/stories/3005-over-200-years-of-service-the-history-of-women-in-the-us-military.
56. Boyle et al., "Changing the Face of Medicine."
57. Boyle et al., "Changing the Face of Medicine."
58. Deborah Balthazar, "Female Surgeons Have Lower Rates of Long-Term Adverse Outcomes Than Their Male Peers, Study Finds," *STAT,* August 30, 2023, https://www.statnews.com/2023/08/30/surgery-outcomes-male-vs-female-surgeons-data/.
59. National Science Board, "The STEM Labor Force of Today: Scientists, Engineers, and Skilled Technical Workers," Science & Engineering Indicators 2022, NSB-2021-2, National Science Foundation, August 31, 2021, https://ncses.nsf.gov/pubs/nsb20212/participation-of-demographic-groups-in-stem.
60. U.S. Bureau of Labor Statistics, "Labor Force Statistics from the Current Population Survey: Table 11. Employed Persons by Detailed Occupation, Sex, Race, and Hispanic or Latino Ethnicity," last updated January 29, 2025, https://www.bls.gov/cps/cpsaat11.htm.
61. "Frances Arnold: Nobel Prize in Chemistry 2018," NobelPrize.org, accessed August 12, 2025, https://www.nobelprize.org/stories/women-who-changed-science/frances-arnold.
62. National Aeronautics and Space Administration, "Astronauts," accessed August 12, 2025, https://www.nasa.gov/humans-in-space/astronauts/.
63. CBS Evening News, "Astronaut Christina Koch on her journey in

space," Facebook video, February 12, 2020, https://www.facebook.com/watch/?v=247670999565690.

64. "Oprah Winfrey's Golden Globes Speech Transcript," *The New York Times,* January 7, 2018, https://www.nytimes.com/2018/01/07/movies/oprah-winfrey-golden-globes-speech-transcript.html.

Index

About the Author

NORAH O'DONNELL is a multiple Emmy Award–winning journalist with nearly three decades of experience covering the biggest stories in the world and conducting impactful, newsmaking interviews. She is a senior correspondent for CBS News, focused on big interviews and projects for the network, and spent five years as the anchor and managing editor of the *CBS Evening News,* the oldest and most revered evening news broadcast in America. O'Donnell anchors CBS News Election Specials and is a *60 Minutes* contributing correspondent. She is married to the bacon-loving Geoff Tracy, otherwise known as Chef Geoff, and is the mother of three children.

X: @NorahODonnell
IG: @NorahODonnell